PROPERTY
ERNEST J. KING SCHOOL
Book No. _____

GETTING THE MESSAGE

The Technology of Communication

J. Barry DuVall
Central Michigan University

Ernest G. Berger
Florida A & M University

George R. Maughan, Jr.
West Virginia University

Paul W. DeVore
Consulting Editor

Delmar Publishers, Inc.

NOTICE TO THE READER

Publisher does not warrant or guarantee any of the products described herein or perform any independent analysis in connection with any of the product information contained herein. Publisher does not assume, and expressly disclaims, any obligation to obtain and include information other than that provided to it by the manufacturer.

The reader is expressly warned to consider and adopt all safety precautions that might be indicated by the activities described herein and to avoid all potential hazards. By following the instructions contained herein, the reader willingly assumes all risks in connection with such instructions.

The publisher makes no representation or warranties of any kind, including but not limited to, the warranties of fitness for particular purpose or merchantability, nor are any such representations implied with respect to the material set forth herein, and the publisher takes no responsibility with respect to such material. The publisher shall not be liable for any special, consequential or exemplary damages resulting, in whole or in part, from the readers' use of, or reliance upon, this material.

Copyright 1981
Delmar Publishers, Inc.
For information, address Delmar Publishers Inc.,
2 Computer Drive West, Box 15-015
Albany, New York 12212

All rights reseved. No part of this publication may be reproduced or transmitted in any form or by any means, electronic or mechanical, including photocopying, recording, or any storage and retrieval system now known or to be invented, except by a reviewer who wishes to quote brief passages in connection with a review written for inclusion in a magazine, newspaper, or broadcast.

Printed in the United States of America
Published simultaneously in Canada
by Nelson Canada,
A division of The Thomson Corporation

Library of Congress Catalog Card Number: 79-57016

ISBN: 0-87192-123-5 Student Text
      0-87192-125-1 Teacher's Handbook

Graphic Design: Karen Mason

10 9 8 7 6 5 4 3

ACKNOWLEDGMENTS

Special thanks to our families for their support and encouragement, to Paul DeVore for his continuing faith and enthusiasm for the project, to the many individuals, companies and agencies who provided photos and technical materials, and to Dr. John Mateer for his technical review of materials pertaining to human physiology and perception.

PREFACE

Today we live in a world where the tools, techniques, and technical systems for communicating between people and machines have become a necessary part of our way of life. In fact, few technologies have had as great an impact on the human condition as the inventions and discoveries in the field of communications. During the last quarter of the twentieth century we have developed new communication channels between people, input links with complex banks of data, worldwide computer networks enabling exchanges of resources between international corporations, and hand held computers. Other discoveries in microprocessor technology, fiber optics, checkless banking, satellite communications, space exploration, and thin film transistors provide more clues on what is yet to come.

Getting the Message has been created to help you understand communication technology and use it more effectively. New discoveries in communications are occurring at such a rapid rate that it is becoming increasingly important to be able to make informed decisions about communications and communication technology. It is our hope that these materials will open the doors to further exploration of the exciting world of communication technology and that they will better prepare you for life in tomorrow's world when we will be even more dependent on communication technology.

Editor's Preface

The creation and use of technical means have been the critical factors affecting the survival potential, choices and characteristics of all societies. This use includes our ability to adapt to the natural environment and to communicate, produce food, clothing, shelter and other necessities, and to transport raw materials, finished products and people. Central to our adaption process has been the ever increasing ability to use and control information.

Throughout the evolutionary process of humans and civilization, the transmission, storage, retrieval, use and control of information have affected the survival and development of individuals, communities and nations. Successful political leaders have long been aware that effective governmental and social controls extended only so far as they could maintain an effective and efficient flow of information. Today, however, with our advanced technical means, it is also necesssary to have specially designed communication systems to maintain and control many aspects of our lives, including monitoring the health of individuals, our life-giving and life-sustaining environment, and our production, transportation and social systems.

We are entering a new era in civilization, based largely on innovation, invention and development in the field of communication. The exploration of outer space, control of manufacturing processes, monitoring of emergency health care situations, the advent of microprocessors and the age of robotics, signal a new beginning based on the technical ability to obtain, process, and use information in unique ways for human purposes.

Each advance in our ability to transmit, receive, process, store, retrieve, and use information impacts on what the future can be. It also impacts on the way we think about ourselves, our society and our future in relation to changes in our technological potential.

Those who use this text as part of their education now will live and work in the twenty-first century. It will be a far different century from the one we live in today. The technical choices and decisions being made today are determining the nature of life then. The study of technology is concerned with the creation and utilization of adaptive means, including tools, machines, materials, techniques and technical systems and the relation of the behavior of these elements and systems to human beings, their societies, the environment, and the civilization process. Knowledge and understanding of technology are basic to being a literate person capable of functioning effectively in the twenty-first century. This book and accompanying program materials are developed and written for use at the secondary and young adult levels to contribute to this goal. Other programs in the series are concerned with production and transportation systems. This secondary program is part of a series prepared for learning levels ranging primarily from kindergarten through grade twelve. Professional books for teachers are also part of the series.

The purpose of the publications for this level is to structure the study of communication, production and transportation technology by identifying and analyzing the component parts and examining the technical means of these systems as critical variables in the affairs of people and society.

The goal of this entire series is to help each of us determine the most appropriate technical means for our social purpose and to more effectively manage that means to attain our personal and social goals both now and in the future. If we all can prepare ourselves to contribute to this goal, we will enter the twenty-first century more by choice than by chance.

Paul W. DeVore, Consulting Editor
Morgantown, West Virginia

CONTENTS

Acknowledgments iii

Preface(s) v

Module One **COMMUNICATION TECHNOLOGY: FRAMEWORK FOR STUDY** **1**
Our World of Communication 1 · The Technology of Communication 3 · Communication as an Area of Study 5 · The Process of Communication 7 · The Senses and Technology 10 · The Development of Communication Technology 11 · Systems of Communication 12 · Communication Technology Today 13 · Concept Focuser 14 · Food for Thought 15 · Expanding Experiences 15 · Locator Tools 16

Module Two **MAJOR SYSTEMS IN WHICH COMMUNICATION OCCURS** **17**
Animal Communication 18—*Communication and Survival, Complex Animal Communication Systems, Communication in Birds, Communication in Higher Animals, Tactile Communication in Animals, Visual Communication in Animals, Acoustic Communication in Animals, Chemical Communication in Animals* · Machine Communication 28—*Machine Communication and Technology, Machine/Machine Communication, Instrumentation and Control* · Anomalous Communication 41—*Extrasensory Occurrences, The Kirlian Aura, Dream Research, Color Hearing, Moving Objects with the Mind, Biofeedback in Humans, Plant Communication* · Concept Focuser 45 · Food for Thought 46 · Expanding Experiences 46 · Locator Tools 46

Module Three **HUMAN COMMUNICATION AND PERCEPTION** **47**
The Sensory System 47 · The Senses 49—*Sight, Hearing, Smell, Taste, Touch* · Extrasensory Perception 60 · Sensory Mixing 61 · Interpersonal Communication 61 · Nonverbal Communication 62—*Environmental Factors, Personal Appearance, Physical Behavior* · Verbal Communication 67 · Perception 70 · Concept Focuser 70 · Food for Thought 71 · Expanding Experiences 71 · Locator Tools 71

Module Four **COMMUNICATION AND SYSTEMS FOR PROCESSING INFORMATION**   **73**

Information Processing System 73 · The Theory of Information Processing 77—*The Encoding and Decoding Process, Measurement of Information* · Cybernetics and Information Processing 80—*Cybernetics in the Human Mechanism, Control of Information Processing Machines* · Concept Focuser 83 · Food for Thought 83 · Expanding Experiences 84 · Locator Tools 84

Module Five **TECHNOLOGY-BASED VISUAL SYSTEMS**   **85**

Our Visual World 86 · Visual Literacy and Our Visual Languages 87 · Phases in the Development of the Visual Message 88—*Message Analysis and Design, Concept Formation and Image Reproduction, Image Preservation* · An Effective Design 91—*The Dot, The Line, Visual Texture, Color, Shape* · Building an Effective Concept 98—*The Thumbnail Sketch, The Rough Sketch, The Final Concept* · Mass Communication Systems 100—*Visual Seals, Early Writing, The First Paper, Early Printing, Raised Surface Printing, Plane Surface Printing, Sunken Surface Printing, Through-the-Surface Printing, Reprography, Photography, Radiography, Color Photography, New Technology, The Moving Image, Illusionary Depth* · Image Preservation 130—*The Microform Industry, Microforms* · Holography 133 · Laserphoto 135 · Lightwave Communications 136 · Summary 136 · Concept Focuser 137 · Food for Thought 137 · Expanding Experiences 138 · Locator Tools 138

Module Six **TECHNOLOGY-BASED ELECTRICAL TELECOMMUNICATION SYSTEMS**   **139**

The Beginnings of Electrical Communications 139—*Early Sources of Electron Generation, Electron Carriers, Components for Electrical Control and Transmission, Circuit Measurement, Early Electromagnetic Discoveries, How We Used Electricity in Telecommunications* · Concept Focuser 171 · Food for Thought 171 · Expanding Experiences 172 · Locator Tools 172

Module Seven **TECHNOLOGY-BASED ACOUSTICAL SYSTEMS**   **174**

Acoustical Messages 174 · The Nature of Sound 175 · Information Transmitted by Acoustical Energy 177—*Techniques of Music, Instruments* · Acoustical Information Transmitted by Energy Other than Sound 183—*Electric Telegraph, The Diaphragm, Telephone, Radio* · Light 194 · Acoustical Information Storage and Retrieval 195—*Mechanical Techniques, Magnetic Techniques* · Concept Focuser 200 · Food for Thought 200 · Expanding Experiences 201 · Locator Tools 201

| Module Eight | **TECHNOLOGY-BASED ELECTRONIC TELECOMMUNICATION SYSTEMS** | **202** |

The Beginnings of Electronic Telecommunications 202—*Early Radio Developments, Early Regulatory Attempts, Thermionic Emission, Electronic Circuits, Modern Radio Receivers, Crystal Set, Tuned Frequency Receivers, Superheterodyne Receivers, Modern Radio Transmitters, Television, Radar, Radio Astronomy* · Modern Advances in Telecommunication Systems 216—*Microwave Transmission, Masers, Forward-Scatter Systems, Pulse Code Modulation, Lasers, Space Communications, Communication Satellites* · Basic Elements of Electronic Telecommunication Systems 224—*Semiconductors, Review of Semiconductyor Physics, Molecular Electronics, Integrated Circuits, Computers* · Electronic Measurement and Instrumentation 236—*Digital Volt Meter, The Signal Generator, The Oscilloscope* · Concept Focuser 238 · Food for Thought 239 · Expanding Experiences 239 · Locator Tools 239

| Module Nine | **COMMUNICATION TECHNOLOGY AND ITS EFFECTS ON SOCIETY** | **241** |

Technology and Society 241—*Stage 1—Primitive Era, Stage 2—Craft Era, Stage 3—Mechanical Era, Stage 4—Modern Era* · Communication Technology Utilization 247 · Effects on Society and the Individual 249 · Effects on Institutions 251—*Government, Economics, Family, Education, Religion* · Effects on the Individual 256—*Values and Attitudes, Perceptions, Emotions, Learning* · The Law 259 · Freedom of Expression 260 · Rights of Privacy 261 · Freedom of Information 262 · Censorship 262 · Regulation and Control 264 · International Control 266—*Copyright, Advertising, Antitrust* · Concept Focuser 269 · Food for Thought 269 · Expanding Experiences 270 · Locator Tools 270

| Module Ten | **COMMUNICATION TECHNOLOGY AND THE FUTURE** | **271** |

At Home, A.D. 2030 271—*The Automated Home—A Scenario, Diagnostic and Prescription Computers, The Automated Plant, Shopping from Home, Mobile Communications Systems, Home Entertainment Center, The 3-D Television System, The Electronic Visitor* · Technology Forecasting 282—*Personal Communications Radio Links, Advances in Telecommunications, The Muon Beam, Liquid Electricity, Computer Technology, Language Translation by Computers, Behavioral Modification by Computer, Large Scale Computerized Data Systems, Biomedical Communications, Global Satellite Communication Systems, The Global Patent Office,*

Interstellar Communications, Other Technology Forecasts, The Decline of Print as a Communication Mode, How Forecasting Can Help · Concept Focuser 298 · Food for Thought 299 · Expanding Experiences 299 · Locator Tools 300

Appendix A **Contributions or Inventions Leading up to Technology-based Electrical Telecommunication Systems**   **301**

Appendix B **Contributions to Technology-based Electronic Telecommunication Systems**   **306**

Glossary of Terms   311

Symbols and Abbreviations   324

Index   325

COMMUNICATION TECHNOLOGY: FRAMEWORK FOR STUDY

Module **ONE**

The walls of the room glistened, like a pool of water reflecting moonlight. The input was from a cluster of optical fibers and lasers, all controlled by a computer in New Orleans. Our host asked his guests, "What will you have?" One said, "San Francisco." Another replied, "Hong Kong." And I said, "Bluegrass and banjo pickin' in the spring." Our host said, "We'll have them all. Let's start with San Francisco." He reached over and pushed a button—and we were there!

In the years ahead, it seems quite likely that we will be able to transmit "matter" in a manner similar to that used today to send 3-Dimensional pictures from one place to another. Patent applications for this process have already been filed in several countries and the process has been demonstrated in laboratories in Europe.

OUR WORLD OF COMMUNICATION

At this time our attempts to "reach out," to communicate, are much more limited. When the United States launched Pioneer 10 from Cape Kennedy in 1972 we were trying, among other things, to communicate—to tell others about the launching, its origin, and the beings that created the system.

The significance of this event becomes apparent when we realize that we are not the only life forms on this planet with a need to communicate. Nearly everything that happens in our world, every object, every plant and animal organism, continuously emits its characteristic identifying signal. Our world is made up of all kinds of messages, each competing for its own chance to communicate. All living things contribute to this confusion, but each transmits its own message and selectively screens out those trying to come in.

Over many thousands of years all forms of life as we know it have undergone successive stages of evolution. This evolution has enabled each species to develop modes of communication that permit selective screening of messages. Accordingly,

2 COMMUNICATION TECHNOLOGY: FRAMEWORK FOR STUDY

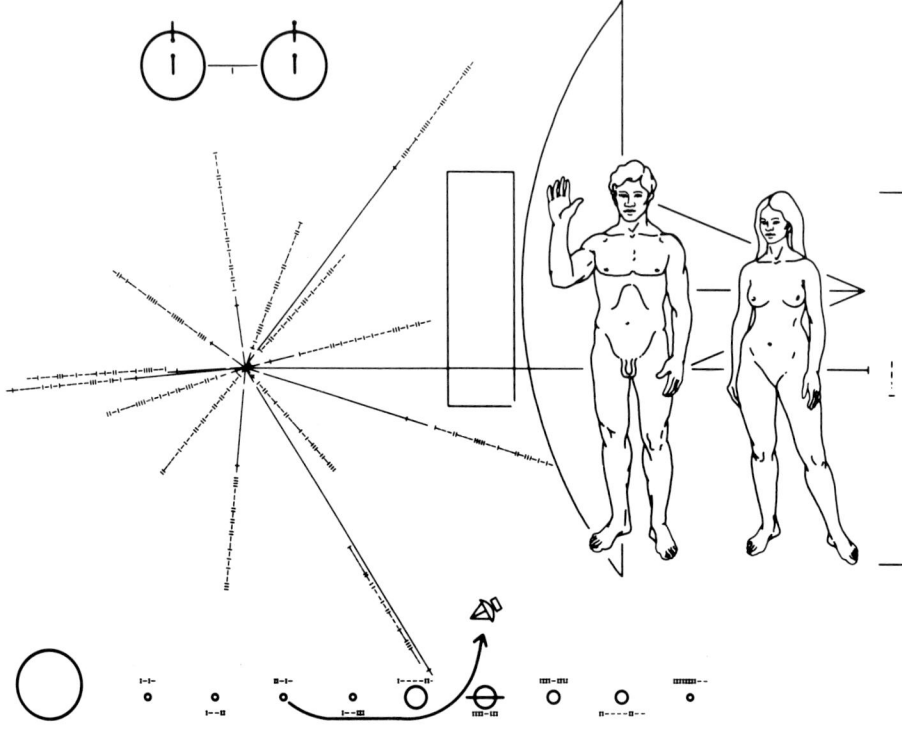

Figure 1.1

The Pioneer 10 Plaque was an attempt to communicate with possible inhabitants of other worlds. The plaque was attached to the supporting struts of the Pioneer 10 spacecraft's antenna. The plaque can be interpreted as follows: The radiating lines at the left represent the locations of fourteen pulsars arranged to indicate that our sun is the home star of the civilization that launched the craft. The bar and hypen symbols at the end of these radii are numbers representing the frequencies of these pulsars at the time of launching. The frequencies are given in relationship to that of the hydrogen atom shown at the upper left with (1) symbol. The hydrogen atom is used as a universal clock, which will help another civilization to determine the time elapsed since the launching.

The hydrogen atom also serves as a universal meter stick giving size to the human figures shown standing in front of the craft's outline. The figures shown indicate the type of beings that made the spacecraft. The man's hand is raised in a gesture of good will.

Across the bottom are the sun and its planets with Pluto at the reader's right.

The plaque chosen was designed by Carl Sagan, director of the Laboratory for Planetary Studies, Cornell University; his wife, Linda Salzman Sagan, a painter and filmmaker; and Frank Drake, director, National Astronomy and Ionosphere Center at Cornell.

The time necessary for the craft to reach the nearest star will be about 80,000 of our years.

certain types of birds, reptiles, and even barnacles, rely on the reception of information important to their species in a specific geographical territory.

We have done the same. We have all developed personal languages, which are modified by our culture, country, neighborhood, occupation, personality, and even our mood at the moment. The process is further complicated when we consider the fact that each of our own unique sets of meanings are constantly changing throughout every waking moment of every day. Current research on dreams has pointed out that the process even goes on while we are asleep.

Almost every day new discoveries are adding to our understanding of communication. Many of these new forms of communication had been broadcasting all the time, but we did not hear until someone chose to listen. Then we all heard them!

Consider the as yet unheard messages that are broadcasting right now. We have only recently become interested in studying the sounds of the sharks and whales, the chirps of the dolphin, and the chatter of the crickets. (For about 60 European species of crickets over 400 different songs have been discovered.) In time we will probably discover an infinite variety of such messages, still waiting to be heard.

Without communication life as we know it would not be possible. Without a program of genetic messages we would not be who we are, and without our internal communications network (between our cells and organs), we could not begin to function as we do. All of us are totally dependent on these processes of internal communication.

When we think of communication we seldom consider these internal systems. We tend to look at communication only as a process enabling people to exchange information with each other. But there is much more to it than that.

Most living things live without knowing how they live and how they communicate. In the main, so do we. Not many of us understand the operation of all of the devices in a weather satellite, a computer network, or a television station; but many of us have at least a **general understanding** of their functions. We cannot say the same for our understanding of the **process** of communication.

The Technology of Communication

There are no "experts" today in the whole field of communications. Our technology has become so sophisticated, and new developments now occur at such a rapid rate that it is no longer possible for any one person to "know all" about any broad area of technology. All that we need to do is take a look at the length of time necessary from the initial discovery of a technical innovation to the manufacture of the actual product to recognize what has happened.

As an example, the beginnings of photography occurred around 1727. It was more than 100 years later before the first photograph was actually produced. The telephone took more than 50 years (1876), the radio 35 (1902), radar 15 (1940), television 12 (1934), the transistor 5 (1953), and the integrated circuit 3 (1960). The time span between the initial development of the idea and production has become shorter and shorter. The world of communications is a lot bigger today than it was in 1950.

Yes, there are experts in specialized technical areas, such as: color television, radio, telephone, or satellites, but few people are knowledgeable about technical communication **systems.** That is the purpose for this text.

In spite of the growth in the number and complexity of new developments, each day we are collecting new information that eventually will lead to improving our understanding of the process of communication. In the main, however, we have learned to live and communicate not through our understanding of these processes, but in spite of our ignorance about them.

To us, communication has become flashes of real-life experiences like an argument between sister and brother, a "far out" TV commercial, or an ad for a custom van in the want-ads. We live in a time where information (television in the evening, billboards on the way to the game, music to get up to, and the morning paper) is heaped on us at a fantastic rate.

It is difficult for us to picture what life was like before the technological developments that made such rapid communication possible. Try to put yourself back in time to the 1860s. Before the Atlantic Cable was completed on July 30, 1866, a person in New York could communicate with a person in London either by visiting or by letter. That letter would be on board ship for weeks or months before reaching port. The Atlantic Cable, suspended deep in the Atlantic Ocean, and the telegraph system that was linked to each end of it enabled persons in New York and London to communicate with each other within minutes.

In our time we cannot fully appreciate the significance of the Atlantic Cable. It was part of a new type of technology, a total system that joined the old and new worlds. But if it is hard for us, what would a person living in 1866 think of our INTELSAT IV, a communications satellite that could transmit up to 9000 phone conversations at the same time? (Compare this to 750 telephone circuits that were possible with the fifth and most sophisticated transatlantic cable first providing service in 1970.)

Communication technology has come a long way since the first Atlantic Cable in 1866. In fact, the rate of growth has been so rapid that even those who tried to

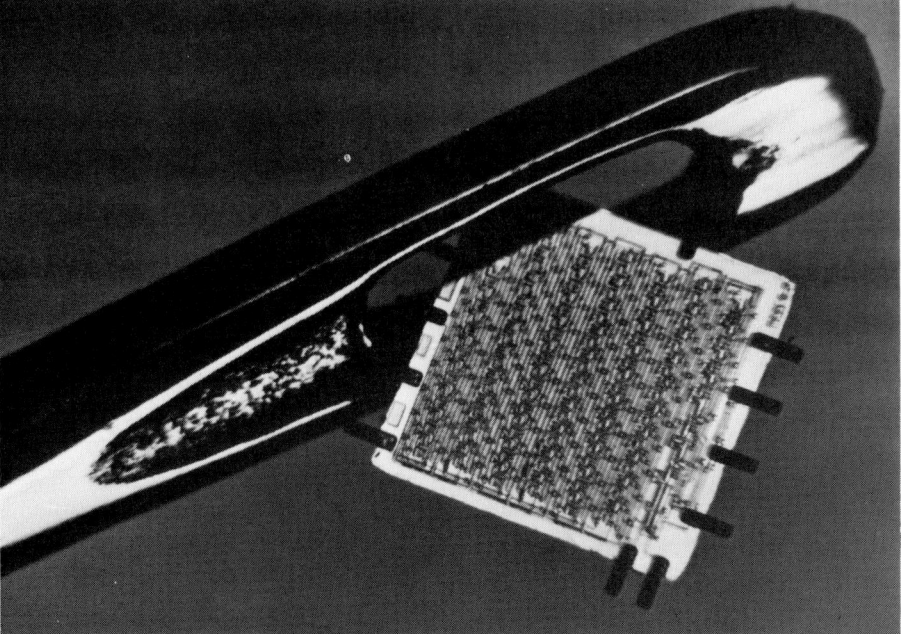

Figure 1.2

New techniques in micro-miniaturization have enabled us to construct integrated circuits with as many as 100 transistors, resistors, and diodes, all being small enough to pass through the eye of a needle. Courtesy, Western Electric

predict what might be possible today from a point in time, say ten years ago, could not imagine the full potential of what we would be up to. Let's take a look at some of today's realities.

Today it is possible for man to communicate with the dolphin, or for chimpanzees to talk with man (see Module Two). **Today** the *Encyclopedia Britannica* markets a series of "Resource and Research Libraries" in ultrafiche. The entire set of 20,000 volumes will fit on the top of a card table (see Module Five).

Today the technique of micro-miniaturization has enabled the development of complete circuits that will pass through the eye of a needle (see Module Eight).

Today new research in radio astronomy may eventually result in our communicating with extraterrestrial intelligences (see Module Nine).

Today early research in the realm of plant physiology seems to indicate that plants may be able to communicate, may have emotions, and may even have memory (see Module Two).

One day all of the functions of the human brain may be simulated in a computer the size of a pack of matches.

In the not-too-distant future machines will be able to understand and respond to human speech in some form of language. At some far-distant point in time it may even be possible for us to communicate with a computer, using ordinary human language.

We have shown that communication takes place in many different forms, and that it is essential to the survival of many different species of life in today's world. Let's take a look at what communication is about.

COMMUNICATION AS AN AREA OF STUDY

In this text, communication technology is presented through a series of modules which, like a communications network, can be joined to represent a total system. The system in this case can be viewed as the world of communication.

The reader should keep in mind that a total understanding of any complex system is seldom possible. Innovations in any technology will occur each moment. This means that the study of technology will never be complete. This text should only be regarded as a stimulus for that study.

Communication is a never-ending process that takes place in a constantly changing environment. Think about it! Communication between persons changes as they go through stages of being alert and friendly to tired and cranky. The process changes; so does the environment in which it takes place.

Communication is more than just a **transmission** or **sending** process. Communication involves sharing, trading, and modifying.

Let's see if we can develop an analogy that puts the process into perspective. When your teacher speaks, your mind does not automatically open a switch that allows knowledge to be poured in. **Communication** has to occur before learning can take place. You have to hear and listen to what is being said. The fact that you listen and hear the message does not mean that your teacher has communicated. Communication does not occur until the incoming information causes some change in your behavior. The process of communication may provoke an immediate reaction on your part or you may receive new information that you (consciously or unconsciously) store in your memory for later use.

We have pointed out that communication involves a giving and taking relationship. There is much more to the process than this, however. The information being transmitted to the receiver must be interesting enough for him or her to consider what is being communicated. In other words, the switch has to be turned on at the receiving end before any information can come in. Once the incoming information has been received it can be used immediately or be stored for later use. If the information is used at the time of reception, the process of communication has caused some change in behavior (a reaction on the part of the receiver).

Let's stop for a minute, and think about what has been said. Communication is a process involving some sort of transmission. A question remaining is, communication of what? If one scans a variety of books on communication many different responses to this question will be found. Let us try to solve the problem using a systems approach, considering some key words that have been used to describe the process. Communication has been viewed as a process that involves the **transmission** of:

- Meaning
- Information
- Thought
- Understanding
- Influence
- Images
- Attitude
- Emotion

These key words express two different perspectives that are found in books on communication. Many authors with the first perspective describe the process as something that deals with the "transmission of information." These authors are most supportive of the theory of communication developed by Claude Shannon and Warren Weaver of Bell Laboratories. Their theory, developed around 1947, portrayed communication as a highly predictable process involving a message sent from a transmitter to a receiver. The theory, and the graphic model they used to explain it, was designed for the purpose of showing how the process of electrical communication occurred. The theory had some drawbacks when it was used to describe the process of human communication. Humans just seemed to be too unpredictable for the model. Nevertheless, many theorists used the early model to describe the communication process in humans and animals.

During the early sixties a second group of individuals began to describe communication as a continuing process, which cannot be described completely. Most of the writers in the field of communications today can be found in this grouping. They believe that the transmission of information by itself does not constitute communication. Communication occurs only when the behavior of the receiver is changed, however small, as a result of the communication act. This second group of communications theorists would use words such as meaning, understanding, influence, and emotion to describe communication.

Let us return to our analysis of communication. We pointed out that communication is a process involving the transmission of information, and that for communication to occur this information has to be used by the receiver in one way or another. How about this for a working definition? "Communication is the transmission of information." No, we know that this is incomplete because the receiver may not be listening. How about this one? "Communication is the **expression of meaning**." The word **meaning** implies that the receiver is listening or receiving the same information that is being transmitted, and that something is being done with the information that has come in. Yes, that should do it.

Now we know quite a lot about the process of communication. We know that it is **continuous** and that it is **action oriented**. We also know that it involves the expression of **meaning**.

Figure 1.3

Communication is. . . ?

THE PROCESS OF COMMUNICATION

Let's take a look at how communication takes place. How is it all accomplished? The process is simple. When the sender (me) transmits information (via this page) to the receiver (you), information is taken in through the senses. At this moment you are receiving information through at least four of your senses. As you read this text you are using your sense of sight. At the same time you are receiving sensory impressions from the environment around you. Your senses of hearing, smell, and touch also can provide inputs that influence the effectiveness of our communication act.

For communication to take place the senses must receive information. Although the information input is channeled to the brain via the senses, our technology provides us with tools, techniques, and, technical systems that extend our human capabilities.

Early communication theorists tried to make sense of the process of communication by inventing the **black box** concept. The make-believe black box had an input and an output. What took place inside of the box was sort of mysterious and unpredictable. The black box concept is a good beginning for the study of the process of communication. We will call the input the **sender** and the output the **receiver**.

It would be nice if we could stop here, with a sender and a receiver, but there is much more to the process than that. For one thing, there has to be a way that the information is transmitted from the sender to the receiver. We will call this the transmission channel. A communication channel is the medium **through which** the information is transmitted. A communication channel might be the printed page, the human voice, electrical wires, a TV picture, or light pipes, to name just a few. Most communication between people takes place verbally at a distance of a few feet. In this instance the channel is air—sound transmitted across molecules of air from one person to another. Keep in mind that the communication channel is what the information is transmitted through, not in what form it is transmitted.

We now have the basic parts for understanding the process of communication, the transmitter, a channel, and a receiver. Refer to Figure 1.4.

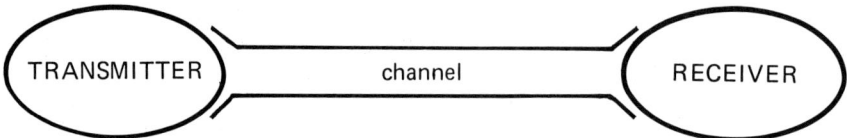

Figure 1.4

Basic elements of the communication process.

To understand communication as a process involving the transmission of information we need to introduce some other factors into the system to make it complete. These factors are called **noise** and **feedback**. Noise is what happens when you are watching TV and a bolt of lightning outside causes interference and the picture on your TV screen not to appear. Noise is what happens when you try to talk on the phone and a fire truck with howling sirens races by. But noise is not always loud sounds. Noise is just interference—things that get in the way of the receiver getting the same information the sender is transmitting.

Feedback takes on many forms. Feedback is a word that describes information that returns from the receiver to the sender as a reaction to a communication. Feedback is used to control chemical processing plants and to keep commercial planes on course. In animals, feedback mechanisms are used to keep their body temperature relatively constant, despite temperature changes in the outside environment. In the area of communication we rely on feedback in almost everything we do.

Suppose that one of your friends liked wearing purple shoes. Everyone in school knew that the shoes looked weird, but only you had the courage to tell him that purple shoes were not the thing to wear. So you told him! He received the information, and responded by giving you a punch in the nose. His response to you is an example of feedback. Not only did you find out how he felt about what you communicated, his response probably affected you in such a way that you will likely alter your communication to him next time around.

Two other factors are important to the process of communication. These can be called **purpose** and **context**. **Purpose** is the intent behind the act of communication. It is something that influences the effectiveness of the process. You may recall instances where you were angry and tried to communicate. Something seemed to be lost in the process. You may have not been able to get your information across to the person you were trying to communicate with. This failure to communicate was not due to noise. Your purpose simply did not match up with that of the receiver. The receiver "turned off the switch." You were transmitting information but the person was no longer receiving.

In communication, **context** refers to the setting where the process takes place. No act of communication can exist in isolation. Many factors in your environment are affecting the process of communication between us right now. Consider the colors around you, the sounds, the smells, doors shutting. The fly crawling up the wall even contributes to the context of the act of communication. Think of it another way. Consider talking to your principal about a class activity that you enjoyed. Imagine communicating with him in his office, and then change your setting to the hallway. Do you think that your effectiveness as a communicator will be different in these two settings? More than likely it will, depending largely on the content of the information you are trying to communicate.

To sum up, now we have a process involving: sender, receiver, channel, feedback, noise, and purpose. The entire process is affected by the context or setting. But because communication involves the expression of meaning, many things often hamper the effectiveness of the process. Let's take a look at some of these.

Transmitter	Receiver
weak signal transmitted	"I can't hear you."
wrong channel	"My thermometer can't hear, only sense temperature."
noise in the system	"I thought you said twink, not think."
transmitting fine, loud and clear	"I can't hear you." (This may be because I wasn't listening, or maybe because I don't understand Spanish)

Figure 1.5

What. . .a failure to communicate?

A failure to communicate can occur for many reasons. These may be intentional or unintentional, conscious or unconscious. Why are there so many failures, particularly in human or animal communications? Why can two people read the same news article and come up with different meanings? The problem is that meaning is in the mind of the perceiver. When we receive information we try to make sense of it using information or data gained from our own past experiences. This means that each one of us interprets the data that we receive in a different way. There are so many factors that influence the effectiveness of the process that it is really remarkable that we can communicate at all.

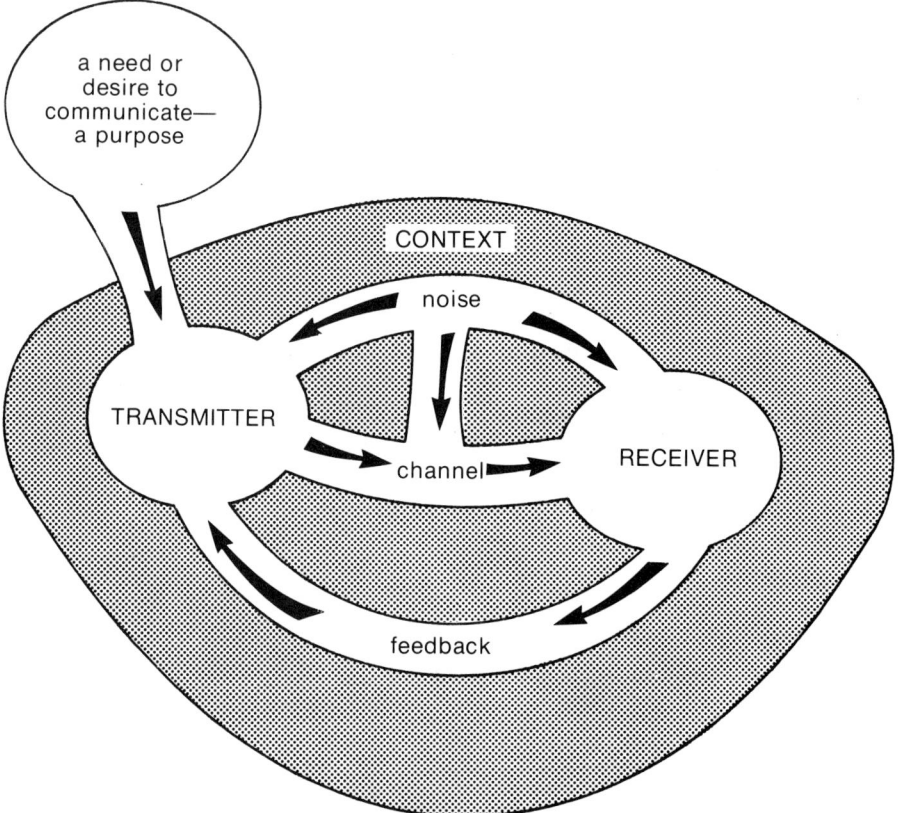

Figure 1.6

A communication model.

THE SENSES AND TECHNOLOGY

We rely heavily on both the senses and technology to function successfully in today's world. Much of the information that we receive comes in directly through our senses. Remember that dog that you saw last evening getting into your neighbor's trash? You received the information through your sense of sight. In this instance you relied on your senses alone to receive information. Technology could have extended your capacity to receive information. If you had used a camera to photograph the dog you would have received the same information input but would have had documentary evidence to show your neighbor. In this way the camera would have provided you with an extension on your sense of sight.

The relationship between our use of the senses alone for information input and our use of technology to assist us in the reception of information has changed drastically over time.

Primitive peoples relied heavily on their senses to receive and transmit information. Then communication technology was poorly developed, consisting mainly of devices for creating crude sounds or scratching primitive symbols on cave walls. Whereas the sense of smell was important to them for sensing danger or receiving other types of information, today we are more dependent on our senses of hearing and sight.

As time progressed people began to depend more and more on technology. In today's world information is transmitted and received at an astounding rate. Most of it is made available to our senses through our technology. As we become more and more dependent on technology and less reliant on our senses, we may wonder if we will ever reach a point where technology will begin to replace the senses. Now technology is used primarily to provide extensions on our senses and assist us in processing information. Will technology some day be used to receive and transmit information directly to our brain as well? Will future generations be created without senses? Be careful before you laugh! Contrast our use of our senses against how they were used by our primitive forerunners. Their senses were much more developed than ours. They had a keen sense of hearing and an acute sense of smell. Today we rely heavily, about 60-70 percent, on our sense of sight to receive information. Our sense of smell has become much less sensitive, simply because we do not use it as much. Future generations might develop without ears if sound vibrations are **heard** by the fingertips and ears are no longer needed.

The Development of Communication Technology

Communication technology relates to our sensory extensions: the way we use tools and techniques to create, transmit, receive, process, preserve, and retrieve information. Communication technology did not just happen overnight. It has been developing for a long time.

Cave people used their senses to communicate, and they also used technology. Over the years they learned much from their environment. They began to notice that certain species of animals used chemical or physical signs (markings on trees, piles of feces, or tracks) to mark the boundaries of their territories. When game became less prevalent around the camp, primitive people began to venture farther and farther away on hunting trips. As they ventured farther away, they needed communication systems to mark their own tracks and to tell others about their activities. Gradually the primitives became inventive enough to devise simple communication systems (primitive forms of communication technology) such as simple markings on trees (signs) and small piles of stone (cairns).

Gradually it became desirable to preserve records of events for later use. Cave drawings (pictographs) emerged as the system for describing slain animals or enemies. These simple drawings evolved into more complex illustrations (ideographs) which were used to portray a series of events in progression around 30,000 B.C.

Figure 1.7

Pictographs on cave walls were often used to communicate important happenings to others. The pictograph was found in a cave in California.
Courtesy, Field Museum of Natural History, Chicago

Gradually humans became more and more adept at using technology to communicate. Today we still use our senses to transmit and receive information, but we also use our technology to help us to reach beyond the limits of our senses.

Systems of Communication

When we really became proficient at using our technology to communicate, many new types of communication activities became possible. Today we transmit information not only to other people but also to machines. Machines even transmit information to us and to other machines.

Today there are several major categories of activity where communication occurs: person/person, person/machine, machine/machine, and machine/person. These labels show relationships which take place in the technology of communications today. Let's take a closer look at what individual acts of communication might be like in each of these groupings.

We all know how people communicate with people. We do it every day, but how might we communicate with a machine? Well, do you remember what communication is? Communication is concerned with expressing meaning and changing behavior. Viewed in general terms then we might say that you are communicating with a machine if you tune in a TV program. In effect, when you adjust the volume control you transmit to a machine (television) a signal that you want to increase the volume. Today it is not too difficult to design machines that a human can set up to recognize words spoken by another human. It has proven to be far more difficult, however, to design a machine in such a way that it can recognize words spoken by any speaker with any accent. In some not too distant future, even this will likely be possible.

What about machines communicating with us? It would be difficult for us to go through a whole day without any machines communicating with us. If on your ride to school this morning a light came on indicating that your car was low on oil, this would be an example of a machine (oil light) communicating with you.

Without machine/machine communication many of our industries would not be in business. Many routine and monotonous tasks that require no creative effort today are accomplished by machines controlled by other machines. Many production processes are directed by one tape control unit controlling the production machine.

Today we rely heavily on many machines that perform robot-like functions. As we drive along the road we obey the signals given to us by robots (traffic signals), which have replaced the policeman waving his arms. Even in the kitchen many of our chores are done with robot helpers (washing machine, trash compactor, dishwasher).

Actually the idea of one machine communicating with another is not new to our time. The Jacquard Loom (1801) used an endless belt of punched cards with holes arranged in such a way as to produce the desired woven pattern in the fabric. The cards, or a primitive type of programming machine, controlled the weaving operation.

In terms of machine/machine communication we have come a long way from this simple device. One interesting development, called the Philips Dog, was invented around 1925. The dog was a much more sophisticated example of a machine-to-machine communication system. The device was a watch dog with two photoelectric cells for eyes. When either of these was exposed to light, it switched on one of two motors, which moved the dog toward the light. When the light intensity reached a certain brightness, the motors switched off and an electrical relay switched on a howling siren.

The heating system in your house is another example of machine-to-machine communication. The temperature of the house is determined by a thermostat. When the temperature drops below what is indicated at the thermostat, a message in the form of an electrical impulse is transmitted to the furnace so that the furnace will turn itself on. Through this simple communication system the temperature of the house is kept at a comfortable range.

We have discussed major systems where communication occurs—in people and in machines. Every day we engage in acts of communication involving both of these system groupings. In societies that are less developed than ours, communication takes place mainly between people, with fewer acts of machine communication occurring.

There is a reason for this. It was not possible, to any great extent, for one machine to communicate with another until many accomplishments were made in the field of energy. Energies such as chemical, thermal, electrical, and mechanical really formed the basis for machine-to-machine communication. The Philips Dog would not have been possible without a combination of electrical and mechanical energy.

Communication Technology Today

The sophisticated state of today's communication technology has been realized by the many new directions taken by communication research. Today we are experimenting with machines that can simulate many of the behavioral processes which, in an earlier era, had been possible only in humans. Today we can create "decision making" machines that in turn can create other machines. This area of study is called cybernetics and will be discussed in greater detail in Module Four. The possibilities for the future are scary—machines creating other machines creating other machines creating. . . . What is the likelihood that we will reach a point in time when machines can think without us?

The beginnings of this cybernetic era emerged during World War II in devices such as self-correcting guidance and control mechanisms for anti-aircraft guns and in response to other military problems. Increased developments in the military, coupled with new innovations in electronics, prompted the computer revolution of the past several decades. Today we have succeeded in using the computer as an efficient clerical assistant. Portable computers for the home are even gaining in popularity. The trend seems to be toward an even closer person/machine relationship, so that the computer may eventually become a generalized intelligence amplifier. (Further explanation of how machines work together [interface] will be provided in Module Two and Module Four).

There are also other forms of communication around us. Nature provides atmospheric changes that communicate with us such as changes in the weather, lightning, a drop in humidity, and tides. Animals also communicate with us. Take a minute and think about what happens when your cat wants his dinner. He doesn't sit there quietly and wait for you to discover that he wants to be fed.

We even communicate with ourselves. Often we think about one thing, and the idea causes us to think about some plan of action to change our behavior.

Almost every day new discoveries are made that will likely lead to an expansion of the world of communication. The results of early experimentation in areas such as: inorganically "grown" photographic emulsions, dream research, psychokinesis (mind control), energy fields, and others seem to indicate that new system areas will soon emerge.

In terms of our study we will deal with many of these developing areas under the category of anomalies (not completely explainable phenomena) in Module Two.

We have introduced many concepts in Module One. A thorough understanding of these concepts is important before we can move on. Let's take a few minutes to review what we have covered.

⟫ Concept Focuser

- Communication involves **transmitting information,** but for communication to occur the information must be **received** and eventually **used.**
- When transmitted information **conveys** some **meaning** to the receiver, and is used by the receiver, it causes some **change in behavior.**
- **Communication** is the **expression of meaning.**
- **Primitive communication** took place largely **between one person and another.**
- **Basic systems** where communication occurs are: **person/person, person/machine, machine/machine,** and **machine/person.**

- When mankind learned how to combine various forms of **energy, communication between machines** became **possible.**
- The **technology of communication** has **gradually evolved** since the days of the primitive cave dweller. Today we are **reliant** on both our **senses** and **technology** to communicate.
- Our **technology** has provided **extensions** on our limited **sensory capabilities.** Technology has enabled us to **transmit** and **receive more information** in ways that were not possible without it.
- Some **societies rely more** heavily on the **senses than** on **technology.** Others depend on **technology** to such an extent that **some** human **sensory capabilities** are **becoming less effective.**

 FOOD FOR THOUGHT

1. Distinguish between the concepts of transmitting information and communication.
2. Of the basic systems where communication occurs: person/person, person/machine, machine/machine, and machine/person, which have been made possible by the development of technology?
3. How does communication technology provide extensions on our senses?
4. Are societies that are more dependent on technology less dependent on their senses, or do they use them differently?
5. What does the concept of using energy have to do with machine/machine communications?

 EXPANDING EXPERIENCES

1. Take a field trip to an airport, satellite tracking station, telephone company, military installation, or local industry. Keep a record of each example you can find where machine/machine communication systems are used.
2. List all of the businesses, industries, and government installations in your phone book where you would say communication was the major activity. Then report your findings to the class.
3. Visit a school for the blind, deaf, or special needs learner; observe the systems used to communicate. Work with a small group of your classmates in teaching parts of the communication system observed to your total class.
4. Read a book on transactional analysis, then make a slide show that could be used to explain the various "communication states" pointed out in the book. Photograph your friends acting out each part.

📖 Locator Tools

Huxley, Sir Julian, ed. *Language and Communication.* New York: Curtis Publishing Company, 1968.

Scientific American, (Special Communications issue), Vol. 227, number 3, September 1972, pp. 30–163.

MAJOR SYSTEMS IN WHICH COMMUNICATION OCCURS

Module *TWO*

Most of the time when we think about communication, the first thing that comes to mind is two people talking with each other. Since spoken words play such an important role in our way of life, it seems natural to think that this is all that there is to the process of communication. In Module One we pointed out that communication is all around us; in fact, almost every object, thing, creature, worm, or protozoa produces its own identifying signal.

This makes the world of communication so big that it seems almost impossible for anyone to make sense of it. We introduced the idea of "systems" so as to organize our study of communication and communication technology. In Module One we touched on a number of major systems where communication activity occurs. Systems are like headings in an outline; they help us to arrange the body of knowledge into a coherent whole.

In this module we will study three of the **major** systems in which communication occurs. Here we hope to provide examples that should help you to recognize the importance of communication to many forms of life on our planet.

We will deal with the communication systems labeled animal, machine, and anomalous. In Module Three we will discuss another major communication system — human. All of these major systems have three essential parts: (1) an information source (the sender), (2) some information to be transmitted, and (3) the information receiver.

Animals transmit information in many ways. Most of this information is transmitted either through the sense of touch (tactile communication), through the sense of sight (visual communication), or through sound transmission (acoustical communication). Some animals also transmit chemical signals, ultrasonic impulses, and olfactory stimuli (smell).

New knowledge of animal communication has enabled us to find solutions to many human problems and has aided us in more effective design and use of our technology. Let's take a look at how the study of animal behavior might have helped us to solve a problem we once thought was unique to humanity.

ANIMAL COMMUNICATION

Benjamin Franklin, a famous inventor and statesman, was blessed with a brilliant mind but terrible eyesight. Indeed, his sight was so poor that he needed two pairs of glasses. He used one pair for observing distant objects and the other for looking at things close to him. Ben was a keen observer, always looking at everything in his environment. He also loved to read so he was confronted with the problem of constantly taking off one pair of glasses and putting on the other. Finally he got tired of this wasted action and took the lenses from both pairs of glasses, cut the lenses apart, and glued them back together. He put the lenses for looking far away on top and the close-up lenses on the bottom. What he had done in the year 1760 was invent bifocals.

What he probably did not know at the time was that bifocals had actually been around for millions of years. The whirligig beetle, a black water beetle that hangs out in ponds and can be seen on warm days spinning out over the surface of the water, was really the first to take advantage of bifocular vision.

Figure 2.1

Whirligig beetle, found on many farm ponds, was really the first to take advantage of bifocular vision.

The whirligig beetle has eyes with two sections. The top portion of its eyes sticks up above the surface of the water and is designed to see in the air. The lower part of its eyes, the section under water, is adapted to seeing in water.

Many other animals have adaptations that rival our most sophisticated technology. Some capabilities, even in the lowly insects, surpass those of humans. Nevertheless, careful study of how animal communication takes place has enabled us to understand more fully our own behavior and develop technology more appropriate to our needs. Further study may some day help us to discover new dimensions in communication, which will be available to us in some distant future.

Communication and Survival

In animals, particularly in the higher animals (apes, dolphins, birds, fish) communication between members of the same species takes place from the moment of birth until death. Without communication most species would not exist.

In the animal kingdom communication occurs mainly for purposes of survival. In this regard many animals rely heavily on communication for purposes of identifying other members of their species. This is particularly essential in some fish and birds, social insects, and barnacles. Many of these animals communicate chemically or acoustically with other members of their species. Other animals use communication to inform members of their group of danger and to interact with other animal groups outside of their own.

In all forms of animals, communication is essential for the reproduction of the species. Few types of animals depend only upon chance wandering to bring the sexes together. Most animals are attracted to one another either chemically or acoustically. In grasshoppers and crickets this is done with songs, and in mammals and moths with odors. Even in the protozoa and slime molds attraction takes place through chemical signals.

In general, the type of communication used by animals depends on their own potentialities. Animals with well-developed eyes rely heavily on visual communication whereas those with well-developed ears rely on acoustical signals. Since most animals are sensitive to chemicals, these systems are the most heavily used of all. The channels available to each species, therefore, determine the nature of the communication process employed.

The simplest way to view animal communication systems is to compare these systems with our own human language. Using our own unique verbal system as a point of reference, we can define the limits of animal communication in terms of those characteristics they have or do not have.

Consider the way that we are communicating right now. Each word that we are using has been assigned a specific meaning by our own particular culture. This meaning has been handed down to us through many generations and has become a part of our life as a result of learning. What is unique about this system of communication is the great number of words and their potential for creating new words and new meanings. We use words in phrases and sentences that produce a great variety of new meanings.

Complex Animal Communication Systems

Let us contrast this to one of the most sophisticated of all animal communication systems, the waggle dance of the honeybee. The waggle dance was first interpreted in 1945 by the German biologist Karl von Frisch. The dance goes something like this. When a foraging worker bee comes back to the hive after finding a new food source, she tells her fellow workers where the food is by performing the waggle dance. The pattern of the dance is performed over and over again in the middle of a crowd of sister workers. The pattern of the dance is conducted in a repeated figure eight. During the straight run movement in the center of the figure the forager waggles its abdomen rapidly and vibrates its wings. This movement is conducted thirteen to fifteen times per second. At the same time the forager emits a buzzing sound by vibrating its wings. The straight run represents the line of flight directly to the food source and the number of gyrations per second shows the workers how far to fly. In the Carniolan honeybee, a straight run lasting about a second indicates a food source about 500 meters away, and a two-second run indicates a target two kilometers away.

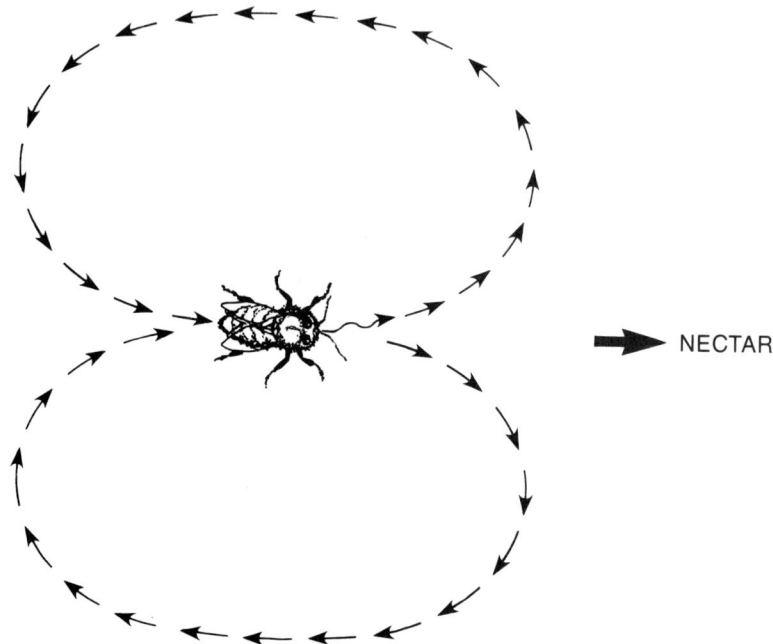

Figure 2.2

The honeybee performs the waggle dance over the hive. The line formed between the two circles acts as a directional indicator showing other bees the way to the source of nectar.

The waggle dance of the honeybee seems to possess some of the more sophisticated elements of human language. Meaning is created through the straight run part of the dance. The communicating bee can generate new meaning at will by altering the pattern. Nevertheless, messages created by the waggle dance are severely limited in comparison to our patterns of verbal language.

Except for humans, by far the most highly organized societies are found among the bees and ants. Just as man seems to be the culminating point in the social evolution of vertebrate organisms, so the ants and bees seem to represent the top of the ladder in the invertebrate category. With ants and bees survival demands a high level of cooperative effort. It is almost impossible for us to understand how such sophisticated patterns of social organization can exist unless each individual can communicate effectively with all of the others.

Nearly thirty-five species of ants depend to some extent on slave labor for their existence. The techniques that they use to raid other ant colonies to get new workers rank among some of the most sophisticated behavioral patterns anywhere in the insect world. These ants use more than brute force to get workers into their colonies. Research seems to indicate that raids are organized by the laying of odor trails to target nests. It appears that this form of communication may be widespread among slave-making ant colonies.

In other insects, fishes, and amphibians, the communication systems used are also limited but impressive. For each signal only one of a very few responses would be possible.

By our standards the quantity of signals transmitted to each species of animal is limited. The communication capability in most social animals is limited to around thirty to thirty-five separate displays (messages).

Communication in Birds

Communication in birds is an interesting phenomenon. Dr. Masakazu Konishi of the California Institute of Technology has pointed out that many birds inherit the ability to sing, whereas others learn to sing by mimicking the songs of adult birds much as we learn our language. In some species of birds the song pattern differs with locality, like accents and dialects in humans.

Research has shown that chickens are among the types of birds that inherit their vocal sounds. Even if chickens are deafened at birth they will still develop normal vocalization patterns.

Experiments with other birds, such as the white-crowned sparrow, have shown us that if they are raised in a soundproof room they will develop a type of song different from that found in nature.

Evidence seems to indicate that there is a parallel between the songs of birds and human speech. We do know that there is a critical period of learning in both. If the white-crowned sparrow doesn't hear normal song, either from an adult bird or a tape recording of another sparrow's song, between the second and seventh week after birth it will develop an abnormal song which cannot be changed.

Communication in Higher Animals

For many years researchers have been interested in dolphins and their ability to communicate. In the air or under water, the dolphin produces a great variety of sounds, which many scientists feel represent a complex language of chirps and barks. Interest in human/dolphin communication has recently been rekindled when officials of the United States Navy acknowledged that they had been using black dolphins for a classified surveillance and detection mission in Vietnam.

A well-known scientific researcher, Dr. John C. Lilly of Marineland of the Pacific in California, recorded dolphin noises with a conventional tape recorder. Many of these sounds were too high pitched to hear, so he slowed the recorder down to one-fourth the normal recording speed. What he found was that the dolphin appeared to be trying to imitate Dr. Lilly's own voice.

Communication in other underwater mammals is equally fascinating. Whales use a **sonar** system in the water. It has been known for many years that whales can hear and that they produce sounds. British sailors referred to one talkative species, the arctic Beluga Whale, as the "sea canary." The full story regarding their activity and observations was not known until World War II, when hydrophone systems developed for the detection of enemy submarines picked up the whale's unusual noises. Today we know that whales can transmit ultrasonic sounds as highly pitched as those of the bat, but we do not know how they produce these sounds. The whale has no vocal cords. We do know that the whale uses echo location as do the bats for avoiding obstacles and finding prey. We also know that whales have their own unique vocal language.

We can learn much about our own ability to communicate from studying animal behavior. Many distinctions can be made between humans and animals. Some of the most interesting studies on animal communication have occurred in experiments with the chimpanzee.

Many of the early studies with apes seemed to indicate that language was unique to humans and that the apes, like other animals, were helpless prisoners in their own physical environment. Early thinking stressed the theory that cries from chimpanzees were shrieks and hoots that represented some type of simple alarm system.

Over the years, however, experimenters have become increasingly intrigued by the possibility that animals other than humans can communicate using complex language systems.

One of the first of these experiments was conducted by William Furness in 1916. The Furness study showed that it was possible to teach an orangutan to speak. Through much patience he taught the ape to say "papa" and "cup." The orangutan seemed to use the words correctly. This was supported when the orangutan contracted influenza and was reported to have said, "cup, cup," in asking for a drink.

After the Furness experiment many experimental studies followed. These studies investigated many aspects of behavior using countless stacks of matches, unlocked doors, color exercises, and other problem solving activities involving apes and chimpanzees.

Early attempts to teach apes to communicate centered on the attempt to get them to talk. It was Robert Yerkes who first suggested that gestures might be a more appropriate way of establishing communication between the chimpanzee and the human. In 1966 his suggestion was acted upon.

The research, called *Project Washoe*, was conducted by Beatrice and Allen Gardner of the University of Nevada. The subject, a young chimpanzee named Washoe, was nearly a year old when the project began. To make Washoe's life as near as possible to that of a developing child, the Gardners kept her in her own trailer behind their home in Reno. The trailer was equipped with a stove, refrigerator, dinette area, bathtub, toilet, and bedroom. Outside was 5000 square feet of open area for the chimp to play in.

In the project the Gardners taught Washoe *Ameslan*, the American sign language used by the deaf. Her training was conducted in an enriched environment. She had constant human and animal visitors and lots of toys and games to play with and occupy her attention. Training sessions were paced to her attention span, and all human conversation was done in Ameslan.

Each Ameslan gesture comprises basic signal units. In total, Ameslan has fifty-five of these basic signal units. Nineteen of these identify the placement of the hand or hands when making the sign; twelve indicate the place where the sign is made; and twenty-four indicate the action of the hand or hands. Figure 2.3 shows what a typical sign might require. Ameslan signs are put together to make sentences.

The object of the experiment was to determine at what point in the process of developing a language the human child outpaced the chimpanzee, and to determine what language abilities the child has that the chimp doesn't.

In April of 1967 Washoe used her first combination of words. She said, "gimme sweet." She was then between eighteen and twenty-four months, which is around the age that human infants begin to form two-word combinations. Gradually the chim-

Figure 2.3

Ameslan (American sign language of the deaf) sign for "really"

panzee began to use three-, four-, and five-word phrases, in a manner much like young children. At the age of fifty-one months Washoe had acquired 132 signs of Ameslan. Later the chimp was moved to the University of Oklahoma's Institute for Primate Studies, and increased her vocabulary to more than 160 signs, including her own slang inventions.

In a follow-up to Project Washoe (1972), the Gardners began experimentation with two infant chimpanzees. The chimps, named Moja and Pili, began to make their first recognizable signs (again using Ameslan) when they were about three months old. In contrast to this project, Washoe began when she was one year old and after six months of exposure her vocabulary consisted of two signs. At the age of six months Moja's vocabulary consisted of fifteen signs.

An experiment conducted by the Yerkes Primate Center took on a different slant. The experiment was done in a room with Plexiglas walls. Panels of multicolored buttons, and umbilical cords of wires leading to a computer were also found in the environment. Inside of the transparent room Lana, a young chimpanzee, began talking to people on the outside. It was all accomplished by pushing keys with symbols on them, observing a display panel situated above the console to check sentences she had written, and waiting for the answers.

This experiment in animal communication was similar to the experiments of the Gardners, in that symbol languages were used as the method of communication. The experiment was different in that technology (a computerized display panel) was used as the link between the human and chimpanzee. The computerized language machine remains ready twenty-four hours a day to relay the chimp's requests for food, drink, games, or entertainment, that is, if the chimp's requests are grammatically correct.

About ninety symbols appear on the keyboard. Each of these represents a word or concept. The keyboard is then connected to a computer and teletype machine. The printout, which comes off the computer onto the teletype machine, is checked by the human researcher. Responses are provided.

With this system Lana has been able to construct sentences and communicate in a complex but limited way with her human observer. All of her responses are based on stimulus-response learning. If she fails to construct sentences properly, she will not get a reward.

Another pioneering experiment with animal communication is being conducted at the University of Pennsylvania. The chimp's name is Sarah, and her initial training

Figure 2.4

Koko, the first gorilla to talk in sign language, uses 225 signs effectively.
Courtesy, *Stanford Observer*

began at the University of California in Santa Barbara in 1966. The study was conducted by Dr. David Premack and his wife, Ann. The Premacks taught Sarah to read, write, and type. Instead of letters, they used different shaped and colored plastic shingles, each representing a word. Sarah learned how to move them around on a magnetized board to create sentences.

The experiment is now being conducted in a research laboratory at Honeybrook Farms, about seventy miles west of Philadelphia, Pennsylvania. Sarah and her protege, Peony, are developing their communications skills on a daily basis. Sarah's vocabulary consists of more than 140 words and Peony's around 100. In fact, the chimps even have a pinball machine, which they get to use by using a computer-activated language correctly.

In Sarah's vocabulary are signs representing verbs, colors, foods, objects, concepts, adjectives, and adverbs.

Other studies are uncovering new knowledge regarding the potential of animal communication. Many of these studies will help us to find solutions to human problems like dyslexia, a common reading disability in humans, or heart disease, mental health, drug research, and many other areas.

In a project sponsored by the Spencer Foundation and the National Geographic Society, research is being done with a four and one-half year old female gorilla named Koko, who communicates using Ameslan. In fact, she communicates so well that she has been given a variety of intelligence tests. The young gorilla's score ranges from eighty to eighty-five, compared to a human child's score of one hundred. The project is significant because Koko has already surpassed the achievements of Washoe, having mastered 225 words. Prior to this study it was believed that gorillas were not able to learn sign language. The project was conducted at the San Francisco, California Zoo, by a doctoral student from Urbana, Illinois, Penny Patterson.

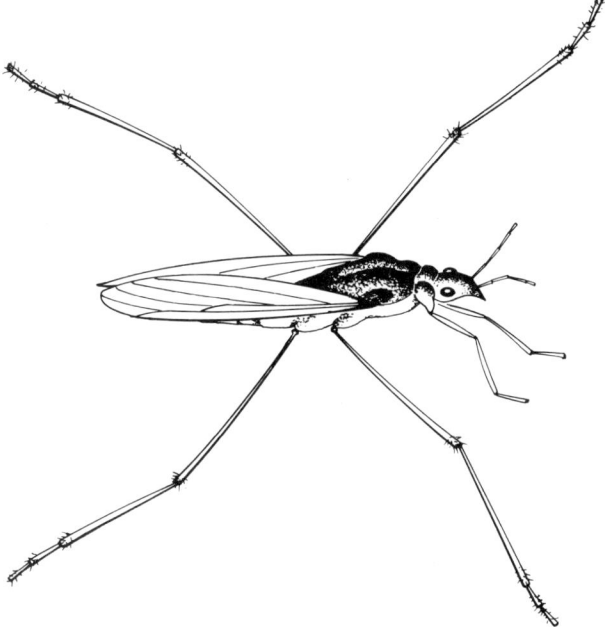

Figure 2.5

The Water Strider has sensory hairs attached to each leg segment.

At the beginning of this section we pointed out that animals communicate for several reasons. In the main, these relate to safety, food, or reproduction of the species. These are inborn characteristics essential to the continuation of their species on the earth. We also mentioned that animals communicate tactilely, visually, and acoustically. Some communication even takes place through chemical signals, ultrasonic impulses, and olfactory stimuli. Let's take a look at how animals communicate in each of these categories.

Tactile Communication in Animals

This communication channel is used by animals in physical contact with each other. Activities in this category vary from simple contact to elaborate dances (honeybees).

Sense organs that respond to touch, pressure, or other mechanical action make up an important part of the basic equipment of most animals. Many insects rely on sensory hairs to give them information about what is happening around them. Often groups of sensory hairs and dome-shaped organs are found at the joints of a leg segment. These hairs touch the next segment so that any bending of the joint will move the hairs and trigger a response in the sensory nerves.

Touch, or simply sensitivity to pressure, is an important feature in the lives of many animals. Animals such as snakes and dolphins caress each other during courtship, while lower animals react to touch or vibration as a sign of approaching danger. A good example of this can be seen by watching snails retreat into their shell when they are touched by an external object.

In many animals, whiskers are also linked to the organs of touch. In animals the senses are best developed that enable them to function more effectively in their environment. Consider the cat. The cat has whiskers sprouting from each side of the nostrils and others around the chin. It seems that their purpose is to warn the cat of obstacles as it prowls about at night. Seals and otters also have whiskers, probably to help them to sense the presence of prey or obstacles in muddy water.

Other animals are sensitive to vibrations. The earthworm comes to the surface at night but pulls back into its hole at the slightest ground movement.

Whirligig beetles rush madly about on the surface of the water but never run into each other. The reason for this is that the antenna of each beetle rests on the surface of the water and vibrations pass through the water to receptors at the base of the antenna. Stimulation in the antenna is used to detect activity around them.

Visual Communication in Animals

Not all animals see the same things, because they are not all sensitive to the same colors of the spectrum. Bees and many other insects may be sensitive to ultraviolet light, but are far less sensitive to red. Most of the light that we recognize as red cannot be seen by them.

Vertebrates, or animals with backbones, are more advanced animals that have developed eyes containing optical mechanisms such as a lens. A lens projects an image on the retina. Insects, on the other hand, have compound eyes comprised of a number of cone-shaped tubes, which give the insect a wide field of vision. Each of these tubes provides one point of the image, and all of these points fit together to create a mosaic picture.

As we study the animal kingdom, from simple to the most complex animals, it becomes apparent that the sense of vision is most important for the higher animals. For them many of the other senses are less well developed.

Sharpness of the sense of vision has many advantages to these animals. Predatory animals use sight to spot their prey from far away. In fact, falcons are able to see a single dragonfly about twenty meters distant. We could not see them much farther away than twenty-seven meters.

Acoustic Communication in Animals

Acoustical signals, like visual signals, require the use of specialized receptors. Specialized phonoreceptors, organs that can receive or detect sound waves, are present only in vertebrates and insects, so acoustical communication in animals is limited to these.

Many animals produce stridulatory sounds. These are sounds produced by drawing a tooth-like structure over a rough surface. Many fish and most grasshoppers and crickets make stridulatory sounds.

By far the finest development of the mechanical senses we know of can be found in the organs of hearing. Different insects are sensitive to various parts of the sound spectrum. Some can even hear sounds in the ultrasonic range, which is more than we can do. Moths can hear ultrasonic sound. This is how they detect the presence of their enemies, the bats, whose calls are mainly ultrasonic.

For many years humans failed to recognize the sounds of bats, which are pitched several octaves above what humans can hear. What is significant about the sounds of bats is not the sound itself but its echo. The sound bounces off obstacles like cave walls, trees, and even flying insects. The echos of the cries keep the bat informed as to obstacles in its way and food in its vicinity.

The bat cries out at a high frequency (40,000 to 80,000 cycles per second). Our ears are sensitive only to a maximum of around 15,000 to 20,000 cycles per second. The bat is able to distinguish between surfaces such as silk or paper in complete darkness.

The bat uses a sonar-type system similar to that used in submarines. Whales use a similar sonar system in the water. We now know that some whales can transmit ultrasonic sounds as high pitched as those of bats.

Animals produce vocal sounds largely by passing air over or through vibrating or resonating structures. The most common animals relying on this means of communication are the mammals and birds. Except for the lower aquatic invertebrates, acoustical communication systems are almost universal in animals. Together with chemical systems, acoustical systems are the most important means of communication used between animals separated by distance.

Chemical Communication in Animals

Acoustic and echo-locating devices used in animals are largely mechanical, but the capabilities of taste and smell are more difficult to understand. Taste and smell are usually classified under the general heading of the chemical senses. Whereas the sense of smell is usually used for examining things at some distance, the sense of taste is used for things actually touched.

Chemical signals are usually transmitted through the air or water currents. Protozoans are attracted to other members of their species through chemical communication. Even slime molds have chemical signals that attract others to them. One individual releases clouds of a chemical acrasin, which causes others to crawl to the caller.

Oysters and marine worms release chemical substances in the water. Body odors for purposes of identification of the species or sex are common among fish and salamanders, mammals, and most insects.

The capability of recognizing other members of the same species is an essential aspect of life for most animals. Most species form social aggregations (clusters). In the case of the barnacle, for example, it is important to recognize other members of the same species. It seems that they are attracted to each other by chemical signals released from certain members of their aggregation.

Earlier in this module we pointed out that humans differ from animals in that animals do not use symbols. Today we are beginning to find out that some animals can and do use symbols effectively. This is not true of most animals, but no longer is it possible to differentiate between the human and animal just on their ability to use symbols.

Some time ago we felt that animals could not learn, and that all of their reactions to particular stimuli were based on instinct. Today we know that even the simplest of animals like the common earthworm learn extremely well.

We do know that animals do, in many primitive ways, seem to show that they are aware of the future. It is a fact that our powers of problem solving and reasoning, of distinguishing between cause and effect, are similar to the abilities that we observe in animals to a less sophisticated extent.

We are now on the brink of new discoveries that are likely to change our world of communications. Advances in the sciences and technologies have enabled us just to scratch the surface. Animal behavior is one area where we have a lot to learn. Future discoveries will continue to help us in understanding our own senses, and how we use them to receive information around us.

Machine Communication

Fifty years ago it would have seemed absurd to have considered the idea of machines communicating with other machines. The mere thought of humans communicating with machines would surely have been just cause for considering psychiatric help for the human, and surely the sledge hammer and junk heap for the machine. Today machine communication is a necessary, if disconcerting, part of our modern way of life.

In 1949 George Orwell wrote the book *1984*. The book described a world where people are controlled by numbers, computer data banks of information, and television surveillance—a place where there is no longer any privacy for "big brother" is always watching you.

Over the years many people have begun to fear their machines. At the turn of the 1980s many of these fears have become more intense. Many of us have become fearful that Orwell's prophecies may come true.

In fact, in June of 1975, nineteen countries representing the industrialized nations of the world met in Paris to address the topic of "data protection and privacy." The conference was organized by the Organization for Economic Cooperation and Development to consider possible laws regulating the collection of computerized information on individuals, personal identification numbers, and surveillance of society.

In West Germany, surveillance of traffic by radar and of factories, banks, and apartment entrances by TV is now common practice. In New York state, experiments have been conducted with television cameras monitoring street intersections.

Machine Communication and Technology

Before we knew how to use technology, it was not possible for us to think about machine communication. Since technology is such a vital part of our way of life, we often try to point the finger toward technology as the cause of all of our current problems. This is an unfair accusation. Our technology has given us new potentials for a better life on our planet. Our technology has enabled us to extend the limited capabilities of our senses. Our senses feed information to our brain, but machines can gather the information that we receive through our senses.

Problems (privacy, surveillance, control, and others) have come about because most of us were not concerned enough about the need for directing and controlling our rapidly developing technology. Technology and machines are not bad; it is those who use them that must assume the responsibility for their actions.

For many years we had to stand in long lines at the supermarket waiting for our groceries to be checked out, one item at a time. Today, thanks to our information processing technology and machine-to-machine communication systems, this problem seems about to be eliminated. The solution has emerged in the form of a system called UPC, or the Universal Product Code. The system consists of a series of closely spaced lines, bars, and numbers printed on all over-the-counter items. The code symbol is different for each product. The code is read by a laser beam scanning device. A message is then sent to the store's computer, which identifies the item, rings it up on the terminal at the checkout counter, and prints an item description and price on the sales receipt. The system has many advantages. Stores across the nation are now experimenting with the system.

Other examples of machine communication are all around us. A dictating machine transmits information from a tape casette through the headphones to the senses, in this case the sense of hearing of a typist. The information is received (heard). The process could stop here. Information has been transmitted from a machine to a person. We are pretty sure that communication has taken place because the machine information has caused a response, in this case the production of typed copy. We will go on to analyze the process in greater detail later.

The situation we have just described represents communication from a machine to a person (dictating machine to typist) and communication from a person to a machine (typist to typewriter).

Machine communication is difficult to understand. Part of this difficulty is created by the fact that we often think of a machine as a metal monstrosity created to perform some factory process. Machine communication refers to nonsensory systems used to transmit and/or receive information. These systems could be machines, instruments, or devices. It makes little difference what we call them. They all share a common purpose; they provide us with extensions on our sensory capabilities.

We know a little about how we communicate using our senses, but we know much less about how we use our technology to help us communicate.

Machine communication is different from human communication because machines do not rely on senses to receive or transmit information. Information is transmitted from a sender to a receiver through a channel, but information is never received through the senses. Instead of human senses we have created artificial senses for machines, ways that machines communicate with each other.

Most machine communication today has been developed for the purpose of obtaining information (instrumentation) and/or for affecting the behavior of other

Figure 2.6

Aerial photograph of the NASCOM Goldstone Deep Space Tracking Station in California. The site is located on the Mojave Desert and has a giant 64.5 meter antenna shown at top right, and a smaller 26 meter antenna located at lower left in the picture. These antennae are modern-day examples of machines that receive information from deep space and then transmit this information to other machines. Courtesy, NASA

machines (control). Some machines such as thermometers, speedometers, and satellites are designed primarily for purposes of instrumentation. That is, these devices have been created to record information and enable humans or other machines to make certain adjustments in their environment.

We can think of many ways in which machines provide us with information. In most cases this information transmitted to us by machines falls under the general grouping of instrumentation. Here information is provided for use by our senses, so machines, or instruments which collect information for us, are of necessity restricted to human sensory capabilities. It would be of little value for us to design instrumentation that would gather information our senses could not interpret.

These machines all enable us to gain more information about our world. They help us to make more sensible decisions. Without their assistance we would be strangers in a foreign world.

Machine/Machine Communication

In addition to our use of machines for transmitting information to us we also use machines to control other machines. Machines transmitting information to other machines for purposes of instrumentation and/or control are widely used today.

The laser beam luggage-handling system being used by Eastern Airlines at the Miami International Airport takes your bags from you in the parking lot. A small label is fastened to each bag. As the bag passes under a laser beam reader, information from the tag on things like destination, flight number, and departure is transmitted to a computer. The computer interprets the code as the flight number for the bag. The computer then checks all of the flights for the day to see if all is in "go" condition. If everything is all right, the bag is sent through a robot-like delivery system of mechanical arms until it reaches the correct location. Eastern officials claim that the system is eight times faster than their old baggage transfer methods.

In the system described above there are hundreds of little communication systems ranging from simple switches to complex computer networks. All of these are concerned with transmitting information from one point to another; all of these systems function for the purpose of either instrumentation or control. Failure in any of these subsystems could shut down the entire system if the system was created without sufficient support systems.

Consider some of the complex communication systems developed by the National Aeronautics and Space Administration (NASA). On July 5, 1976, the first of two Viking Landers set down on the surface of Mars. Thirteen experiments were on board to collect information that was to be transmitted back to earth. Let's take a closer look at one of these systems—the camera system used to photograph the Martian environment.

The two cameras used on the Viking mission are simple devices compared to most of the communication systems aboard the lander.

The Viking Lander had many sophisticated communication systems and subsystems. Each of these systems had to work properly before the mission could become a success.

32 MAJOR SYSTEMS IN WHICH COMMUNICATION OCCURS

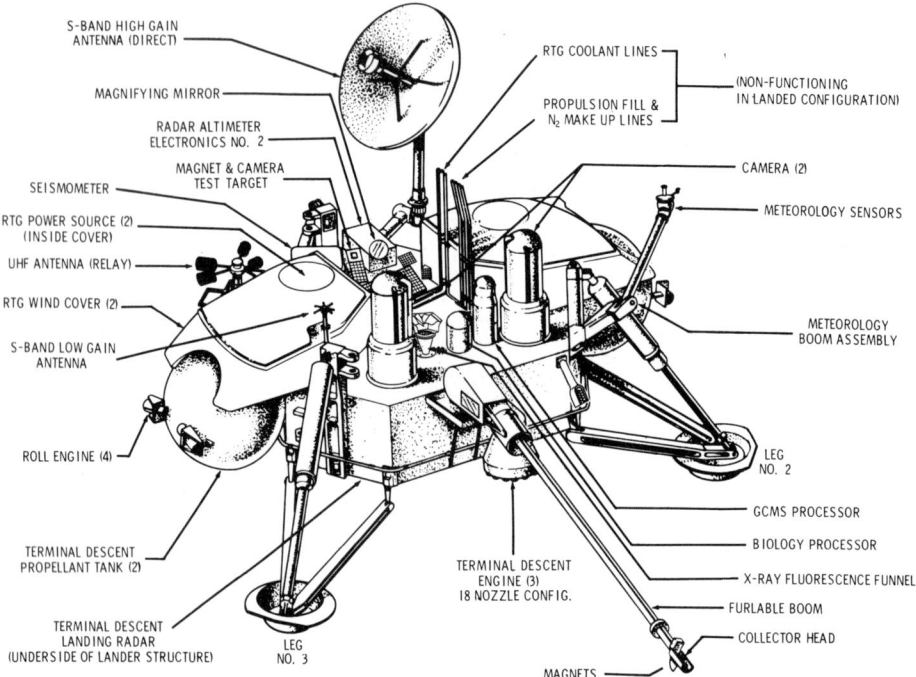

Figure 2.7

This simplified drawing of the Viking Lander shows the location of the two cameras used to collect data on the mission.
Courtesy, NASA

Have you ever wondered how the telemetry, or the task of transmitting findings back to earth is accomplished? On the Viking mission it was done in this way:

1. Information in the form of electrical voltages was received from instruments on board the craft.
2. These electrical voltages were then changed into digital pulse patterns, which were stored on magnetic tape in a multichanneled tape recorder. The digital signals enabled the computers on earth to tell which instrument was sending the information.
3. At preset times the recorder unloaded the recorded information into a radio transmitter.
4. The transmitter sent out information to the Viking Orbiter and the Orbiter transmitted to the dish-shaped microwave antenna in California, Australia, and Spain.
5. At the receiving stations computers sorted out and made sense of the information.

Communication from machines to other machines is important in many other areas. Since the early 1960s we have been concerned with gathering weather infor-

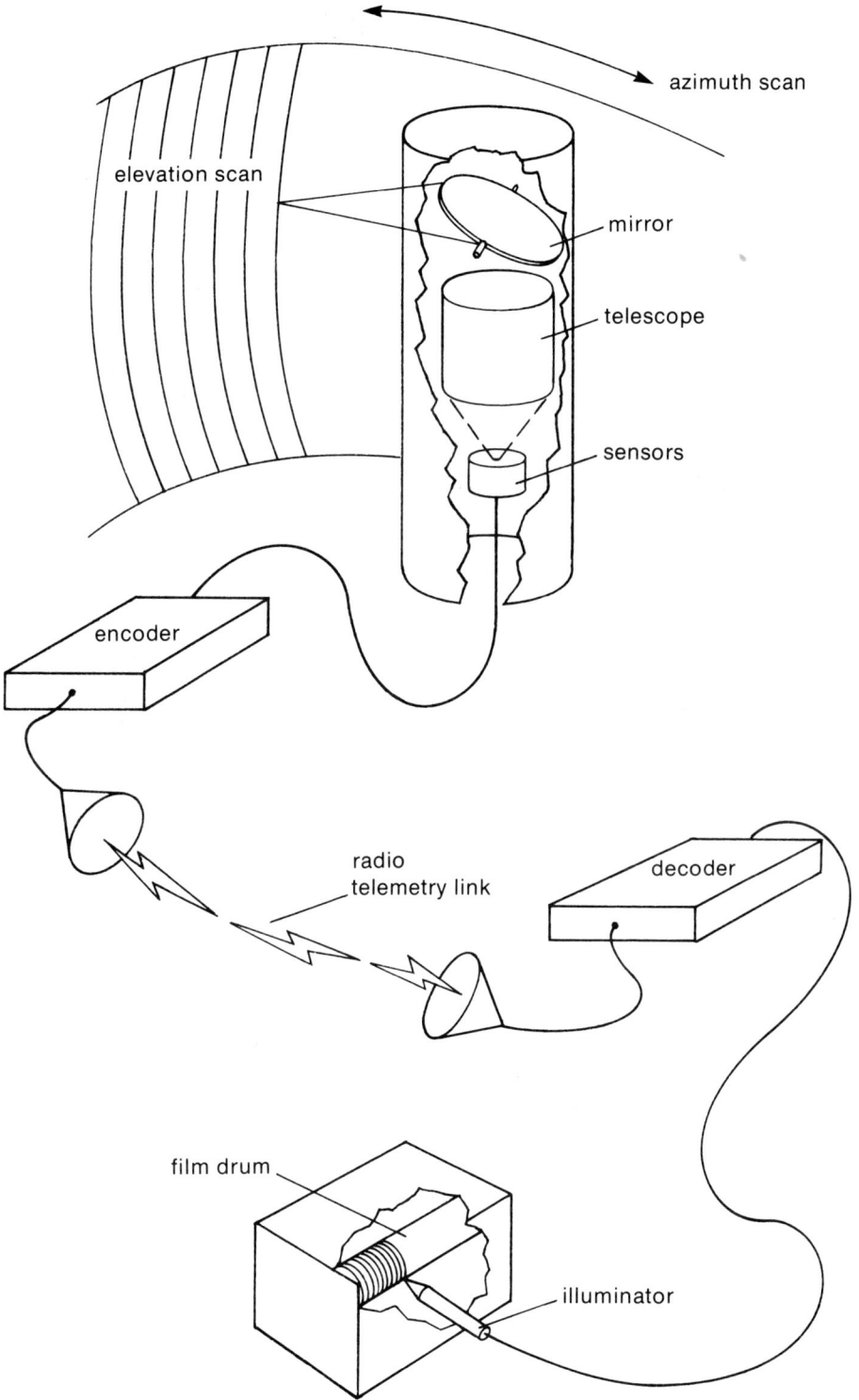

Figure 2.8

On the Viking Mission two cameras collected visual information and fed the information back to earth.

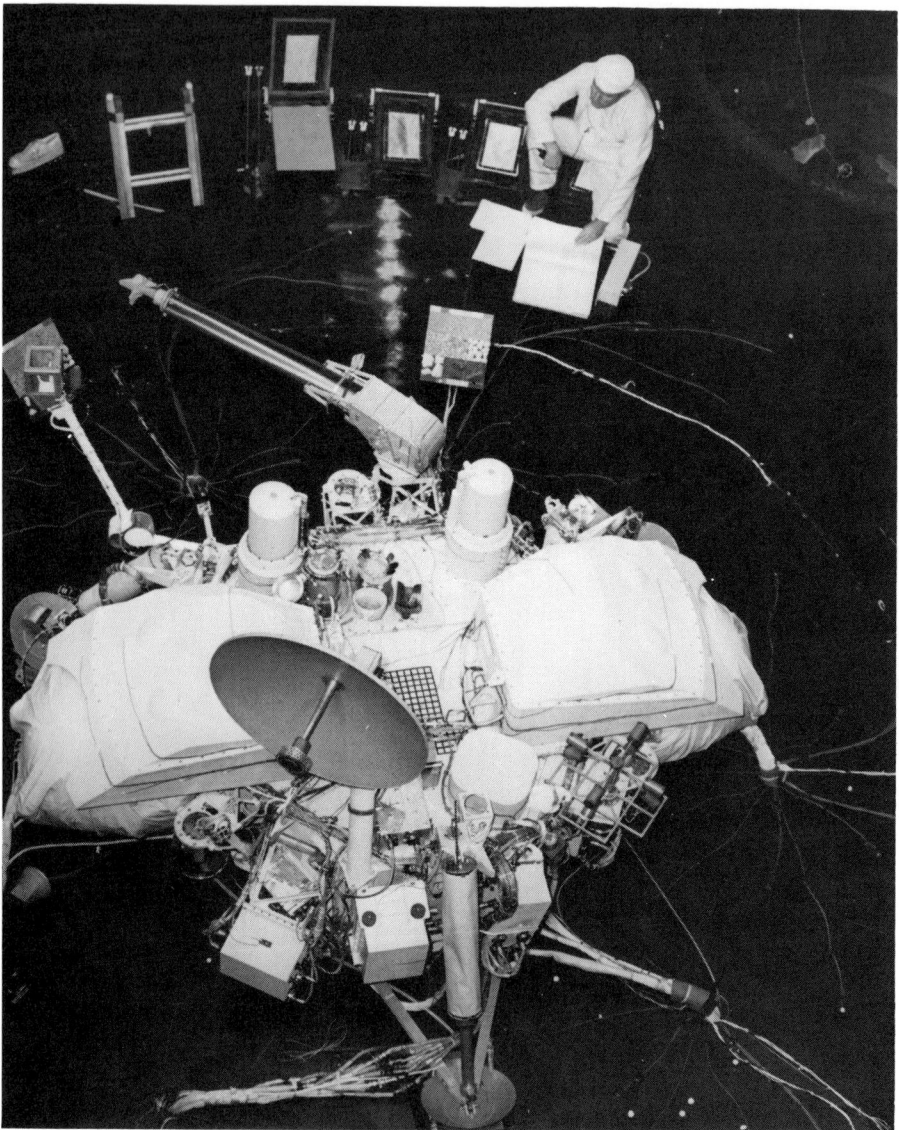

Figure 2.9

Many systems and subsystems underwent rigorous tests in a vacuum chamber at space center facilities in Colorado before the Viking spacecraft could depart for Mars.
Courtesy, NASA

mation on a global basis. To accomplish this, environmental data buoys have been developed. An environmental data buoy is a floating platform anchored in deep water. The buoy must contain sufficient electrical power to operate for about a year without attention and must be durable enough to survive 150 knot winds and 180 meter high waves.

The first such buoy was moored off the coast of Florida in 1964. The buoy, referred to as BRAVO, housed sensors that monitored air and water temperature, air pressure, dew point, wind and water current velocity, insolation, precipitation, wave heights, and amount of salt in the water.

On environmental data buoys the electronic/electrical on-board systems consist of sensors, a data acquisition and control system, a telemetry system, and a source of power. On a typical environmental data buoy information from as many as 200 sensors is received, processed, stored, and transmitted with the help of an on-board digital computer. In the Environmental Data Buoy there are thousands of instances where

Figure 2.10

This buoy transmits weather and pollution data from its location in the Gulf of Mexico to Miami every three hours.
Courtesy, National Oceanic and Atmospheric Administration

information is transmitted from one point to another point, and from one machine to another.

Other examples of machines controlling other machines can be found in the satellites now collecting information or data for our use back here on earth. Have you ever wondered just how this information gets back to us? Telemetry, or the process used to transmit data from a spacecraft back to earth, is all made possible through the use of sensors. Here's what happens. Data (satellites collect over 200 million bits of data each day) is converted into electrical signals. These signals are transmitted to earth where they are received and used to reproduce the original data. Data may be either transmitted continuously or stored on magnetic tape until the ground station requests a **read out.**

One such ground station, the Etam satellite station in northeastern West Virginia, monitors hundreds of information circuits around the clock. Etam provides the major link for communications between the United States mainland, Central and South America, the Caribbean, Europe, Africa, and the Mideast. The station receives and processes information from satellites situated in synchronous orbit over the Atlantic.

Information is transmitted and received at the same time through the station's dish-shaped antenna. The antenna is 29.57 meters in diameter and stands higher than a ten-story building. Signals received from a satellite are directed from the dish-shaped reflector to receiver amplifiers. They are then boosted again in power and are finally processed at the control station.

Figure 2.11

The Etam control station in West Virginia receives most of the satellite information used in the United States. Careful monitoring of incoming information from satellites makes viewing of international events such as the Olympics possible.
Courtesy, Communications Satellite Corporation.

The Etam control station enabled around 500 million people in four countries and five continents to watch the first steps on the moon in July of 1969. Without sophisticated types of machine/machine communication none of this would have been possible.

Today we use communication satellites and sensors to detect conditions that formerly we could only guess about. From space we are able to measure temperatures, colors, shapes, distances, and climatic conditions. From these measurements we can determine environmental conditions. Let's look at some of the accomplishments of machine communication today.

Weather satellite systems are regulated in the United States under the management of the Department of Commerce. Satellites provide weather data used to make TV weather reports. The satellites can also be used to monitor water pollution. Studies are being conducted using the Chesapeake Bay oyster. The oyster is a good monitor of water quality because its heartbeat varies with the amount of oxygen in the water. Since oysters cannot survive in polluted water the quantity of oysters in the region gives observers a good indicator of the conditions of the water. The heartbeat of the oyster is transmitted to a stationary Environmental Data Buoy (EDB) which in turn relays the data via satellite to a receiving station.

A similar study is being conducted using the blue crab. The crab's bloodstream responds to the degree of salinity of the water and its heartbeat is an indicator of its health. A miniature transmitter sends information to an EDB and on to the satellite. Both studies may help us to understand the degree of pollution and its effect on valuable food species.

Pictures taken from satellites are also used as environmental monitoring systems. In addition to sources of industrial pollution being spotted, oil spills and other ocean dumping are quickly recognized. Federal lawsuits against polluters have been the result of antipollution monitoring systems.

Satellite imaging systems have also been used to determine turbulence of water, measure degree of snow cover, ascertain drainage patterns, detect earthquakes, prospect for minerals, monitor crops, and even record the behavior of California gray whales.

Most of the communicating machines that are important to us, no matter whether they are just instruments or control devices, could be looked at as robots. They help wash our clothes, compact our trash, and even tell us when to get up in the morning and go to bed at night.

It seems likely that in the 1980s robots with sensors and computer control systems will be able to adapt their behavior to changing environmental conditions. This means that they will be able to handle many new tasks in conditions that are unsuitable to humans. Tasks such as mining, tunneling, exploring the great ocean depths, and conducting production tasks in ultrahot or ultracold temperatures can and will be done by machines.

In many factories throughout the world there are now thousands of devices that could be called robots. Most people would not think of these devices as robots. People have the idea that robots look like humans and move about in a jerky sort of semihuman way.

Industrial robots are just machines that pick and place objects, and demonstrate only the simplest kinds of motions. They have little or no capability of sensing conditions in the environment. When they are turned on, they only execute a preprogrammed plan of action.

38 MAJOR SYSTEMS IN WHICH COMMUNICATION OCCURS

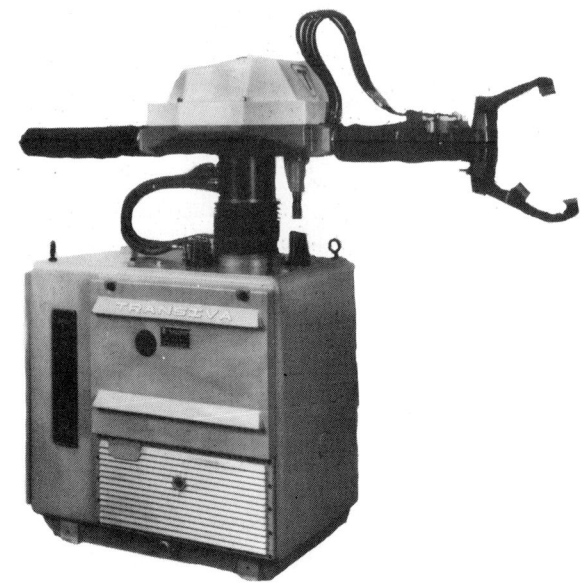

Figure 2.12

The Transiva industrial robot is used for repetitive loading and unloading operations and in hazardous areas where human operators could not work.
Courtesy, B & R Ltd., London, England

Figure 2.13

This child's drawing of a robot shows that most people think of robots as human-like in appearance.

For years we thought that this was how humans were distinctly different from machines. Humans learn how to do things from experience; machines do not learn but only have been programmed to perform specific tasks.

In 1952 Claude E. Shannon, then of Bell Telephone Laboratories, devised an experiment to illustrate the potential of telephone relays. What he did was design a maze-running electrical mouse. The mouse was able to find its way through the maze by "remembering" information through the switching relays like those used in the old dial telephone systems.

In order for a machine to learn to do anything it must, like a human or animal, anticipate what will happen as a result of its behavior. For example, a computer can be programmed to play chess—and win. If the computer knows when it wins or loses the game it can decide whether the moves it makes are good or bad. It can then store good moves in its memory for later use in similar situations. By collecting information from a number of games it could "learn" how to make better choices.

Several fairly simple machines are sensitive to the results of their own actions. One good example can be found in Ross Ashby's homeostat. Ashby pointed out that much of the success of mammals is due to our ability to control and maintain a constant internal environment. If all is working well, we automatically control the temperature of our bodies and the chemical composition of our bodily fluids.

The homeostat consists of several electrical controllers joined by relays. When the controllers fluctuate from the preset range, relays switch creating a new circuit arrangement. If the new circuit is unstable, new combinations will be tried randomly until a stable circuit is found. The device has no memory but is adaptive because it changes its internal connections.

Another example can be noted in the **flyball governor** invented for the steam engine by James Watt. The governor was fastened to the vertical shaft of the steam engine. As the shaft turned, the steel balls were drawn outward by centrifugal force. Their action on the levers served to shut down the throttle lever, which turned off the steam to the boiler on the engine. This is how the device regulated the speed on the engine.

Although this simple governor is an excellent example of automatic control, like the homeostat it is an adaptive machine capable of changing its own behavior. Neither of these machines are what might be called thinking machines. Both of these are representative only of automatic control devices. They cannot learn to control their own behavior.

Instrumentation and Control

Machine communication is a by-product of our technology. We have developed systems of machine communication for the purpose of obtaining information (instrumentation) or affecting the behavior of other machines (control).

Instrumentation is used to provide new information for our senses. In most cases this information has been obtained with much greater precision than our senses would have ever provided. Quite often this instrumentation is used to record critical variables such as temperature, pressure, or humidity.

A good example of how instrumentation provides extensions or capabilities beyond our senses is a development that has occurred in the realm of fiber optics.

Research and development in the field of lightwave communications has resulted in several different types of optical fibers being produced. Light tubes all transmit light from one point to another, just like a copper wire would transmit electrical energy. One of the basic principles of fiber optics is that light travels in a zigzag path through the transparent core of each fiber because of the intensity of the light source, the type of sheath and core structure, and the length of the guide itself. Fiber optic devices are used in all sorts of applications where there is a need to carry light from one point to another. The concept has already found use in home appliances, vending machines, electrical controls, signs, communications equipment, surgical and medical instruments, and many other markets. One of the interesting features about light guides is that they can carry light around bends and tight angles without resorting to lenses, prisms, or any other optical devices.

The potential for light wave communications extends far beyond the realm of providing light to instrument panels in automobiles. According to recent developments being made by Bell Labs, telephone calls will soon be carried through glass fibers the size of a human hair. The system is called **Lightwave Communications,** and is being developed as an alternative to the copper wire now used to transmit phone calls. It will have real advantages over copper because the fibers are thinner and can carry as many calls as a big and bulky copper cable. This will be an advantage in underground conduits where conditions are already very crowded. One other advantage of the glass fiber system is that it requires fewer natural resources to make it; all that it requires is sand.

Instrumentation is different from control. Control is not necessarily linked to our human senses. It is related to the "senses" of the interpreting machine. Let's take a closer look at it.

It is easy to confuse a control system, or **servomechanism** as it is often called, with a power drive. The idea of a power drive may be grasped by thinking about the bicycle. The power drive is the system from the pedals and drive sprocket through the chain to the rear wheels. Anyway, this is a much different type of thing than a control system, which enables one machine to control another through electronic instrumentation and electromechanical devices.

The old mechanical lift is an example of a power drive. It required a human operator to bring it to the right floor by turning a speed control lever. The power was provided by the lift, but the idea of guidance and judgment was left to the operator.

Consider the modern elevator. In this system the operator pushes a button indicating the desired floor and the rest is automatic. An interesting aspect of this servo system is that new information can be put into the system, by pushbutton or other means.

There are three important aspects of most control or servo systems: (1) a sensing device, (2) accuracy, and (3) rapid response. In addition to these, other unknown variables serve to muddy the picture.

In the flyball governor there was some delay in getting to the final response. It was possible for the balls to move up and down for some time before the boiler was finally shut off. In modern servo systems, amplifiers increase the sensitivity of the response so that the efficiency of the total system is improved.

The technology of control in machines and animals is called **cybernetics**. A servo system is an adaptive mechanism in that it is capable of modifying its behavior to changing conditions in its environment. Since a servo system can react to changing conditions we often refer to it as "intelligent." Machines are only intelligent in that they are capable of processing information. Machines are now available that can read typed copy and speak with a midwestern accent. Others are performing well as musical composers, medical diagnosticians, and maxi librarians.

Even though machines can do just about everything, some problem areas have emerged that are hampering progress in the realm of adaptive machines. One of the most difficult areas is that of machines being able to recognize pictorial information such as shapes, sizes, colors, or irregular outlines. In time machines will undoubtedly be able to be "trained" to read handwriting. Machines developed by the United States Air Force Research Laboratories at Cambridge, Massachusetts, are now available that can be trained to produce printed words in response to spoken sound.

Other research being conducted at Massachusetts Institute of Technology, the Advanced Research Projects Agency (ARPA), and at a number of major universities, is investigating the possibilities of creating a machine that can even read a person's thoughts. Reports from the ARPA have indicated that the machine can already determine five emotional states by reading a person's brain waves—with an accuracy of 90 percent.

Machines are poorly equipped to deal with abstractions such as love, beauty, or pleasure, but it does seem likely that in the near future they will even be able to deal with these types of issues.

Today many of our machines are becoming distinctly more human. Some of these robot machines (vacuum sweepers, dishwashers, trash compactors) have already found their place in our homes. Some say that their successors, the robots of the future, will be much more lifelike. It is even possible that they will have their own pleasant but identifying smell. We are only just beginning to scratch the surface in creating complex machines with adaptive characteristics. What the future will hold we can only guess. What we can be sure of is the fact that as our machines become more and more sophisticated, communication will be there. Without instrumentation and control, machines would be no more than figments in our imagination.

Anomalous Communication

One of the most exciting features about the study of communications is that researchers are making new discoveries every day. Many of these discoveries cannot be explained within the framework of our past experiences and knowledge. Because of their unexplainable nature they can best be referred to as anomalies. An **anomaly** is something that occurs, but we have little information on which to base our judgment of why it is occurring.

If one looks hard enough anomalies can be found in all communication systems. Today anomalies are prevalent in human and animal communication.

In discussing communication anomalies, the most important thing is objective analysis and keeping an analytical but open mind. Most of the discoveries that we will mention at first glance may seem ridiculous because, based on our current knowledge base, they do not fit. We do not have answers to explain how and why the anomaly occurs. Eventually many of the topics mentioned in the following pages will be accepted as stable knowledge or accepted fact. Some other areas will be disproven or explained away. They will make little contribution to the total process of communication and our development and use of communication technology.

Extrasensory Occurrences

Several years ago (1972) the Stanford Research Institute conducted research on Uri Geller. Geller is a controversial Israeli who claims that he can predict the future, read the thoughts of others, and even move objects by using thought processes alone. The Stanford Project, conducted over the span of five weeks, sought to find out once and for all if there was any truth in Geller's claims. In the tests Geller accomplished the following:

1. He transmitted a number he was thinking of to Stanford Research Institute's vice president for research (telepathy).
2. He predicted the throw of dice each of eight times he tried (precognition).
3. He indicated twelve times with no mistakes which one of ten cans contained objects (clairvoyance).
4. He caused a calibrated laboratory balance inside a bell jar to change its reading without touching it (psychokinesis).

The final reports of Stanford Research Institute regarding the findings of the experiment indicated that certain phenomena were observed that seemed to have no scientific explanations.

The Kirlian Aura

During early transatlantic voyages sailors were kept at ease by the presence of the patron saint of seamen, St. Elmo. When they stared out at the mast on dark nights they could see him represented as a violet glow against the sky. What they did not know was that they were observing the electro-discharge or corona-discharge phenomenon. Today researchers know that the glow that sailors saw was nothing more than ionized air created by electrostatic potential. This glow is now known as the Kirlian aura, or Kirlian corona.

There are several interesting features about the aura, which is really just an energy field, surrounding everything around us. Researchers found that the aura, or corona, could be captured on photographic film by a technique now known as Kirlian photography. The technique was developed by Russian electronic experts Seanyon and Valentina Kirlian during the late 30s. They found that by striking a subject with a small amount of high-voltage, high-frequency current and monitoring the static discharge on photographic film an aura (pattern surrounding the object) would be produced.

The Kirlians also reported that if one were to cut a section out of a leaf and then photograph the leaf with the technique, the aura of the entire leaf would appear on the film. This is known as the **phantom leaf effect**.

Most Kirlian researchers feel that the aura around a hand, finger, or even fingerprint reveals changes in the emotional state of the individual. Many of these researchers claim that the technique may offer new possibilities for diagnosing illness and treating disease.

Others claim that these auras are nothing more than patterns created by moisture, and do not represent emotional states or physical conditions. A 1976 study conducted by the Logical Technical Services Corporation in New York concluded that most of the variations in the aura of living objects can be accounted for by the presence of moisture. Scientists conducting the experiment (John O. Pehek, Harry J. Kyler, and David L. Faust) photographed human fingers and specially coated objects. They found that the objects produced auras similar to the real fingers but they did not vary. By soaking the fingers in alcohol and then measuring increased levels of perspiration they found that reduction of moisture resulted in changes in the aura.

The technique of Kirlian photography should not be discounted yet, however. Conventional polygraph machines (lie detectors) used by the medical profession and police departments are based on the principle of moisture, and they still are used to detect emotional states.

Dream Research

The Maimonides Medical Center in Brooklyn, New York, was the first in the United States to set up a laboratory for the specific purpose of conducting research on dreams. Since 1964 a number of formal studies have been conducted investigating dreams and other anomalies. The findings of these studies indicate that telepathy (sending or receiving information without the use of the five senses) does exist in dreams.

Color Hearing

Color hearing, or **synesthesia,** also offers new potentials for communication explorers. Synesthesia relates to the fact that some people see colors as a result of nonvisual stimuli. The most common of the characteristics of synesthesia is "color hearing," where the hearing of a sound results in a visual impression. For individuals with this capability, hearing certain sounds results in seeing colors, even with their eyes blindfolded.

In most cases individuals experiencing color hearing seem to rely on a dermo-optic sense. This appears to be an unknown sense which relies on light just like normal vision and on heat transmitted from certain colors.

In any case, the subject's eyes are covered or an opaque wall is placed in front of him. He detects colors placed before him by the hands.

According to the researchers about one individual in six seems able to refine the development of this dermo-optic sense.

Moving Objects with the Mind

Telekinesis or **biogravitation** is the power of moving objects through mental processes. Proponents of this idea claim that telekinesis is only possible in a gravitational field. They claim that biogravitational fields exist around all living things.

Most researchers experimenting with biogravitation admit that it cannot be understood within the framework of present-day science and technology. According to these researchers the great problems of studying biogravitation are caused largely by the lack of instruments to measure the phenomenon. It is true that demonstrations have been given and research has been conducted on the idea of transmitting matter through thought processes. To date little conclusive evidence of what is really going on has been uncovered.

Biofeedback in Humans

Another anomaly of human communication can be seen in the area of biofeedback. Already biofeedback has been instrumental in fighting such ills as asthma, heart disease, ulcers, and insomnia. New research has shown that people can learn to control activity of most, if not all, bodily systems. This could be heartbeat, blood pressure, gastric acid, or brain waves.

Biofeedback deals with the control of bodily functions as a result of information being "fed back" from the bodily part (subsystem) to the individual (total system).

Specially designed electronic instruments monitor bodily activities while the individual takes in this information and then uses techniques to alter mental and physical behavior. Tension and anxiety are characteristics that can be reduced using biofeedback. The control system functions something like a household thermostat. The instruments monitor body states while the mind can be used to control the physical body. How the mind operates to cause states of relaxation, excitement, or even stimulate learning is yet to be explained. The future of biofeedback is unknown, primarily because no one knows the limits of mental control over bodily functions.

Some scientists think that living cells communicate with each other through some sort of electromagnetic wave language, while others feel that this occurs through chemical messages sent to nerve centers. Successful interpretation of our communication systems inside the body will enable us to use biofeedback techniques effectively. The result will be longer, happier human lives.

Plant Communication

Other researchers report that some type of biofeedback system can be found in plants. In fact, some have even gone so far as to state that plants do have emotions and can communicate—not just with other plants, but with humans as well!

Early plant communication experiments began in 1966 when C. Backster, an American lie detector expert, decided to hook his philodendron up to a polygraph machine. Through several experiments Backster concluded that humans, animals, and plants are interconnected by some unknown energy, and that all living organisms can instantly communicate, even at a distance.

The reported results of his initial experiments went something like this. He used a galvanometer, the part of a lie detector that will cause a pen to make a tracing on a moving roll of graph paper when attached to a human by wires through which a weak electrical current is run. When used with a human even the slightest change in emotion results in movement of the pen. When Backster observed a plant hooked up to the instrument, he found that it produced a tracing on the paper similar to that made by a human. What was interesting was that when he dunked the plant's leaf in hot coffee there was no response on the printout. He then decided to burn the leaf with a match. Before he could pick up the match he looked at the printout and observed that the pen had jumped all around on the paper. He concluded that he had telepathically communicated to the plant. Further experimentation **supposedly** supported his conclusion.

Another one of his experiments was carried out in a locked laboratory with no people present under totally automated conditions. At preset times small brine shrimp were dumped into boiling water. In rooms located elsewhere in the laboratory, plants hooked to polygraphs reacted sharply when the shrimp died from the boiling water.

Over the years Backster's published findings served to create much interest in the scientific community, both in the United States and abroad. Currently scientists in universities and research laboratories are exploring the phenomenon. Reports of activity have been published in *American Scientist*, *National Wildlife*, *Sputnik*, the *Ladies Home Journal*, *Atlanta*, and *Science*, among others.

We have touched on some of the anomalies in communication. It should now be clear that there is much that we do not know, and much left to discover. Many of the reported findings on anomalies are unreliable because of faulty experimentation and careless research. Experimentation must be conducted with proper controls. If the experiment cannot be re-enacted with the same results, the evidence is not conclusive; and rational judgments must not be made.

On the other hand, be leery of shutting out areas of exploration because they do not seem possible. If no one had the courage to investigate the unknown, we would not have science and technology. The biggest roadblocks to discovery have often been caused by too much or too little knowledge about the problem, or incomplete and obsolete knowledge forcing the individual into rejecting consideration of a new option.

We have seen that communication is important to almost everything that exists in our world. We know now that communication takes place in machines and animals, and that we have just begun to scratch the surface on what might be known about the process.

In Module Three we will deal with human communication, the last of the major systems where communication activity occurs. We will then be ready to concentrate on the major emphasis of this text—communication technology.

In Module Two we have attempted to put the world of communications into proper perspective. Let's step back a bit now and review the highlights of what we have covered.

⫸ CONCEPT FOCUSER

- **Animals** and **humans** communicate using the **senses** to interpret information.
- **Machines** receive information through **nonsensory systems** made possible by our technology.
- **Machines receive information** in the form of **energy** through **instrumentation**, rather than the senses.

- **Without instrumentation** and **control** systems **machine/machine** communication would **not** be **possible**.
- **Evidence** seems to indicate that there are **senses beyond** the **accepted five**.
- There **are** many **anomalies left to be discovered** in the world of communications.

 FOOD FOR THOUGHT

1. Which of the following communication relationships, person/person, person/machine, machine/machine, and machine/person, have been made possible by technology?
2. Since machines do not have senses how do they receive information?
3. How can the study of animal communication be of value to the communication technologist?
4. Why do we rely on machines to assist us in communicating?
5. List an example of something that was a communication anomaly ten years ago and is a reality today.

 EXPANDING EXPERIENCES

1. Team up with one of your classmates. Make arrangements to spend a day in the country observing how animals communicate with each other in their natural habitat. Keep a log of your findings and discuss them with your science teacher and communication technology teacher.
2. Read some magazine articles on the behavior of ant colonies. Then as a class project make a self-contained anthill of plexiglass. Observe the behavior of the ants and conduct experiments to find out more about their patterns of communication.
3. Read a book or series of articles on telepathic communication. Then design a class experiment to find out if telepathy really exists, and if ESP powers can be developed. Ask your teacher to help in designing the experiment.
4. Develop a resource list of people and places in communication that deal with animal or anomalous communication. Share these with your classmates. Then speak with your teacher about inviting some of these people to class to speak on their aspect of communication.
5. Investigate all of the industries dealing with automated manufacturing or machine communication and talk to your teacher about taking a field trip to visit them.

 LOCATOR TOOLS

New Horizons, NASA, Superintendent of Documents, U. S. Government Printing Office, Washington, D. C. 20402, stock number 033-000-0631-4, 1975.

Tinbergen, Niko. *Animal Behavior*. New York: Time-Life Books, 1970.

HUMAN COMMUNICATION AND PERCEPTION

Module
THREE

The purpose of this module is to discuss the various ways human beings communicate and how information is received and perceived. The process of **human communication** is the conscious or unconscious transfer of meaning from one human mind to another, by the means of some kind of message.

The reception of a message, in human communication, occurs through the human senses of sight, sound, taste, smell, and touch. Whatever message is received by the senses is then interpreted by the brain. How a receiver interprets the message depends on his or her perception. **Perception** is the process by which an individual understands information fed in from the world around him. There is a distinction between the reception of a message via the senses and the perception of a message via the brain. This distinction can be illustrated by considering the difference between hearing and listening, seeing and looking, smelling and sniffing, touching and feeling, and tasting and savoring. This information may help us understand and improve the process of human communication.

THE SENSORY SYSTEM

For the sensory receptors to be of value, they must function as part of a total system. The sense of sight receives visual signals via the eye, but the reception of the visual signal does not mean communication has taken place. The eye serves merely as the receptor of visual signals for the rest of the system. In the case of the sense of sight, the remaining part of the system is the optic nerve. It changes the visual information to chemical-electro information through a complex network of nerve endings that go to the brain. Once at the brain the information is interpreted or decoded into a message that is perceived by the individual. So then, the eye as a sensory receptor is only one part of the total system that enables human beings to understand visual images.

The senses open doorways to information, to new and more complete views of the world around us. The senses are body systems that take in various kinds of stimuli. **Stimuli** are signals that are sensed by our bodies. These stimuli incite us, or at least certain parts of our bodies, to action. This action is commonly called the **response.**

For example, when you change class late in the morning and smell the aroma of food from the cafeteria, your stomach may suddenly feel empty or your mouth may water in anticipation of eating lunch. Perhaps, depending on the quality of food in your cafeteria, a different feeling may overcome you, one of nausea or panic! Whatever response the aroma of food has created, it is dependent in part on your past experience with similar stimuli. This is a simple example of a very complex stimulus/response function basic to all animals, including human beings. But, let us take it one step beyond the sense of smell and analyze how this stimulus/response function works with our senses in general.

Each sensory system has certain organizational features in common. Collections of sensory cells in different body locations are called **receptors.** These receptors pick up various signals from the environment around them. The receptors act as receivers of particular signals and relay this information along. The information passed on by

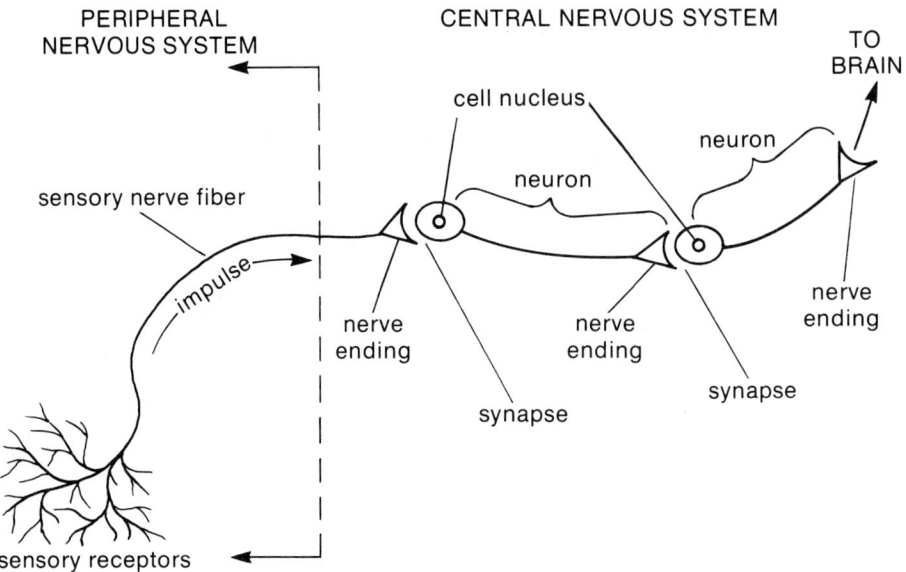

Figure 3.1

Sensory stimuli (information) received by the sensory receptors create an impulse that is carried by the sensory nerve fiber to the central nervous system. The nerve impulse travels across synapse gaps from neuron to neuron until the impulse reaches the brain.

the receptors is conveyed by a sensory nerve composed of many individual fibers to more central parts of the nervous system. This information must be passed between a series of nerve cells (**neurons**). Neurons are located at the end of each nerve fiber.

At the level of the sensory receptor the original information (in the form of odors, light waves, sound waves, pressure) is transformed into electrical impulses. These impulses are transmitted along the sensory nerve fiber toward the central nervous system. When these impulses arrive at the ending of the sensory nerve fiber they cause the release of a chemical substance (termed **neuro transmitter substance**) into a gap called the **synapse**. The transmitter substance then, by a complex process, causes electrical impulses to be generated in the next neuron. This sequence is then repeated at each synapse and permits transfer of information along the series of neurons. Electrical energy transmits information along nerve fibers, whereas chemical energy is responsible for the transfer of information between nerve cells, or neurons.

Coding of information in this system is based primarily upon the rate or frequency of electrical impulse firing along the nerve fiber. For example, very light pressure on the skin may produce two impulses per second to be conducted along the sensory nerve fiber, whereas heavy skin pressure may cause as many as 100 impulses per second to be conducted. This entire process of sensory communication takes place automatically within milliseconds.

Noise, or interference, in human communication is a variable that is important in all biological activity. Noise in communication occurs quite frequently. It can come from within the individual's sensory processing system or outside the sensory system. To clarify the idea of noise occurring outside of the human system let's return to our example of the aroma of food in the hall outside the cafeteria. Many elements affected your accurate reception of the signals of food being prepared. Besides your sense of smell being bombarded with the aroma in the building itself, it also might have contended with the smell of the aftershave on the boy across the hall, perfume on the girl next to you, or those gym clothes you forgot to take home for washing. Your other senses were also being fed various signals not related to lunch or the smell of food and perfume.

Noise within a sensory system (interval noise) can alter information just as easily. It is currently unknown what causes interval noise, but scientific research has determined that there is noise in the form of inaccurate information coding and in the firing of information signals between the nerve endings. What results from inaccurate sensory information and the confusion of the senses will be discussed later.

THE SENSES

In order to better understand the five basic senses of human beings, the foundation of human communication, let's analyze each in more detail.

Sight

Sight is the individual's most efficient means of sensory communication. The human faculty of vision surpasses all others in determining complex relationships of information. As the sensory receptor of visual information, the eye is the first group of cells in the optic system to receive a stimulus.

The eye is a sense organ that contains photoreceptors capable of image formation. A photoreceptor is any group of cells sensitive to light. The eyeball is basically a hollow sphere of tissue about 1.5 centimeters in diameter. As light enters the eye it passes through the external transparent tissue called the **cornea** into a clear fluid, the **aqueous fluid**. Light then passes through the **lens** which is a flexible structure partially covered by the iris. The **iris** regulates the amount of light that enters the eye by acting

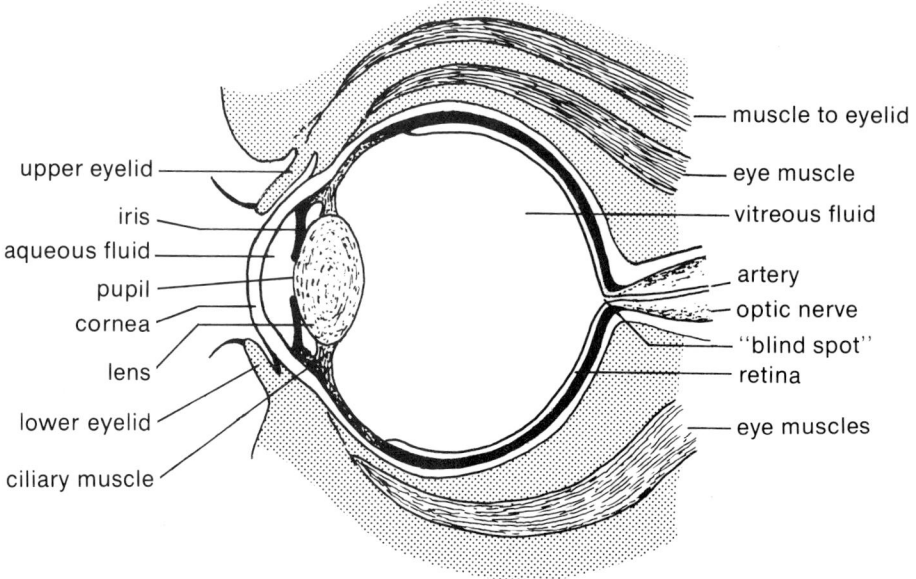

Figure 3.2

The eye is a photoreceptor capable of forming images from visual stimuli.

as a circular diaphragm. It is also responsible for the color of one's eyes. Light continues through the center of the eyeball, (a jelly-like substance called the **vitreous fluid**) until it is brought into focus on the back wall or **retina**. The retina, which acts as a very sensitive screen, is the site of the optical image.

Focusing of the image on the retina wall is done in part by the cornea, but mainly by the lens. The ciliary muscle has the ability, through contraction, or relaxation, to change the shape of the lens and thus can adjust the focus of the visual image on the retina. The retinal layer contains photosensitive sensory receptors called rod and cone cells. These receptors are specialized sensory neurons whose nerve fibers enter the optic nerve on their way to the brain. The optic nerve is simply a collection of all of the individual nerve fibers originating from the retinal rod and cone cells. These specialized cells contain a complex biochemical substance (called **visual pigment**) whose structure is altered when light strikes the cell. This chemical alteration causes electrical impulses to be sent along the nerve fiber, thus transmitting information from the retina to the brain. This information in the form of electrical impulses, however, must be passed across several synapses before arriving at the region of the brain responsible for receiving and interpreting visual information.

Most other mammals have visual systems similar to those of human beings. However, most human beings, through their visual sensory system, have a refined capacity to respond to color, texture, shapes, and spatial relations. We also have the capacity to retain visual information. Before we can study the human communication process in terms of types of visual communication, we must know a little more about light itself.

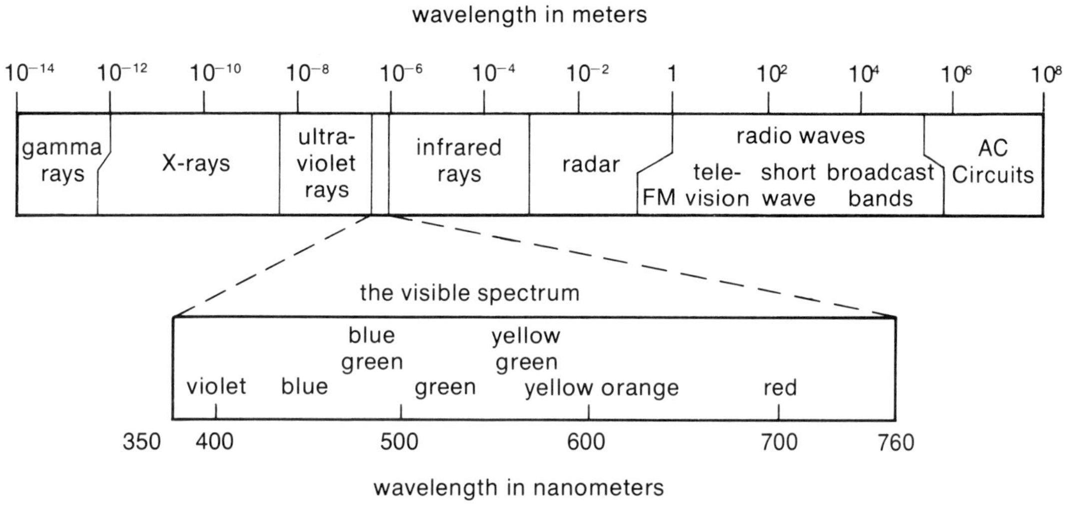

```
wavelength in meters
10⁻¹⁴  10⁻¹²  10⁻¹⁰  10⁻⁸  10⁻⁶  10⁻⁴  10⁻²   1    10²   10⁴   10⁶   10⁸
```

| gamma rays | X-rays | ultra-violet rays | infrared rays | radar | radio waves (FM tele-vision, short wave, broadcast bands) | AC Circuits |

the visible spectrum

| violet | blue | blue green | green | yellow green | yellow | orange | red |

wavelength in nanometers: 350 400 500 600 700 760

Figure 3.3

The visible spectrum of radiation exists only between wavelengths of approximately 375 nanometers and 760 nanometers for most humans.

The light waves necessary for vision occupy only a small range of the total spectrum of waves that exist in our environment. The visual range falls between waves of a very short length (10 trillionths of a centimeter) called **cosmic rays** and long **radio waves** (many kilometers) at the opposite end.

Under normal situations, without a smoke-filled room, the eye is the recipient of many different wavelengths, intensities, and purities of light. These different qualities of light are interpreted by the normal adult eye subconsciously unless the qualities are at extremes such as bright flashes, underwater, or fog.

One's interpretation of a visual stimulus changes from infancy to adulthood. Small children know the color of red because at some time or other someone has told them to associate red with a particular visual stimulus. If they had not had accurate guidance they could just as easily have labeled that same stimulus "zuwarp."

A remaining characteristic of our sense of sight is our ability to retain visual images. This is very important to our ability to obtain information in today's world.

In 1844 one of the foundational discoveries of human visual communication occurred. Joseph Plaeau investigated the concept of creating the illusion of moving visual images. He painted a series of slightly different single images of a running horse and arranged them sequentially around the perimeter of a circular disc. He then viewed the disc through a single port so that only one image could be seen at any given time. By rapidly rotating the disc, the illusion of motion was created; the horse appeared to be running. This principle forms the basis for today's animated cartoons and motion pictures.

Hearing

Next to sight, hearing is our most important sensory link with the world about us. Like the eyes, our ears contain complicated sensory receptors, which transfer information to the brain. Phonoreceptors in the ear contain structures that are capable of detecting vibratory motion in the form of sound waves in the environment. They relay this information to the brain. Auditory information consists of sound wave vibrations, some of which can be heard (are audible) by humans. Auditory information can be transmitted to the ears through a medium of liquids, gases, or solids. We cannot hear in a perfect vacuum.

The communicative information offered to us by our sense of hearing can hardly be overestimated. For just a few minutes, pull yourself away from this book and try to identify and list all the different sounds you can detect. Our ears are pelted by the entire spectrum of sound, but generally we can detect only twenty to 20,000 sound vibrations every second. Because of our ability to "focus" or tune our auditory systems we are not constantly bombarded by extraneous auditory input. This is why we are able to concentrate on the sounds of certain instruments when listening to a concert or stereo record.

Once auditory information reaches the brain, it goes through a complex process that enables us to locate accurately the source of any given sound. This is how you can tell without looking if your teacher is coming down the aisle behind you or on your right or your left.

The auditory system functions much like all sensory systems. Let's begin to analyze the system with a closer look at those external flaps attached to the side of your head. All ears are divided into three parts: an external, a middle, and an inner ear. The function of the external ear of human beings is to receive and direct sound or acoustical stimuli through the auditory canal, which is about 2.5 centimeters in length. Other mammals have additional uses for the external ear: elephants use them to swat flies and some animals wiggle them as part of their mating ritual. However, the human's restricted use of the external ear is limited to catching acoustical information in the form of wave disturbance and vibration usually through the air.

The middle ear is a small irregular chamber lying between the external and inner ear. It is lined with mucous membrane and contains three separate but connected bones whose peculiar shapes have earned them the names **stirrup, anvil,** and **hammer.** Sound transmitted down the external ear sets up vibrations in the thin membrane known as the **tympanic membrane** or **eardrum,** which forms the outer border of the middle ear. The eardrum is connected to the first of the three bones (the stirrup). This arrangement allows for transfer of vibrations from the eardrum to the stirrup and in turn to the remaining two bones of the middle ear. The last bone of the series, the hammer, is connected to the **cochlea**. This structure constitutes the inner ear and consists of a fluid-filled sac shaped very much like a snail's shell. Specialized receptor cells form the inner lining of this sac. Vibratory impulses transmitted from the eardrum through the series of bones eventually arrive at the cochlea. These vibrations set the cochlear fluid in motion, and this fluid motion causes activation of the specialized sensory receptor cells. Once activated, these cells send electrical impulses toward the brain along their nerve fibers. The collection of all nerve fibers originating from these receptors makes up the acoustic nerve. These impulses, like those from the visual system, must be conducted across a series of synapses in the brain until they reach the area of the brain responsible for reception and integration of auditory information.

The mechanism of hearing is dependent upon the reception of sound waves. A wise person once asked this question: "If a tree falls in the deep forest, but no one is

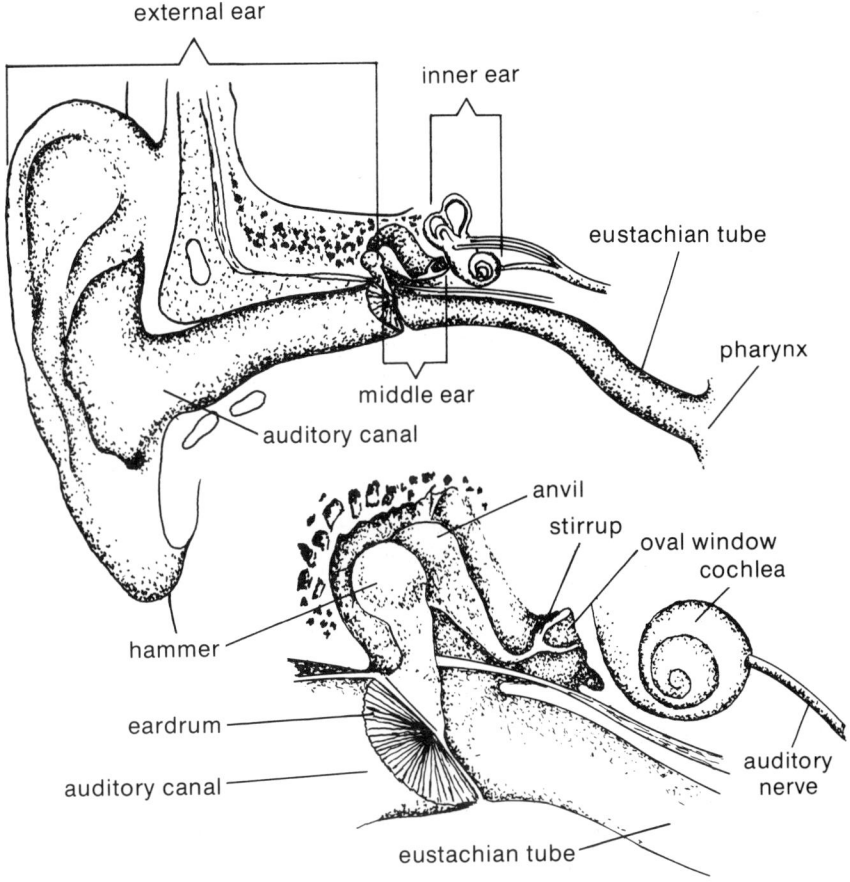

Figure 3.4

The human ear is divided into three parts: external ear, middle ear, and inner ear. Acoustical information, whether transmitted by electronic means (telephone, radio) or by sound energy alone (human conversation) is received as wave vibrations by the ear.

there to hear it, is there a sound?" Perhaps an investigation into what sound is will provide us with the insight to answer this question, and what it is that humans hear.

Human communication by acoustic modes deals with the properties and physics of sound. The word **sound** can be interpreted several ways. Some individuals view sound as the sensations produced in the organs of hearing when certain vibrations are caused in the surrounding air or other elastic media such as gases or liquids by a vibrating body. Here sound is a sensation interrupted in the mind of the listener. But there are sound waves that are not audible. Others feel that sound is the effect of vibrations of sound waves, that is, the physical phenomenon occurring in any elastic medium.

To continue our investigation of sound let's pursue the second definition. It is entirely true that the human ear (each individual threshold of hearing varies) can detect and hear only a small part of the entire spectrum of sound wave vibrations.

Each individual has a different threshold of hearing, that is, the point at which hearing begins or ends.

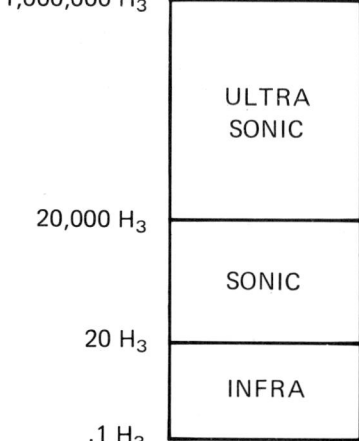

Figure 3.5

Sound wave vibrations are generally classified as infrasonic (below the human range), sonic (the human range of hearing), and ultrasonic (above the frequency range of human hearing.)

The most common method of analyzing sound vibrations is to identify the frequency of sound. **Frequency** (f) of a sound wave is determined by the speed of each vibration, **velocity** (v), divided by the distance the wave travels in one cycle. For example, if a sound wave travels 3.4 meters at 340 meters per second in an air medium, it will have a frequency of 100 cycles per second or Hertz (Hz).

$$\text{frequency} = \frac{340}{3.4} = 100 \text{ c or } 100 \text{ H}_z$$

Depending on their age, human beings can hear sonic tones within a range of about 20 Hertz to 20,000 Hertz. Sound waves of only 0.1 Hertz up to about 20 Hertz are below the normal range of hearing and are called **infrasonic** waves. The range above human detection is the **ultrasonic** range up to as high as one million Hertz. The following scale will show the decibel (dB) rating (a sound level ratio) of some sounds familiar to the human ear (figure 3.6).

Smell

Recently, the dog's sense of smell has again become a valuable tool for humans. Dogs have been used to detect various elements potentially dangerous to humans. They are used to detect hidden or secretive items such as explosives and narcotics in airport terminals, train stations, and border crossings. Long ago sight replaced a keen sense of smell as the dominant human sense. This is all for the better. Instead of running around like a dog sniffing at fire hydrants to determine the environment, we can stand erect and use our eyes to view the unknown.

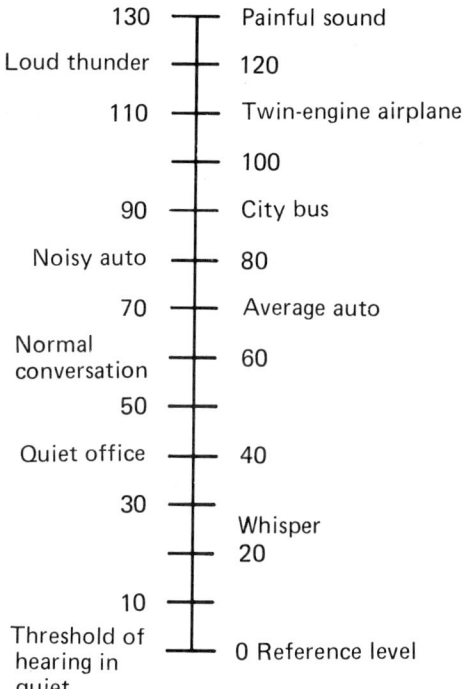

Figure 3.6

Decibel scale showing the relation of some common sounds within the sonic range.

Like taste, the sense of smell appears to be more important in the communication of lower organisms than in human communication. Nonetheless, the human sense of smell (olfaction) is an important sensory system, which we use to receive information about our surroundings. **Olfactory** receptors are groups of cells that can receive and detect the presence of scents and odors. The reception of information via the sense of smell is a chemical process involving sensory receptors located in the **nasal passages**. Up to 600,000 cells in an average nose are capable of distinguishing between 17,000 different odors. A trained nose can tell the difference between various kinds of wines, foodstuffs, and even people (by such stimuli as their clothes, perfumes, or aftershave). Our sense of smell plays a large role in our habits of eating, drinking, and mating.

The elements of our olfactory information system are quite simple compared to those in our senses of sight and hearing. The nostril area acts in a manner similar to that of the external ear since it directs and filters air from the environment. Some olfactory information also enters the nasal passage from the mouth/throat area. The air carrying the odors must reach the top of the nasal cavity where the olfactory receptor occupies an area of about 6.25 square centimeters in each nostril (not depending on nose size).

In normal breathing, only a small portion of air reaches the olfactory receptor. Most of the air is taken into the lungs via the streamlined lower nasal passage. This does not interfere with the reception of olfactory signals because only a small amount of odor-ridden air is necessary to activate the sensory receptors.

Once a particular smell reaches the top of the nasal cavity it affects the sensory

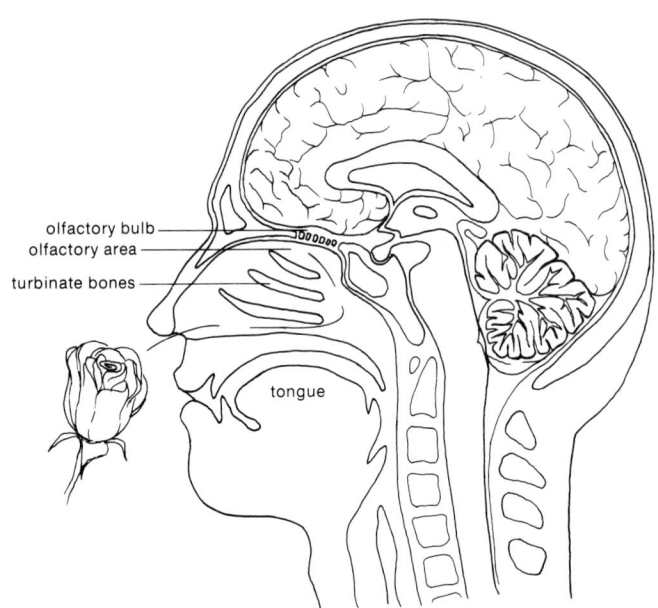

Figure 3.7

Odorous molecules suspended in air are sniffed through the nasal passage and passed to the olfactory area where the sensory receptors receive the chemical information.

receptors. The olfactory cells are located within the side walls of the cavity but receive information from hairlike extensions that pass through the supporting cells and into the mucous covering of the walls. See enlargement section in figure 3.8. These nerve endings passing through the supporting cells to the surface are called olfactory rods. The type of molecule of odorous material that is received at the rods is reflective of what the smell is. Molecules of the same shape, size, and weight tend to have a similar smell. The information received at the rods is transferred through the olfactory cell itself, which is combined with other olfactory nerve endings to form a direct link to the brain.

The sense of smell is often used in cooperation with our sense of taste. In fact, quite often the olfactory system enables us to like or dislike the flavor of the food that our taste buds receive in the mouth. (Try holding your nose and distinguishing between the taste of an apple and a potato.) Without our sense of smell, eating would cease to be an enjoyable experience and would be reduced to a nutritional necessity. The sense of smell can communicate many things, mainly to our subconscious. This explains why people in the industries of perfumery, food manufacture, and packaging are concerned about olfactory systems. Who wants a candy bar wrapper that smells like wax or a sweater that smells like a sheep?

Taste

Our discussion of the sense of taste follows our investigation of the sense of smell because the two are often inseparable. If the sense of smell can be considered as a

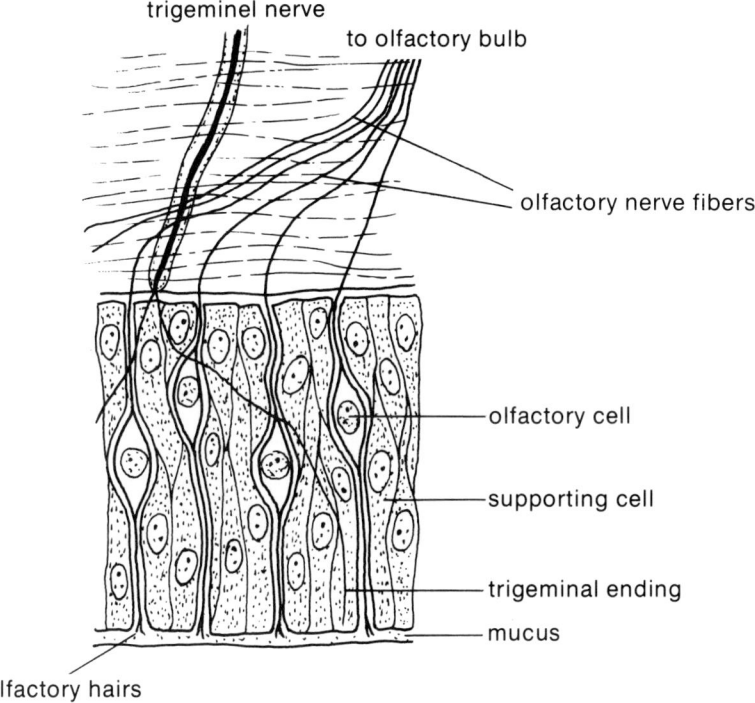

Figure 3.8

Once the odorous molecules are intercepted by the hair-like receptors inside the nasal cavity, the information is transferred to the olfactory bulb and then on to the brain.

primitive system, then our sense of taste can be considered as a very poor supplier of information. The sense of taste rarely provides human beings with information that influences communication among people. However, it is full of mysteries and contains supportive information that complements our understanding of the body's capacity to process sensory information. Taste, like smell, should be considered as a chemical type of sensory system.

The sense of taste is initiated by the **taste buds** (gustatoreceptors) which in all mammals are found in the oral cavity. It is here that flavored objects stimulate the taste receptors. Located mainly on the human tongue, up to 50,000 taste buds discriminate between only four major tastes: sweet, salty, sour, and bitter.

Small round structures on the surface of the tongue called **papillae** are activated when flavored substances come into contact with the mouth. Clustered about the papillae are many taste buds that are receptors to a specific taste. This means that there are papillae containing taste buds which respond only to sweet tastes, sour tastes, and so on. Gustatory receptor cells located on the tongue transfer information to the brain via two nerves. In addition to taste receptors, the lining of the oral cavity and tongue also have receptors sensitive to touch. Nerve impulses arising from these receptors reach the brain via another nerve. Thus, when one eats a strawberry, it not only tastes like a strawberry but also feels like one.

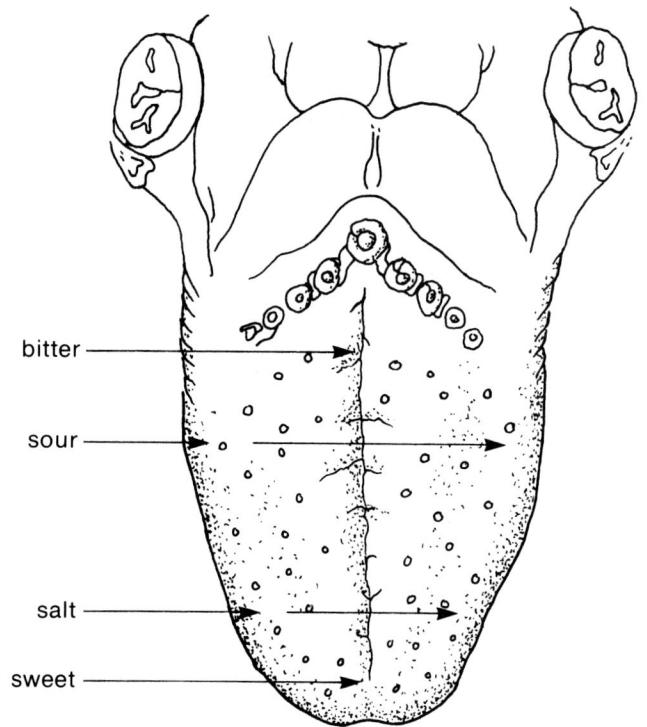

Figure 3.9

The human tongue and taste receptors often cooperate with the olfactory system to provide two sensory interpretations of complex information.

Touch

Any sensation of feeling such as pain, heat, cold, pressure, itch, tickle, or others is associated with the human sense of touch. These stimuli are identified by nerve endings called **cutaneous** receptors, located in the surface skin of an individual. These receptors are not distributed evenly over the body. They appear to be more heavily concentrated in areas such as the fingertips and lips. This explains why these areas are sensitive enough to distinguish between a smooth glass and an etched pattern only .01 millimeter deep.

Animals, as well as humans, respond to **tactile** stimuli (something that arouses our sense of touch). The next time you step on a German shepherd's tail, you will have relayed a message to him via his sense of touch. Perhaps the dog's response will communicate information to your cutaneous receptors. Regardless of how we communicate with animals, human communication, through the sense of touch, enables us to receive information necessary in our work and play.

We all know that sensations from a punch or a kiss provide information to our brain. Just how this is accomplished demands a closer look at the human skin.

The human skin has three major layers: the **epidermis** or external layer, the **dermis,** and the **subcutaneous** tissue. In the epidermis are to be found tactile discs and free nerve endings. These cutaneous receptors are the first to receive any tactile stimulation, but it is theorized that our acute sense of touch stems from the larger and more responsive receptors found in the dermis. The subcutaneous tissue contains the largest nerve endings.

THE SENSES 59

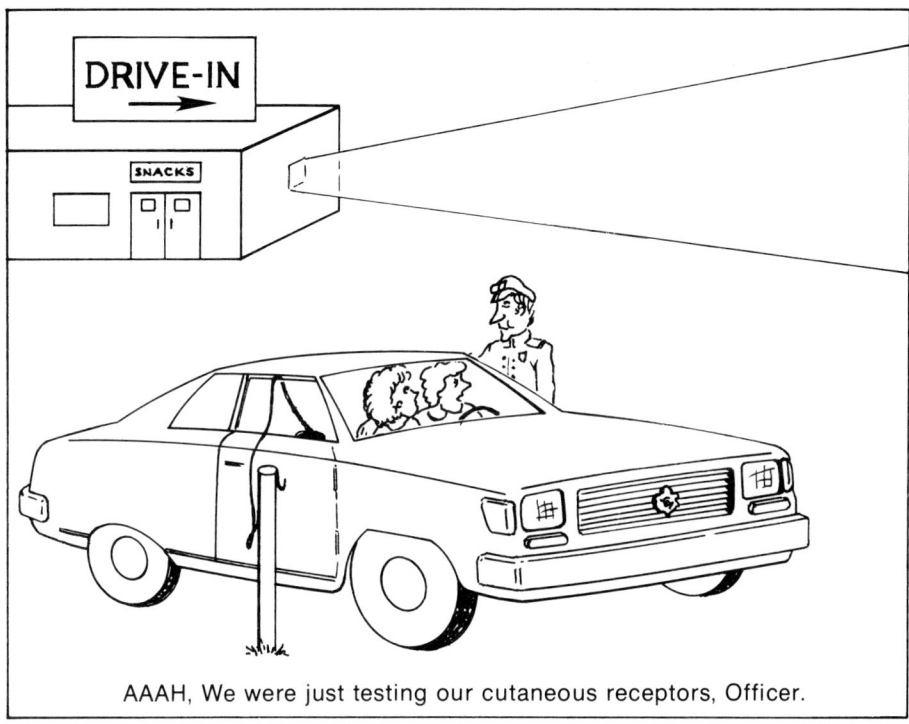

Figure 3.10

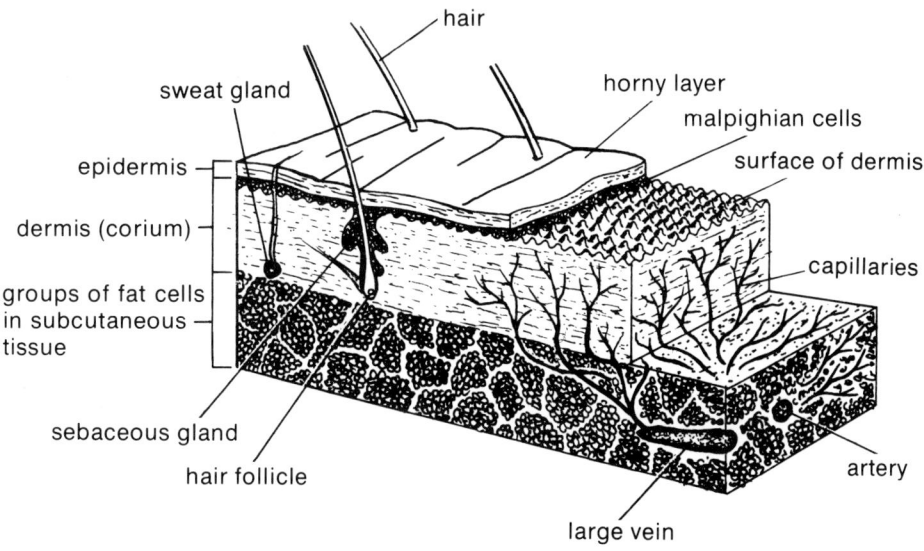

Figure 3.11

The human skin (in toto) is the largest sensory organ of the body, containing unevenly distributed cutaneous receptors that create a vast network of nerves.

It is through this vast range of different sizes, types, and locations of sensory receptors that we receive tactile stimuli. Whenever our cutaneous receptors receive information, they send messages to the brain through a vast nerve network.

One way to describe this would be to imagine a tree-like structure with the leaves and branches interwoven through the three layers of the skin. When the tactile information is passed to larger nerve bundles it is like the outermost leaves and branches waving in the wind and passing the movement to larger branches below. Once the receptors pass the information to larger bundles of nerves, the nerve trunks carry it to the spinal cord. Fortunately, the chaotic nerve network becomes more organized as impulses travel through central pathways in the direction of the central nervous system.

There are two major pathways to the brain through the spinal cord. These are used to relay different types of tactile information, from different parts of the body to the sensory projection area in the brain. The area called the somatic sensory projection area receives all information from the cutaneous receptors in the skin.

EXTRASENSORY PERCEPTION

There are sensory phenomena that cannot be fully explained within the confines of normal human sensory communication. Prior to this section, you have seen how people communicate when they are stimulated by something they see, hear, smell, taste, and feel. Many people also suggest that individuals could have other senses beyond the basic five. Senses in this category were referred to as anomalies in Module Two. Often they are discussed under the descriptor, Extrasensory Perception (ESP) and have fascinated people of many countries for centuries.

The term ESP has been a catchall for many kinds of unexplainable forms of human communication and has been at the mercy of "quacks" and scientists alike. Extrasensory means just what it says—senses outside of our normal senses. Whereas our normal senses are concerned only with receiving information, anomalies in the extrasensory category include transmission as well as reception of information. Many people, including some scientists, tend to explain extrasensory phenomena as a kind of emotional communication like music, dance, and art. Others seem to feel that

Figure 3.12

ESP

these phenomena have something to do with energy fields. In any regard, researchers in Europe (fewer in the United States) have met with some success in making sense of some extrasensory phenomena.

Further discoveries may someday provide a change in consciousness that will enable new vistas in human communication. Who would need to write notes or telephone friends, if telepathic communication were capable of being developed by everyone? Persons could just "tune in" and receive any and all information held in anyone else's mind. This possibility raises some problems, however, such as the invasion of privacy. Perhaps you don't want your friends or parents to know everything you are thinking! Aside from the possible drawbacks of using telepathy and other extrasensory communication processes, some researchers are trying to train persons to use these senses more effectively.

SENSORY MIXING

Whether a person possesses five or more senses there is a slight chance that they may suffer from **synesthesia** or sensory blending. For a person who experiences synesthesia, a voice could produce not only sound but also tastes and colors. It is the overstimulation or confusion of sensory receptors that produces illusions. Children are more likely to possess a blending of the senses than are adults, although some research claims that all persons have some small capability of sensing synesthetically.

Since all of the senses may be involved in a blending mixture, there are many types of synesthesia. The two most common types are when a sound arouses visual images, or "color hearing," and when taste stimulates visual images. This phenomenon does not include the preconceived image a student has when he hears the word "teacher," rather, the rare occurrence of a rainbow of colors when the word "teacher" is heard. Or perhaps, when listening to the high school band, a certain sound produces the taste of chocolate pudding or baked beans.

An adequate understanding of the process and effects of synesthesia is lacking. Further research will need to be conducted to ascertain whether synesthesia really provides valid modes of human sensory communication. To date, a lack of accurate measurement and evaluation techniques has hampered research in this area. However, we do know that there is much left to discover about human communication.

INTERPERSONAL COMMUNICATION

Effective interpersonal communication is dependent, in part, upon one person's relationship with another.

Research has shown that children who are twins seldom need to conduct formal exchanges of verbal (expression in spoken words) messages to communicate. For this reason, twins usually develop a verbal vocabulary later than single children of the same age. It is also common for people, beginning at about the junior high school age, to identify the "mood" of a friend by the way he or she walks, talks, gestures, sits, or dresses. Communication among people today is unavoidable. Fortunately so, for without it we would quite possibly lose a foundational element of civilization.

Interpersonal communication is a complicated process. It mixes aspects of the conscious and the unconscious self, of fact and fancy. Interpersonal communication is nontechnical, in that it requires no devices or special training; we all are involved with it whenever we are in contact with other people. Let's take a closer look at the process and attempt to "stop the action" of a real life situation in identifying some of the elements of interpersonal communication.

> The time is 1:15 p.m.; the place is the assistant principal's office.
> **THE SENDER** becomes Joe Tuffguy—mind, body, and spirit.
> **THE TRANSMITTERS** become the voice, appearance, posture, and smell (slightly of smoke) of Joe Tuffguy carried by the air and light waves in the office.
> **THE RECEIVERS** become the sensory receptors of the assistant principal—mind, body, and spirit (complete with a mildly upset stomach after eating in the school lunchroom).
> **THE CONTEXT** includes the details of the office, black telephone, large wooden desk, dusty bookshelf, wall picture of the 1959 championship team and file cabinet (that holds the expulsion slips). The situation is also affected by the fact that Joe Tuffguy has frequented this office before and still receives "bad vibes" from such visits, and that the assistant principal never did like Joe's older brother.

Whatever message is about to be transmitted verbally, it will have to overcome the messages that are in existence through nonverbal communication. It becomes evident that interpersonal communication consists of just about everything about an individual. In order to expand our understanding of human communication, let's investigate the elements of nonverbal and verbal interpersonal communication.

NONVERBAL COMMUNICATION

Two great American designers, Buckminister Fuller and Frank Lloyd Wright, had tremendous success in their profession because they were aware of physical space and the effects of environment on people. Both coordinated structures to be built with their surroundings, according to size, shape, and materials. Mountainous terrain demanded hard edges and elongated vertical lines in buildings that were constructed of elements natural to that setting, such as stone, wood, and glass. Not only were their structures aesthetically attractive, but they were also enjoyable for those who lived and worked in them.

Environmental Factors

Many sensual clues are derived from the physical space around us. Architecture and room design have a great deal of influence on our moods, our personalities, and our expectations. Oftentimes, the style and arrangement of a room reflect the kinds of activities intended to occur there. Even the organized seating arrangement of a typical classroom affects the behavior and attitude of the students using it. Experiments have been conducted in creating stimulating rooms with the use of particular furniture, wall and floor coverings, windows, and door openings. Care in selecting the correct blend of textures, colors, shapes, and sizes has resulted in rooms that enhance human communication.

Figure 3.13

Shelters of unique design offer new and different experiences in human interaction and communication by offering living spaces in the round. Courtesy, The Yurt Foundation, Bucks Harbor, Maine

64 HUMAN COMMUNICATION AND PERCEPTION

Figure 3.14

Children and adults develop a personal space around them when interacting with others.

With the creation of new types of living environments, new and different styles of living are emerging. The open concept of "living in the round" evident in shelters such as yurts and geodesic domes has caused people to become more interactive with one another. Various service (bathroom, workroom, kitchen) and living (entertaining, sleeping, playing) areas have replaced the traditional private corners and rooms. A marked change in personalities and attitudes of individuals living in these alternative structures may provide some answers to problems arising from living in highrise boxes in urban areas.

Personal space (**ackistics**) is a crucial factor dictated by our environment. The personal space of an individual is carried with him or her. It is this invisible boundary that determines how close we wish to be to others. The best way to learn about personal space is to start walking. When walking or standing, persons reflect a personal space about them that they may not wish to have invaded. If you begin to invade someone's personal space they will feel uncomfortable and usually back away. In the United States, distances of conversation zones have been identified. For example, 8 cm to 16 cm could be regarded as very close and top secret; 50 cm to 90 cm is neutral and personal; 5 m to 8 m is public distance and information for others to hear.

If you were an exchange student in South America, you would possibly experience a difference in personal space. As cultures differ, so does the distance of personal space. A Latin American prefers to be closer to you in conversation than you are accustomed. Each time you might feel uncomfortable and back away, your hosts would move a little closer to speak. This two step, without music, could be incorrectly interpreted as a display of the stereotype of "cold, arrogant North American attitudes" and the "aggressive Latin American."

The distance you remain from someone is an effective mechanism for conveying information. This nonverbal communication element of personal space is critical when we exchange information on an interpersonal basis.

Related to the element of personal space are cultural factors involving interpersonal communication. Briefly, the cultural element is only of concern when people of different cultures are involved in communication. Some of the cultural areas identified by the interpersonal environment might be:

- the embrace of adults of the same sex
- touching another's arm while speaking to him
- violation of one's personal space
- attitude toward a person's race
- attitude toward a person's socio-economic status
- attitude toward the way a person dresses
- expression of emotions such as crying or laughing

Personal Appearance

When was the last time you wore a dress, or coat and tie, to school and your teachers wore faded blue jeans and a cowboy shirt? However often this may happen (if ever), you would notice a distinct attitudinal change in yourself and teachers, as well as any visitors to your school. Clothing is a major source of information about a person's character and identity. It affects the way that we feel about ourselves and others. Say, for instance, you were getting ready for a house party that you thought was to be really informal. So, you show up in your jeans and T-shirt only to find your friends wearing their new knit shirts, suits, and dresses. Aside from the first reaction, you may receive snide remarks about your attire, or you may make comments about how strange everyone else looks. Unfortunately, the old saying, "Clothes make the person," is true to some extent, especially beyond your high school days. The idea of making an impression such as being casual, rich, sexy, or athletic by the way you dress is not a new one. Nor does it seem likely that it will ever completely disappear from the American scene.

Just as a person's dress produces certain stereotyped attitudes from others, so does the physical attractiveness and physique of a person. Researchers have found that people believe that different personalities and temperaments go along with certain body builds and facial attractiveness. Three classes of body builds have been found to convey certain kinds of information. The distinct classes of body builds most often identified are: thin and light (ectomorph); husky (endomorph); athletic (mesomorph). Most people form initial impressions concerning characteristics of being neat, sloppy, bossy, timid, ambitious, nervous, and good-looking from the way you look.

It has been found that the physical appearance of an individual has something to do with the success they have in certain professions in life. Such a guideline is not always a good one to follow. Often the interpretation of a person's abilities based on appearance has been found to be incorrect. Nevertheless, appearance is an influential factor in the human interactive process.

Physical Behavior

If you were to pass the back of your hand a few centimeters from your face, you should be able to detect slight variances of heat. This heat differential is oftentimes used by persons who have lost their sight, as signals of their surroundings. The heat from a brick building could identify the street a person was walking on and the temperature change surrounding a window may assist a blind person to navigate around furniture without touching a thing. Our emotional state can also be identified through the sense of touch. A flare of anger or embarrassment can oftentimes be felt, as well as seen, by the rise of temperature on one's face.

The effect of physical behavior on communication goes beyond the sense of touch. If you quietly observe a fellow student, or teacher, and pay careful attention to the way they sit, stand, walk, and move about, you can tell a lot about them. They

Figure 3.15

A simple gesture can often communicate to a very large group of people.
Courtesy, West Virginia University Sports Information

have communicated to you just by their body movements, even though the message you received was probably unintended. There are, however, body movements that are intended. Anyone who is a sports enthusiast can identify what has happened in the playing arena by the signals or body movements of the officials and players.

To small children, the use of body movements is critical in their interpretation of the world. Children learn through a continual flow of parental signals that teach them what is right or wrong, good or bad, or many other messages.

The study of the language of the body is often referred to as **kinesics** or body language. Thousands of individual movements of the body have been identified as having specific meaning. Just like any other language, kinesics must be interpreted within a particular context, or it does not represent any meaning. The prime areas of movement in the American culture that are used to convey information are the eyes and the hands.

Suppose a young woman offers to get a Coke for a young man at a party. Perhaps what she is really doing is offering him her attention. Even beyond that, she is leaving room for a response. If he is receptive, he may say something like, "Haven't I seen you somewhere?" or "Don't you live outside the city?" which indicates little interest in where she is from, but more interest in gaining a closer acquaintance. How has all of this been communicated? The verbal message really contained neutral information; the real message was conveyed through body language and facial expressions.

This example offers additional clues to our study of nonverbal communication. The amount of information offered by speaking in this situation is similar to that which might occur in a normal two-person conversation. In our example only about 35 percent of the social meaning was conveyed verbally. This is pretty typical; normally about 65 percent of the meaning in a communication act is conveyed by nonverbal communication. When there is conflicting information from the verbal and nonverbal, we tend to rely on the nonverbal as being the "real" message.

Let's rerun our party scene and zoom in on the facial expressions of each subject. The fact that the participants faced each other indicates interest in one another. Perhaps while talking to the young man in our scene, the young woman saw an old boyfriend walk past. The girl could have broken eye contact with her new acquaintance, smiled and spoken by turning her head over her shoulder looking at her old friend and establishing eye contact with him, while retaining the interest of her new acquaintance by having her body remain facing him. Obviously, eye contact is an important factor in facial gestures. Others include the eyebrows and their movement, and the region of the lips. It would be through these elements of expression, body movement and position, and the concept of personal space, that the couple in our party scene would "get the message."

One additional element of nonverbal communication could be identified in our party scene. You will recall that verbal information was exchanged between the boy and the girl. We pointed out that **what** was said contained neutral information. **How** it was said, however, is very important. The tone, volume, rate of speech, and pauses between words, are oftentimes more important than the words being spoken.

VERBAL COMMUNICATION

People talk to each other without using words. But more often than not, when people attempt to transfer information on an interpersonal basis, it is usually with the spoken word. Often the ability to communicate became a matter of life or death for primitive people. As social animals, human beings out of necessity developed verbal messages to survive. Whether planning a hunt, or rallying to the defense of the family, early communication was usually a combination of verbal and nonverbal messages.

Primitive human beings are believed to have used some kind of verbal language as long ago as 100,000 years—long before the advent of writing. Ironically, even today we have few real ideas of how people generate or understand speech. Speech and verbal communication depend upon a symbolization process not involved in nonverbal communication. The conscious attempt to convey a mental thought by the means of a verbal message is a symbolic process. This process occurs during the preverbal state of an individual. Usually, but not always, a person thinks before he speaks.

This thought process is an organizational period that enables us to identify words to be used in representing what we are thinking. These words are symbols. Neither the word **green**, nor the letters that make up the word, exist in nature. They are only elements of a language that human beings created. However, what the word **green** represents does exist in the natural world. Language codes are culturally distinct. The meaning for a particular symbol or word may differ from one country to another, from one culture to another. Within a particular culture various subcultures or counter-cultures have various connotations for some elements of language: for example, words like wolf, bike, tough, grass, truck, and class.

As small children, we experienced/learned to associate certain verbal symbols with objects in our environment. **Mama, daddy, cat,** and **baby** were some of the words we heard and identified. Anyone with small children in the family can verify that once a child has learned to control his/her speech patterns, he/she can repeat almost any word said. These words have no meaning to a child, suggesting that symbolization then develops only as fast and accurately as the perception of the child grows. Beyond the development of an ability to organize abstract ideas into elements of a language (words), we must have the capacity to express these words in the form of a verbal message (speech).

The speech center is located in the left hemisphere of the brain. If injury occurs to the speech center, one person might suffer from a distorted speech pattern or lose the ability to speak. Experts do not really understand the mental processes of speech, and as yet have great difficulty in restoring useful speech to a person who has suffered injury. Considering the brain, then, as a vital element of speech, let's examine the remaining body organs that enable us to speak.

Anyone who has ever run, or walked very fast, knows that it is difficult to speak when you are out of breath. We can logically guess that speaking has something to do with a person's lungs and air passages. Athletes, particularly football players, often conserve air, and time, by relaying a symbolic message to the other players. A quarterback uses code names and numbers for plays and strategies, such as "44 slant right on 2." Sound is emitted only when previously inhaled air is slowly released from the lungs past the larynx. Due to the movement of air past the vocal cords (which are housed in the larnyx), a pattern of vibrations is created. These vibrations are a lot like those created on a reed when air passes over it. When pronouncing vowel sounds (a, e, i, o, and u) the vocal cords vibrate in a natural pattern. To achieve the consonant sounds, control over sound vibration is achieved by the movement of the mouth, jaw, tongue, and soft palate. Notice this by the lack of specific movement of these elements when quietly pronouncing vowel sounds. The vowels and consonants are the basic units of articulation. Articulation is the movement and adjustment of the speech organs involved in producing a sound.

Let's investigate how sounds are achieved. The sound of air passing through the vocal cords is first modified by the soft palate, located at the back of the throat. This acts in conjunction with the placement of the tongue and the shape of the lips. It is through the action of these, along with the teeth and nasal cavity, that consonants are formed. What actually takes place is that the air flow from the lungs is periodically stopped or reduced by these system elements. Proper articulation results in the alternation of the vowel and consonant sounds to make syllables. Syllables combine to make words, words to phrases, phrases to sentences, and the whole thing hopefully ends up in the transfer of grammatical meaning. As this occurs, the symbolization process also develops in a similar manner.

When a person speaks, a listener hears word sounds, but he or she also hears other things. The acoustic properties of speech are often the vehicles of additional information important in human communication. The intensity of speech is in part determined by the amount of air expelled from the lungs. Intensity is measured from the lowest sound pressure that can be identified as a sensation of hearing. Intensity should not be confused with loudness. This relationship might be explained as similar to the one of the power of an automobile and the speed of an automobile. Intensity, at the upper level, might affect the listener who experiences a ticklish sensation or pain from it.

Loudness of speech is referred to as a complex function of intensity. It can be measured by the discriminatory capabilities of the listener. The threshold, or first sensation of hearing, varies from a drummer in a rock group to the keeper of a cemetery.

Pitch is the dimension of speech which varies primarily as a function of the frequency of sound. It is often referred to as the high-low quality of speech. A female's voice is often referred to as one of a higher pitch than that of a male. This difference in sensation is due to the physical property of the frequency of sound wave vibrations from the vocal cords.

The intonation of sound refers to the rise and fall of pitch. This characteristic of speech is apparent when we speak with emphasis or singsong. Some word phrases change pitch in an obvious fashion. For instance, "Who said that?" illustrates a rise in pitch at the end of the phrase. In contrast, a statement of fact often realizes a lowering of pitch—"During the night, about four inches of snow fell."

How much impact a message has can depend upon factors other than the physical makeup of speech quality. How a message is presented can affect its clarity, credibility, and retention. The following often affect the interpretation of meaning transferred through human speech.

- **Pauses**—spaces between words or phrases
- **Repetition**—words or phrases said again
- **Stuttering**—interrupted rhythm by blocks of spasms of pronunciation
- **Omission**—neglect or failure to verbalize all expected information

You might disbelieve something that is said because of these items or because you disagree with the content of the message.

It should be apparent by now that we communicate in many ways. The channels of interpersonal communication are complexities of the physical and psychological nature of the human being. But perhaps the key to human communication, regardless of channel, is perception.

Perception

Perception can be defined as the process by which an individual understands. In addition to just receiving information about our world with our sensory receptors (physiological mechanisms), we understand beyond that information. The ability to do this, to perceive, enables us to organize and make more meaningful the impressions we receive via the nerve pathways of the sensory organs. There are many levels of perception. Perception of reality finally takes place in the brain.

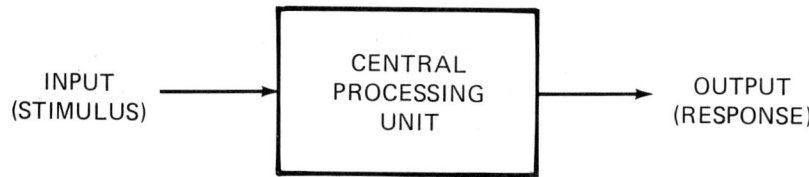

Figure 3.16

Basic elements of any perceptual system: input, central processing, and output.

Considering this information, let's examine the following example. The way we view or perceive a dirt bike is based on our experiences and attitudes. It can be seen as merely 212 kilograms of metal, rubber, and plastic. This may be the way an engineer would perceive the object if he had no past experiences or future expectations of the bike. However, this interpretation is a far cry from a motorcycle enthusiast who perceives the bike as something that can leap tall buildings, travel faster than a speeding bullet, and scare the pants off of you if you're not careful!

Human beings are communicative animals. Everything we do and how we do it conveys information about us. Our ability to hear in stereo, see in moving color, and to taste, smell, and feel has enabled us to cope with our changing world in an effective manner. However, we must realize that the power of human communication and perception is finite.

Concept Focuser

- **Human communication** involves the **transfer of meaning**. **Perception** involves **understanding**.
- **Human** sensory **receptors channel information** via the synapse **to the brain**.
- Most of our **visual input** is taken in via our **visual** receptors. The senses of **smell, taste** and **touch** are more **refined** in the **lower organisms** than in humans.

- Sensory **receptors** take in information and **transmit** it down a series of **nerve fibers** to the **synapse**.
- The **human sense** of smell is often **used** in conjunction with the **sense of taste**.
- **Tactile stimuli** are **identified** by **nerve endings** called **cutaneous receptors**.
- **Extrasensory perception** refers to **perception** of information **outside** the **normal sensory channels**.
- **Interpersonal communication** can be **accomplished** through **verbal** or **nonverbal** stimuli.

FOOD FOR THOUGHT

1. Describe in outline fashion the path that visual information follows in going from the optic nerve to the brain.
2. What would be examples of techniques that could be used to gather nonverbal information on your friends?
3. How do you suppose the process of synesthesia or color mixing occurs?
4. What is body language?
5. Why do you think it is possible for blind people to develop more sensitive receptors in areas such as hearing and touch?

EXPANDING EXPERIENCES

1. Conduct a limited experiment of sensory deprivation using such items as blindfolds, ear plugs, or gloves.
2. Observe small children at a nursery school or day care center and note their actions about: (1) personal space; (2) nonverbal communication; (3) language symbolization.
3. Research and report on Frank Lloyd Wright's contributions to modern architecture in terms of environmental communication.
4. Design and build a cardboard yurt or dome and experience the sensation of communicating in the round.
5. Write a one-page description of what you perceive a **diffident dif** to be.

LOCATOR TOOLS

Benge, Ronald C. *Communication and Identity.* Hamden, Connecticut: Linnet Books, 1972.

Carr, Donald F. *The Forgotten Senses.* Garden City, New York: Doubleday and Company, 1972.

Harms, Leroy S. *Human Communication: The New Fundamentals.* New York: Harper and Row, 1974.

Perception: Mechanisms and Models, readings from *Scientific American*, W. H. Freeman and Company, San Francisco, 1972.

Schwartz, Barry N. *Human Communication and the New Media*. Englewood Cliffs, N.J.: Prentice-Hall, 1973.

COMMUNICATION AND SYSTEMS FOR PROCESSING INFORMATION

Module
FOUR

Information Processing System

The key element in modern information processing systems is the conversion of information into a mode for transmission which, when received, conveys to the receiver or final user the same shade of meaning originally conceived and initiated by the sender.

In Module Four, we will explore the system of information processing in detail so that we may completely understand how organic and inorganic systems effectively communicate with each other.

In its broadest sense the primary functions of an effective information processing system is the acquisition-transmission-interpretation of intelligence. To support this primary function a basic system would have: (1) a message source, (2) a transmitter, (3) a transmission channel, (4) a receiver, and (5) a user at the destination. However, if we include both human and machine information processing in our study, then we must modify the above support system to include memory and feedback functions as well.

Since effective processing is really the transfer of meaning from one person to another through the medium of a transmission system, let us consider figure 4.1, which is a two-way model for the successful achievement of this transfer. Each of these elements are functions of the human and machine act of communication.

Let us consider each of these stages in their proper sequence so that the whole process can be better understood. An example of a short and effective message might be your terse reply, "nuts!" to your chess partner when he puts your king in jeopardy. This brief message is an example of good communications because it would convey complete understanding from one person to another with the least number of words and communicative effort.

Returning to figure 4.1, let us go to the first stage of the model which is the source

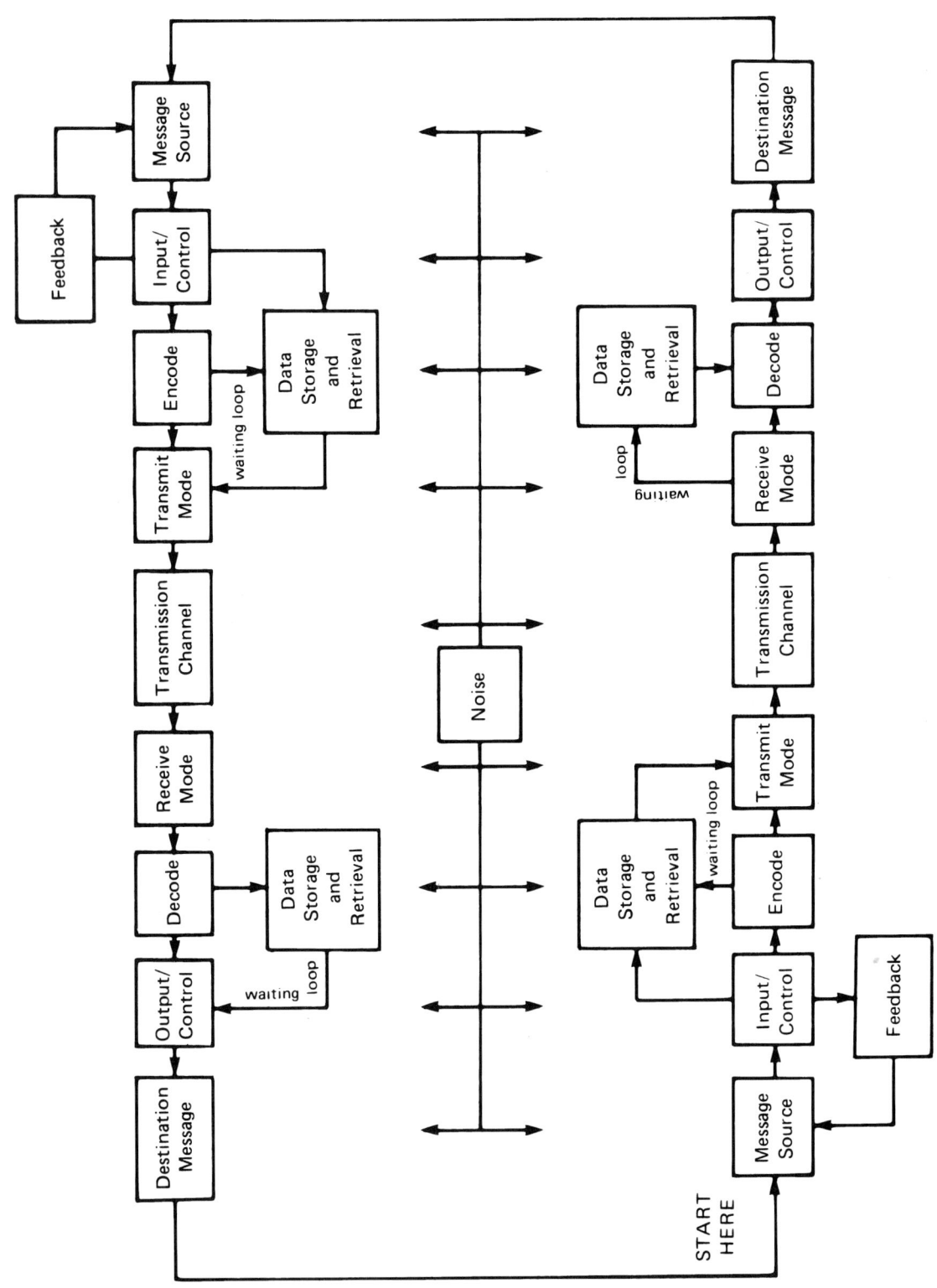

Figure 4.1
Information Processing System Model

of the message. The function of the message source is to create meaning of the message to be conveyed. By definition, a message is an arbitrary amount of information with a beginning and end. It usually originates in one place and is intended to be transmitted to another place. Messages can take on many forms such as symbols, speech, writing, pictures, drawings, codes, or can even be mathematically expressed in bits of information. The transfer of meaning into messages can only be accomplished by the cognitive or thinking process of the human brain.

The transfer of a message might be analyzed in the following manner. When a source (person) wishes to send a message to the destination (user), he or she usually speaks, types, or otherwise inserts a pattern of message symbols into the appropriate input device. The input device has provisions for a feedback link to the sender so that he or she can check the accuracy of the message being sent.

Machine language differs greatly from human language. Therefore, the function of the encoder stage is to transform the human language of words and symbols into the proper machine language of digital bits, which is generally expressed as a single pulse in a group of pulses or, the smallest unit of machine language. Digital bits are sometimes called digital pulses.

The binary system of numbers is one method of changing message content into machine content. Because of the possibility of a backlog of traffic in a system, the source person may desire to route the machine information to the Data Storage and Retrieval Unit until the traffic clears.

Data Storage and Retrieval Units do not work in real time as does the direct input/encode/transmit function of information processing. Rather, it functions in machine time. Machine time is a fraction of the real time equivalent. Real time is the actual time we live in. Control of the storage and retrieval function is accomplished at the Input/Control stage.

Assuming the traffic has cleared, the operator of the system routes the machine information to the fourth stage of the system—the Transmit Mode. The modes of transmission that could be selected are either visual, electrical, acoustical, or electronic, as indicated below.

The fifth stage in the information processing system is the transmission channel which links the transmitter and receiver together by a variety of paths. For example, the transmission channel might be a transistorized cable, a submarine cable with repeaters every few miles, a pair of telephone wires handling pulses at the rate of 1.5 million per second, or a radio circuit. It all depends upon the transmit mode that was initially selected. Other channels might be the sophisticated satellites or the microwave and forward scatter systems that beam information from one point to another.

The sixth stage in the information processing system is the reception point at the other end of the transmission channel. This stage performs the function of receiving the machine information and routing it. Machine information is routed either to the Data Storage and Retrieval Unit if the circuits are busy, or directly to the decoder unit where it is converted in real time from digital machine language to the original source message. The source message can be displayed at the output/control unit terminal and is now considered the destination message.

Once the message is received by the destination user, it must be interpreted and transformed into meaning. When this occurs successfully, reliable communication or information processing is said to have taken place.

Although we have traced a message in one direction only, that is, from source to destination, communication is actually a two-way street. After the destination message is received and interpreted, a response may be indicated. In this case, the cycle is repeated as indicated in figure 4.1.

The achievement of information processing and communication is always somewhat less than perfect. During processing, some messages lose their full meaning due to system noise. As indicated in figure 4.1, it can affect every stage of the processing system, because intelligence and the unwanted noise are often transmitted together.

We know that noise is anything that tends to obscure or impair a message. Some examples of noise are simple mechanical failures or interference from other motor-driven equipment. In humans, noise might be caused by cultural differences or physiological differences such as indistinct speech or language barriers. Noise can even be a semantic problem, with a single word having several meanings. Or it could be a loss of meaning attributed to the use of technical terms not normally familiar to most people. Therefore, it is important for the destination reader (receiver) to have a clear understanding of the subject matter as well as the source language if full meaning is to take place.

Several other factors can cause problems within a radio or television information processing system. One of these is atmospheric, or interference caused by magnetic storms associated with the sun. Some of this interference appears in the form of spikes, which sometimes can be misinterpreted as a pulse by the receive mode.

There are two ways to help reduce noise caused by this type of electrical interference and human error. One is the use of digital pulses for the transmit/receive/mode link, and the other is the use of system redundancy. System redundancy is the identical duplication of equipment in a system that can be immediately substituted for the prime system in the event of sudden outage or excessive interference. Both measures can improve a system's reliability and accuracy of message transmission.

One way to determine the efficiency of an information processing system is through its input/output ratio as shown as follows:

$$\frac{\text{Output messages}}{\text{Input messages}} \times 100\% = \% \text{ of message efficiency}$$

Primary System Only:

If the source sends out 100 messages and the destination receives the 100 messages, then we have achieved 100 percent system efficiency. However, if system noise interfered with twenty messages, then the ratio of system efficiency would be reduced to 80 percent.

$$\frac{100}{100} \times 100\% = 100\% \text{ message efficiency}$$

If a high order of system efficiency is essential then the messages should be sent over a primary and alternate channel to insure at least 100 percent system efficiency as shown below.

Primary System:

$$\frac{80}{100} \times 100\% = 80\% \text{ efficiency}$$

Redundant System:

$$\frac{80}{100} \times 100\% = 80\% \text{ efficiency}$$

Total: 160% system efficiency

This formula can work just as well as an indicator of individual message efficiency. Using the word "Nuts" from our previous example of a perfect message, assume a letter was lost in transmission as shown in the following example.

Message Transmitted	Printout Display
Primary System	Primary System
$\frac{3}{4} \times 100\% = 75\%$ efficiency	N____TS
Redundant System	Redundant System
$\frac{3}{4} \times 100\% = 75\%$ efficiency	NU____S
Combined: 150% system efficiency	NNUTSS
Total: 150%	NUTS

If the input was four letters and the output only three, then we would have attained a message efficiency of only 75 percent on the primary system and the redundant system. However, chances are that the same letter would not have been garbled and the total meaning of the message would have got through to the destination. An on-line computer would have compared the messages from both channels, detected the missing letters and made the appropriate corrections on the printout display unit.

THE THEORY OF INFORMATION PROCESSING

The information processing system is the means of communicating data from one person to another, from person to machine, from machine to machine, and from machine to person. In this process two terms stand out that confuse people and often are used interchangeably. These are "information" and "communication." You will recall from Module One that communication involves more than transmitting information. Information transmitted from the sender must convey meaning to the receiver before communication occurs.

The Message	N	U	T	S
A. Morse Code	— ·	· · —	—	· · ·
B. Modified Morse	▮▮▁▮	▮▮▁▮▮	▮	▮▮▮
C. On-Off Mode	10	001	1	000
D. Numerical Equivalent	14	21	20	19
E. Binary Equivalent	1110	10101	10011	10100

= 19 digits

F. Information Content Comparison

H	E	L	L	N	O	I	M	N	O	T	G	O	I	N	G	T	O
8	5	12	12	14	15	9	13	14	15	20	7	15	9	14	7	20	15
01000	00101	01100	01100	01110	01111	01001	01101	01110	01111	10100	00111	01111	01001	01110	00111	10100	01111

= 90 bits

S	U	R	R	E	N	D	E	R
19	21	18	18	5	14	4	5	18
10011	10101	10010	10010	00101	01110	00100	00101	10010

= 45 bits

TOTAL: 135 bits

Figure 4.2

Sequential steps in the development of a digital code system.

THE THEORY OF INFORMATION PROCESSING 79

Information is the result of a processed message or communication. In its very narrowest sense, it is the encoding and decoding of message content.

Information theory deals with a collection of mathematical concepts relating to the measurement of transmitted information. It treats the measurement and flow of information as being analogous to those of matter and energy. Specifically, it deals with the problems associated with the coding and decoding of message content so as to establish criteria for comparing the effectiveness of different communication systems.

The Encoding and Decoding Process

Of the many encoding/decoding schemes that exist, the simplest is the Morse Code. It is composed of a series of dots and dashes. If we can reduce the 39 symbols shown in the code, we can decrease the possibility of error in the transmit mode. The Morse Code can be reduced to 34 symbols if we would be willing to use only capital letters and have 1 represent both number one and the letter "l." This can be carried a step further by having 0 represent both the zero and the capital letter "O." By the above changes and eliminating the comma, period, and question mark, we have reduced the code without destroying the message capability.

Assuming we wanted to informationally process the message "Nuts," we still could select the appropriate code for each letter as follows: N (_____ .), U (.. _____), T (_____), S(...), and transmit the full message as shown in figure 4.2, line A.

To modify the code so as to better match our modern digital systems, we might want to stand the selected code symbols on their ends, lengthening the dots to one-half of the length of the dashes as shown in figure 4.2, line B. We have now created a pulse code system from the Morse Code. To improve on the system still further, we must change the elongated dots to full sized Os as shown in figure 4.2, line C. Unfortunately, the Os represent time the transmitter is not modulating so that the letter "S" in our message would not have been transmitted.

If we were to convert the Morse Code from letters to equivalent numbers such as A = 1, B = 2, C = 3, then our message code would be 14 for N, 21 for U, 20 for T, and 19 for S as shown in figure 4.2, line D. Using the binary equivalents for these numbers we would have developed a digital code system suitable for the transmit mode. (See Binary Code and figure 4.2, line E.)

Measurement of Information

Effectiveness of the information processing system is measured in terms of the number of digital bits that must be transmitted in order to send a message from one point to another. This is called the information content. Returning to figure 4.2, line D, the information content of the message is only 19 binary bits of information. However, if you had been more verbal in your denunciation at the chess table and said, "HECK, NO! I'M NOT GOING TO SURRENDER!" then we would have seen a rise in information content to 135 bits as illustrated in figure 4.2, line F. Obviously, the more lengthy message was less efficient than the short one and required more transmit mode time to get the same message meaning across.

All information processing systems and transmit modes have a saturation level, which is measured in bits per unit time. As an example, the typical upper limit capacity for a telephone speech circuit is 20,000 bits per second as compared to a television broadcast channel which has a capacity for 50,000,000 bits per second.

CYBERNETICS AND INFORMATION PROCESSING

Cybernetics is the study of communication and control of living things as well as organizations and machines. The term was originally coined by Andrè Ampére from the Greek word for control. Cybernetics is a relatively new science within the field of automation. It is interdisciplinary in nature and involves such disciplines as mathematics, anatomy, neurophysiology, and engineering. The interrelationships between engineering and biology are often reciprocal in that the principles developed and applied to communications and control, such as information theory and feedback, have been effectively used to understand the various processes of the human nervous and muscular systems.

One of the principle concepts of cybernetics is feedback. By means of feedback, corrective action can be taken by man or machine to correct an error. A biological example of feedback being used to correct an error occurs when a person reaches for an object. His hand movement is detected by the eye as well as the sense organs in his fingers. If the hand moves too far to the right, appropriate sense organs feed this information to the brain, which sends a signal to the muscles, causing a corrective movement to the left. The fingers will close around the object as soon as sensed and when the brain sends the proper signal. This is the same type of detection-feedback system that is used to control machines.

A control system is a means or device to regulate and direct a process or programmed sequence of events. In its simplest form the device could be a thermostat controlling a heating system. If the heated air is hotter than the control setting, the circuit will be opened and the heating system allowed to cool. If it becomes too cool, the process is reversed. In its most complicated form, the control unit of a digital computer directs the machine to carry out a task in proper sequence in accordance with coded instructions previously programmed. In the event of an error, the control unit will detect it through its feedback loop and direct the machine to take corrective action.

Like humans, sensors are the perceptive organs of machines. They are used to perceive an impending event and automatically transmit a signal to the control system, which must take the appropriate action.

In mechanical devices, there are manual and automatic sensors. Manual sensors are feedback devices such as thermometers and tachometers, which operate in real time. Devices such as photocells, feelers, strain gauges, proximity switches, and transducers are all examples of automatic sensors that also operate in real time.

Automatic sensors must have a method of displaying their output and are normally connected to such readout devices as meters, oscilloscopes, CRT consoles, lights, recorders, dials, and counters.

Cybernetics in the Human Mechanism

The control system for machines somewhat resembles the control function of the human mechanism. It generates nerve impulses, which carry messages that the sight, sound, touch, taste, and smell sensors detect around the human body. The brain, like the mechanical control unit, determines the final meaning and generates the appropriate control signal.

There are other similarities between the machine and the human organism. The machine normally has hundreds of electrical interconnections that control its performance. Similarly, the spinal cord, which is enclosed in the bony structure of the human backbone, functions as a vast telecommunications network as it relays nervous impulses to and from the brain.

Control of Information Processing Machines

Another facet of cybernetics is the control of organizations and machines. The control of organizations is beyond the scope of this book and deserves a book by itself. Therefore, we will move on to the control and communication of information processing machines.

In the previous section on cybernetics and the human mechanism, we discussed some of the seemingly human functions that have a counterpart in the area of information processing systems. Now we will look at a machine designed especially for the function of information processing—the computer.

Like the human brain, the computer accepts information from its environment through its input devices, combines this information according to the instructions programmed in its memory bank, and sends back appropriate signals to its environment through its output devices. Although the computer may seem to duplicate some of the functions of the human mechanism, it only mimics human behavior at best. But what of the distant future? Can the computer ever be made to think for itself or reproduce itself? No one really knows for sure. However, you may want to consider some of the educated guesses in Module Nine about the future of the computer.

The total process from human recognition of a problem to the programming of a computer consists of three steps: (1) the data required must be put into a form the computer can use, (2) someone must tell the computer what to do, and (3) the computer must read the data, process it, and present a readout of the answers, so that the human programmer can read and interpret the output data.

The digital computer used for information processing is made up of five basic functions as shown. They are the input, storage and retrieval, arithmetic, control, and output units. We shall discuss each in turn.

1. **Input Unit**
   The input data is called **alphanumeric**, meaning a combination of alphabet and numerals. Alphanumeric data is usually in the form of coded punched cards or paper tape. This input data is fed to the machine and is converted to the binery format. The input unit can store the data until the machine is ready to handle it.

82 COMMUNICATION AND SYSTEMS FOR PROCESSING INFORMATION

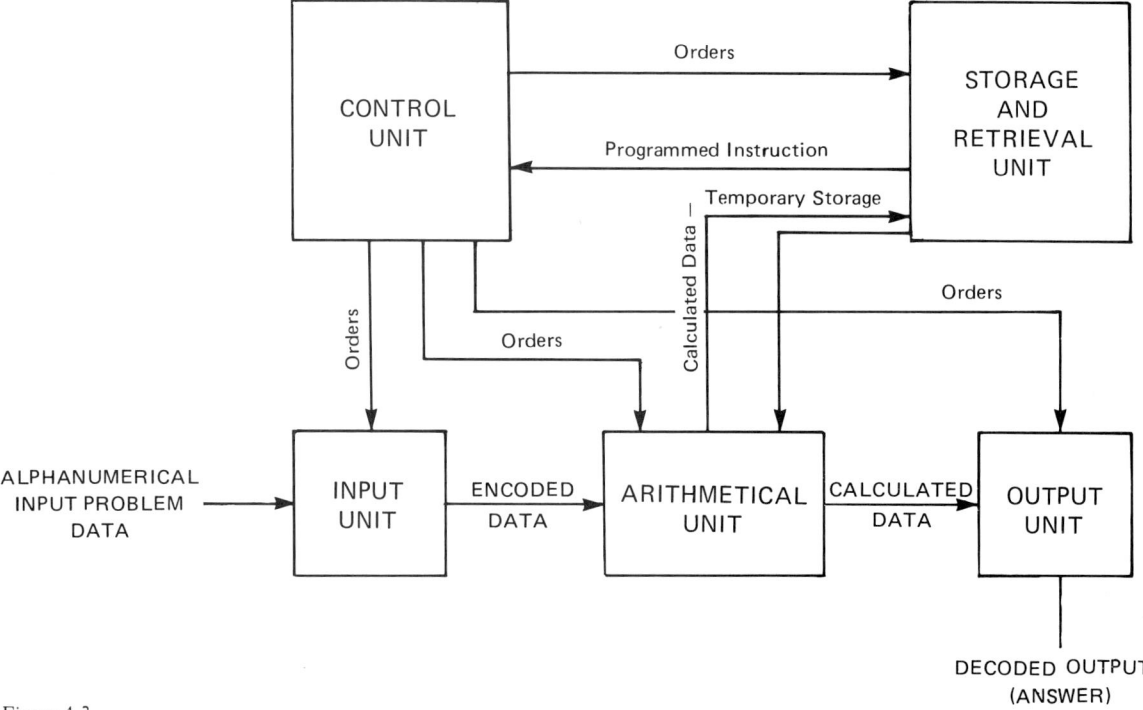

Figure 4.3

Block diagram of the functions of an information processing digital computer.

2. **Storage and Retrieval Unit**
    The program of instruction to the computer is located in the storage unit. The program contains detailed instructions in sequential form and the computer reads each operation and performs the computations indicated. The storage unit consists of three areas: the program storage, permanent data storage, and temporary storage. As previously indicated, the program storage area holds the current program that the machine is performing. Permanent data is used for storing various constants and any other special data the computer will need to complete the problem. The temporary storage area is used internally by the computer to store processed information that it will need later in the final computations.
3. **Arithmetical Unit**
    As the name suggests, this unit performs all of the mathematical functions such as addition, subtraction, multiplication, and division. Any complex mathematical functions use various combinations of the four basic arithmetical functions. The output of this unit can be stored in the temporary storage area or be read out through the output unit.
4. **Control Unit**
    The control unit directs and coordinates the entire computer system as a single multipurpose machine. It controls such functions as the input-output units, the arithmetical operations, and directing the overall machine according to the stored program developed by its human programmer.
5. **Output Unit**
    The function of the output unit is to provide a method of recording data generated by the computer.

From this description of the functions of the individual units, you may have a better understanding of the close interaction between human and machine in this information processing system.

Module Eight has a section devoted to the many other segments of our society that are served by this product of our technological age. The basic functions of all computers are the same—only their programs are different.

CONCEPT FOCUSER

- **Key** to modern processing systems is conversion of information into a **transmit mode** that **conveys meaning as intended** by the **sender**.
- A **basic** information processing **system** contains a **message source**, a **transmission channel**, a **receiver**, and **destination user**.
- A **message has** a **beginning** and **end**. Its **mode** can be **visual, electrical, acoustical, or electronic**.
- All systems have noise. Noise is anything that **impedes, impairs,** or **obscures** the proper reception of **messages**.
- 100 percent **telecommunication efficiency** occurs when **all** the **messages** sent arrive at the **destination undistorted**.
- Information is a **processed message; communication** is the **meaning** contained therein.
- **Cybernetics** is **communication** and **control** of **organisms, organizations,** and **machines**. It needs **feedback** to **function** properly.
- **Control systems** have **sensing, decision,** and **actuation** functions. **Sensors** can be **manual** or **automatic**.
- Human mechanism has **central** nervous system and **peripheral** nervous **systems**.
- Neurons are working **units** of nervous **system**. Nerve **impulses** are **physiochemical changes** in nerve **fiber** membranes. All systems **feedback** to **brain** for storage. This is called **memory** function.
- Basic **computer functions** include **input, storage, arithmetical** processing, **control** and **output** activities.

FOOD FOR THOUGHT

1. If a basic computer system lost its information storage function, could it still process input data?
2. Would deafness in a person be considered to be noise? How about a language barrier in a foreign student—would that be noise? Why?
3. If fifty-two messages were sent out, but only twelve arrived at their proper destination, what percentage of system efficiency would we have? If this were to continue for several months, how soon would the message center chief be expected to become unemployed?
4. Describe the benefits of a Pulse Code System versus the Morse Code System.

5. Explain cybernetics in terms of a car and how you could increase the feedback capability of the machine.
6. Make a list of mechanical sensors and explain how they are used in an electric typewriter.

Expanding Experiences

1. **Case Study.** Ask your teacher to arrange a field trip to several local businesses, equipment supply houses, and stores in your school district that do not have computers or access to data processing centers. Make a list of all the reports, inventories, orders, and personal management papers that are done by hand. Ascertain those that you think could be easily computerized if a computer or data processing center were nearby. Analyze your findings and present them to the class for discussion.
2. **Case Study.** Visit the nearest computer or data processing center serving your school district. Make a list of all the computing or data processing functions the machine is programmed to accomplish. Discuss job opportunities with center personnel and the type of training that is required. Make a list of those jobs represented at your computer center and report your findings to the class.

Locator Tools

Bagdikian, Ben H. *The Information Machines.* New York: Harper and Row, 1971.

Clark, John O. *Computers at Work.* New York: Grosset and Dunlap, 1971.

Information and Computers: Physical Science and Technology Series, New York: Holt, Rinehart and Winston.

Information Technology: Some Critical Implications for Decision Makers, New York: The Conference Board, Inc., 1972.

Meethan, Roger. *Information Retrieval.* Garden City, N.Y.: Doubleday and Company, 1970.

Phillips, James P. and Wolk, Allen M. *How to Build a Working Digital Computer.* New York: Hayden Book Company, 1967.

Rusch, Richard B. *Computers: Their History and How They Work.* New York: Simon and Schuster, 1969, pp. 36-86.

TECHNOLOGY-BASED VISUAL SYSTEMS

Module
FIVE

Today we live in a visual world. It is visual because a great majority of the information we take in through our senses is visual in character. To what extent we depend on our sense of vision is hard to say. Some feel that as much as 80 percent of our learning occurs through our sense of sight (Gesell, 1949), whereas others (Cohen, 1962) feel that as much as two-thirds of the information received by our brain involves vision. We know that each milisecond our brain processes close to three million bits of information. It is important to realize that a great majority of this information relies on our visual receptors to serve as the primary input link to our brain.

In Module Three we discussed how the human visual system functions as an information input link to our brain and how our senses channel this information to the brain.

Here in Module Five we will concentrate on the major developments in visual communication that drastically influenced or changed our capacity to communicate.

Before we can really attempt to understand these technical systems we must understand something about our visual world. Technical systems serve as extensions of our senses. They help us to communicate in ways that were not possible without them. Visual communication technology refers to the systems we have developed that help us in creating, controlling, and using visual information.

Many people think of technology as machines or tools—things that we have created to make our lives more pleasurable. Synonymous with communication technology are things with the prefix "tele" meaning "over a distance"—developments like the telegraph, telephone, or television. Sometimes, we also consider as technology newer accomplishments like the satellite or holography, but seldom do we give much thought to the "what," "why," and "how" of these developments.

In addition to the study of "things" we will also deal with technology humans use to communicate with others and to transmit information between people and machines.

Before we can attempt to understand the systems used to transmit and receive visual information we must know how to effectively create a visual symbol. We will study the development of the visual symbol as part of the concept we will call visual literacy.

Visual communication begins with the birth of an idea—a stage we will call "ideation." For visual communication to occur other phases are also necessary. We will study these phases by revisiting some of the major developments which have had significant impact on society.

OUR VISUAL WORLD

Our sense of sight is nearly ten times as sensitive as our other senses. Consider the twenty-six letters of our alphabet. With this system alone we deal with 620,448,-402,733,239,360,000 possible combinations in which these letters can be arranged in relationship to each of the others. It doesn't take long to realize that during a normal school day a fantastic amount of visual information enters the brain.

In Module Three you learned how the eye works as a receptor of visual information. It is important to keep in mind how the rods and cones function in channeling visual messages to the brain.

The size of the visual image at a certain distance is an important factor in the reception of visual information. At 30 centimeters away the eye can make sense of a visual image only 10.2 millimeters high, whereas at 54 meters away the image must be nearly 50.9 centimeters in size to be recognizable. This is the factor that regulates our perception of visual images.

Have you ever wondered why headlines in magazine advertisements, writing on billboards, and symbols in airports are the size they are? All of these attempts at visual communication must keep in mind the viewer's distance if they are to be effective.

Another factor that is important to the designer of a visual message is contrast. Visual shapes can create problems for the viewer by being too thin or too thick, out of proportion length to width, too black or too white, or displayed in a background environment too similar to the color they are. Such messages confuse the rods and cones and slow down the process of communication.

Agreed-upon meaning is another important factor of visual images. For many years gypsies have arranged grass and sticks in patterns near campsites to communicate certain messages to others who could interpret their language. Tramps and hobos also have their own unique symbol language. They draw chalk symbols on fences, sidewalks, houses, and boxcars to indicate the conditions in the area. Many seemingly unknown visual messages can be found all around us. We just need to be able to interpret their own, often unique, systems of meaning. Even the position of a postage stamp on an envelope, the location of headlines on an advertisement, or the color of stationery have a certain degree of universal or agreed-upon meaning.

Agreed-upon meaning is important. It is also hard to tell when we have it. Hardly any word has the same meaning when used in a different way (context). How about the word "hit?" Think about some of the meanings it has associated with it. You can hit a ball, or become a hit with your friends. You can listen to a hit song, or hit the right note. The word "hit" has few meanings. Some words have hundreds of different meanings attached to them.

Communications research has shown that even the color of an object affects the length of time we will use it and whether we would buy it in the first place.

We rely so heavily on the visual message as our primary channel of communication that we have created an information explosion. The era of information explosion began somewhere around twenty years ago. It is likely that it will continue for another ten to fifteen years before it will end, probably as a result of people reacting harshly against too much information at a given time.

Chances are that we are closer to this point right now than we might think, and things may get worse. Since it is becoming easier to produce information, less care will be taken in separating out what is essential from what is not. Much of what we print today is not essential; it is simply cheaper to say it with a lot of words than it is to use a few. A message restricted to the essence takes more time to create, and for businesses and industries time means money.

If history is any indication of what will likely transpire, our reliance on today's visual media (newspapers, magazines, road signs, television) will not come to a halt overnight. Our emphasis on them will simply shift over time. The invention of photography and the camera did not eliminate painting; they simply caused painters to redirect their focus. When portrait painters were almost entirely replaced by portrait photographers, they shifted to other types of painting. Painting as an art form was not disturbed. Neither were the newspaper and book wiped out by the motion picture.

So, the question remaining is: "Given our knowledge of past accomplishments and likely futures, how can we strive for better and more effective communication?" The answer seems to be that we must become more skilled at understanding and absorbing visual information.

VISUAL LITERACY AND OUR VISUAL LANGUAGE

Methods for enhancing visual literacy are equally valuable in Rome or Cairo, New York or London. To create visual messages that communicate one does not even have to know the language of the locale.

Symbol systems are one of the basic inventions of human beings. There are many symbol systems and many languages. Some of these are related since they were derived from the same source. Each symbol system is based on its own meaning and unique set of ground rules. There are more than 3000 different languages in the world.

The language of vision is not as difficult to understand as are most others. To use most languages means that one must understand all of the components of the language, as well as the total language system.

Look in a magazine for an advertisement that communicates a particular feeling—something like friendship, brotherhood, or love. Ask some of your friends what the picture communicates. Chances are that most of your friends will pretty much agree on what the photograph means. If you showed them a picture of someone eating, the photograph would communicate a universal meaning. If you said the words "eating rice" to the same group, many might not understand.

A well-designed symbol can often communicate more effectively than other communication mechanisms. For many centuries the signs of the zodiac have been interpreted as explaining certain aspects of the human personality. For those who believe that our personality is affected by the stars this symbol helps to provide clues to human behavior. For example, a Leo (person born between July 22 and August 21) would have traits of generosity, would be proud, and more than likely would be extravagant. Do you know any Leos? Do they fit this pattern?

Phases in the Development of the Visual Message

The capacity to produce and understand visual messages is not the same today as it was 30,000 years ago, but many of its components are still the same.

In early times the message was intended largely to communicate to "spirits" or gods rather than to other human beings. In primitive times when human beings wanted to communicate, they did so at the time of need through the use of their senses. Today we are able to replay messages for viewing at a later time—thanks to our technology.

Throughout time, the visual message has evolved through four stages or phases of development. All cultures did not progress through each of these phases. When our ancestors first began to express themselves visually only the first of these phases was involved. Today, when we create visual messages we often become engaged in all of these phases, or a few, depending on the purpose of our act of communication and our need to communicate. The phases are called: message analysis and design, concept formation, image reproduction, and image preservation.

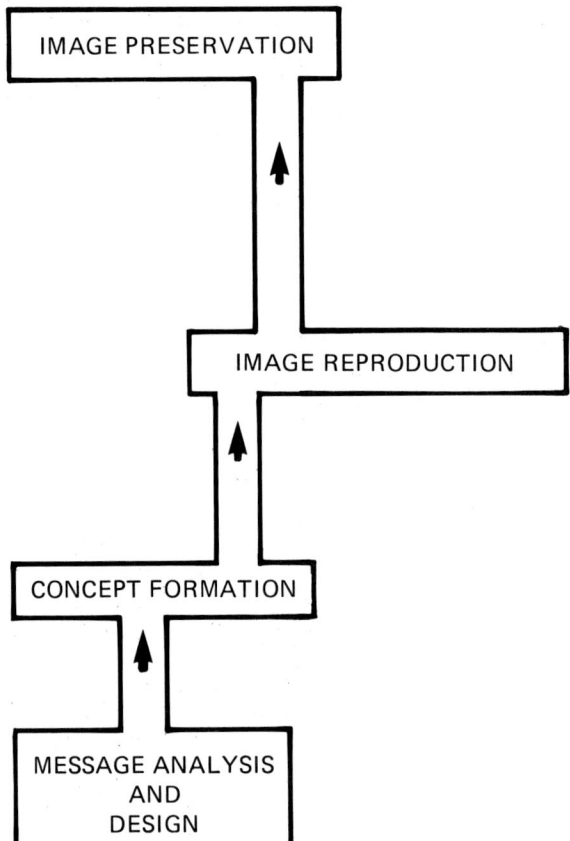

Figure 5.1

Four phases are involved in the creation of the visual message.

PHASES IN THE DEVELOPMENT OF THE VISUAL MESSAGE 89

Message Analysis and Design

Phase I shown in figure 5.1 is where the visual message begins. We call this phase message analysis and design. This step involves making sense of what is to be communicated. What is it that you want to say? What is the information to be transmitted?

Sometimes in the message analysis stage we decide what information we want to communicate without any help or verbal comments from others. We simply review all of the available information that might help us in creating an effective design solution.

After message analysis comes design. Humans have probably always gone through this phase in creating a visual message. In fact, evidence shows that our Cro-Magnon ancestors invented ways to string together a series of events to tell a story.

Today we call this technique "pictography," or picture writing. For many centuries entire civilizations have been able to communicate with each other using pictography, even though they spoke different languages and belonged to totally different cultures.

Cave painting was an important development in the evolution of communication technology. Figure 5.3 shows some of the important developments that were direct spinoffs from this one development.

With a development like cave painting it is difficult to tell exactly where message analysis stops and design begins. In fact, it is likely that the two occur almost simultaneously. After the design of the cave painting was completed, it was produced on the cave wall as the final concept. The transmission of information from a sender to a receiver was almost complete when the painting was put on the wall. All that was

Figure 5.2

This cave painting was found in a cave in France. Note the detailed rendering of the artist's concept. Courtesy, Field Museum of Natural History, Chicago, Illinois

left for communication to occur was for the receiver to view the painting and get the message.

Today we have many examples of acts of communication that occur in the same way. For example, when you bring a note from home to your teacher only the phases of message analysis and design and concept formation are involved in the process. The sender (your parent) has a need to communicate (message). He or she thinks about the best way to do this, decides on the channel to be used (written note), and then creates a few sentences (the design) that will transmit the desired information to the receiver.

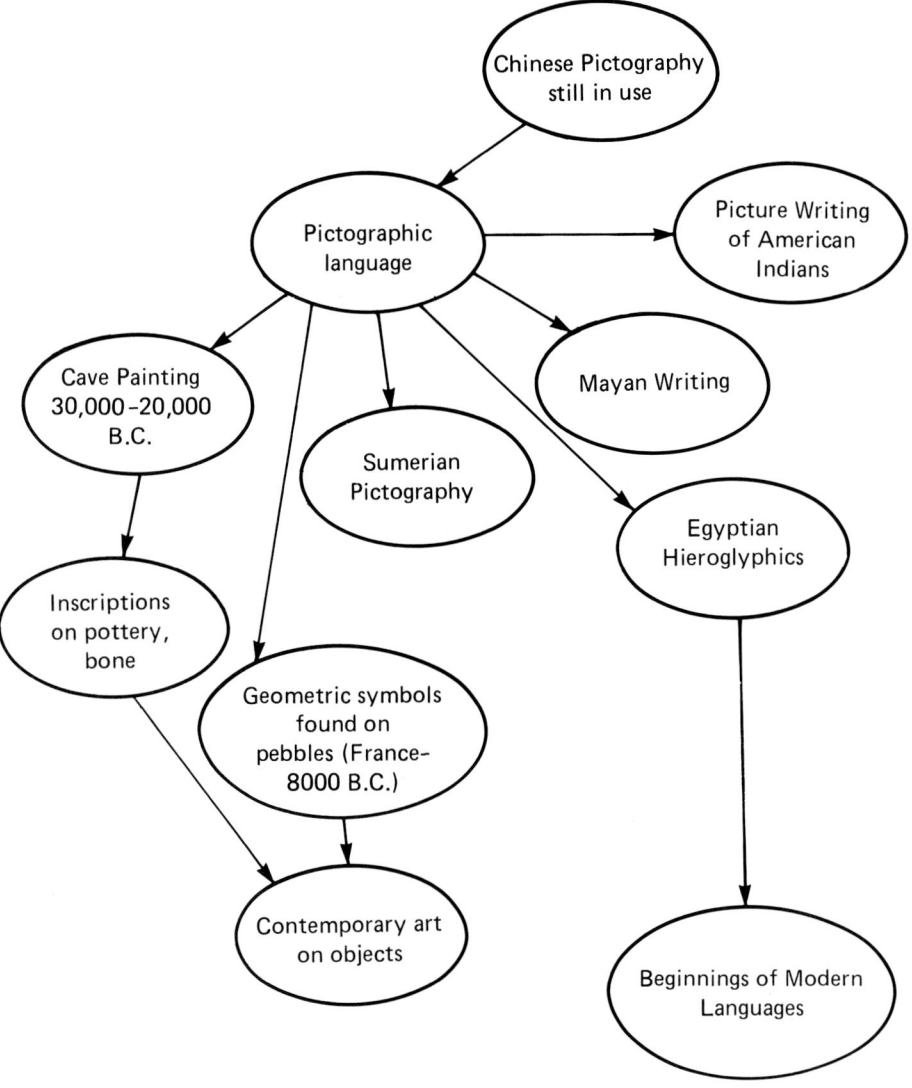

Figure 5.3

Many technical developments occurred as a result of the advent of early cave painting.

Concept Formation and Image Reproduction

Many times each day we go through the process called message analysis and design, and then move on to produce a message in the form of a drawing, painting, or photograph. What is important to keep in mind is that in the concept formation phase only one copy of the desired visual message is produced by the designer (printing, camera-ready layout, cave painting).

On other occasions we have a need to communicate to more than one individual (small group or mass communications), or for some other reason need to produce multiple copies of the original visual concept. What happens in this phase (image reproduction) is that many copies of the visual message may be made available, enabling more receivers to get the message.

Image Preservation

At times it is necessary to use techniques to preserve information for use at a later point in time. This is called image preservation and is often a necessary step for several reasons: (1) security—protecting important records; (2) conserving space; (3) cutting costs for reproducing more information; and (4) improving the speed of retrieving information. We will deal with techniques used to preserve vital information later in this module.

Let's take a few minutes now to look more carefully at the actions we might become involved with in phase I, message analysis and design, and phase II, concept formation.

There is more to creating a visual message than just creating a design for others to see. There are many factors that affect what it is about the visual message that we do see, and what it is about it that makes an impression on our senses.

AN EFFECTIVE DESIGN

A design will communicate if five elements are properly considered. They are called: **dot, line, texture, color,** and **shape.** These elements enable us to attract the viewer to the visual image, and then emphasize the part of the message that we want to make the greatest impact.

Our understanding of the relationship of each of these essentials to each other and how human beings perceive visual information is based on a great amount of research, much of which has occurred in the field of Gestalt psychology. The notion of Gestalt psychology is based on the theory that an understanding of any total system (the visual message is a system) is not possible without understanding the fact that it is made up of interacting parts. That is, each of the parts, or subsystems, influence one another and lead to the development of the total system. This means that none of the parts can be changed without causing the total system to change. What this means to us in terms of designing an effective visual message is that if we fail to use any of the design essentials correctly we are likely to create a design that once again fails to communicate.

The Dot

The dot is the simplest part of any design. The dot is the most natural of all shapes. We can find many examples of dots in nature but not of the square or the rectangle. When liquid drops on any solid surface a dot results. Even when we poke a stick into the snow to draw a design the first action results in our creating a dot.

Dots are often used to create a feeling of movement. When they are presented together in a visual pattern, they quite easily lead the eye. When they are displayed against a strongly contrasting dominant background their impact is strengthened.

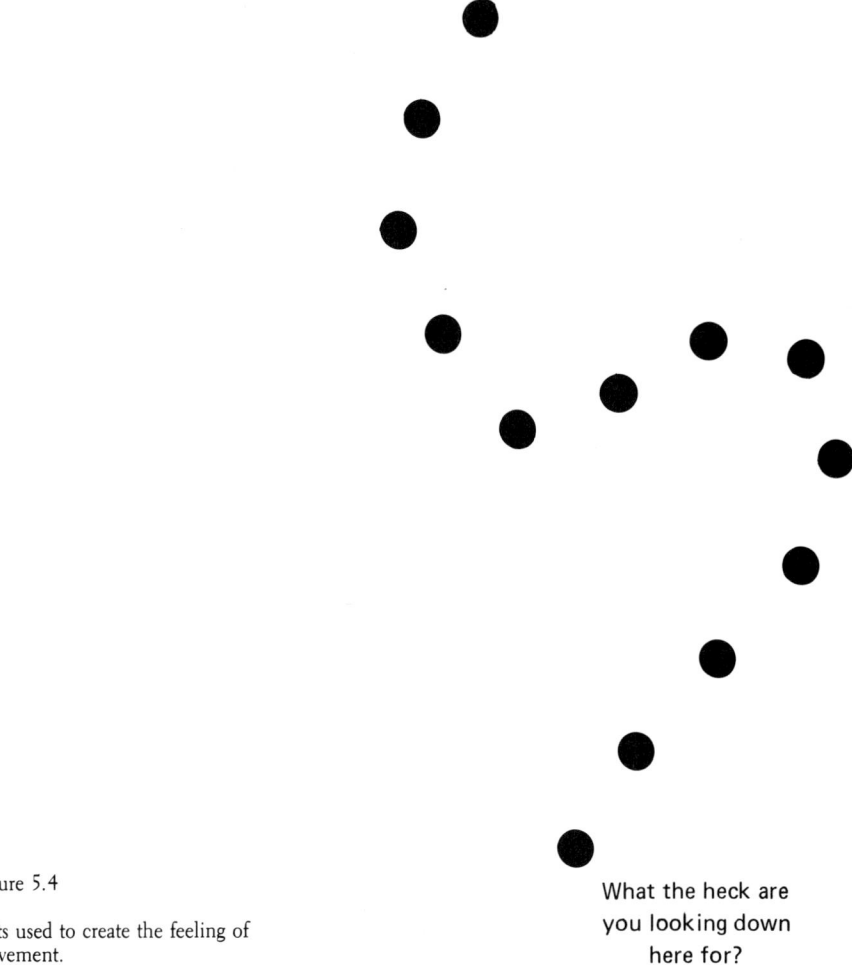

Figure 5.4

Dots used to create the feeling of movement.

What the heck are you looking down here for?

Today we use the dot for purposes other than to create emphasis or the feeling of movement. One of the most important uses of the dot is in the area of halftone photography. Take a minute and look closely with a magnifying glass at a color picture in any magazine or book. You can see that the picture is made up of many different colored dots. There are really only four colors of ink used to print the picture: yellow, red (magenta), blue (cyan), and black. These four colors create all of the different shades and tones in the picture. We will go into how this works later. What is important for us to note here is that these dots positioned properly together are what make it all possible.

The dot can also be used to attract attention, or act on one's perception of balance. Figure 5.5 shows how the dot can be used as an attention-getting device. Some basic ground rules to keep in mind when using the dot to attract attention are:

Figure 5.5

Dot used to attract attention.

- The dot is natural and simple; keep your design simple and to the point.
- Do not overload the design concept. Use few dots and position them where you want to focus attention.
- Contrast your dots against a very different colored background; use a dark dot on a light background for best optical visibility.

Dots are also used to give the illusion of depth or texture to drawn objects. The technique when used in this way is called stippling. **Stippling** is a technique used to produce shaded areas on drawings. The technique is done by covering the surface to be shaded with a series of dots made with the point of a soft pencil or inking pen. When the artist wants the appearance of dark shading the dots are placed closer

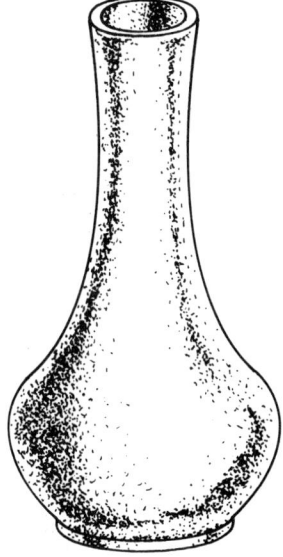
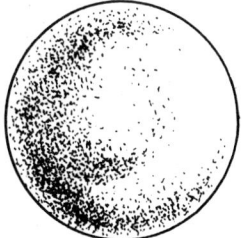

Figure 5.6

An example of stippling.

together; for light areas they are positioned farther apart. The technique, as illustrated here, is often used to create realism in drawings of cast parts and unmachined surfaces.

When dots are placed closer together, the eye moves from point to point much easier than if they are located far apart from each other. If the dots are placed so close together that they cannot be distinguished from each other, the feeling of direction or movement is even more apparent. When this happens we have progressed beyond the concept called dot and are talking about a new visual element. We call it the line.

The Line

The line is really what is created by a dot in motion. If we photograph the movement of a bouncing ball, using high speed film and multiple exposures, the moving ball (a dot) will have created a line. A line is the mark which is made when two dots are connected. Lines are seldom static; they provide the feeling of action in the visual message. The line is what gives us our first look at what could not be seen, at an idea which before had existed only in the imagination.

It is possible for us to create a perfectly good design without using any design elements other than line. Figure 5.7 shows examples where line has been used to create unique letter styles.

Figure 5.7

Figure 5.8

Lines are found all around us in our world. How we view them affects the way we use lines in a graphic design.

Figure 5.9

Light and dark shading can be accomplished by varying the spacing of the lines.

The letter styles or typefaces shown above are representative of the moods that can be created using the concept of line. Line is much more than a mechanism for establishing direction or movement. Lines can be used effectively to create many different types of feelings or emotional responses.

Horizontal lines often are used to create a feeling of restfulness, whereas vertical lines are often used when the designer wants to create the feeling of awe or inspiration. Diagonal or slanting lines are often used to suggest trouble or chaos. It is interesting to note why we feel as we do about the positioning of lines. Most of our reaction to certain elements of design is related to the way we see things in nature. Figure 5.8 shows how certain shapes we find in nature reflect the use of line and directly influence the type of feelings we get when we view these lines in a visual design. Lines can take on many forms to express different moods. They can be loose and undisciplined, as in the sketches above, to create the feeling of spontaneity of expression. They can be thin and delicate, or bold and coarse. Lines can be questioning, hesitant, and even personal, as in your own mark of uniqueness, your signature.

Lines can also be used to add the appearance of shading to a visual design. When used this way it is referred to as **visual texture**. Visual texture is achieved by using lines spaced close together for dark shading, and far apart for lighter effects. Figure 5.9 shows how shading can be accomplished using lines.

Visual Texture

The key behind texture in visual design is variety. Keep things simple and make the visual element you want to emphasize different from the other elements. Visual texture is found all around us. We accomplish it in a variety of ways: the printed design of many fabrics, the use of type styles on a printed page, the texture of the surface of writing paper, and even the weave of the fabric in your clothes.

Color

Often we think that a good visual design means a colorful design. This is not true; a good design can be created without using a variety of colors. It is true, however, that very few designs lack color. Even a black and white design involves color. Black is made up of all the colors mixed together, whereas white is the absence of color. In any regard, we will refer to color here to mean the use of colors other than black and white.

Today we know a great deal about color and how it affects us. Of all of the design elements, color is the most flexible. It can change the entire character of a visual message. In fact, even with all of the other design elements used properly, the design may fail to communicate if the wrong color is used. It is also the most difficult to understand and manage properly. We rely heavily on the proper use of color all around us. We paint the offices of doctors and dentists colors that help to calm the nerves. Some restaurant owners even paint their walls stimulating tones that cause the customers to eat more food.

There are some interesting features about color that we must keep in mind when we are creating visual messages. These relate to what colors are most legible (recognizable) when contrasted with others and to the moods that particular colors create. A lot of research has been conducted to find out just what consumers really think about color and how it affects their buying habits. The psychology of color varies among different cultures and nations. Color preference is even different between people living in large cities and those living in rural areas.

Generally people with many emotional outlets (things to do to occupy their time) prefer conservative and neutral colors. Often these are people in the higher educational grouping and income levels. Poorer and less educated individuals usually favor bright colors, such as orange or red. Studies related to color preference of people living in the inner cities of large metropolitan areas show that they prefer rainbow colors. People who do not have grass in their yards, or do not have yards, prefer green, and so on.

These psychological aspects of color are important to package designers. In fact, when planning a package, most often they consider its size, then its shape, and then its color. It is the color, though, that makes the first and greatest impact on the consumer.

It is difficult to make sense of the concept of color. This is so because we all view color differently and have our own preferences and feelings toward certain colors. It is possible, however, to generalize on the attitudes or feelings that are created in the minds of most Americans when certain colors are used. Here's what it looks like.

REDS = exciting/irritating/sexy
BLUES/GREENS = tranquilizing effect, calming or relaxed feeling
BLACK LETTERING on YELLOW = greatest optical visibility; can be seen from the greatest distance away
RED/ORANGE = catches the viewer's attention first
YELLOW = increases apparent size of container
VIOLET/PURPLE = depressing effect

Shape

Shape is the result of lines enclosing space. There are many shapes that are possible in a visual design. In the end, however, all of these are the result of alterations made on three basic shapes: the triangle, the square, and the circle.

Each of these shapes has its own unique sets of meanings. The triangle means action, conflict, tension, and movement. The square is more associated with meanings like conventionality, honesty, and integrity. The circle often creates feelings of endlessness, warmth, protection, and security. Each of these basic shapes also convey feelings of movement. Movement is created according to the direction of the lines making up the shape.

Each of these visual directions is helpful in creating the desired feelings from a visual design. Since horizontal and vertical lines appear to be stable and well-balanced, these feelings are transferred to all visual symbols using vertical and horizontal lines. The triangle is made up of diagonal lines. Diagonal direction is the most unstable of all directional lines. Since it is the most unstable it is helpful in causing the viewer to take notice. It introduces a sort of threatening and upsetting meaning in the visual design.

Circular and curved lines create the feeling of repetition and reaching out. Of all the basic shapes the circle is the least threatening. It even stimulates feelings of pleasure and warmth.

We can all become more visually literate if we know how to design and create visual messages effectively. Constructing a visual message that communicates effectively is never a simple task. It is possible however, to become more competent in creating visual messages by developing an awareness and experimenting with design elements. The process takes time and is complicated. It is complicated because each of the major visual design elements acts in a competing way with all of the others.

Now that we know what is needed to create an effective visual message, let's take a closer look at phase II (concept formation).

BUILDING AN EFFECTIVE CONCEPT

Usually any visual idea begins with a sketch. The idea of sketching to communicate information is not new. We cannot be sure just how long humankind has relied on the technique to express ideas, but we do know that as early as 2200 B.C. sketches were used to show internal design characteristics of buildings and other structures.

The Thumbnail Sketch

Most often one does not just start out to represent a visual idea with a sketch in detailed final form. Usually a designer considers a number of alternative possibilities before narrowing in on the one alternative that seems to offer the most promise. The thumbnail sketch is a series of small quick sketches and is used to illustrate the positioning of certain design elements. Details are not provided on the thumbnail sketch. In fact, quite often the thumbnail sketch is made up only of lines or shapes.

The Rough Sketch

The second stage in the preparation of a sketch illustrating a visual concept is called the rough sketch. The word "rough" should not be misleading. Essentially the rough

Figure 5.10

Thumbnail sketches are used by the designer of the visual concept to show a variety of possible solutions to the problem. The thumbnail sketch is used primarily to show the placement of design elements.

sketch is a working representation of the final design. The rough sketch lists all of the details necessary to communicate what is to be developed, but it is not polished and "suitable for framing" like the final design concept.

Often several rough sketches are completed for the designer and client to consider. The client is the person for whom the visual concept is being created.

The Final Concept

After the rough sketch or sketches are completed and evaluated the one winning idea emerges. This marks the beginning of the phase called **concept formation**. The rough sketch is used as a model guiding the preparation of the final visual concept. It is in the stage called concept formation that the final inking, rendering, painting, or illustration takes place.

The final visual concept is what often does the communicating. The visual concept may be prepared in the form of an artist's proof called a comprehensive layout. The **comprehensive layout** is a graphic layout made up of design elements pasted up on a layout board for photographing. The design elements might be hand lettering, drawings or illustrations, photographs, or other artwork, all arranged in the proper position and in correct size relationship on the layout. Except for the final color, the comprehensive layout in every way resembles the final printed result.

Not always is the final visual concept developed for the purpose of photographing and reproducing in quantity. Oftentimes the visual concept is prepared on the actual object and only one copy is ever made. Examples of visual concept formation are paintings, photographs, final design sketches, designs on pottery, and even images carved on leather belts. In each case the visual message is the end product that must do the communicating.

Prior to the middle 1400s this was about the only way a visual message could be transmitted. Today we still engage in acts of communication that stop at this point.

Mass Communication Systems

It was technology that finally enabled us to extend our communication capability. Instead of society being dependent on information being transmitted through single drawings, paintings, or art, technology made it possible to reproduce as many visual images as were necessary to ensure satisfactory communication. Let us take a closer look at processes used to reproduce the visual message.

Many important technological discoveries took place before it became possible for us to produce multiple images of the initial visual concept. In fact, nearly 5000 years passed between the development of early pictographic languages and image reproduction techniques.

Visual Seals

One of the earliest true pictograms was called a **visual seal**. A seal is a design that is used to indicate ownership. Early social groups used seals to stand for their own protective totem or to label their clan. Even today we rely on seals to mark our national identity and to legalize documents.

As the Sumerians and Egyptians spread the technique of making seals, a picture language began to develop. In the earliest pictographic writing seals often showed animal masks, animal deities, and zodiac signs. The use of the seal led to the gradual evolution of the signet or stamp-seal. The cylindrical seal is still used by the people of Nigeria to impress designs on pots and ceramic objects.

The system of marking symbols or ideas onto surfaces evolved in stages. The earliest attempts do not seem to have involved drawing and counting nor were they attempts to communicate with others located far away. The primary purpose of these early pictographs was associated mainly with record keeping, recording how many animals one had to trade, or keeping track of time.

Early Writing

Real writing evolved from drawing and cutting pictures into tree bark or stone to representing ideas.

Early cuneiform writing, a name derived from the wedge-shaped characters that characterized it, became popular throughout the Middle East during the fourth millennium B.C. It is unknown just who invented the script, but it is known that the Sumerians were instrumental in its development.

At about the same time (3100 B.C.) the Egyptians set out to develop their own cuneiform writing, which they called **hieroglyphics** (sacred writing). The writing was a fairly abstract script. Its "letters" were pressed into wet clay tablets with a stylized wedge-shaped stylus.

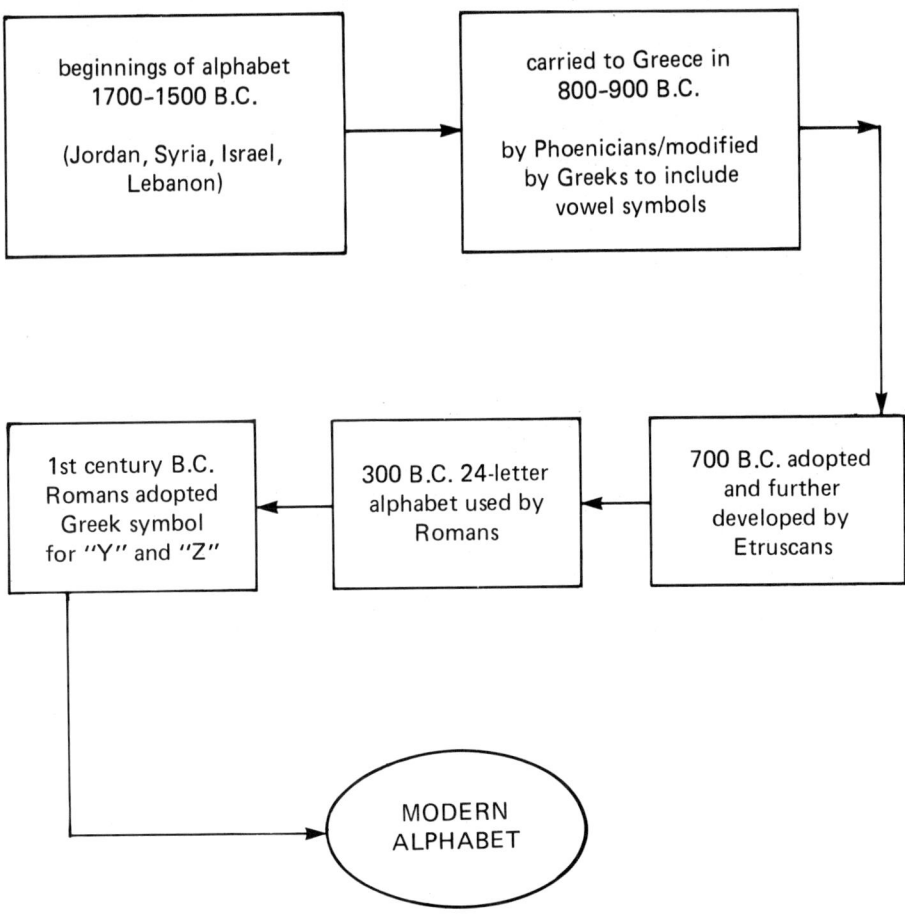

Figure 5.11

Major developments that led to the birth of the modern alphabet.

Like cave writing and pictography, the development of hieroglyphics as a communication system offered the culture new potential. Hieroglyphics consist of ideograms, symbols that are capable of recording ideas and abstractions as well as objects.

Pictograms can be distinguished from hieroglyphics in this way. If four wavy lines can only mean or stand for water, the system is pictographic. If the same lines can also mean wetness, saturation, or humidity, then the system is ideographic. A hieroglyphic illustration of a bird could be interpreted three ways: to stand for the bird itself, to stand for the characteristics associated with birds, or to represent the sound of the dominant consonant of the word itself.

Ideography has advantages over pictography, but both systems are capable of communicating effectively to people of different cultures and language backgrounds. The best example of an ideographic language is the script used by the Chinese. In China the more than 50,000 ideographic symbols have served the nation since the fifteenth century B.C. Eight thousand symbols are currently in use. To this day Chinese writing has not evolved beyond the ideographic form.

It was not until the discovery of the famous Rosetta Stone in 1799 that sense could be made of Egyptian hieroglyphics. The stone was prepared in 196 B.C. in hieroglyphic, Demotic, and Greek. The French scholar Jean Francois Champollion deciphered the stone in 1822 and provided us with a new link to understanding the ancient Egyptian culture. He deciphered the stone by first translating the Greek, then comparing it to the hieroglyphic.

Hieroglyphics were significant because they formed the basis for language, linking sounds and ideograms, but it was not until the sixth century B.C. that a real "sound language" emerged. The beginnings of our modern script emerged along the Mediterranean in an area that now comprises the countries of Jordan, Syria, Israel, and Lebanon. Written language went through many stages of evolution between the eighteenth century and the first century B.C. as shown in figure 5.11.

The First Paper

Significant for the popularity of hieroglyphics was the Egyptian development of papyrus, the first form of paper. Papyrus was made from the thin fibers of the papyrus plant. The fibers were matted together into sheets.

Before papyrus was developed about 2500 B.C., visual information was produced either by carving designs on bones, stones, or clay, or by hand-printing them on cave walls and pottery. Papyrus made communication via visual media available in much less time for many persons, not just the artist.

The development of papyrus led to further developments. Parchment, a paper made from the skins of animals, was perfected by the Greeks about 200 B.C. Paper similar to our modern linen paper was perfected by the Chinese around A.D. 100 and was further developed by the Spanish in Europe between A.D. 1100 and 1300.

Early Printing

It was not until 767 that Empress Shotoku of Japan began real exploration of the process of printing. Wood blocks were used to imprint one million Buddhist charms that were placed in miniature pagodas. The visual image to be printed was in relief, or raised away from the wood background surface. The printing was done on a paper similar to the linen paper we use today. The process probably involved grasping the block in the hand, stamping it in the ink, and then pressing it onto the parchment. The wood block printing process was later called **xylography.**

Wood block printing in China and Japan was popular long before it appeared in Europe. Its principal market was to produce playing cards, or sheet dice, as they were then called.

The year 1450 marked the birth of a new era—a time when printed communication became readily available to the average person. The individual most generally given the credit for the development was the German printer, Johann Gutenberg. Actually all of the components of the communication system were developed prior to Gutenberg, but he was instrumental in putting it all together. Let's take a look at what was needed.

First on the list of needs was the development of a technique for creating visual images, particularly words, quickly and inexpensively. The solution was found in wood block printing.

The problem with wood block printing was that it was not a medium that could be effectively used by the average person. One needed to be an artist to create the wood cut, and the process was tremendously laborious and time consuming.

The development in China of moveable type made from clay occurred between A.D. 1034 and 1041. Around A.D. 1250 both China and Japan first began to experiment with casting moveable type of bronze from molds. Although the concept of moveable type emerged in the East, there is really little indication that the development had any significant impact there. It is likely that news of the development leaked to Europe. In any event, the concept of moveable type was essential to Gutenberg's development of a total printing system. What Gutenberg did was to develop molds from which individual letters could be cast. This eliminated the time-consuming process of hand cutting each letter.

Another essential element to the success of Gutenberg's printing system was the development of high quality paper at a low cost. During the middle 1300s paper mills were established in Germany. By the 1400s there were paper mills in Spain, France, and Italy. Without the development of this economical form of paper in sheets of uniform thickness, surface texture and flexibility, Gutenberg's printing system probably would not have been possible. In fact, some have estimated that if he had been forced to use vellum to print his famous 1282-page Bible, nearly 165 animal skins would have been needed to produce a single copy.

Also essential to the success of the Gutenberg system was the development of a printing ink that would stick to the surface of the moveable metal type and also be legible when printed on paper. The ink used for printing wood cuts was made from a pigment made from lampblack suspended in a vehicle, usually watery gum. This type of ink was good for wood blocks but it did not stick well to metal type. Ink with some sort of adhesive property was needed. Inkmakers of fourteenth century Europe experimented with vehicles made from nut or linseed oil to suspend the pigment. This ink was what Gutenberg needed, but to be useable it had to be printed with a very firm, even pressure. The casual contact used to print with water soluble inks was not sufficient.

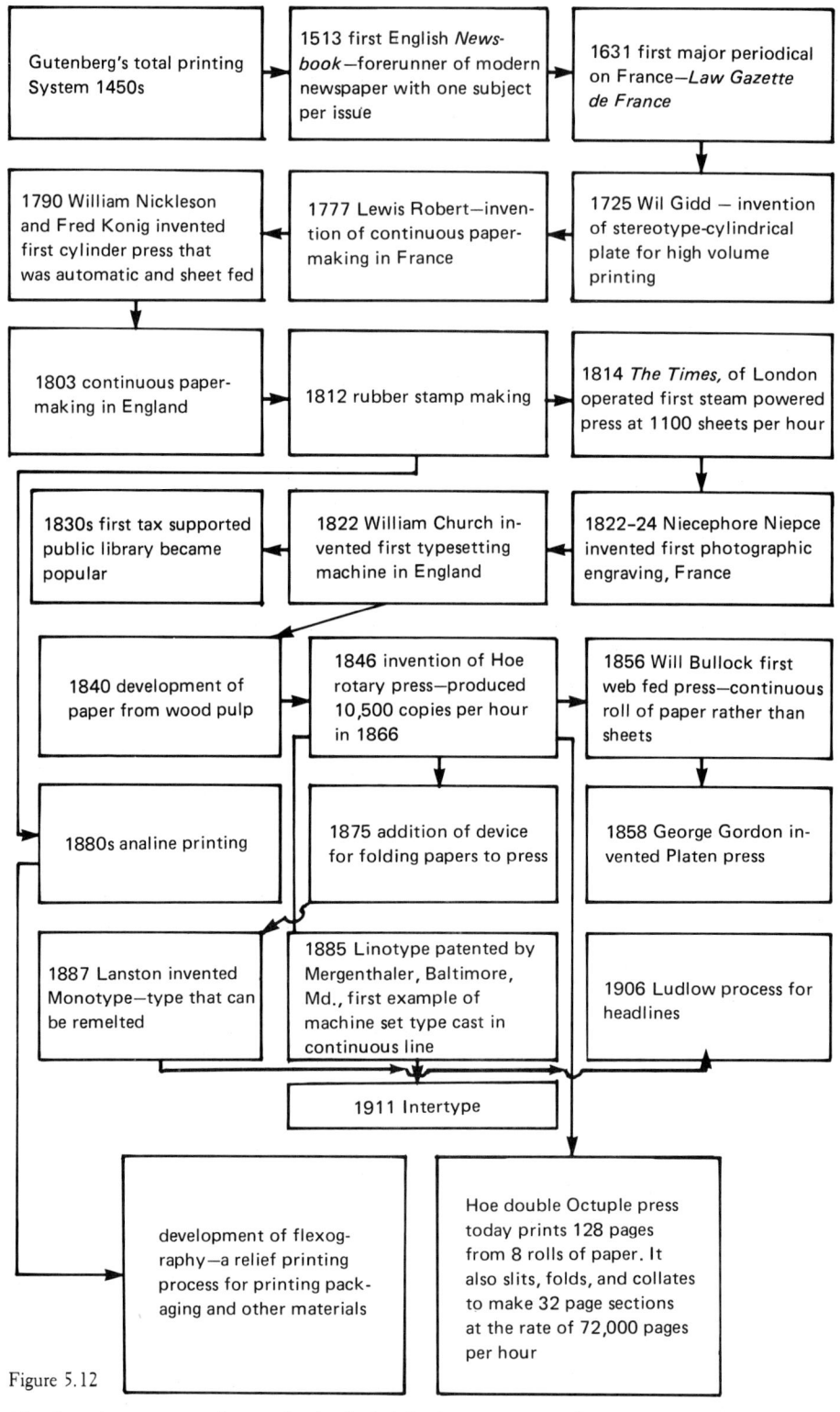

Figure 5.12

After Gutenberg a great explosion of technological developments occurred.

This leads to the final element in Gutenberg's total system, the printing press. The press that was to be used was already available as a tool for printing wood engravings. It was a simple screw-press like those used to squeeze the juice from grapes for making wine. Screw-presses had for some time been used to print wood block images on textiles and for flattening covers to be used in the book binding process.

These are all of the elements of Gutenberg's system. To us, viewing this contribution in our time, it seems like a rather obvious innovation. But it took a creative genius to put it all together.

Gutenberg's development of a total printing system—moveable type in a frame, ink of a new design, paper, and a printing press started what was later to be known as the communication revolution. It made the visual message readily accessible to the average person, and it served as the beginning of a vast array of image reproduction processes that were to follow.

Before Gutenberg there were fewer than a million books in existence anywhere in the world. By the end of the fifteenth century there were more than 9,000,000 books in circulation in Europe alone. Today there are more than 20,000 new titles published each year in the United States alone. Some of the inventions following Gutenberg's discovery are shown in figure 5.12.

Raised Surface Printing

Let's move away from the idea of what was done and take a closer look at the basic concept behind Gutenberg's process itself. Today the process is called **relief,** or **letterpress** printing. It includes any type of printing which is done from a raised printing carrier. The part that is to be printed is raised up from the supporting surface. Figure 5.13 shows how the process works.

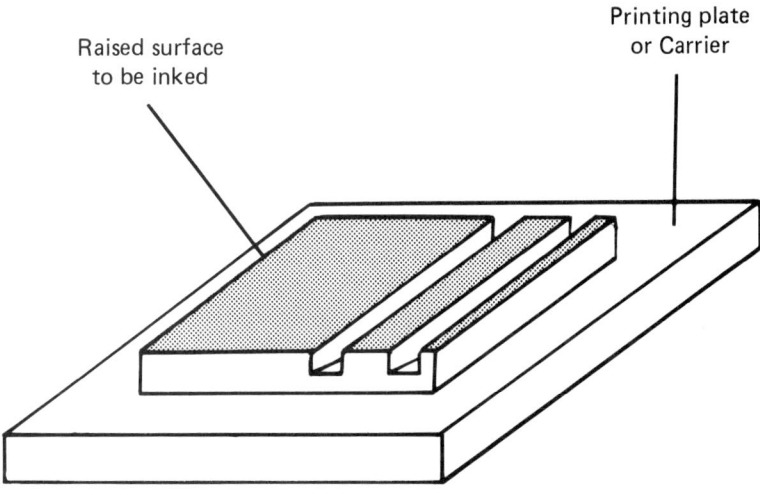

Figure 5.13

Basic concept behind raised surface printing.

In raised surface printing the visual image is inked. The surface to be printed (such as paper, plastic, or cloth) is placed on top of the inked image, and pressure is applied. A good example of the process in action is the rubber stamp used in many of our libraries to stamp due dates on books.

A modern spinoff of the raised surface printing concept is a process developed by George A. Covington of Austin, Texas. Covington's process produces photographic images in relief. The raised surface pictures then are "read" by blind persons touching the pictures with their fingertips.

Many other processes have been developed that enable us to reproduce images. In the printing industry today four major processes are responsible for more than $26 billion worth of production per year in the United States alone. This figure does not include packaging, which by itself accounts for more than twenty billion annually. Think also of the associated industries: chemicals, ink making, paper making, press manufacturing, and photographic, and the thousands of jobs created by these industries. In fact, there are more than 100 industries in the printing and publishing area alone.

We have touched on how raised surface printing, or letterpress printing, is accomplished. Let's take a few minutes to discuss the basic concept behind each of the other major printing processes.

Plane Surface Printing

The biggest producer in the printing industry is plane surface printing or offset lithography, accounting for more than half of the industry's total production. Offset lithography grew out of the discovery of lithography by Alois Senefelder (Germany) between 1796–1799. In the beginning the process was called **lithography**, meaning stone writing.

The discovery happened this way. Senefelder was doing some drawing on a piece of Bavarian limestone found around his home. As he experimented with drawing on the stones he found that he could write on them with a greasy crayon, apply water to the image and then ink, and that the image would retain ink and the non-image area would not.

Let's think about the concept a little closer. It is unlikely that you have any limestone close at hand so in place of the stone plate let's imagine using a flat piece of tin cut out of a large tin can. The tin will serve as our printing plate. Next visualize drawing an **X** on the tin with a black grease pencil. Now imagine running a cotton pad dipped in water over the plate. What would happen? Well, the greasy image would not accept water because of a basic chemical theory that grease and water will not mix. The **X** image then would stay dry even though the water was applied to it. Not so for the nonimage area. In that area water would adhere to the metal surface. Next imagine running an inked roller (called a brayer) over the entire plate. Do you know what would happen? The dry image would be inked but no ink would stick to the area where there was water. Confused? Try it and see what happens.

Senefelder did the same thing. The only difference was that he used a flat stone for a printing plate instead of tin. Later on Ira Rubel (1906) invented the offset press. The press used a flat metal plate similar to what we just described to transfer the visual

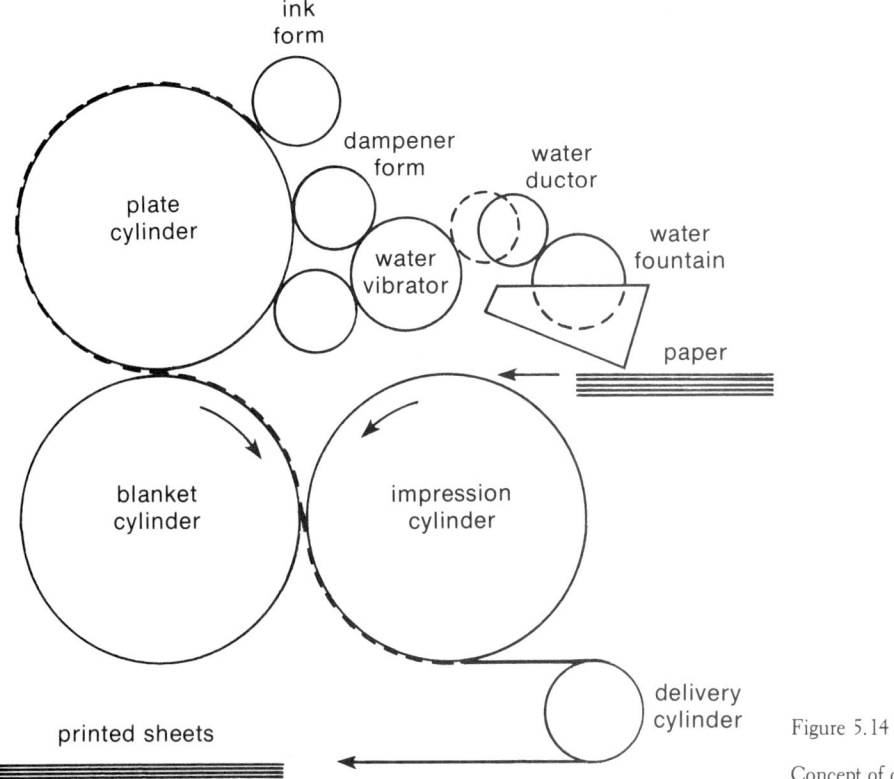

Figure 5.14

Concept of offset printing.

image. Since the printing plate is flat or **plane** the process is often referred to as plane surface printing.

Today offset presses are of several designs. All of them, however, stem from the basic three-cylinder dual system principle. Figure 5.14 shows a simplified schematic of how the offset press works.

Here's how it works. A flat metal plate carrying the image is wrapped around the plate cylinder. The press is turned on, and a sheet is picked up from the feeder and fed into the printing portion of the press. The paper is then grabbed by grippers, metal fingers attached to the impression cylinder of the press. As the cylinder turns, it takes the paper with it, squeezing it between itself and a rubber-covered blanket cylinder and is "offset" from the blanket cylinder to the paper. This is why the process of lithography is often referred to as offset printing. The principle of lithography still remains, however. Think about how the image gets to the blanket cylinder where we want it. After the printing plate has been placed on the plate cylinder and the press is turned on, a cloth or cotton covered water roller contacts the plate. This roller, called the water form roller, puts water on the plate in the nonimage areas. No water sticks to the greasy image area. Next ink rollers are engaged against the plate. This is when the ink is applied to the dry image and is repelled by the areas covered by water. What we have now is a visual image on the plate, which is inked and ready for action. After sheets begin feeding through the press an impression lever is engaged to bring the blanket cylinder in contact against the paper. The image at this point is offset against the paper and the paper is squeezed between the blanket and impression cylinders on its way out to the delivery end of the press. That is all that there is to it! Seems kind of confusing, doesn't it? Go back through this section and think about it. It is really quite simple.

Sunken Surface Printing

The gravure process does not involve a raised printing surface like the relief process or a flat surface like lithography. **Gravure** uses a sunken or depressed image area. The process was first developed around 1879 by Karl Kleitsch of Vienna. Figure 5.15 shows

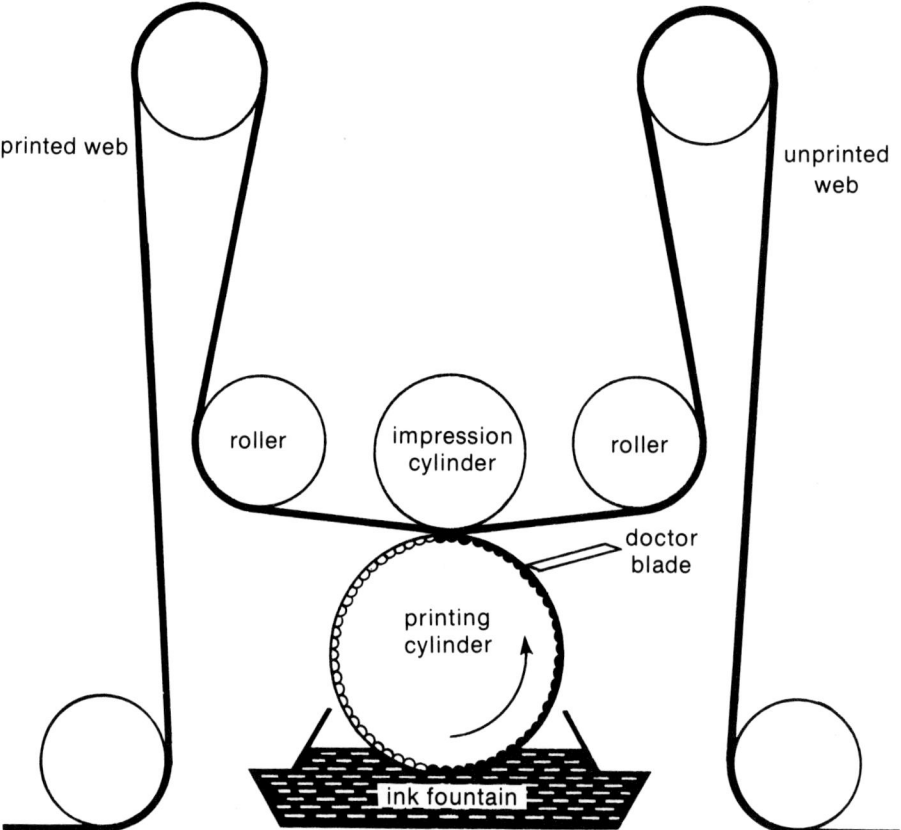

Figure 5.15

Concept of gravure printing.

how the process works. The process started using a flat plate with the printing image scratched into the surface. Then a highly fluid ink was rubbed across the plate. What happens with the process is that the ink is retained in the sunken image areas and is rubbed away in the raised non-printing areas. Paper is then applied using great pressure.

The paper is partially squeezed into the depressions and the ink is pulled from the depressed areas.

The development of the use of cylindrical plates led to the development of **rotogravure,** a rotary gravure process capable of printing cheaper paper at great speeds. Sunday newspaper sections, color sections of newspapers, premium stamp catalogs, and mail order catalogs are examples of uses for rotogravure printing. For years sheet-fed gravure has been the major process used for printing requiring fine illustrations, such as stocks and bonds, and money.

Through-the-Surface Printing

During this past decade screen printing has been one of the fastest growing of all of the major printing processes. It is the oldest of all of the processes, dating back to the Chinese in the Middle Ages. The process has not achieved the success of the other three processes until recently, primarily because of the longer time that was needed for screen printed images to dry. Recently the process has found new potential, mainly because of technological refinements in inks, automatic presses, and improved driers.

The screen process involves through the surface printing. It all begins with a stencil, which acts as the printing plate. The stencil is prepared by hand or photographically. The image area is removed from the stencil. Then the stencil is fastened to a porous screen, usually made of silk, nylon, dacron, or stainless steel. The screen is stretched tightly on a frame. A very thick ink is placed on the stencil, and a squeegee (rubber bladed instrument) is pulled across the screen, either by hand or machine. The ink is forced through the surface of the open image area of the stencil onto the printing material. The process has advantages over the others. It can be used to print on any solid surface, in any size, shape, or thickness. Because of the thickness of ink deposit it is simple to print a light color over a dark color with perfect legibility. With thinner inks used with other processes it is usually difficult to recognize a light color printed over a dark color. Imagine drawing your name with a yellow magic marker on a dark blue piece of paper. It would be difficult if not impossible to read your name. With the screen process it could be read easily.

During the past ten years screen printing has grown at a rate nearly three times that of the gross national product. Figure 5.16 shows the concept of screen printing.

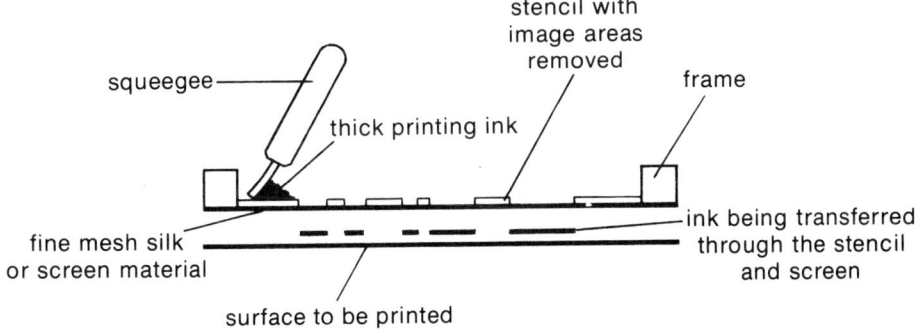

Figure 5.16

This is the basic concept behind screen printing.

Reprography

There are many other processes for reproducing the visual image than the four major printing processes. In fact, a new industry now known as the **reprographic** industry has emerged to try to fulfill the need for mass reproduction of the visual image.

Reprography deals with duplicating and quick copy processes used by business and industry to produce limited numbers of printed copies. Quick copy processes are those responsible for producing twenty-five or fewer copies, whereas duplicating processes are generally used for reproducing visual images in quantities up to 3-5000 copies.

A general rule of thumb for determining whether to choose a quick copy process, a duplicating process, or a printing process for a job is that when cost is a factor and only a few copies are needed, it is cheaper to use a quick copy reprographic process to do the job than to use a duplicating or a printing process. On the other hand, if 1000 top quality copies were required, the offset printing process would probably be the way to go. Several factors influence selection of the best process to use for a job. The final solution all boils down to quality and cost. The process to be selected should be the one that produces the best image for the lowest cost.

Hundreds of different types of reprographic processes have been developed since the beginning of the twentieth century. Many of these processes are variations on one another, but all of them have been in competition for a piece of the market.

All of the processes used in the reprographic field can be grouped under three general categories: (1) processes reproducing copies directly from the original copy; (2) processes reproducing copies from prepared masters; and (3) processes reproducing copies through the use of remote transmission systems.

The simplest processes to use are those that reproduce copies directly from the original copy. Processes in this category are designed primarily to make fewer than twenty-five copies. Today only three forms of quick copy processes are popular: diazo, thermal, and electrostatic.

Copies from the Original

The Diazo Process. The diazo process is heavily used by the drafting industries. The original design is drawn on a piece of translucent (slightly transparent, frosty looking) tracing vellum. The process was originally called the blueprint process, but today many refer to it as whiteprinting. After the original is prepared it is used to make the copy or copies. Refer to figure 5.17 for a simplified version of how the process works.

There are two types of diazo processes, the wet diazo and the dry diazo. With both processes two steps are involved: exposure to ultraviolet light and the development of the image. Some years ago the wet process involved running the exposed diazo paper through a developer where the areas of the diazo surface of the paper that were not exposed to bright light combined with a chemical to form a colored image. In this form the process was called blueprinting, and was an offshoot of aniline printing (a process developed in the 1880s).

Today the blueprinting process has been almost totally replaced with the diazo process. This process relies on an ammonia vapor or a dry powdered toner as the developing agent.

(1.) EXPOSURE

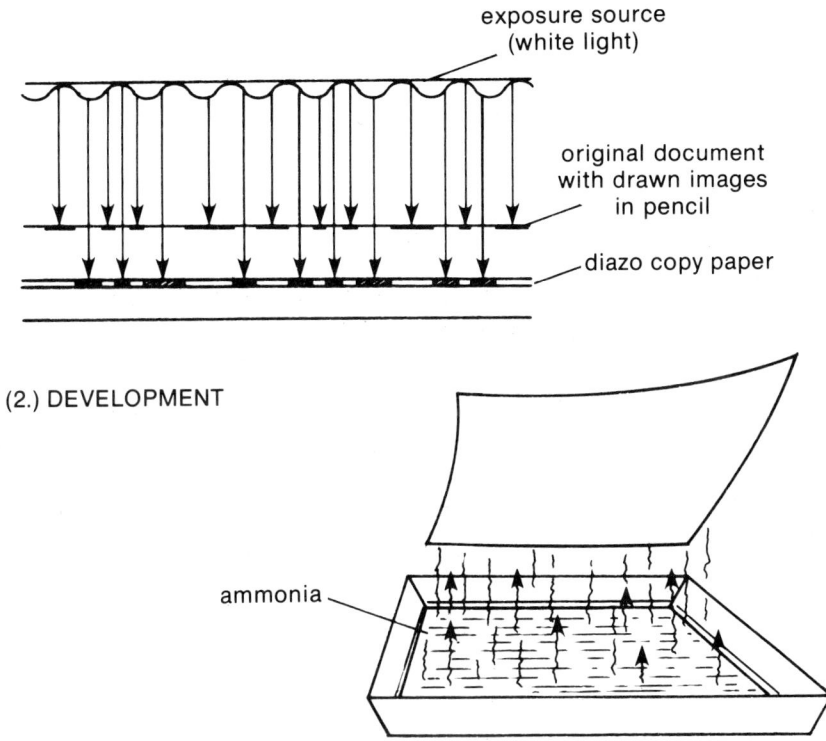

(2.) DEVELOPMENT

Figure 5.17

The Diazo process.

All diazo processes operate in much the same way. First the translucent original with the original design drawn on it is placed in contact with the diazo copy paper. The paper is not as sensitive to light as photographic paper and can be handled in room light for a brief period of time. Both the original and copy paper are fed into the diazo machine. Both sheets of paper feed around a glass tube containing a number of ultraviolet (often fluorescent) lights. The ultraviolet light passes through the master where there is no image and breaks down the light sensitive diazo salts coated on the copy paper. In the image area of the original no light can pass through, and the diazo salt is left undisturbed. In both of the diazo processes, the developing agent neutralizes an acid in the diazo coating and lets the chemical components combine to form a colored image. In the wet process the developer contains part of the colored image, which combines with the diazo compound left on the copy paper.

Let's review what happens with the ammonia-type diazo process. The translucent original is placed on top of a sheet of diazo copy paper, and both are fed through the machine. As they pass through the exposure section of the machine, light passes through the original where no image area is there to block it and affects the diazo salts. It neutralizes an acid in the coating. If we were to take the paper out of the machine at this point, we would be able to see a yellow coloring on the diazo paper where the original image was. The background area would be white, or neutralized. When the copy paper is passed through the ammonia vapor, the area that still contains the diazo salts (the image area) is affected by the ammonia vapor in such a way that the chemicals combine to form the colored image. The shorter the exposure then the darker the background. Where the surface was neutralized no coloring takes place, and the background stays white.

The Thermal Process. The thermal process was developed in 1950 by Dr. Carl Miller of the 3M Corporation. The process is important because heat, rather than the transmission of light, is responsible for producing the image on copy paper. The process is fast (four to six seconds per copy), and it does not require any developing solutions. These features have made it a popular process for office and business copying needs.

The process is limited to making copies from originals having images made with heat absorbent inks that are composed of carbon-based compounds. Typed matter and pencil drawings will work fine, but many ballpoint pen inks contain no carbon and will not make an image with this process. The copy paper is placed in contact against the image area of the original and is fed through the machine. Infrared light (heat) is built up around the image area. This build-up of heat in the image area causes the copy paper coating to turn dark. A slower machine speed will result in feeding the copy and thermal paper through the machine slower, and the end result will be a darker copy.

The Electrostatic Process. The electrostatic process has advantages over the diazo and thermal processes. Its disadvantages are linked primarily to the initial machine cost. However, it can produce copies in black and white or color and the copies it produces are of a quality much closer to the original copy.

There are two major types of electrostatic processes used by the reprographic industries—**xerography,** pronounced "zeer-og-raphy," and **electrofax.** The electrofax process is used to print odd shapes such as lemons, nuts, bottles, cardboard boxes, and packing crates. It is a spinoff of screen printing, using a charged screen to carry the image. A dry toner, which also becomes charged after being placed in contact with the screen, produces the image. A plate with an unlike charge is positioned under the object to be printed, and the charged toner is attracted to the printed object. The image is then fixed by fusing the toner or spraying it.

The xerographic process was first developed by the United States Army for printing maps in the field. The Army process used zinc oxide coated paper and a liquid toner. The process produced the image much like the electrofax process. In the reprographic industry the process has received the most recognition through developments made by the Xerox Corporation. Let's take a closer look at how the process works.

The process uses a light sensitive selenium metal plate that carries a positive electrostatic charge. The electrostatic charge is destroyed in the areas where light strikes it and stays in areas where light does not contact it.

It is necessary to understand the theory behind the reflection and absorption of light before we can really make sense of how the electrostatic process works. A basic principle upon which photography is based states that light colors reflect light and dark colors absorb it. This means that the lighter the color is, the more the light that will be reflected from it. If we were to draw a black **X** on a white piece of paper we would have copy that can reflect light in certain areas and absorb it in others. This is exactly what happens when the original copy is placed in the electrostatic copying process and an exposure is made. Where the copy paper is white, the background area on our imaginary document, light is reflected. Where our black **X** is, light is absorbed. So, now let's return to our basic process.

After the plate is exposed to light, it becomes positively charged. (The plate is sensitive to light like a piece of photographic film.) The white area of the original reflects light to the charged plate, and the light destroys the charge where it strikes it. The plate is then dusted with a toner that sticks only in the areas where the charges remain. Copy paper is then placed against the plate, and a negative charge is applied to the paper. The toner is attracted to the paper, and the image is fixed. That is all that there is to it!

The Xerox 6500 color copier has reportedly triggered a spread in counterfeiting across the nation. The ability of the machine to make fine quality color copies has even caused the McDonald's company to redesign its hamburger gift certificates because so many phony ones were being accepted.

Most of the processes used to reproduce visual messages from the original document are either diazo, thermal, or electrostatic.

Copies from a Prepared Master

Other processes used by the reprographic industries involve the use of a prepared master. These processes are generally called duplicating processes rather than quick copy processes.

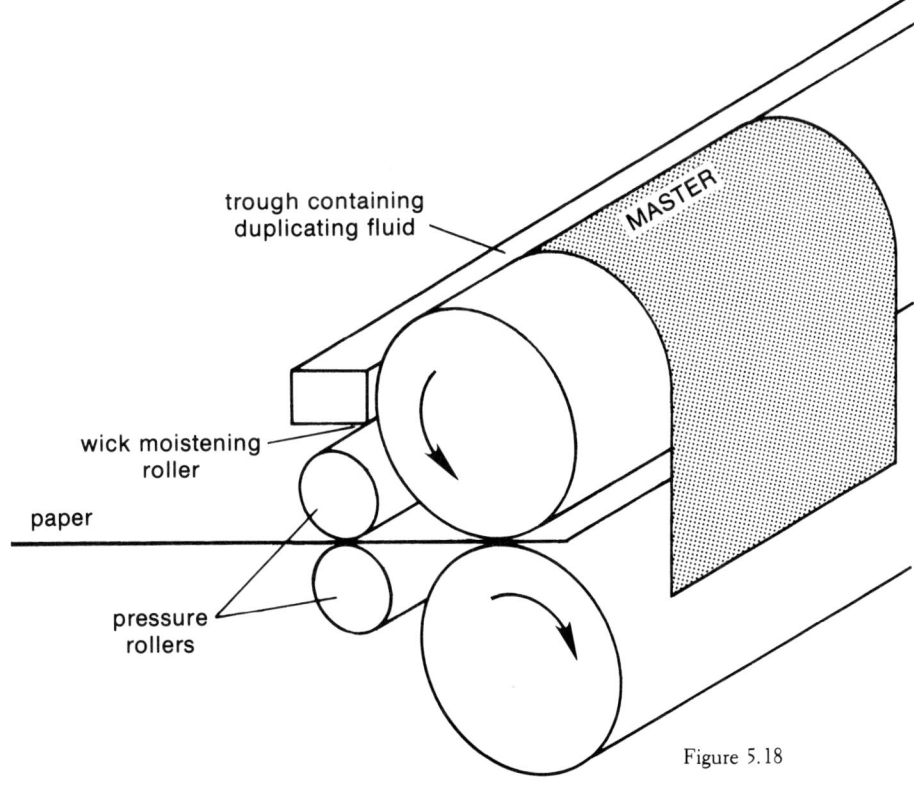

Figure 5.18

Spirit duplication process.

Spirit Duplication. The most widely used duplication process today is called **spirit duplication.** Its origin seems to lead back to aniline dye printing. It got its name (the spirit process) because of the spirits, or alcohol-based liquid used to dissolve the carbon dyes. Here's how it works. The original image is prepared on a paper master. The master consists of two attached sheets, one on top of the other. The top sheet is paper and the bottom sheet is covered with waxy carbon paper. The two sheets are separated with a thin sheet of protective paper. The user removes the separating sheet and draws, types, or otherwise makes an impression on the top sheet. The pressure created causes the carbon dye substance to be transferred on to the back of the sheet. The top sheet is then placed on the master cylinder of a spirit duplicator. When the machine is turned on, a quantity of duplicating fluid is pumped to a felt wick, which gently contacts the duplicating paper as it is fed through the machine. The moist paper, in turn, is squeezed between the master cylinder and impression roller. The moist paper contacts the carbon dye on the master and causes it to be gradually dissolved. The coloring is what comes off on the sheet and produces the image. As the master continues to come in contact with the duplicating fluid, it gradually begins to lose its coloring ability. Masters are rated as short, medium, or long run by the manufacturer. Most manufacturers specify that 200 is about the maximum number of copies attainable with a spirit master. Refer to figure 5.18 for a review of how the process works.

Mimeograph Duplication. Another duplicating process frequently used by business and industry is called **mimeograph,** or stencil duplication. The master consists of a gelatin coating on a fine screen, much like that used in the silk screen process of printing. In fact, the process works just like the silk screen process in principle. The only difference is that the stencil is wrapped around a master cylinder on the mimeograph, rather than being stretched tightly over a wooden frame. The process uses a very thick, pasty ink, held inside of the printing cylinder. As the cylinder turns a rubber squeegee turns around inside the drum forcing ink out through the open image areas of the stencil. Mimeograph duplication has several advantages over spirit duplication. A major advantage is the quality of the printing image attainable. Refinements in stencil preparation, better inks, and improved duplicators have enabled the production of fine quality printed copy. Stencils are prepared by typing directly on them or by hand drawing.

Copy produced using the offset process has always been used as the standard of quality for other duplication processes. The mimeograph process is now capable of producing copy that is close to offset in quality. Another advantage of the process over spirit duplication is that the mimeograph process is capable of reproducing several thousand copies.

There are also disadvantages associated with the process. The process involves printing ink, so it is more messy to clean up the machine after use. Handling used stencils is also more troublesome since excess ink must be removed from the stencils after they have been used.

Remote Transmission

We have discussed methods used to produce visual images directly from the original copy and through the use of prepared masters. It is also possible to create visual messages using remote transmission techniques. The process involves the use of sophisticated electronic technology. Here's how it works. The design to be reproduced is placed under a high intensity light scanner that changes the black and white images into electronic impulses. These impulses are then beamed to a satellite, which beams the electronic signal down to the receiving station. There the electronic impulses are changed to light impulses and exposed on photographic film. The film is used to make offset plates, which are used to reproduce the visual image for mass distribution.

This is the system now used by Dow Jones and Company to publish *The Wall Street Journal* in Orlando, Florida. A facsimile (actual representative) of an entire newspaper page is transmitted from a plant in Chicopee, Massachusetts to the Westar satellite 13,851 miles above the equator. The satellite beams down impulses representing entire pages in about three and one-half minutes. Dow Jones has been experimenting with remote transmission since 1973, when it transmitted a facsimile of the journal page from Clarksburg, Maryland to Intelsat IV located above the Atlantic Ocean. It then took six minutes and twelve seconds to transmit, receive, and reproduce the image at the other end. The real potential for remote transmission is that visual information originating anywhere may be received anywhere else fairly quickly, assuring same-day publication for mass distribution.

Within the next ten years it is likely that the lag between information input and reception will be continually shortened, so much so in fact that we may eventually be able to transmit and receive visual information almost simultaneously. It is hard to imagine how a picture might be transformed into electrical signals and sent through the air over networks of wires.

The technique was first made possible by the discovery of the element, selenium. When selenium is exposed to light, its electrical resistance changes according to the amount of light that falls on it. If a selenium device is inserted into a circuit it will change varying intensities of light into variations of electrical current. The photograph is comprised of various tones of black and white, which in turn reflect varying amounts of light. The selenium device functions as a converter, much as a microphone does when it changes variations in air pressure into variations of electric current.

There is much more to the process than this. Let's think about what we would do if we wanted to transmit a picture of you from your school to a television station in Mount Pleasant, Michigan. Your picture would be wrapped around a drum on the transmitting machine situated in your school. The photograph would be scanned by a very narrow light beam reflecting on only a small part of the picture at a time. The tiny light beam would be reflected off the picture in varying amounts onto a camera lens. Behind the lens a phototube, a modern equivalent of the early selenium cell, would transduce or change the visual information to electrical impulses. These electrical impulses would then be transmitted over telephone lines or by satellite.

Once your electrical impulses were received in Mount Pleasant, a phototube would again be used to change them to light, which would expose photographic paper held on a recording drum.

The beam would scan, both on the transmitting and receiving ends, across the picture from right to left very quickly. At the same time both drums would turn very slowly. Oftentimes Polaroid film, which can be developed without darkroom equipment, is used on the recording end.

Other recording processes based on electrothermal, electrolytic, or pigment-trans-

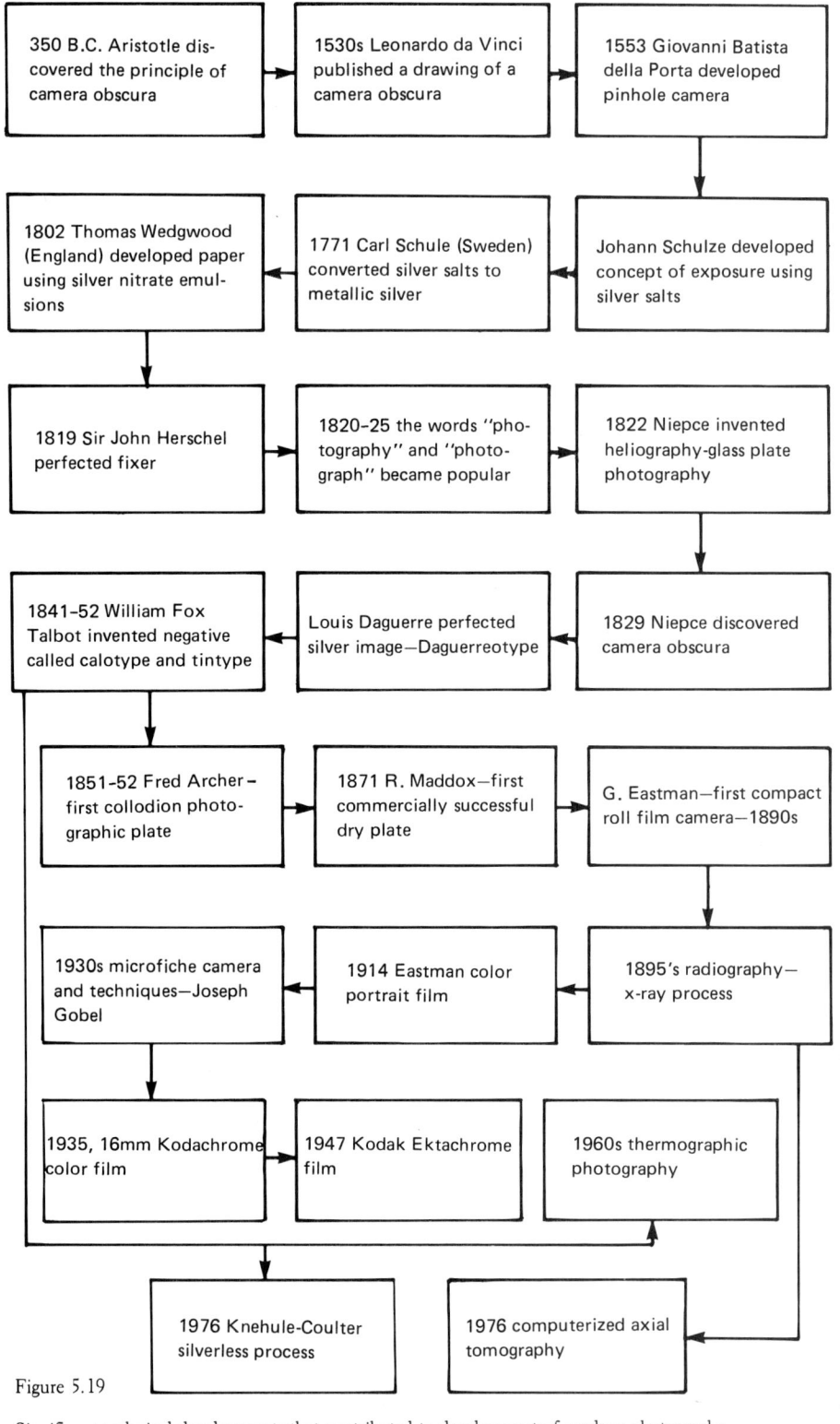

Figure 5.19

Significant technical developments that contributed to development of modern photography.

fer techniques are also used for remote transmission. These processes are often used and are worth mentioning here.

In the electrothermal process a special recording paper, which has a white surface on top of a black surface, is used to record the image. The white coating has been treated so it will conduct electrical impulses. Dark areas, which eventually become representative of the visual image, are produced by passing an electrical current through this area of the paper and burning away the white coating. Weather charts and telegrams are usually received this way.

The electrolytic recording technique uses a similar type of paper, but the electrical current causes chemical changes that result in darkened areas on the paper.

Carbon paper recorders are also used to recreate the visual image. These recorders are examples of the pigment transfer process. With this process the recording is made by a stylus inscribing marks on carbon paper, which in turn marks on a sheet of white paper.

With each of these types of remote transmission processes photographs can be created quickly. When this is done quality is lacking. Normally a picture will be transmitted in seven or eight minutes. To accomplish this about one million areas are scanned in this amount of time.

Much of the visual communication we see each day falls into the category of image reproduction. Today we have so many different processes available to help us in reproducing information that we have been caught in a sort of communication dilemma—we have become less selective in what we produce.

Many technological developments were necessary for us to reach our current level of technological sophistication. Of the most important of these is what we call photography—or writing with light.

Photography

Many discoveries and innovations led to the development of photography. This is why it is difficult to specify the date of its true beginning. There is, however, general agreement on the time period when it all began (1822–1839). Photography is much like Gutenberg's total printing system because it was made possible by a series of independent but somewhat related developments that were joined to form the system we now call photography. Figure 5.19 shows what some of the major developments were that made photography possible.

Photography as we know it was made posssible by six areas of innovation. Each of these are represented in figure 5.20.

Camera Obscura

The camera obscura was initially discovered by Aristotle around 350 B.C. He noticed that the rays of the sun were projected through the leaves of a tree onto the ground where he was sitting. As he thought about it he realized that when he moved a sheet of papyrus closer to the opening in the leaves the image was enlarged. Well, it doesn't seem like much of a discovery, does it? He felt the same way, and the principle was not used for any constructive purpose until nearly 2000 years later.

In the middle 1500s Giovanni della Porta used the concept of the camera obscura to construct a pinhole camera to show his friends. Later on the device was used to

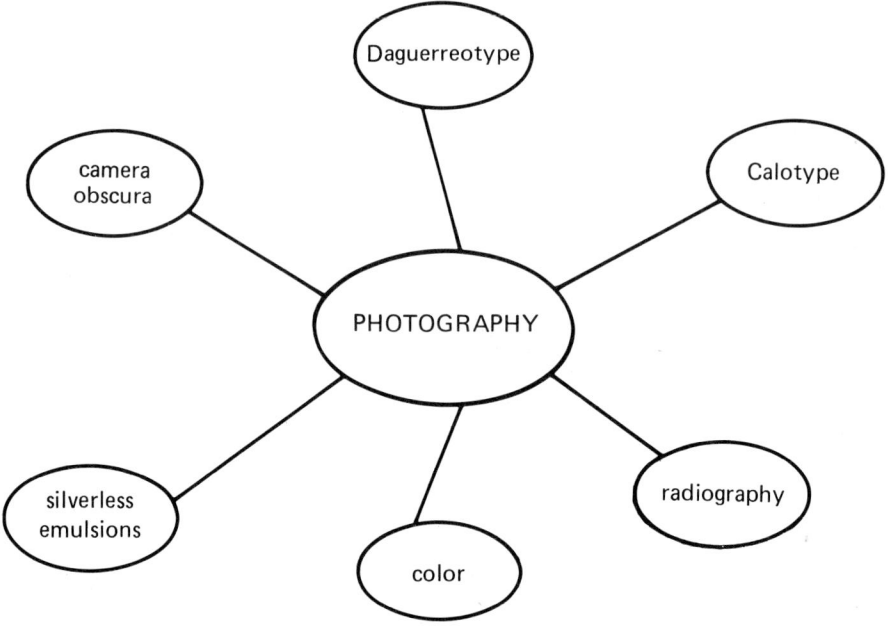

Figure 5.20

Major highlights of the world of photography.

help artists to enlarge and reduce drawings of original objects. No permanent image was captured with the pinhole camera but the concept was important because it established the basis for the development of the camera used today. The outline of the object was projected on a silver reflecting surface and reflected upward to a surface of slightly frosted ground glass. The concept that della Porta discovered works like our own eyes. The image is turned upside down after it is projected through the lens.

Between the years 1822–1839, a French painter by the name of Louis Daguerre, working with Joseph Niepce, was successful in permanently preserving a visual image on light sensitive silver plates. Prior to this time photographic images had been produced on paper and glass, but they were not able to withstand continued exposure to light. Time caused these images to darken and fade away.

Daguerreotype

The development of the process was due largely to the initial ideas of Niepce, but after his death in 1833 Daguerre received most of the credit for the innovation. His form of photography became known as the daguerreotype.

It worked like this. A silver-coated plate was covered with a coating of iodine. This made the plate sensitive to light, much like our modern photographic film. The plate was far less sensitive than modern film and took long exposures. In the areas where the light struck the surface of the plate it affected the silver iodine emulsion surface. This produced an invisible or latent image by hardening the emulsion where it received the exposure to light. The plate was then exposed to fumes of mercury. The mercury was attracted to the area of the plate which had been exposed to light and was not attracted to the nonexposed areas. What was produced was a visual image on a shiny silver plate.

Daguerreotypes were kept in ornate leather cases, which protected them from the elements. The process was significant because it was the first permanent photographic image, but it did have drawbacks. It did not produce a negative. A new exposure was necessary each time an image was desired.

Daguerreotype photographs required long exposures. If a portrait was desired the person had to sit perfectly still, sometimes as long as fifteen to twenty-five minutes, under bright lights, before a satisfactory exposure was made. Crude as the process was, it was an important beginning.

Calotype and Paper Negative

Several years later an Englishman by the name of William Fox Talbot was responsible for establishing the practical beginnings of the process as a form of visual communication that could be used by the average person. In 1852 Talbot developed, after much experimentation with gelatin and potassium bichromate, the calotype process and the first negative. The Talbot negative consisted of paper coated with silver nitrate and sodium chloride. The advantage of having a negative was that other identical copies could be produced from the original visual concept.

Film Negative

Today we use film that has the light sensitive emulsion carried on a support surface called a **base** or **substrate**. Today most of the time we use film with a plastic or acetate base. Seldom do we prepare paper negatives any more. The synthetic bases are much more durable and usually assist in producing a better quality negative.

Types of Film

There are many different types of film in use today. They are classified according to the type of light to which they are sensitive. There are quite a number of general classifications for black and white film. The most common are: panchromatic, orthochromatic, blue sensitive, radiographic, diazo, kalvar, dry silver, and silverless. Of all of these, panchromatic, orthochromatic, and blue sensitive films are the most popular.

Panchromatic film is the type of film commonly used by many amateur photobuffs. "Pan" film is sensitive to all colors of light, although it is a little less sensitive to green, and is slightly oversensitive to blue and violet.

Orthochromatic film is sensitive to all colors except for red. This often gives it a built-in advantage over pan film. It can be processed using red safelights without the red light exposing the film. This enables the photographer to view the negative while it is being processed.

Blue sensitive film is made up of a silver bromide emulsion, which is sensitive only to blue and ultraviolet light. This type of film is particularly well suited for use in high contrast copy work where the copy being photographed has extremely dark and light areas, and few middletones or areas in between.

Specialized types of films such as radiographic, kalvar, diazo, dry silver, and silverless emulsions will be discussed later in this module. Each of these films is sensitive to different ranges of light.

How Film Works

When considering how films react to certain types of light and how visual images are created and preserved on film, it is necessary to look more carefully at the characteristics of film emulsions. Most films used today have silver halide emulsions. Let's take a closer look at how visual images are made using these films.

It all begins with exposure. Light is reflected from objects in varying amounts, according to their surface characteristics and degrees of lightness or darkness. We know from previous discussion that white reflects light and black absorbs light. Where light is reflected through the lens onto film an exposure is made. To a point, more light means more exposure and less light means less exposure.

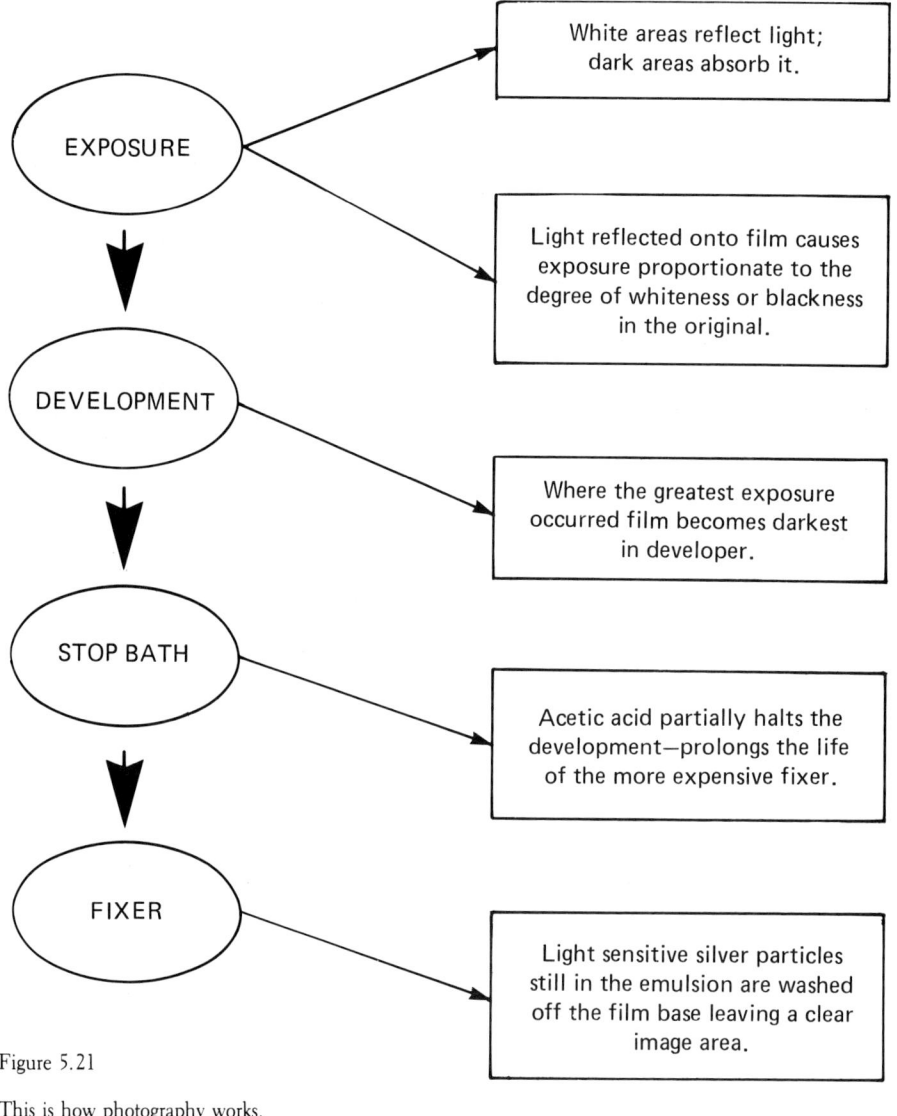

Figure 5.21

This is how photography works.

Next the film is placed in a developing solution. Here the exposed areas become dark when the film is placed in developer. The areas of the emulsion that received light chemically react resulting in a heavy build-up of minute particles of silver in these areas.

After the film has been properly developed it still contains many light sensitive particles that were not influenced by the initial exposure. If we were to turn on the white room lights at this time our film would quickly darken and the visual image would be lost. A solution called **fixer** is used to permanently destroy any light sensitive silver left on the film. Fixing consists of submerging the film in a chemical, usually sodium thiosulfate or ammonium chloride. The fixer removes the unexposed silver salts from the film. The fixer acts like a bleach, turning the unexposed image areas on the negative perfectly clear.

Usually an intermediate step is involved between developing and fixing. This step is called the **stop bath,** and consists of placing the film in a solution of acetic acid. Some of the unexposed silver salts are removed in this step, but a residue of alkaline developer is left on the film. It is the fixing solution that removes all of the developer and unexposed silver salts. After the film has been in the fixing solution about 75 percent of the recommended time the photographer can turn on the room lights and view the film. This makes it easier to tell exactly when the film is adequately fixed. The film will be cloudy, or milky looking, in the image areas but will be cleared when it has been in the fixer long enough.

We have touched on how film works, and the process involved in making and preserving the photographic image. There is really much more to it than this, but one should not be scared away by the many chemicals and solutions available to the photographer. Processing at home is very enjoyable. It is not complicated, despite all of the chemicals and equipment available. Photographic processing is based on some rather simple concepts. Figure 5.21 summarizes the entire process.

The design of a particular photographic emulsion is based on the properties of light it will record. One of the most interesting of the silver halide emulsions is X-ray film, which is based on the process of radiography.

Radiography

Radiography was developed by Roentgen in 1895. Today it is one of the most important of all of the nondestructive tests used in industry. By using highly penetrating X-rays and gamma rays that do not damage the part itself radiography enables a visible film record of what is inside. Objects to be radiographed range in size from microminiaturized electronic components to huge parts used in the space program.

In the medical area radiography is even more important. By passing X-rays or gamma rays through a patient's broken arm a radiograph, or X-ray negative tells of the severity of the break. How it works is relatively simple. Where the area being analyzed is the most penetrable the emulsion receives the most exposure and turns dark in the developing process. Where the rays penetrate to a lesser degree the film receives less exposure and is lighter in the resulting negative. The rays act much like visible light. More exposure results in more hardening of the film emulsion and less exposure results in unaffected emulsion. The unaffected emulsion is cleared in the fixing solution, and the hardened areas become black in the development.

Today it is possible, using a sophisticated new radiographic technique called computerized axial tomography, to photograph an entire cross section through the human body. A number of such "slices" can be taken at any angle desired. This process has enabled the medical profession to treat and diagnose internal injuries much more quickly and more efficiently. The technique will tell the doctor exactly what the problem is and precisely where it is located.

Color Photography

Color film has a different set of characteristics than black and white. Common films used for making positives (right reading images) are Kodachrome and Ektachrome. Both are manufactured by Kodak and are examples of subtractive-type color films.

All subtractive films are made up of three different emulsion layers. These emulsions function like filters, letting the correct color of light pass through to the layer underneath. Ektachrome is an example of reversal film. With reversal films, the three emulsions are first developed as a negative. Then they are re-exposed and redeveloped.

As with black and white film, it all begins with an exposure. Different colors of light affect each of the three emulsion layers in several ways. Let's take a look at what happens.

In the initial exposure the white and blue light affects the blue-sensitive first emulsion layer. The other colors of light do not expose this emulsion layer. The second layer is sensitive to green and the bottom emulsion layer to red. Parts of the second and third layers are exposed during the initial exposure, and other areas are unaffected by the color of light being reflected.

After the first development the film is exposed to white light and is redeveloped. This developer produces dyed images (magenta or red, yellow, cyan or blue) in the proper layers of the emulsion. If the film were to be viewed after the first exposure and development, it would look much like a black and white negative.

Other steps are also involved in processing subtractive-type reversal color film. After this development the film is very dense and very dull. A bleaching process, acting much like the fixer in black and white film, is used to clear off unexposed emulsion areas. After processing, color film often looks like it had been processed incorrectly. The color, while wet, looks dull and dark. The film should be allowed to dry completely before viewing. Subtractive reversal films can be easily processed at home by the amateur.

The additive color process is also important in creating visual images. The additive color process is used to print color photographs in magazines and books. The process involves using four color separation negatives: one to print yellow, another to print magenta, a third to print cyan, and a final black printer to sharpen up detail. Each of these colors are superimposed on each other or overprinted, using transparent inks. The technique enables the printer to produce all colors of the spectrum by using only three basic colors: yellow, magenta, and cyan.

The topic of subtractive and additive color processing is beyond the scope of this text, simply because of the extent of coverage necessary to provide adequate background information. The interested amateur should not be afraid to investigate further, however. A great amount of color experimentation can be done at home without extensive facilities or equipment.

New Technology

Recently many new processes have emerged that promise to revolutionize photography and visual communication technology. One of these processes emerged late in 1975. The process involves a new type of silverless photographic film and was developed by Coulter Information Systems, Inc. The process has been dubbed the Kuehnle-Coulter process. What is most interesting about the film is that the emulsion is comprised of inorganic crystals that are "grown" in a special coating machine and coated on a polyester base. Each of the crystals acts like a photo-transistor. This means that the sensitivity of the film or exposure speed can be influenced by the charge level that is applied to the crystals. The film can be handled in room light conditions prior to being sensitized. After the film has been fixed new information can be added simply by recharging and re-exposing.

The shortage of silver as a natural resource may make the process even more attractive in the years to come. The film relies on synthetic materials.

The concept of photographic images only being possible through wet processing technology is rapidly being displaced, or at least threatened, by new technology. Another type of emulsion and processing system that is becoming more popular today is called **dry silver** technology. The process is based on the dry silver concept, which is an outgrowth of 3M's "Thermo Fax" process. The process relies on heat to develop the film.

Dry silver films really became popular in the middle 1960s. The dry silver process requires only heat and light to produce images on film or paper. An image is produced with an exposure to light, and the image is then made visible through development by heat. Much of the microfilm work done today involves dry silver technology.

Heat has been used in many other ways for producing images. One process, which has far-reaching application in many different fields, is called thermography, or infrared photography. The process is based on the concept that any object or body having a temperature above absolute zero radiates energy in the infrared region of the electromagnetic spectrum. Thermography measures this radiated temperature and determines the temperature of these bodies. In the beginning stages of thermographic photography only macro (large scale) photography was possible. One of the primary uses of the technique was for weather forecasting via satellite. The thermographic photograph represented in figure 5.22 was taken from the Earth Resources Technology Satellite-1 and shows a birdseye view of the land area stretching from New York to Norfolk, Virginia. The three colors, green, red, and infrared, were recorded separately by the satellite and were received at NASA's Goddard Space Flight Center, in Greenbelt, Maryland. The photograph tells us a great deal about the land being photographed. The healthy trees, plants, and vegetation, which cannot be seen by the naked eye from the height of the photograph, appear as a light pink. Barren land areas appear as light gray. Cities and highly industrial areas show up as dark gray and water appears as shades of dark blue.

Today we also use the thermographic technique to take pictures of microscopic targets. Used in this way we refer to the technique as **microthermography**. Using sophisticated electronic technology and computerized scanning systems it is now possible to photograph, or spot check, small areas with great accuracy. In fact, it is even possible to record temperature differences down to 0.1 degree C.

Figure 5.22

The Edison Projecting Kinetograph popular around 1890, was the first motion picture camera.
Courtesy, Edison National Historic Site

Well, technology has come a long way since Gutenberg's total printing system. Photography, like Gutenberg's system, opened up new markets, new tools, and new techniques for communicating, but it was only the beginning.

The Moving Image

Photography gave us realism in creating images, but it could not end here. The advent of motion was the next significant development in visual communication technology. The motion picture is nothing more than a series of still pictures projected in rapid sequence so they give an illusion of movement. The concept of moving pictures was based on a very old idea, that of making drawings on wheel-like devices which when spun gave the viewer the illusion of motion.

Motion Pictures

It was not until around 1870 that photography was well enough developed to take photographs at a rapid enough speed to give the effect of movement.

Figure 5.23

The Peephole Kinetoscope of 1894 used celluloid film. Note the film attached to the spools.
Courtesy, Edison National Historic Site

In the early 1890s Thomas Edison invented two devices called the Kinetograph and the Kinetoscope. The Kinetograph was a motion-picture camera using celluloid film while the Kinetoscope was a device for peep-show viewing. They both met with

Figure 5.24

This was the original Kinetographic Theatre called the *Black Maria*. The theatre turned to face the sun and the roof opened to let light in to illuminate the image.
Courtesy, Edison National Historic Site

tremendous success, and marked the beginnings of the era of the motion picture and the moving image.

The film ran continuously through the Kinetoscope between the lens and a light source. The film length was limited to about 13.5 meters and ran for about thirteen seconds. The pictures for the Kinetoscope were produced at Edison's studio in West Orange, New Jersey. The studio, called the "Black Maria," revolved to keep the stage in the sunlight. The camera (Kinetograph) weighed nearly a ton, and everything had to be brought to it.

The Cinema

Around the year 1895 the Lumiere brothers of France developed the first really practical device for projecting moving pictures on a screen. It was called the Cinematograph. Between the years 1895 and 1914 the French photographer Georges Melies produced more than 4000 reels of film.

A number of refinements occurred, but it was not until the early 1920s that the concept of the motion picture as we now know it really emerged. The development of sound in pictures in the twenties was really what made the technique of moving pictures popular to the American public. Gradually the technique broadened to include wide screens, color, and magnetic sound (1951).

The most important milestone in the history of the cinema, or motion picture, with the exception of the development of sound in 1926, was the opening of the wide-screen cinerama in New York in 1952. Many cities across the world followed suit, and the moving image became even more popular.

Television

Another development which, like the motion picture, photographic imagery, and Gutenberg's mass communication system, opened up a new world and a host of new options for visual communication was television. Developments that led to the development of the system that we call television began in 1873. At that time experiments with the element selenium led to the discovery that its exposure to different degrees of light resulted in varying degrees of electrical conductivity. Other experiments were made by Paul Nipkow (1884), John Baird (1890), Sir William Crookes (1895), and Vladimir Zworykin (1923).

In 1939 the Radio Corporation of America (RCA) presented its refined system at the World's Fair in New York. RCA began a series of semi-weekly TV shows. Further efforts were halted by World War II. After the war developments in TV technology began to soar. In the late 1940s the concept of color television began to emerge.

Sometimes we do not really recognize the great impact of this one development on our lives. We know that 99.8 percent of the more than sixty million homes in the United States are equipped with a television set and more than 25 percent of these have two or more sets. Two-thirds of all American households have color sets. In most of these homes the set is turned on about six hours a day. Television is a big business with operating revenues for radio, television, and telegraphic sectors representing monetary growth from around $11 billion in 1969 to more than $28 billion today.

What impact does television make on the American people? Well, by the time the average child enters the first grade he has already spent more time watching TV than he will likely spend in college earning an advanced degree. By the time this same individual is eighteen years of age he will have spent more time watching TV than he will in any other activity in his life, other than sleep.

Television has directly influenced more American lives than has any other development in our contemporary society. It is more complicated than radio, but many of the basic concepts are the same.

We will discuss television as a visual system here. Specifics regarding the operation of each of the subsystems will be discussed elsewhere in the text.

The television system begins with a visual image that is transmitted by light. Light in the form of detailed images cannot be projected over distances extending much more than 50 to 100 meters. To transmit the visual image over distances beyond this, it is necessary to convert the light impulses to electrical signals. These electrical signals are then transmitted into space, are picked up by receiving antennas, and are finally transduced, or changed into a visual image. The basic difference between television and radio occurs in the complexities that arise in converting visual images into electrical signals and vice versa. This is accomplished by a technique called **scanning.** What takes place essentially is that the visual message is scanned line by line. With each scan an electrical signal is produced in direct proportion to the image brightness recorded by the scan. The scan is done in the television picture tube and is what results in the final picture. The scan takes place across the entire screen in more than

500 lines. All this is done at about the speed of thirty times per second. After the audio and video signals are sent into space by the transmitting antenna and are picked up by receiving antennas the signals are demodulated. The audio signal is then channeled to a speaker and the video signal is converted to a visual image through the cathode ray tube, the picture tube on the television set. The image on the screen is brightened in proportion to the strength of the electrical signal that the set receives.

Color Television

Color television started in the United States in 1954. The concept of color television is based on the idea that color images can be created by combining images of red, green, and blue. When the signal is transmitted, the picture is separated into these three colors using mirrors and filters. Each of the three separate images is projected on a separate TV camera. In the set the color picture tube contains three separate electron guns. The screen of the TV set is made up of very small sets of phosphor dots that eventually create the color image on the screen. A beam from each of the guns projects onto the appropriate phosphor dot, and the picture is created.

There is a whole lot more to television than we have provided in this rather cursory overview. What is important to remember is that television is an example of a total system that has drastically extended our potential to communicate visually. Once we delve deeper into the subsystems that make it all possible we will be beyond the scope of this module. We will deal with the electronic systems that make it all possible in Module Eight.

New Developments in Television

One of the latest developments in black and white television is the miniature TV combination—television combined with tape recorders, AM-FM radios, or digital alarm clocks. The miniature TVs, often smaller than one decimeter, are available from most major electronic suppliers. One of the most promising developments in television is the thin-screen color concept being developed by GTE Sylvania. This screen is less than one centimeter thick and can be produced in sizes measuring nearly two meters diagonally. The new GTE screen may be commercially available in 1981.

Some firms have also perfected techniques for eliminating the picture tube by replacing it with a flat panel using electroluminescent material that glows when an electrical charge is applied. This new system was first introduced by Sharp in 1978. Matsushita, the parent corporation of Quasar and Panasonic, has even demonstrated a set with a picture on a liquid crystal panel similar to that used in digital watches. Sanyo plans on making available by 1981 a set using light emitting diodes to produce a picture on a screen less than one centimeter thick.

Illusionary Depth

There are many ways to create an illusion of movement or of depth in a visual image. We talked briefly about motion pictures and TV. There are other methods that do not require a projector or camera to create the feeling of depth or movement.

In 1692 a young French painter by the name of Bois Clair experimented with the impression of a single picture having depth. The anaglyph differed from the stereoscope in that the two pictures in an anaglyph were superimposed over each other. Each of the pictures was in a different color, usually red for one picture and green for the other. The viewer got a three-dimensional effect when he or she viewed the picture wearing glasses with one red lens and the other green. Some printed matter was produced using this technique. Most of this was in the area of children's comic books. Anaglyph movies were also made. The frames alternated between red and green, and when viewed through red and green glasses gave a three-dimensional effect.

The anaglyph, like the work of Bois Clair, was an example of the stereoscopic concept. Stereoscopic pictures are always flat, and printed in red and green.

Sophistication in the realm of 3-D imagery was not possible until techniques were created that gave the illusion of the viewer being able to see around the object. This technique was known as **autostereoscopic** photography. The technique was refined by *Look* magazine; Eastman Chemical Products, Incorporated; and Pictorial Productions, Incorporated. The technique gradually became known as **Xography**, meaning "to write with parallax." **Parallax** is the effect achieved when the same object is viewed from two different positions.

Xography has been further refined by Pictorial Productions, Mount Vernon, New York. The 3-D effect is created using cameras that weigh more than 800 pounds.

The camera sits on a two-meter by two-meter bed, which insures stability. The photograph is created by placing a lenticular screen in front of the film when the photograph is taken. The screen divides the picture into hundreds of tiny vertical parallel strips. Each one of these strips creates a different view as the camera moves on a track taking exposures from different angles.

After photography the illustration is printed on fine quality coated paper. The paper is then coated with tiny strips of hot-melt clear plastic, and a viewing lens is embossed to each one of the tiny plastic strips. When viewers move their eyes across the picture some lenses come into view and others disappear. Each eye sees a different picture. In this way the viewer is able to actually see around and in back of an object. The first Xograph, or mass-produced 3-D picture to appear in publication was in the February 25, 1964 issue of *Look* magazine. The first color Xograph appeared in April of the same year.

methods for creating an illusion of movement. What he did was paint two distinct pictures on a flat surface over which was fastened a closely spaced grid of vertical laths. These laths were attached at right angles to the surface. If the viewer entered the room from the left one picture would be seen. From the right one would see another. Today an example of Bois Clair's work can be viewed in the Rosenborg Castle in Copenhagen, Denmark or in the Brussels Museum of Art.

This was the first example of mechanical three-dimensional (3-D) representation. Over the years three-dimensional art has developed through several different phases. Early experimentation dealt with hand methods for altering photographs to provide the illusion of depth. In 1950 *Look* magazine began experimentation with a technique called the **anaglyph.** The anaglyph required a viewing apparatus similar to the early **stereoscope.** The stereoscope was a viewing device that was used to combine two pictures of the same object taken from a slightly different point of view, thereby giving

IMAGE PRESERVATION

Because of the great amount of visual information being transmitted today we must be concerned with methods for preserving visual information. Today we are faced with more information to file, to process, and to preserve. This great influx of information has created an information management problem in all areas of public life. Rapid growth in mass communication technology, associated with information presented through print media, the motion picture industry and television, has prompted the necessity of techniques for storing and making accessible great quantities of visual information more effectively. What has emerged is a new industry, and a host of new options for storing and retrieving information. The new industry is called the Microform industry. Figure 5.25 shows the different sectors of the microform industry.

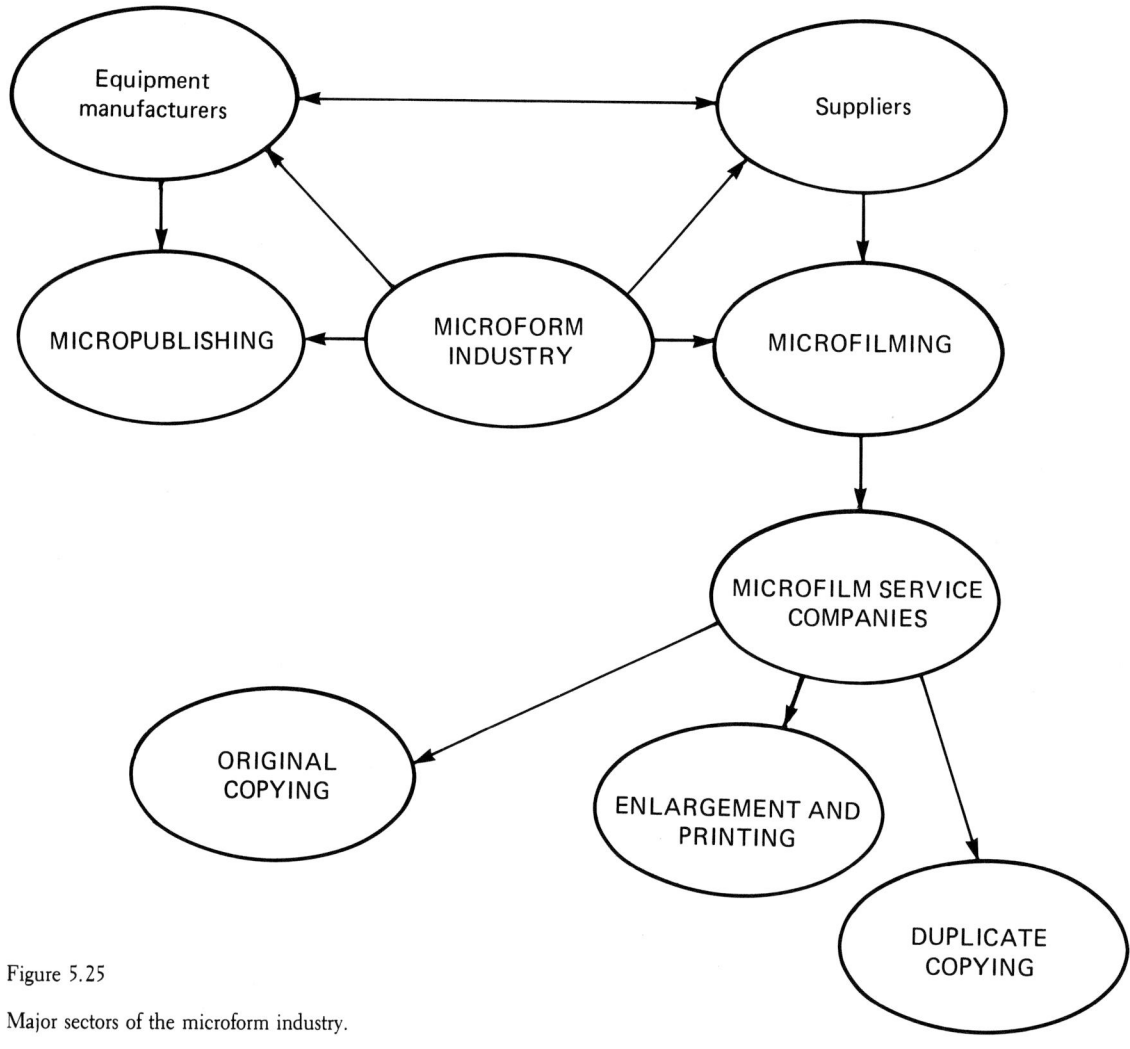

Figure 5.25

Major sectors of the microform industry.

The Microform Industry

Many industries can be classed under the heading of the microform industry. Some of these are:

- printing and publishing industries (magazine, newspaper, book)
- electronics industry
- distribution industry
- chemical industry
- photographic industry
- graphic arts supply industry
- coatings industry
- printing machinery and manufacturing industry
- business and office reproduction industry

Many specialized industries are found under each of these headings. Under the electronics industry heading alone there are several hundred specialized industries. In effect what this means is that there are hundreds of different career fields and thousands of specific jobs associated with microforms and visual communication technology.

Microforms

The word **microform** stands for any technique (on film or paper) that contains microimages. In general there are four major microforms used today: (1) microfilm, (2) aperture cards, (3) microfiche, and (4) ultrafiche.

Often we have a tendency to look at microfilm as something associated with espionage, national security, and other such secretive activities.

Actually the use of microforms dates back to Ninevah in the year 3000 B.C. when cylinders were made that required a magnifying glass to read. Today a single microfilm cartridge can contain as much visual information as it normally takes forty pounds of paper to present. This by far is not the best that can be done, however. At the 1964 New York World's Fair a 1245-page Bible, including both Old and New Testaments, was on display. The entire Bible was preserved on a single 5 cm by 5 cm piece of PCMI ultrafiche. Today it has been demonstrated that 3300 standard letters can be stored on a single fiche at a reduction of 150 times. The associated technology, film quality, sophisticated readers, and reader-printers make return to the original size attainable with very little loss of detail.

Microfilm

Microfilm as we know it today really began with John Benjamin Dancer of Manchester, England. Dancer installed a microscope lens in a camera and was successful in making microphotographs of a document. The first patent for a microform that was commercially useable was issued in 1959 to the Frenchman, Rene Prudent Dragon. Dragon photographed 1000 telegrams on a strip of film small enough to be banded to the leg of a pigeon.

It was during World War II that microforms began to be used widely. In the war effort the microfilming of overseas mail (called V-mail) cut down the weight from 2700 tons to 31 tons. The average transport plane could carry nearly 9,600,000 letters on microfilm reels.

Most of the time when we think about microforms we think that their main purpose is to reduce space. Actually the advantages are also to protect important records, reduce the cost of reproducing information, and improve information retrieval.

Microfilm, the most commonly used microform, is nothing more than film in 16mm, 35mm, 70mm, or 105mm sizes containing images reduced 65 or more times from the original size. Microfilm is stored on reels; each of the microfilm rolls are around 25 meters in length. Microfilm can also be inserted in data processing aperture cards. One roll or cartridge of film is capable of recording as much as 3000 pages of standard letter size information.

The aperture card format also became popular during the war. A standard data processing card was die cut so that a single frame of microfilm could be fastened to the card. The card had the advantage of quick retrieval because of the punched informaton on the card.

Microfiche and Ultrafiche

Microfiche and ultrafiche enable many more reductions of a single film sheet. **Microfiche** generally involves a 24-power reduction, resulting in 98 or more images

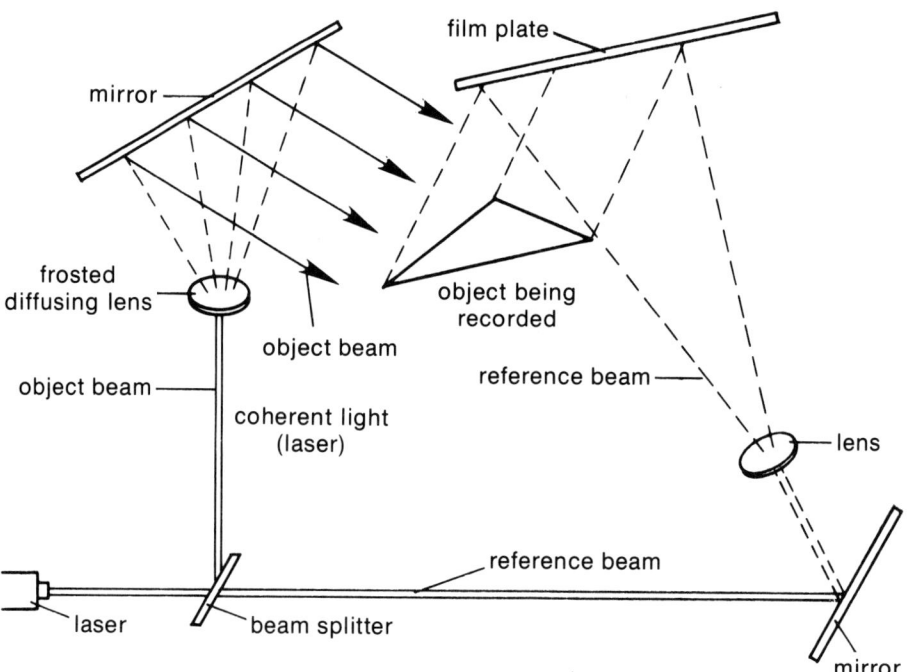

Figure 5.26

This is how the hologram is produced.

on a single letter-size card. Experimentation with reduced formats has resulted in 75- and 150-power reductions. In this microreduced format the technique has been called **ultrafiche.** The possibilities for information storage in the future seem astonishing, but ultrafiche is only the beginning!

HOLOGRAPHY

Much experimentation and testing is now being done with a technique called holography. Holography was invented by Dennis Gabor in 1947. Gabor's development was significant because it marked the beginning of a new dimension in 3-D photography. Although Gabor invented the holographic method in 1947, it was nearly ten years later before the theory was really demonstrable and practically replicable. Holography was made practical by the development of the laser, a means of creating coherent sources of light. The invention of holography was so significant that in 1971 Gabor received the Nobel Prize in physics for his work with holography. (Refer to figures 5.26 and 5.27.)

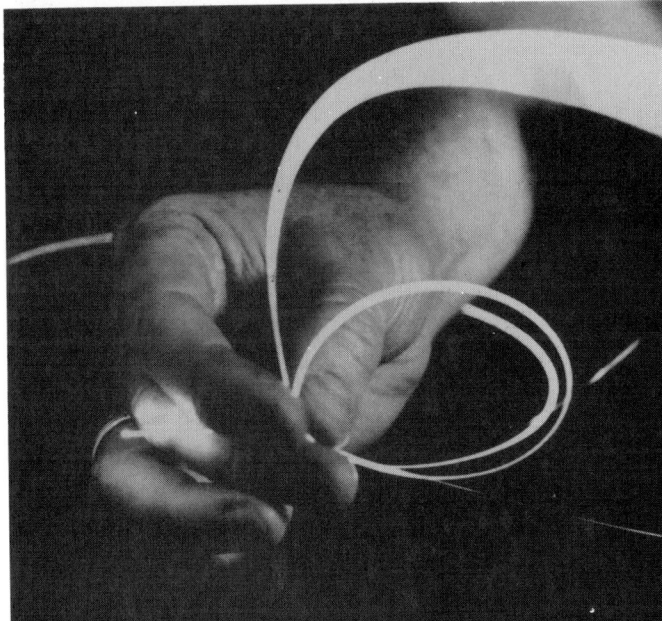

Figure 5.27

Glass fiber optic light guides may serve as "wires" for future telecommunications transmissions systems carrying telephone calls and other communications on beams of light.
Courtesy, AT&T

A hologram is a very unusual type of photograph containing visual information. In producing a hologram no lens is involved, and no image is created. What does happen is that each point of the object being photographed reflects light onto the photographic plate. Coherent light from a laser is what illuminates the object. The light projected onto the photographic film does not just come from the object itself. It is projected from two places. One beam is reflected off the object and another is projected directly onto the film itself. What happens is that the two light beams interfere with each other, and the photographic film records this interaction.

When the two beams of light interfere with each other at some angle it is not possible to visually see any change in either beam. However, where the two beams cross each other the intensity will be different than it would be anywhere else. What happens is that depending on the intensity of each of the beams, either constructive or destructive interference occurs. Destructive interference results in reducing the light intensity that might strike the film whereas constructive interference increases the light projected onto the film. The film records light waves instead of recording an image. The hologram produced does not resemble a photographic image. It shows tiny areas of varying density, dark areas when the object and reference beams cross each other, and light areas where they are out of phase (do not cross). The hologram records the shape of the object and the brightness of each point on the object. It also records the position of each of these points in relationship to each other point.

When coherent light is projected onto the hologram the observer will see a picture in full three-dimensional form. The picture will look like it might in "real life." The viewer will be able to see behind the object and will observe depth and even color.

From an information storage point of view the concept of holography is likely to offer much potential for the future. If one were to cut a small section out of a hologram and reinsert it in front of a laser beam the entire image of the original object would be reconstructed. If you were to cut the hologram into one hundred pieces each piece would produce an entire image. If you were to keep doing this many times each bit would still contain a total image. This occurs because the inference patterns created in effect create many duplicate images of the original object. Any one of these can be used to reconstruct the original object. This means that miniaturized holograms can be used to reconstruct vast amounts of information. The technique will without question permit us to go far beyond anything yet possible with microfilm camera reduction techniques. As many as 10,000 bits of information might be stored on a single one mm square hologram.

Another interesting feature about a hologram is that a number of entirely different holographic images can be produced on one hologram without the images interfering with each other. This is accomplished by simply changing the angle at which the reference beam hits the film plate for each different image.

The beam of coherent light, usually from a laser, is broken up into two different beams using a beam splitter. One beam, which is called the object beam, is projected through a diffused lens and onto a reflecting mirror. The mirror illuminates the object. The points of the object then reflect light onto the film plate or light sensitive emulsion. The other beam, called the reference beam, is projected onto a mirror and lens. The lens diffracts the beam and projects it onto the film plate or light sensitive emulsion. When the object beam reaches the emulsion, it interacts with the reference beam producing the interference pattern.

When a beam of coherent light is projected through the hologram, the wavefront that was originally preserved on the film is again set into motion. When the viewer looks at the hologram the image appears suspended in space on the other side of the hologram. If the viewer changes the direction in which he or she views the hologram, a different perspective of the picture is revealed.

Today new applications for holography are being discovered, which indicate that holography may be our next monumental breakthrough in visual communication technology. Holography has already become nearly a billion dollar business. Holographic and laser technology has been used to discover defects in automobile tires and bonds of unlike materials. It has been used to study particles suspended in gases as well as to produce three-dimensional imaging systems.

LASERPHOTO

In 1973 the Associated Press, one of the largest news gathering and distributing organizations in the world, announced its use of a remarkable new phototransmission system. They called it **Laserphoto.** It uses a laser beam as a light source and creates photographic quality prints on 3M dry silver photographic paper without chemicals or associated processing. The organization claims that it enables delivery of pictures to AP member papers across the nation four times faster than other methods previously used. A standard size photograph can be delivered to a receiving station thousands of kilometers away from the transmitting point in two minutes. At the receiving point a laser beam traces out the visual information on the dry silver paper. The laser is responsible for the exposure, and the image is made visible through heat.

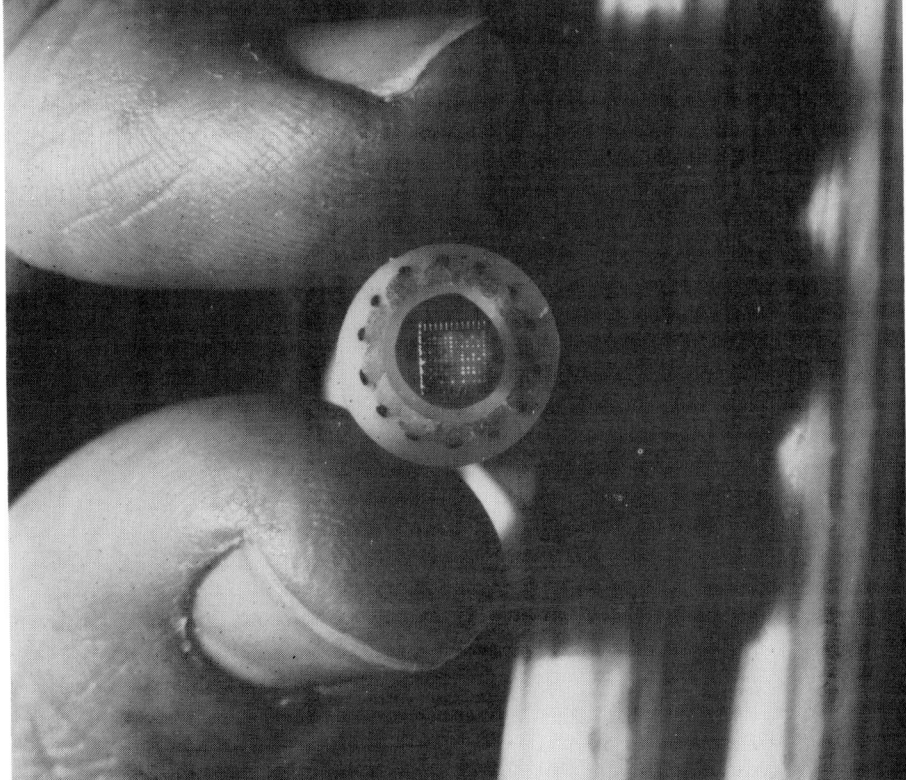

Figure 5.28

A typical lightwave communication system through which messages are communicated by light pulses through cables of glass fibers.
Courtesy, AT&T

LIGHTWAVE COMMUNICATIONS

In May of 1977, the Bell System began evaluating the world's first lightwave communication system designed to carry customers' voice, data, and video signals on hair-thin strands of glass called fiber optics. The system carried pulses of light, made possible through lasers and light emitting diodes, below the streets of Chicago between two Illinois Bell switching offices and a downtown office building. The lightguide cable contained twenty-four fiber lightguides. The cable was only slightly thicker than a pencil. Two lightguides were able to carry 672 conversations at the same time.

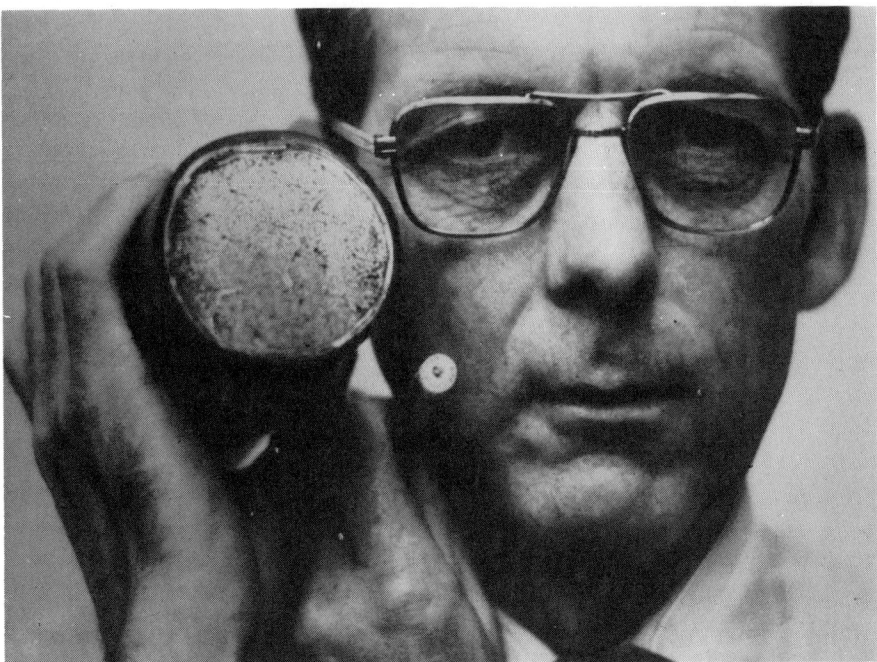

Figure 5.29

The conventional coaxial cable on the left carries the equivalent of 10,800 conversations. The fiber optic lightguide cable on the right will carry nearly 50,000 conversations.
Courtesy, American Telephone and Telegraph Corp.

Testing has been completed on the Chicago system. All indications seem to be that this system may open up many new developments in communication technology in the years ahead. One thing is certain. It won't be many years before most of the unsightly above-ground telephone cables are replaced with optic cables buried in the ground.

SUMMARY

Well, our journey through time is nearly over. We've come a long way—from cave paintings and pictographs to inorganic emulsions, laserphoto, and fiber optics. Who knows what the future will hold? Standing at a vantage point, say in 1880, who would have predicted the developments of today—television, holography, or satellites transmitting visual images back from space? It is unlikely that even the most clear-sighted visionaries could have dreamed of such developments. The beauty of it all is that we are only beginning. Tomorrow will offer new innovations, well beyond our farthest dreams. It is up to us to make sure that we are using our technology effectively and appropriately for the good of humankind.

We have covered a lot of information. Let's step back a bit now and try to summarize the major concepts presented in this module.

CONCEPT FOCUSER

- We are confronted with so much visual information in our daily lives that it is essential that we learn how to **create visual messages** that **communicate more effectively.**
- **Visual literacy** involves the refinement of capabilities for **creating** and **understanding** visual **messages.**
- Our **language of vision** involves human **perception** and then some **reaction.**
- A **symbol** is a visual mechanism that **stands for** a **single concept.**
- The **phases** in the development of the **visual message** are: **message analysis** and **design, concept formation, image reproduction,** and **image preservation.**
- The **design essentials,** building blocks to visual literacy, are: **dot, line, texture, color,** and **shape.**
- The **use of** each of the **design elements influences** the effect of each of the others and the **result** of the final visual concept.
- Developments in **communication** technology that directly influenced **changes in society** were: **cave painting, pictography, hieroglyphics,** the **alphabet,** Gutenberg's total **printing system, photography, motion pictures,** and **television.**

FOOD FOR THOUGHT

1. Explain how certain areas of a photographic negative become black and others clear.
2. Differentiate between each of the major printing processes in terms of the advantages and disadvantages of each.
3. List the most significant technical developments that occurred in one subsystem such as photography or reprographics since 1450 B.C.
4. What are the differences between a thumbnail sketch, rough layout, and comprehensive layout?
5. Explain how the concept of remote transmission of information can take place.

Expanding Experiences

1. Keep a record of all of the different types of visual information that you receive during the day. Bring the list to school and compare it with lists made by your friends.
2. Make a display of primitive devices that people used to communicate.
3. Design a symbol that communicates a particular message as a sign or poster to be displayed somewhere in your school. Be sure to use the essential design elements as effectively as possible.
4. Pick a particular technical development that was mentioned in this module and do an in-depth study of how the development works and how it influences society.

Locator Tools

Conners, J. Richard and Amundson, William M. *Microfilm: Active and Vital*. Minnesota Mining and Manufacturing Company, St. Paul, 1975.

Fabre, Maurice. *History of Communications*. New York: Hawthorne Books, 1963.

Koberg, Don and Bagnall, Jim. *The Universal Traveler*. William Kaufmann, Inc., Los Altos, California, 1974.

Papanek, Victor. *Design for the Real World*. New York: Pantheon Books, Random House, 1976.

Pocket Pal, International Paper Company, 220 East 42nd Street, New York, New York 10017, 1978.

TECHNOLOGY-BASED ELECTRICAL TELECOMMUNICATION SYSTEMS

Module *SIX*

THE BEGINNINGS OF ELECTRICAL COMMUNICATIONS

Since the beginning of time, the growth of civilization has depended to a large extent on the ability of people (and, later, of their machines) to communicate with each other. Contrary to popular belief, people began to communicate with each other over longer and longer distances through the use of electrical phenomena even before the underlying theory, laws, or the technology were discovered or invented. Thus many new modes of electrical communication were opened as humans learned to apply the phenomena of electricity to the solution of their communications problem. Module 6 will deal with the use and development of technology-based electrical modes of communication and trace their evolution over time.

The real beginning of the use of electrical phenomena as a mode of communication is lost in antiquity. Any early electrical phenomenon observed or used by early humans to communicate with one another probably perished with its owner. It is likely that some of the later uses of electrical phenomena may have passed from father to son or may have been rediscovered in other locations only to be just as promptly lost again. Those phenomena that actually survived the evolution of cultures were probably linked with superstition and for that reason managed to survive the ages.

Perhaps the first mode of technology-based electrical communication was the phenomenon of magnetism (see Appendix A). Although there is no record of who first discovered and used the forces of magnetism for communicative purposes, it is known that very early in history a shepherd noticed that certain types of rocks seemed to cling to the tip of his iron staff and the nails in his sandals. However, he found no useful purpose for these strange rocks and promptly forgot about them.

Today, we know that the rocks he found contained a black mineral called magnetite, which is considered a natural magnet. As time passed on, someone else discovered that this particular stone seemed to have the ability to always point toward the North Star. It thus became known as a "leading stone," which was later shortened to "lodestone."

The first legendary account of the use of the lodestone for man-machine communication was attributed to the Chinese about 2637 B.C. According to the early scribes, a Chinese emperor was pursuing rebels in a westerly direction when his troops became hopelessly lost in the fog. Legend has it that the emperor strung a piece of lodestone across the lead chariot and was thus able to determine which direction was west. He followed the rebels through the thick fog and managed to overtake and capture them. This was probably the world's first practical application of an electrical phenomenon for communication (directional) purposes.

Since about 1020 B.C. the lodestone was used quite extensively for directional purposes on land and sea.

Suspending magnetite on a string so that it might indicate directional headings must have challenged the early leaders to seek a better way. It surely must have occurred to them that delicately balancing a sliver of magnetite on a sharpened wooden pin, located in the center of a small wooden box, would provide greater freedom of movement for the indicator while protecting it from wind, dust, and unsteady hands. Similarly, innovative mariners must also have searched for a suspension system that would automatically compensate for the natural motion of a ship at sea. This problem was probably solved by floating a small piece of magnetite on a chip of wood in a wooden bucket set at the helm of their ship.

Although it is not known when people first discovered that pieces of iron stroked by natural magnetite produced artificial magnets, this technological advance must have been discovered, and as a result the bulky magnetite indicators were replaced with small iron (and later, steel) indicating needles. This increased the accuracy of the compass while it decreased the size of the instrument. Its usefulness soon spread from continent to continent—as did the superstition that the invisible magnetic force surrounding the compass needle could cure such things as burns, toothaches, and headaches. The superstitions surrounding early electrical phenomena clouded any real understanding and blocked the search for underlying fundamentals, principles, or properties of electrostatics and magnetism.

It was during the Crusades in A.D. 1269 that the existence of different magnetic poles was accidentally discovered. Experimenting with two lodestones, Perregriunus discovered that the northern-indicating part of one stone attracted the southern-indicating part of another stone and the southern-seeking part, the north. From this early experiment the law of magnetic poles was derived—unlike poles attract, like poles repel. This law is still valid today.

Again, any new discoveries or theories remained at a standstill until the late fifteenth century, when Christopher Columbus discovered that his compass needle, which usually pointed toward the North Star near his home port, varied considerably in different parts of the New World. Columbus had accidentally discovered "magnetic declination," which must be compensated for by global navigators.

In the seventeenth century Gauss, a German mathematician, conducted extensive studies into magnetism and its measurement. He determined the strength of a magnet as being the number of lines of force that exist in a one-square-centimeter area. This unit area is now called gauss in his honor.

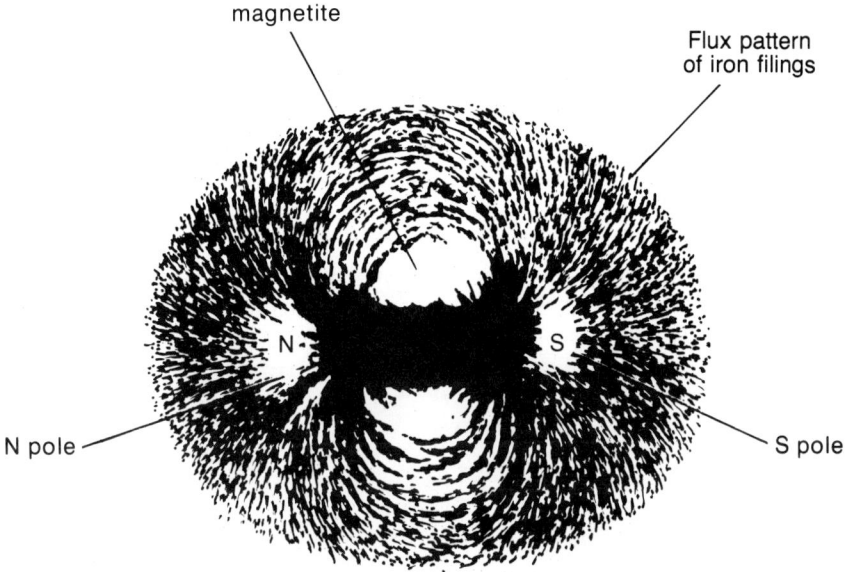

Figure 6.1

If a piece of lodestone were placed under a sheet of paper and iron filings sprinkled on top of the sheet, the pattern of magnetic lines of force would probably look like this if the sheet of paper were tapped several times.

Today we know that the magnetic attraction of any type of magnet is concentrated at its north and south poles.

Every magnet has invisible lines of force that always travel from the north pole to the south pole. If we could see them, they might look like hundreds of rubber bands under tension. However, the effect of these lines of force can be seen in the alignment of iron filings placed along the long axis of a magnet. These lines of force are called **flux lines**; the shape of the area they occupy is called the **flux pattern.**

One important characteristic of the flux pattern is that the lines of force never cross or unite with each other. As a matter of fact, magnetic lines of flux tend to repel each other, especially when two north or two south poles are brought together. The opposite is true when two unlike poles, such as a north and south pole, approach each other. Although magnetic flux does penetrate some materials better than others, there is no known insulator for it except distance.

Although not apparent at this time, the concept of magnetism was the first, most important discovery that led to the later development of electrical modes of communications.

At the start of this module, we learned about the discovery and first use of natural and artificial magnets. Later, more effective artificial magnets were produced and used in various types of communications applications. These artificial magnets were made of a steel alloy called Alnico, which is the combined chemical symbols for aluminum, nickel, and cobalt. Today, almost all of the artificial magnets produced are made from ceramic materials and, therefore, are more economical to produce and use.

Early Sources of Electron Generation

In the evolution of communication modes, the second most important discovery was the generation of a source of electrons.

Thales, a Greek philosopher who lived in Miletus, discovered that amber, a translucent fossil found near seashores, exhibited unusual properties of attraction when it was rubbed. He discovered that amber would attract such things as bird feathers, bits of paper, and other light materials. It was also discovered at this time that certain hard substances, such as glass, attracted the same type of light materials when they were rubbed by silk. Based on these early observations, the existence of what we know

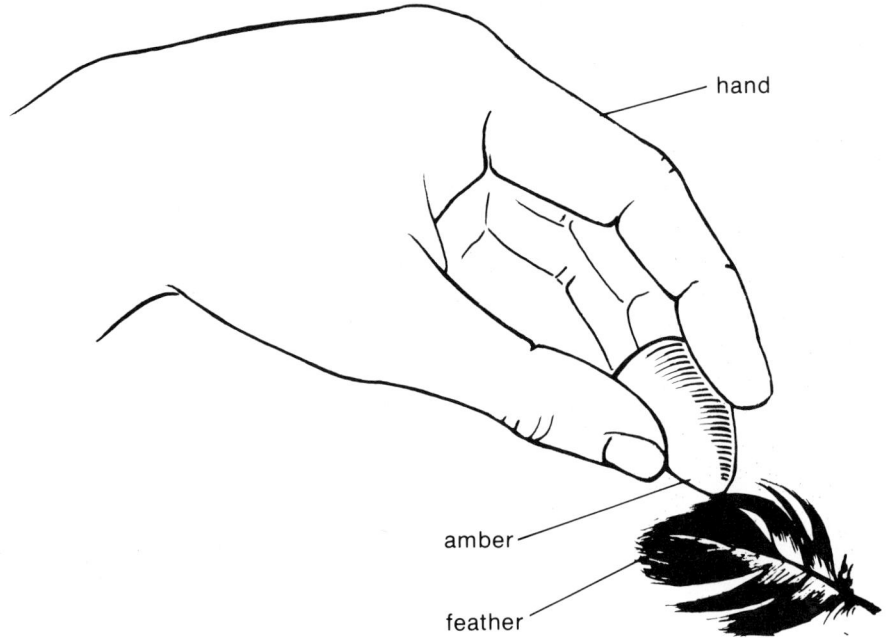

Figure 6.2

When the surface electrons are rubbed, amber will attract light objects like feathers and small bits of paper.

today as static electricity was discovered. Somewhat later, Thales tried to explain the phenomenon as invisible streams issuing out of bodies and expelling the surrounding air, thereby causing whirlwinds, which tended to draw certain materials inward. This explanation was the first known attempt to try to explain the early mysteries of electricity.

The second account of the attraction properties of static electricity occurred much later in Rome. However, no other known electrical phenomena, theory, law, or technology was discovered or developed for the next 2200 years. Perhaps this could be attributed to the fact that in the then known world the desire or need for a person to communicate beyond his or her village was not yet very important.

Figure 6.3

This huge Tandem Van DeGraaff Accelerator employs the basic principles of electrostatics in its operation. The large gas-filled tank (top center) contains the charging belt that generates up to 10 million volts used to strip electrons from the 3-6mm source electron beam. The beam emerges toward the reader and is deflected 90° by the large electromagnet in the center of picture. It is then directed to the target room where it is used to bombard particles for fundamental and applied research purposes.
Courtesy, Florida State University

In the sixteenth century William Gilbert, a court physician to Queen Elizabeth and King James I, began his early experiments with magnetism and independently discovered that many other hard materials—such as diamonds, opals, and sulfur—would attract lightweight materials when rubbed. On the basis of his findings, he proposed the theory that all matter consisted of either "electric" or "nonelectric" materials. This theory was later disproved. However, he is credited with coining the name **electricity**, which he derived from the Greek word **elektron** meaning amber. He also advanced the theory that the world was a giant magnet and later wrote six books summarizing all that was known about electricity up to A. D. 1600.

Another significant discovery along the road to an understanding of modern electrical modes of communication was the development of the first electrostatic or frictional generator by Otto Von Guericke, the mayor of Magdeburg, Germany. By rotating a large ball of sulfur and rubbing it with his hands, he was able to generate static electricity and make it travel the length of a short linen thread. This crude electrostatic generator became the first electron source to energize the primitive types of telegraph systems that were to follow.

The method used today for generating huge amounts of electrostatic force is through the use of Van de Graaff friction-type generator. Other than for scientific purposes, very little use is made of this method for communications.

Several other methods of electron generation appeared a bit later. One was the discovery of bioconductivity by Professor Galvani, an Italian physician. Galvani thought he had discovered bioelectricity after his accidental contact with a laboratory frog. This led to his erroneous conclusion that there was such a thing as animal-generated electricity, when in fact all biosubstances (such as skin tissue) conduct electricity much as a wire does. Galvani's theory of animal electricity was disproven by Volta a few years later.

By themselves, the bioconduction capabilities of biosubstances did not play a role in communications and only served as the conducting link with modern day bio-instrumentation such as EKG machines, lie detectors, and the like.

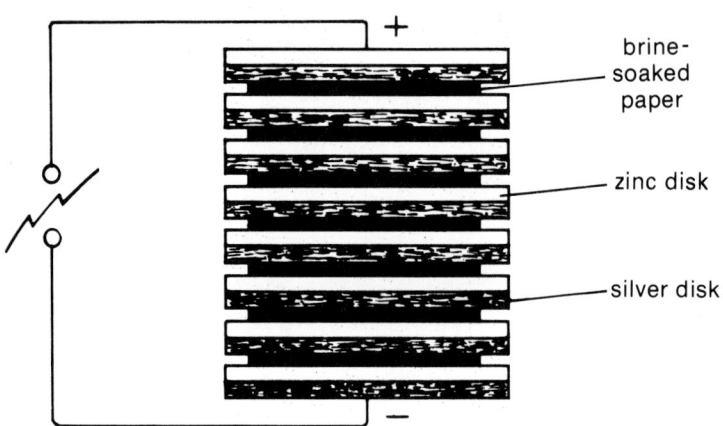

Figure 6.4

Sketch of Alessandro Volta's original voltaic pile which soon became the first reliable energy source to power early telegraph and telegraph systems.

Alessandro Volta, a physicist, was the first to succeed in producing a steady flow of electricity by chemical means. During experimentation he produced a sizable spark from a silver and zinc electrode "pile." In later experiments he used copper and zinc disks as the electrodes and diluted sulfuric acid as the electrolyte. He had produced the world's first reliable chemical battery—the **voltaic pile**. The voltaic pile is the forerunner of today's modern batteries.

About fifty years later, Gaston Plante designed the first lead-acid battery, which effectively converted chemical energy to electrical energy. Eventually, Plante's battery was to become the power source for the telegraph and the telephone systems yet to come.

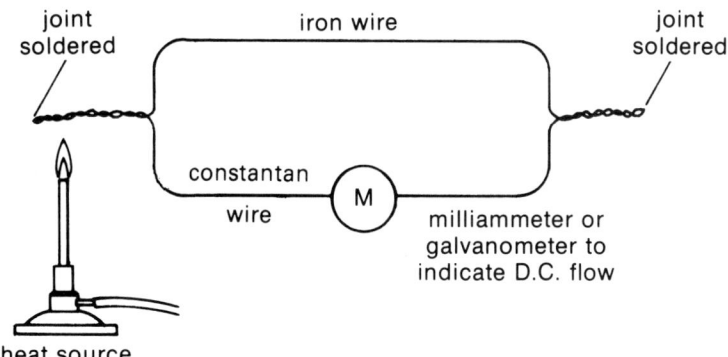

Figure 6.5

The thermopile (or thermocouple) is made up of two dissimilar metals twisted together. When the junction is placed over a heat source, the molecules vibrate and allow the electrons to move freely through the circuit thereby producing a small amount of direct current.

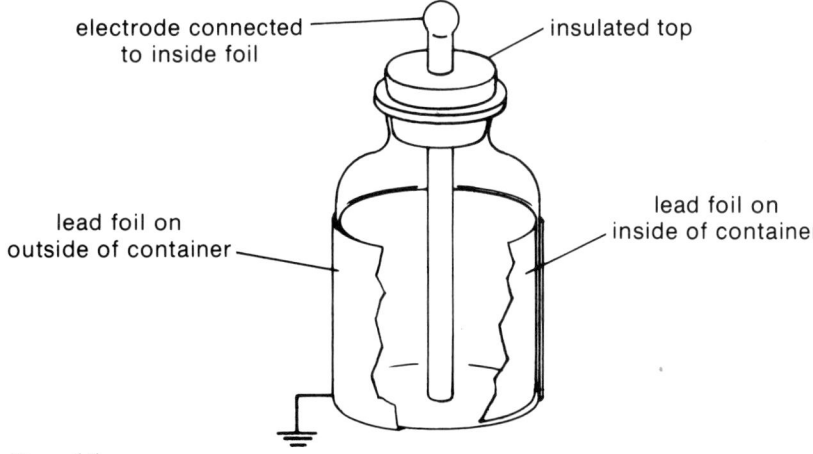

Figure 6.6

The Leyden jar, named after the city in Holland where it was first discovered, is the forerunner of the capacitor. The jar was used to energize the early telegraph systems.

In another milestone of electrical communication progress, Thomas J. Seebeck, a German physicist, pursued Volta's earlier observations about the effect of temperature on different metals. In 1822, Seebeck developed a thermopile, which consisted of two dissimilar metal strips, joined at one end. As heat is applied to the joint, a small amount of direct current will flow. The name thermopile was later changed to the more descriptive term **thermocouple.** Another researcher named Jean Peltier independently produced electricity by heating the junction of two dissimilar metals.

Early experimenters discovered that electricity could be stored for short periods of time. One of these, Professor Pieter Van Musschenbroek, a Dutch scientist, covered a glass jar with tinfoil on the inside and outside and then applied an electrical charge. The charge held for some time. His electron storage device became known as the Leyden jar.

Devices that are used to store electrons are called **capacitors.** This term is often confused with the term **condenser,** with which it is used interchangeably. The early Leyden jar was a capacitor in that it stored electrical energy for a short period of time.

In today's practice, capacitors are used to store energy or to block the flow of direct current in a circuit.

Capacitors consist of two plates that are separated by an insulating material called the **dielectric.** Wire leads connect the end plates to an external circuit.

There are three factors that influence the capacity of a capacitor: (1) the area of the plates, (2) the distance between the plates (which is generally controlled by the

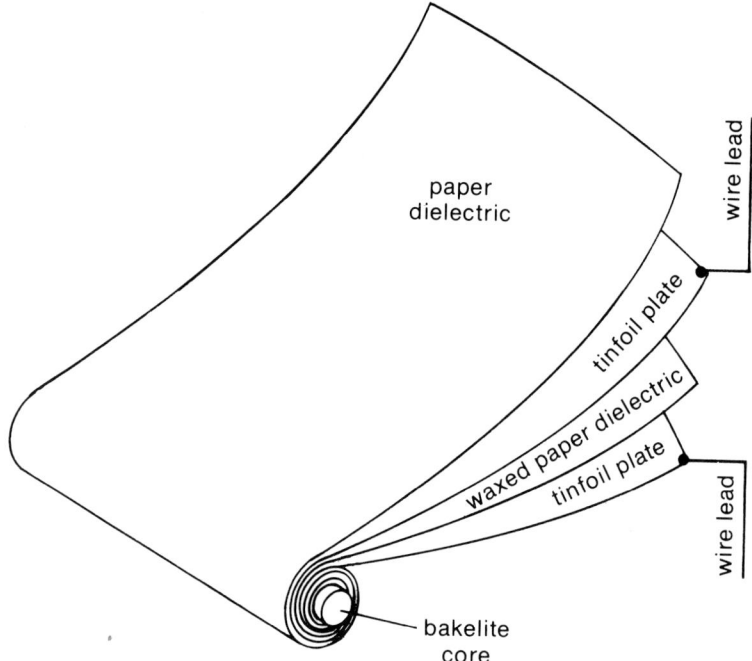

Figure 6.7

All capacitors are made up of two plates separated by an insulating material, such as air, mica, or paper. Wire leads are connected to each of the insulated plates. When fully charged, they store electricity for short periods of time.

Chart A

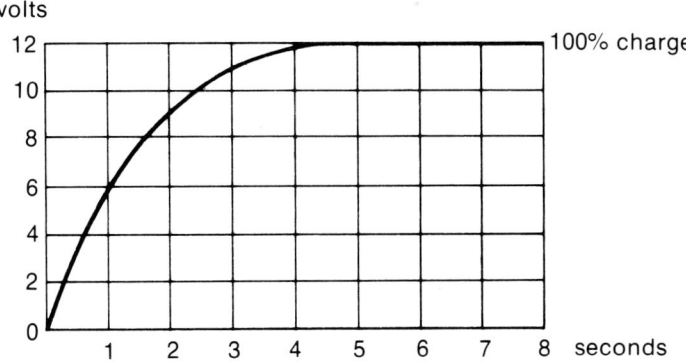

Schematic B

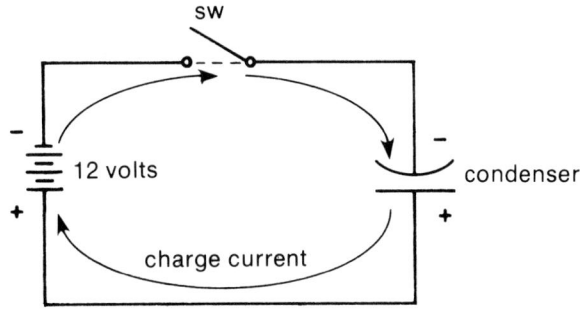

Schematic C

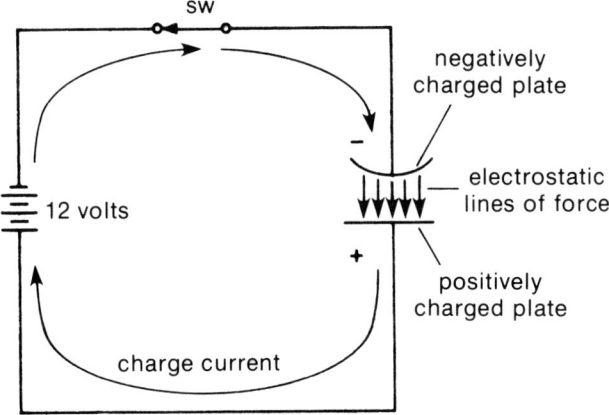

Figure 6.8

Chart A reflects the voltage charging pattern across the condensor in Schematic B. When the switch is closed, the electrons from the battery flow through the condensor and charge it. In Schematic C, the charging current has driven all the protons to the opposite plate. Now we have negatively and positively charged plates separated by electrostatic lines of force.

thickness of the dielectric), and (3) the material used for the dielectric. We will consider each of these factors in turn.

Plate Area. The size of the plate area is very important in determining the amount of capacitance since capacitance varies proportionately with the plate area. For example, a large plate area would have room for more free electrons than a smaller area and, therefore, would hold a larger charge.

Distance Between the Plates. The effect two charged bodies have on each other depends on the distance between the two bodies. As an example, the capacitance between the two plates increases as the plates are brought closer together. Conversely, the capacitance decreases as they are moved apart. The reason for this is that the closer the plates are to each other, the greater the effect a charge on one plate will have on the other.

Dielectric Thickness. Air is the basis for determining the dielectric constant for capacitors. The dielectric constant of air is always one.

Different materials have different dielectric constants. If the dielectric is waxed paper—as it is in so many of the smaller capacitors—then the dielectric constant is three. This means that if waxed paper is placed between the two plates, the dielectric constant for that capacitor will be three times greater than one with an air gap. All materials contain some free electrons.

In order to charge the plates, an electrical source such as a battery is required. To charge the plate negatively, it is necessary to force extra electrons onto it from a negative source. The first few extra electrons forced on the plate oppose, or try to repel, the addition of any other electrons. As more electrons are forced onto the plate,

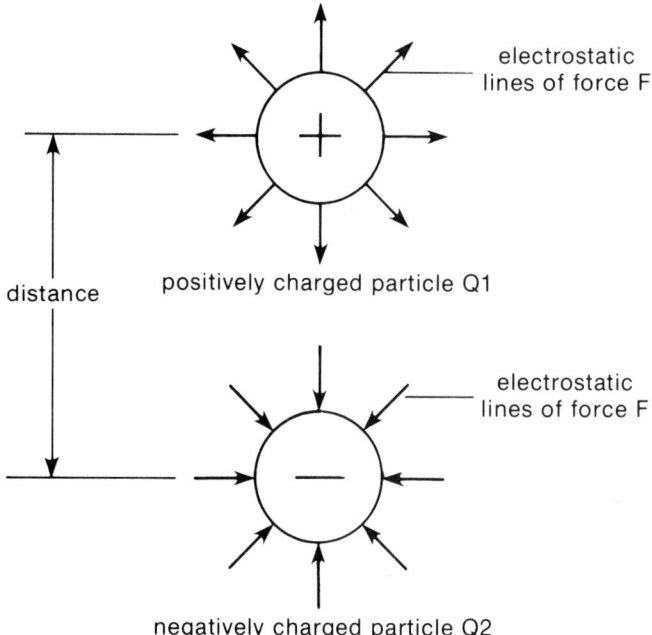

Figure 6.9

Sketch of electrostatic lines of force that exist between any two charged bodies.

the repelling force increases so that a greater force is required to move additional electrons. When the negative repelling force equals the charging force, no more electrons will move onto the plate.

There are many different kinds of capacitors used in electrical circuits. They are generally classified according to their dielectric material. The most common type is the fixed or variable air capacitor. Other types are the electrolytic, vacuum, variable mica, fixed mica, molded paper, bathtub, metal-encased paper, oil filled, and ceramic capacitors.

As will be discussed later the storage capability of a capacitor is an essential electrical component for electrical control in a circuit. Many manufacturers print the capacitance on the capacitor; others print a manufacturer's number. Many use the color code system, which is similar to the color code for resistors. The surest way to determine the capacitance of a capacitor is to measure it with a capacitor checker.

Still trying to explain the evasive phenomenon of electricity, Charles Augustin Coulomb, the French scientist, formulated the "law of forces" that exists between charged bodies as being directly proportional to the product of the charges and inversely proportional to the square of the distance between them. To make this valid law easier to use, it can be expressed mathematically as:

$$F = \frac{Q_1 Q_2}{d^2}$$

in which

F = the electrical charge

Q_1 = the amount of one charge

Q_2 = the amount of the other charge

d = the distance between centers of charges

This relationship between charged bodies has never been disproved.

Another researcher named Charles Francis Du Fay suggested that there might actually be two different kinds of electricity. One he called "vitreous" and the other "resinous" fluids, both having the characteristics of repelling and attracting each other.

John Dalton stated his new theory for electricity. He believed that all materials were composed of particles, which he called **atoma**. He reasoned that since the earth was made up of many basic elements, such as iron, copper, and zinc, each would have its own special type of atom. His theory of atomic structure is still in use today.

A scientist named Joseph J. Thomson announced that he had discovered proof that atoms, under certain conditions, shoot out smaller particles of matter, which are now called electrons. This gave rise to the **electron theory**, which states that all matter is composed of three types of particles—the electron, the proton, and the neutron. This is the current electron theory in use today.

Another important electrical law was discovered by Dr. Georg Simon Ohm, a German physicist, who explored the fundamental relationship between voltage, current, and resistance. Using the analogy of water, he showed how electricity in wires acted much like water in a pipe. Both flow and pressure are controlled by a resistive

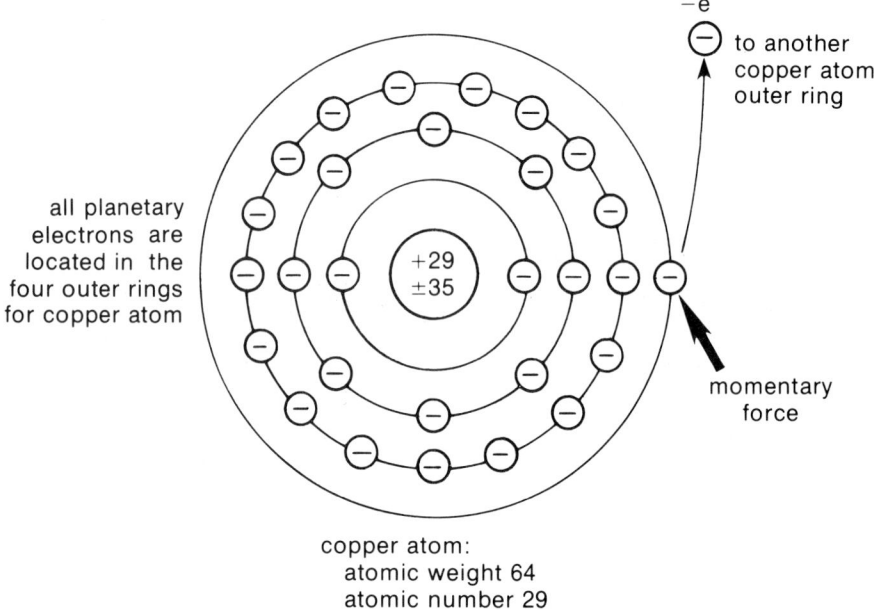

Figure 6.10

Sketch of a theoretical copper atom shows a free electron being dislodged from the out planetary ring and shooting off to join another copper atom. This movement of electrons is called current flow.

device. The unique relationship between voltage, current, and resistance became known as Ohm's law and is used today to calculate the value of circuit elements.

There are four electrical terms that confuse people most. They are often erroneously used interchangeably, although each one has a specific meaning. Carefully study the chart in Figure 6.11 and learn the difference between the terms **voltage, current, resistance,** and **power.** This will assist us as we discuss the relationship that exists between voltage, current, resistance, and power in a circuit.

Benjamin Franklin was the first person to develop the theory of positive and negative charges of electricity or direct current. When Franklin sent up his kite during

Electrical Term	What It Really Is	Basic Unit of Measurement	Formula Symbol
Voltage or Electromotive Force (EMF)	Electrical Pressure	Volt	E or V
Current	Electron flow	Ampere	I or A
Resistance	Opposition to current flow	Ohm	R or Ω or —⋀⋀⋀—
Power	Rate of usage of electrical energy	Watt	P or W

Figure 6.11

Chart of voltage, current, resistance, and power relationships.

a storm, he observed that lightning seemed to act like electricity and concluded the clouds contained only negative charges. He believed the path of electricity ran from the positively charged ground. His erroneous theory about what was positive and what was negative causes much confusion even today.

Although these theories tended to explain the observed phenomena, none of them contributed directly to the development of electrical modes of telecommunication.

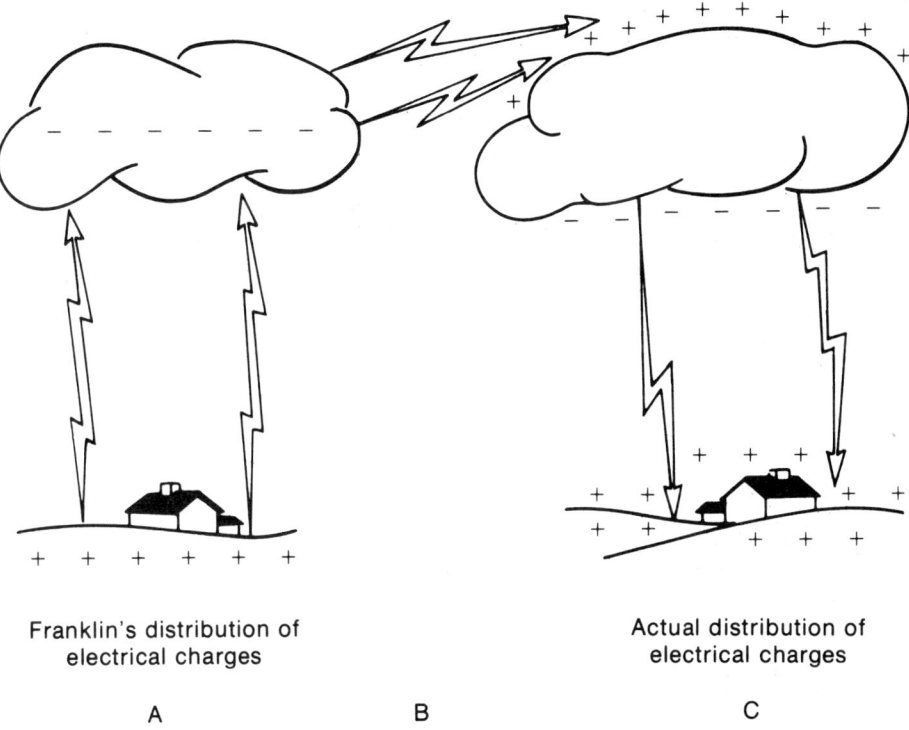

Figure 6.12

Ben Franklin erroneously believed that the distribution of electrical charges looked like A; whereas it is now known that the distribution of charges is more like B and C during a storm. Lightning bolts can go from cloud to cloud as in B or cloud to ground as in C, or even ground to cloud if the bottom side of the clouds is more positive than the ground.

Electron Carriers

According to Dr. Ohm, electric circuits are considered to be complete electrical pathways which carry electrons. There are three basic types of circuits to be considered: (1) series circuit, (2) parallel circuit, and (3) series-parallel circuit. We will briefly discuss each one in turn.

In a series circuit having one or more circuit elements as its load, the resistor values add together to form the total resistance or total load of that circuit.

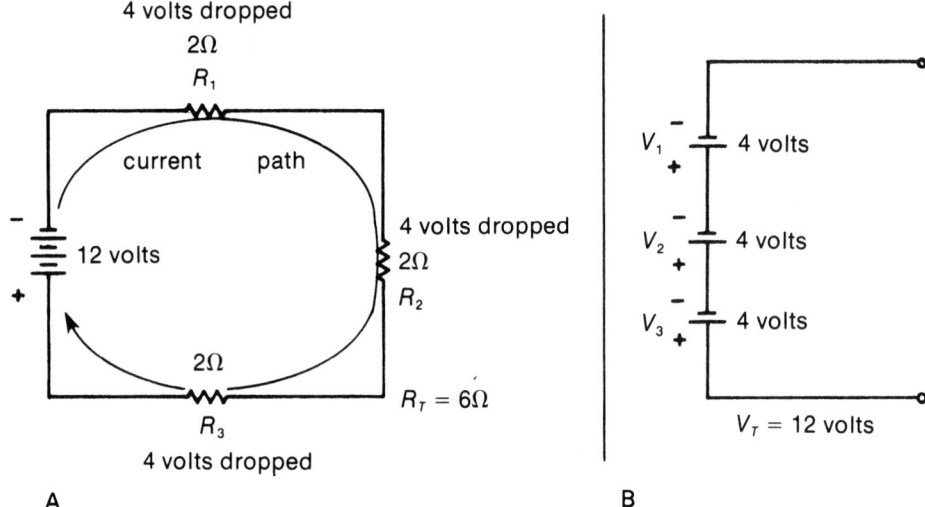

Figure 6.13

In series circuit A, the sum of the resistive elements equals the total resistance of the circuit, or RT = R1 + R2 + R3. Similarly, batteries connected in series B add, or VT = V1 + V2 + V3.

If resistors of equal value are connected in parallel, this effectively increases the cross-sectional area, and thus reduces the total resistance or circuit load by the value of one of the resistors. Ohm's law works just as well for parallel circuits as it does for series circuits.

The series-parallel circuit has the electrical properties of both series and parallel circuits, depending upon where you are in the circuit. The value of a different branch or leg can be calculated using Ohm's law.

Series, parallel, and series-parallel circuits all played a very important part in the development of early telegraph and telephone sets and systems.

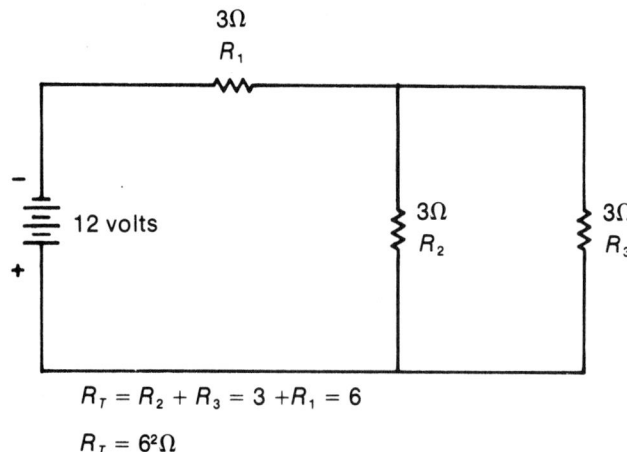

Figure 6.14

In a series-parallel circuit, the rules for both series and parallel circuits apply. For example, R1 is added to the resultant of R2 + R3 divided by 2. In this circuit, RT = 6 ohms.

Components for Electrical Control and Transmission

An eighteenth-century English experimenter, Stephen Gray, was the first person to correctly classify materials (such as metal) as conductors of electricity and other materials (glass) as nonconductors. Conductors are one of the major components for electrical control and transmission of energy.

Insulators	Conductors
Air	Platinum
Glass	Silver
Porcelain	Copper
Rubber	Gold
Bakelite	Aluminum
Wax	Tungsten
Amber	Iron
Sulfur	Constantan
Paper	Nichrome

Figure 6.15

Comparative list of materials best suited to be used as insulators and conductors.

Noting the success Gray had with wire conductors, Henry Cavendish, an English chemist and physicist working in the last half of the eighteenth century, conducted further experiments with iron wire, which became the principal conductor of electricity at that time.

Henry Cavendish's experiments and research studies with the capacity of conductors were an outstanding achievement for his period of time. He developed the concept of "degree of electrification," which later became known as "potential energy."

As pointed out by the early experimenters, the opposition to electron flow is not the same for all materials. This is because atoms of some materials, such as metals, give up their outer electrons more easily than other materials, such as ceramics. The materials that give up their electrons easily are called **conductors**; those that don't are called **insulators.**

Conductors

From the preceding paragraph you may have gathered that a conductor is a poor insulator and that an insulator is a poor conductor. This is because the electrical properties of each are so completely different from each other. For example, good conductors are materials that offer very little opposition to the flow of electrons and, therefore, are used to conduct electricity. The best conductors are gold, silver, platinum, copper, aluminum, and iron wire. Even though gold, silver, and platinum are the best, they are also the most costly. Therefore, copper and aluminum wire represent a compromise and are used for most applications.

Materials that are good conductors have a plentiful supply of free electrons. Even the very best conductors have some small resistance to electron flow over a long distance. The resistance of wire conductors depends upon four factors: (1) the material from which the wire is made, (2) its physical length, (3) its cross-sectional area, and

(4) its temperature. Therefore, all conductors can be assigned a relative value of "resistivity," which would indicate how well a wire conductor would carry electrons under given circumstances—such as length, thickness, temperature, and material. The table in Figure 6.16 shows the relative resistivity of copper wire. Note that as the gauge size increases, so does the resistance value. Let us consider each of the factors that affect the resistivity of a conductor.

The longer the length of a wire, the greater its resistance to electron flow. For example, if we were to select 300 meters of 20 gauge copper wire from the chart in Figure 6.16, we would note that the resistance would be 10.35 ohms. If we were to double the length of wire, the resistance would also double—becoming 20.70 ohms.

The thickness, or cross-sectional area, affects the resistance of a given length of conductor. The greater the area, the lower the resistance. Conversely, the smaller the area, the higher the resistance because, in a smaller area, there are less free electrons to flow in the conductor. This is evident when you compare the diameter of gauge 20 copper wire (31.96 diam mils) with the diameter of gauge 40 copper wire (3.145 diam mils) in the table in Figure 6.16.

Gauge No.	Diam. Mils	Circular Mil Area	Ohms per 300 Meters of Copper Wire at 25°C	Gauge No.	Diam. Mils	Circular Mil Area	Ohms per 300 Meters of Copper Wire at 25°C
1	289.3	83,690	0.1264	21	28.46	810.1	13.05
2	257.6	66,370	0.1593	22	25.35	642.4	16.46
3	229.4	52,640	0.2009	23	25.57	509.5	20.76
4	204.3	41,740	0.2533	24	20.10	404.0	26.17
5	181.9	33,100	0.3195	25	17.90	320.4	33.00
6	162.0	26,250	0.4028	26	15.94	254.1	41.62
7	144.3	20,820	0.5080	27	14.20	201.5	52.48
8	128.5	16,510	0.6405	28	12.64	159.8	66.17
9	114.4	13,090	0.8077	29	11.26	126.7	83.44
10	101.9	10,380	1.018	30	10.03	100.5	105.2
11	90.74	8,234	1.284	31	8.928	79.70	132.7
12	80.81	6,530	1.619	32	7.950	63.21	167.3
13	71.96	5,178	2.042	33	7.080	50.13	211.0
14	64.08	4,107	2.575	34	6.305	39.75	266.0
15	57.07	3,257	3.247	35	5.615	31.52	335.0
16	50.82	2,583	4.094	36	5.000	25.00	423.0
17	45.26	2,048	5,163	37	4.453	19.83	533.4
18	40.30	1,624	6.510	38	3.965	15.72	672.6
19	35.89	1,288	8.210	39	3.531	12.47	848.1
20	31.96	1,022	10.35	40	3.145	9.88	1,069.0

Figure 6.16

Resistivity table for copper wire.

For most materials, the hotter they are, the more resistance they offer to the flow of electrons for a given length and cross-sectional area. Conversely, the colder a

Color	Number	Tolerance
Black	0	—
Brown	1	—
Red	2	—
Orange	3	—
Yellow	4	—
Green	5	—
Blue	6	—
Violet	7	—
Gray	8	—
White	9	—
Gold	—	5%
Silver	—	10%
No Color	—	20%

Figure 6.17

This chart shows the resistor color code. Note the letter each color begins with: B, B, R, O, Y, G, B, V, G, W. Using these letters, can you devise a saying that will help you to remember the sequence of these letters?

material the less resistance it offers to the flow of electrons for the same length and cross-sectional area.

Some special materials such as carbon and electrolyte solutions are exceptions to this basic rule. Their resistance to electron flow decreases as their temperature increases. The converse is also true.

Insulators

Insulators are materials that offer a very high opposition to the flow of electrons. Therefore, they are used to block, or insulate, a wire or circuit from the flow of electrons. All materials, including insulators, conduct current to some degree, but the electron flow in insulators is so small that it is usually considered to be zero.

Resistors

If you were to connect a one-volt battery to a gauge 10 copper wire 300 meters long, you would have 1.018 ohms resistance. Using Ohm's law, we could calculate this to be one ampere of electron flow in the circuit. Adding long lengths of a conductor to achieve the proper resistance in a circuit is obviously foolish. There is a more effective method that takes up less space and costs less money. That method involves using a resistor.

Most of the resistors used in small electrical devices are made of carbon. Carbon resistors are constructed of compressed graphite and binding material; they have wire leads attached to each end. They are generally covered with an insulated coating of ceramic material.

There are many other types of resistors used in different applications. Some of the most common types are large carbon resistors, metal-film resistors, wire-wound resistors, and variable resistors in carbon or wire configurations. All of these have different color coding schemes.

When too high a rate of electron flow goes through a resistor, the temperature can rise above the power-handling capability of the resistor, causing it to change its chemical composition, expand, contract, or burn out. Therefore, most resistors are rated in watts—the product of the current and voltage applied to the resistors. This is expressed by the formula:

$$P = I \times E$$

in which

P = power (in watts)
I = current (in amps)
E = voltage (in volts)

Carbon resistors are normally rated as 1/3, 1/2, 1, and 2 watt. Resistors of greater than 2 watts are generally wire-wound and are manufactured in ranges from 5 to 200 watts. Generally, the larger the physical size of a resistor, the higher its wattage rating. This is because the larger surface area will give up its heat to the atmosphere much better.

The basic unit of resistance is the **ohm**. One ohm is equal to the amount of resistance that will allow exactly one ampere of current to flow when one volt of electrical force is applied. Ohm's law for calculating the resistance of a resistor or a circuit is:

$$R = \frac{E}{I}$$

in which

R = resistance (in ohms)
E = voltage (in volts)
I = current (in amps)

It is almost impossible to tell the value of a resistor without using an ohmmeter unless we know its color code. Most of the carbon-type resistors have their color coded values painted on them in end-to-center band markings. Let's think about how you would use the code to determine the value of a resistor. You have been given a resistor with a body color tan and three bands of color—let's say red, green, and yellow—from the end to the center of the resistor. What is its value? If you consult the color code table shown in Figure 6.18, you will note that red = 2, green = 5, and yellow = 4 zeros. The tan body color represents nothing. Therefore, the value of the resistor is 250,000 ohms with 20 percent tolerance. This means that the resistor can vary as much as 20 percent of 250,000 in either direction.

Many times you will need to express resistor value in ohms greater than one, as in this case, or less than one. The smaller values are expressed in microhms, while the larger values are expressed in megohms. One microhm equals one-millionth of an ohm, whereas one megohm is equal to 1 million ohms. Resistances above 1000 ohms generally use the letter **K** in place of the three zeros. Thus, 15 K ohms means 15,000 ohms.

Switches

A switch is a device to open or close a circuit. It is used in every electrical and electronic mode of telecommunication to energize or de-energize circuits.

Figure 6.18

It takes all types of fuses to protect the wide variety of circuits used in the electrical and electronic industry. Pictured in the background are the larger fuses as used in heavy, current-carrying electrical circuits; in the foreground are grouped the smaller type of fuse found in most electronic circuits.

Switches are designed in different shapes and sizes to suit particular applications or configurations. There are many types of switches, including the toggle switch, the combination variable resistor and switch (volume control with an on-off switch), the slide switch, and the knife switch with single and multiple contacts.

Fuses

When current passes through a circuit with several circuit elements—such as resistors and coils—a certain amount of ambient temperature is attained. If excessive current is drawn because of a short circuit, some of the circuit elements may be damaged unless a safety device is added to the circuit. This is the purpose of the fuse. It is designed to "blow out" or melt when the power consumed by the circuit exceeds safe levels. It is usually connected in series at the start of the circuit so that it will protect the more expensive circuit elements from burning out.

Fuses come in many different sizes and shapes according to their intended use. The glass cartridge, screw plug, and solid cartridge fuses are the most common types used today.

All fuses are rated by the amount of current they will safely conduct without burning out. Values are usually stamped on the fuse. For example, 2 or 2A would mean that a fuse is rated at 2 amperes.

Circuit Measurement

In order to comprehend what is taking place in an electrical circuit, an understanding of the proper use of instrumentation is essential. Sometimes the only way to detect a problem in a circuit is by taking measurements of the voltage, current, or resistance.

There are many different kinds of instruments for measuring the presence of voltage, current, and resistance. One of the most common and effective instruments is the multimeter, which combines the functions of separate meters for measuring voltage, current, and resistance. In addition to the multimeter, the galvanometer, wattmeter, and megger are common measuring instruments. Other instruments associated more with the electronic modes of communication will be discussed in Module 8.

The **multimeter**, or VOM as it's most commonly called, is one of the most versatile basic instruments in electrical communications. Current is measured with the VOM inserted in series with the circuit, while voltage measurements can be taken across the load. To obtain an accurate reading, resistance measurements must be taken with no power in the circuit and with one of the circuit leads disconnected.

Switching the VOM to either the voltage, current, or resistance position connects the meter movement and its circuit to the probes. If you are measuring voltage or current, be sure always to start at the high-value end of the scale to avoid damaging the meter. You will have an opportunity to use the galvanometer and VOM in conjunction with the instrumentation activities in the ACT manual.

Early Electromagnetic Discoveries

Hans Christian Oersted, a Dutch scientist, accidentally discovered electromagnetism while he was teaching one of his classes, when he accidentally applied current to a wire that was lying over a compass. Each time he applied current, he noted that the compass needle moved at right angles to the wire, indicating that some type of invisible force was being exerted on the compass needle. On the basis of this accidental discovery, he developed his theory of **electromagnetism**, which he defined as a field of force around a wire or the forces exerted by a current-carrying wire. The unit of magnetic intensity, the **oersted**, was named for him.

A year later, Michael Faraday, an English scientist, produced alternating current by moving a coil of wire near a magnet, thereby discovering electromagnetic induction. Using the principles of electromagnetic generation of current and electromagnetic

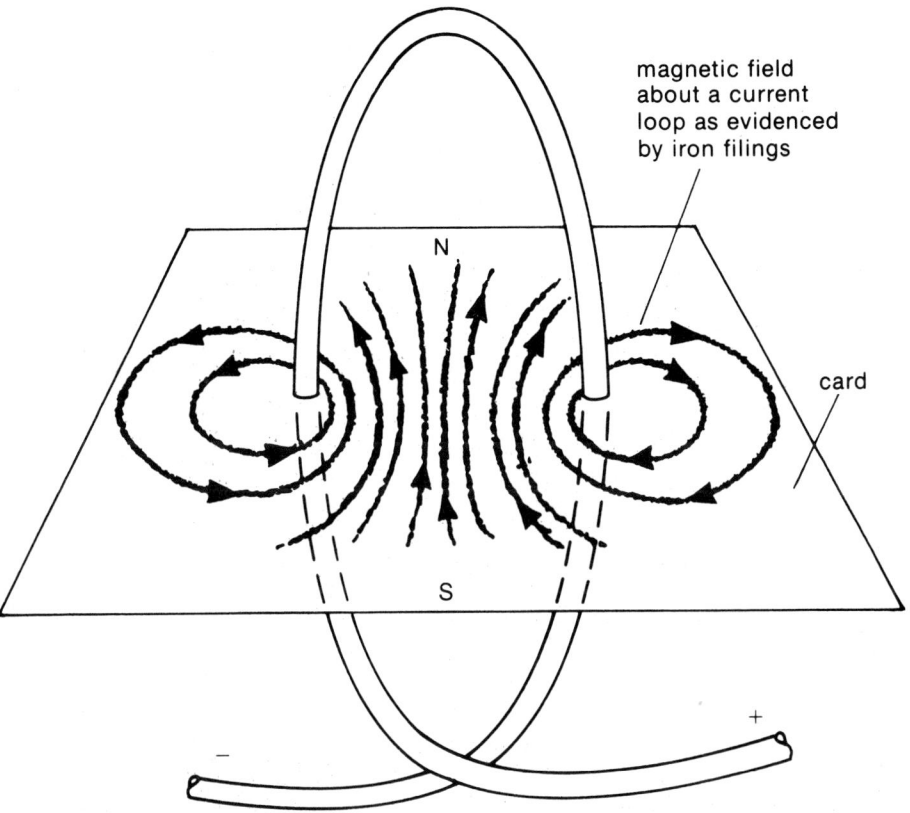

Figure 6.19

A looped wire carrying current will produce a magnetic field in direct proportion to the amount of electron flow through the wire. If it is looped through a card and iron filings are added to the surface of the card, when the card is tapped the pattern of the magnetic field will look like the above sketch.

induction, he built a 35-centimeter copper disk, which he rotated between the poles of an electromagnet. With this device he proved that if electricity could produce magnetism, then magnetism could produce electricity.

Joseph Henry, an American school teacher, was the first to discover the force of induced currents caused by the self-induction of current-carrying coils. In honor of his discovery, the unit of measurement for the electrical size of coils was named for him.

While most of the earlier discoverers and experimenters were either physicians or physicists, people from other walks of life also made contributions to the expanding field of electromagnetism. One of these persons was William Sturgeon, an English shoemaker, who applied the properties of the electromagnet to pick up nails that had fallen in the dirt. He built his electromagnet by coiling a long piece of insulated wire around a soft iron horseshoe. When he applied current, the horseshoe attracted the loose nails to the pole piece.

A physicist, André-Marie Ampère, continued experimenting with Sturgeon's earlier horseshoe magnet and soon discovered that any coil of wire with current flowing

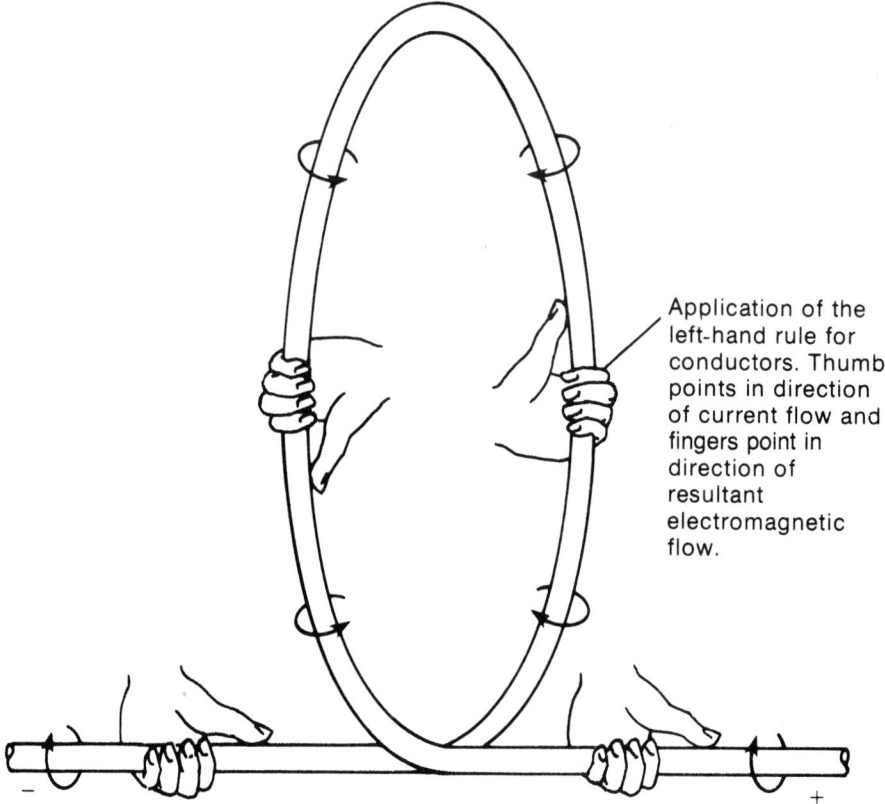

Figure 6.20

To determine the direction of an electromagnetic field in a coil of wire, use the "left-hand rule for conductors," which states that if the thumb of the left hand points in the direction of current flow, then the fingers will point in the direction of the magnetic field.

through it acts as a magnet. When he inserted an iron core in the coil, the magnetic field seemed to intensify. In his writings, Ampère explained the true nature of electric current and its relationship to magnetism. The unit of current was named for him. Based on the previous discoveries of Sturgeon and Ampère, Dominique Arago produced the first commercial electromagnet.

Later studies proved that a flow of electrons through a single conductor sets up an electric field around that conductor in direct proportion to the number of electrons flowing through it. If that single conductor is looped to form a coil and a flow of electrons is forced through it by a battery, then it takes on the properties of an electromagnet, having two poles and the power of attraction.

A very definite relationship exists between the direction of electron flow in a wire, wire loop, or coil, and the resultant magnetic field. This relationship can be determined by the "left-hand rule for coils." If we grasp the coil of wire in the palm of our left hand, with the fingers pointing in the direction of the electron flow, then the thumb will point toward the north pole of the coil. This rule is important for the design of electromagnets used in telegraph or telephone circuits.

THE BEGINNINGS OF ELECTRICAL COMMUNICATIONS 161

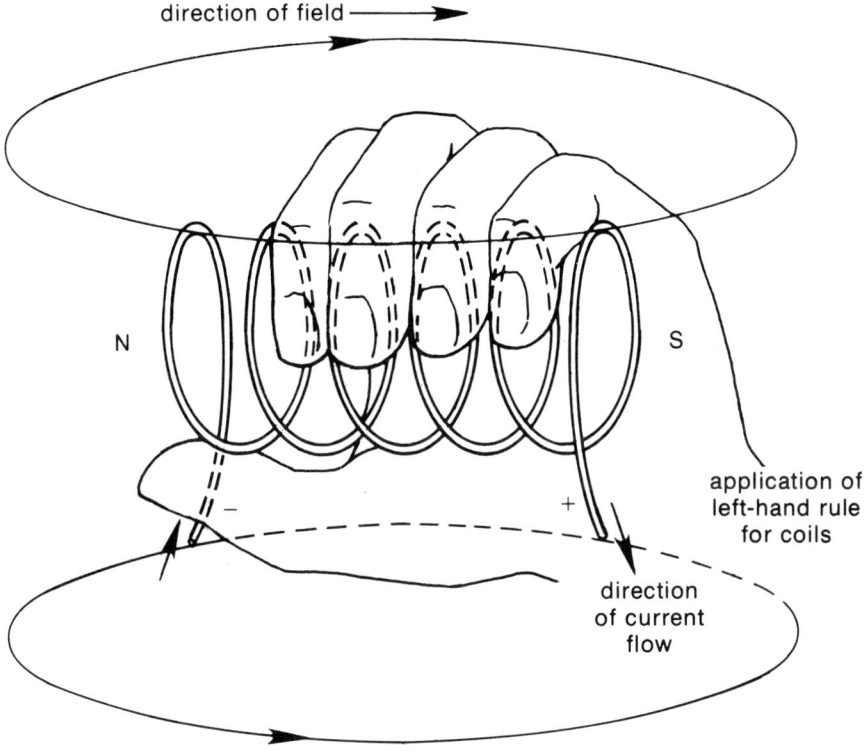

Figure 6.21

The application of the "left-hand rule for coils" to determine poles.

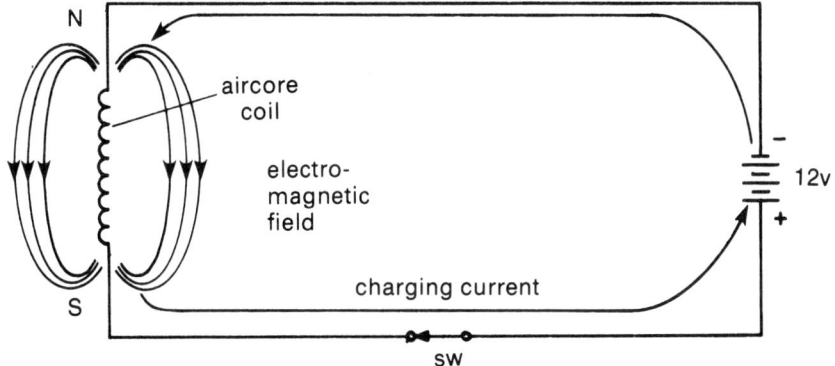

Figure 6.22

Creating an electromagnetic field in a coil by the application of a 12-volt battery. If the power source remains connected as shown in the sketch, then the magnetic field will remain as shown. As soon as the switch is opened, the circuit will be broken and the magnetic field around the coil will collapse.

The number of lines of magnetic flux is represented by the Greek letter **phi** (pronounced 'fye'). Phi occurs in direct proportion to the force **F** in gilberts producing it. The formula that expresses this relationship is:

$$\Phi = \frac{\text{Force}}{\text{Reluctance}}$$

$\mathcal{R}$ represents the reluctance, or REL, which is the resistance offered to the passage of the lines of force through one cubic centimeter of air. As the flux path increases in length, the REL increases. This is called Rowland's Law.

Another important property of electromagnetism is that it may be induced or introduced into an adjacent wire or coil without any direct connection. For example, if we were to move a permanent magnet past a wire connected to a galvanometer, we would note a deflection of the needle indicating the induction of a force that caused free electrons to flow in the wire. If the wire were coiled many times and the same action taken, then the galvanometer would register an even stronger swing of the needle. A rapid back and forth movement of the magnet over the coil would produce a rapid positive and negative movement of the needle. This illustrates the basic principle of the production of alternating current.

If we can generate a current in a coil of wire by moving a magnet, then it would seem equally possible to reverse the process and create an electromagnetic field around a coil by connecting it across a power source. If we wish to increase the field strength of the flux pattern, then we must either increase the number of turns in the coil, increase the current through the coil, or insert an iron core through the center of the coil. The relationship between magnetic force (**F**) and the product of ampere-turns is expressed by the formula:

$$F = 1.257 \: I \times N$$

in which

F = the force in gilberts

I = the applied current to the coil

N = the number of turns of wire of the coil

One of the more familiar electromagnetic devices is the buzzer. The rapid making and breaking of the circuit causes the contact points to buzz. This is the basic principle behind the "sounder" used in Morse's telegraph circuit. The bell-ringing circuit in a telephone instrument also makes use of a modified electromagnetic buzzer. In the telephone a striker is added to the vibrating end of the armature and the bells are arranged so that they are struck each time the circuit opens and closes.

Another familiar device is the transformer. Transformer action is the transferring of energy from one circuit to another. This action is also called mutual induction. Refer to Figure 6.23. Coil A is the primary circuit and coil B is the secondary circuit. When the switch is closed, the electrons start to flow and a magnetic field starts to build up on the outside of coil A. As the magnetic field of coil A is expanding, it cuts across coil B, thereby inducing an electromotive force (EMF) in coil B. The galva-

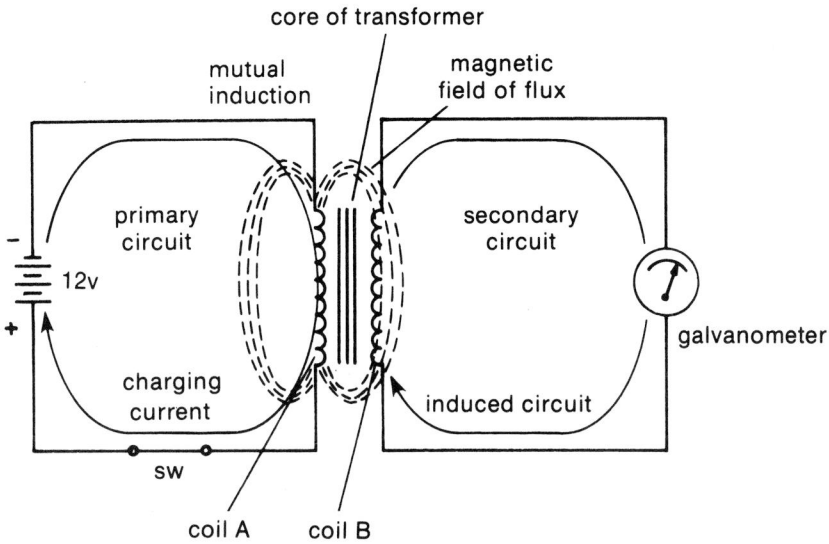

Figure 6.23

Sketch showing transformer action, or mutual induction.

nometer in the secondary circuit indicates that there is electron flow in the secondary circuit. The magnetic field in coil A has now expanded to its fullest point and then remains constant as long as the current from the battery is flowing in the primary circuit. As the field of flux from coil A is no longer moving and cutting coil B, no force is being mutually induced, so the field of the secondary coil B collapses, and the galvanometer needle reads zero electron flow in the secondary circuit.

When the switch in the primary circuit is opened, the magnetic field around coil A starts to collapse and this movement cuts across coil B, causing an electron flow in the opposite direction in the secondary circuit. The galvanometer shows that electron flow only takes place when the magnetic field is either building or collapsing. The energy source used in this demonstration transformer circuit is for explanation purposes only. A transformer is normally used in a circuit having a constant changing flow of electrons—such as alternating current, voice frequencies impinging on a microphone diaphragm, or pulses from the making or breaking of a telegraph key.

There are many applications for the transformer in radio and electronic circuits. These will be discussed in detail in Module 8.

How We Used Electricity in Telecommunications

At this point in our study of electrical concepts we have learned about the basic theories and early discoveries of electrical phenomena and how people tried to harness this energy for their own use. Yet, with all of the discoveries, people still had not learned to combine their knowledge so as to extend the limited range of the human voice.

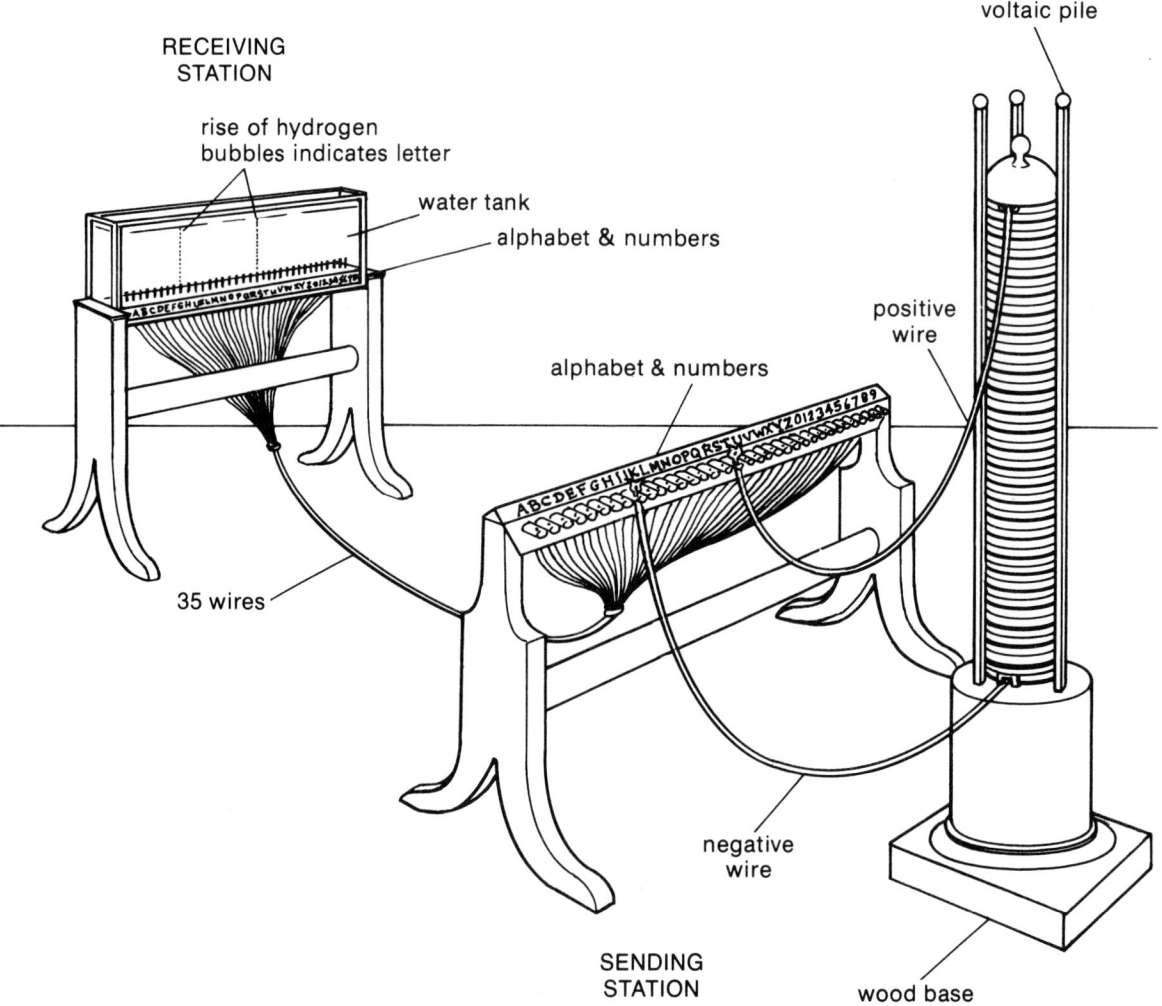

Figure 6.24

The Soemmerring chemical telegraph system utilized the earlier discovery of the principle of the decomposition of water into its two basic elements — oxygen and hydrogen. To send a message, a voltaic pile was connected to a letter at the sending station and hydrogen bubbles were seen to rise above the same letter at the receiving station.

The first mode of electrical communication was the compass, which extended humans' traveling range half way around the world.

From earlier experiments it was known that electrostatic forces could attract light pieces of paper. It was a simple matter to combine a source of power with wire conductors and a method for relaying the intelligence to another location. This was accomplished by putting the letters of the alphabet on tiny pieces of paper. When electrostatic force was applied to the paper, it would move, thereby indicating which letter of the alphabet was being transmitted. This first electrostatic telegraph system did not prove too practical and soon gave way to experiments with the chemical telegraph system.

The chemical system was based on an earlier scientific discovery that water could be electrolytically decomposed into its two basic gases, oxygen and hydrogen. During this process, the hydrogen gas would form bubbles on the positive electrode. Combining the hydrogen-bubble technique with the alphabet on pieces of paper and thirty-

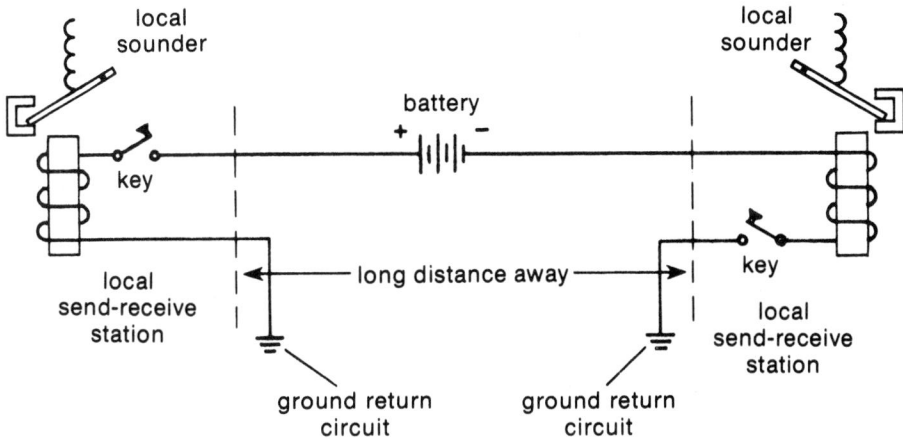

Figure 6.25

The sketch shows a two-way telegraph circuit using duplicate instruments at each remote sending-receiving stations. Note the ground return to complete the series circuit.

five wires connecting two stations together, an effective system for communicating was devised. Each frame at a receiver station had a small tank of water under each letter and the hydrogen bubbles indicated to the operator which letter was being sent. Although a very interesting device, it had limitations and finally took its place in history as an important experiment without significant practical value.

Later, an electromagnetic-compass needle telegraph system was proposed based on Oersted's accidental discovery. This device combined a power source, wire conductors, and two compasses attached to a backboard on which the letters of the alphabet were placed. Electric current from a distant station would cause the compass needles to move. The line of intersection indicated the letter of the alphabet. Several varieties of this method were developed, the most successful of which used five compasses to indicate the letters. This system was used for many years as the communication system for the early European railroads. The elecromagnetic-needle system was slow at best, and inventors continued their search for a better and faster mode of communication.

It was Samuel Morse who first conceived of combining a battery, as the power source, with a switch (key) and an electromagnet to which he attached a sounder. He produced the first reliable telegraph instrument. It functioned like this: If the key is closed, the circuit is completed. The electrons flow from the negative terminal of the battery, through the key and electromagnet, to ground and back again to the positive terminal of the battery. As a result, the soft-iron armature is attracted to the electromagnet and produces a metallic click. In Figure 6.26, we note that the armature is

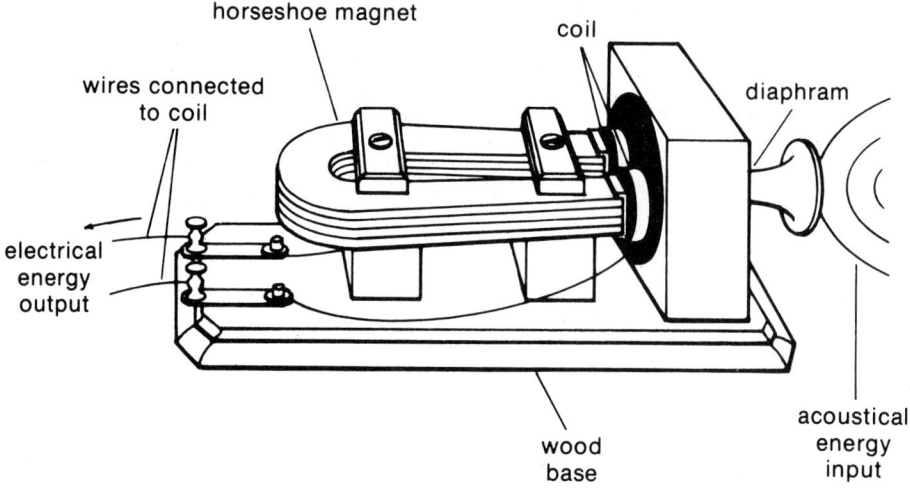

Figure 6.26

A model of the original experimental telephone instrument invented by Alexander Graham Bell. In this model, he used a horseshow magnet, coil, and diaphragm to change acoustical energy into electrical energy.

pivoted, as well as spring loaded, and rides in the U-shaped metal stop. When the key is opened, the electromagnet loses its attraction and the spring pulls the armature to the top of the stop, which makes another click. This part of the electromagnet is called the sounder.

The device by itself is useless unless there is some way to convey meaning.

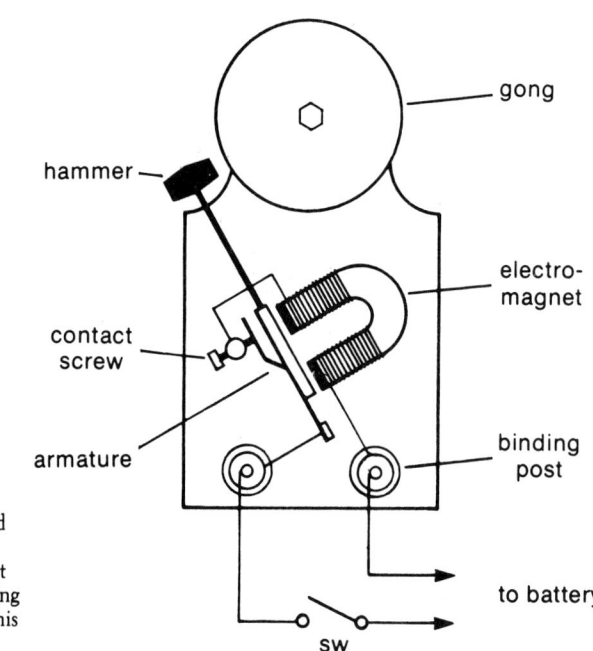

Figure 6.27

A single ringing circuit that would alert a person at the other end of the line was an electromagnet that made and broke the circuit, causing a small hammer to hit a gong. This ringing device completed Bell's telephone system.

Figure 6.28

One of the earliest of the Teletype tape printers. On this machine a perforated tape was cut and sent out to a distant station over telegraph quality lines. At the distant station, the received signal was printed on paper tape that was gummed on the reverse side. It could be cut to the width of letter paper, pasted on a sheet of paper in a series of lines, and delivered to the addressee.

Therefore, Morse was forced to develop a code to convey intelligence by means of the clicks. Inasmuch as the interval of time between clicks can be made short or long by an operator, he reasoned that a short interval would represent a "dit" (·), and a longer one would be a "dah" (-). So he arranged a code that made use of the short and long time intervals between clicks. By adding another sounder and key at a remote location, he established the first telegraph net. This system of electrical communication spread far and wide and soon became the communication mode by which railroad stations and even the entire nation was linked together. The expansion of the network was aided by the expanding railroad system because the telegraph system could use the steel rails as conductors. Like the steel rails, the transatlantic cables linked nations together in one gigantic communications network.

Looking back at the technical developments that predated the early telegraph, one can conclude that the telegraph was the invention that advanced the technology of telecommunications as well as communication of basic ideas. As an example, when the literature announced the development of a new and more effective semiautomatic (tape) telegraph printer, the conversion to the new technology was almost immediate.

As people continued to use the telegraph system to transmit messages, they soon

Figure 6.29

Facsimile messages are automatically received and transmitted by the modern Xerox Telecopier 410 transceiver. The 410 system automatically sends or receives by telephone as many as 75 documents without an operator in attendance. The system answers calls, starts the sending and receiving process between two points, and hangs up when transmission is complete. It operates at four or six minutes a page and is completely compatible with all other Xerox Telecopier units.
Courtesy, Xerox Corporation

Figure 6.30

Pictured above is one of the huge tracking antennas used to follow deep space probes on their way toward Mars. Essentially, the high-gain, parabolic "dish" reflects the signal into the feed horns where it is directed to the receiver for amplification, recording, and retransmission to Houston, Texas or Pasadena, California. Courtesy, NASA

began to wonder if it would be possible to send the human voice over the telegraph wires. Although many people on both sides of the Atlantic were working on this new problem, Alexander Graham Bell is credited with the invention of the telephone, the device that launched the communication explosion. The major problem was how to convert sound energy into electrical energy. If Bell could accomplish this, he could reverse the process and transmit-receive the spoken word. Reasoning that the human voice originates with the vibrating vocal cords, which compress and expand the air in front of them, he experimented with sound waves vibrating a diaphragm. Remembering that resistors regulate electron flow in circuits, Bell obtained some carbon granules and encased them in a container having a fixed carbon plate on one side and a movable plate on the other. He then attached a flexible diaphragm to the movable carbon plate and connected a battery to each plate to complete the circuit. As the sound waves impinged on the diaphragm, it caused the movable carbon plate to move in and out in accordance with the sound wave pattern. When he pushed the diaphragm inward, the attached carbon plate tightly packed the carbon granules, thereby decreasing the resistance and permitting more current to flow. Conversely, if he allowed the granules to return to a loosely packed condition, the resistance of the circuit increased and the electron flow decreased. Bell had invented the first microphone.

With the problem of superimposing the human voice on a wire solved, all that remained was to devise a ringing circuit to alert an operator at the other end of the line. Once he solved this problem, he produced a workable telephone system that was destined to reach around the world.

As the need for telephone and telegraph networks expanded, many new problems were introduced. Applying the same human ingenuity in the application of scientific discoveries for the benefit of people, many of the early problems were solved by the inventors of communication devices.

One of the problems involved the resistance of long runs of wire between communities. As we learned, the resistance of wire doubles every 300 meters. This tends to reduce the signal strength over long runs so that it can't be heard. This necessitated the development of repeater stations along the way to amplify the signal when it was required. The repeater stations helped expand both telephone and telegraph networks and made coast-to-coast communication practical.

As more and more subscribers began using the telephone and telegraph nets, new problems became evident as long-distance telephone calls and messages began to pile up at central stations. It was no longer practical to add more circuits to link different communities, because they too would become saturated with the backlog of calls and messages. A more efficient technique for using the existing lines had to be developed. Thomas Alva Edison developed a method for "quadruplexing" circuits so that four messages could be sent over the same wire simultaneously. This soon reduced the backlog, and the communication explosion was on its way.

By 1920 many new types of telegraph printers with transmission speeds of 60 words-per-minute were introduced into the nation's communication network. This was followed twenty years later with the new 100 words-per-minute teletype machines using new high-speed switching centers to relay millions of calls and messages daily.

With the expansion of communication networks and the increase in the number of calls and messages, other technical developments were introduced. One of these was the facsimile telegraph machine, a device that can scan a page and use electrical impulses to flash it to distant stations by telephone circuit for conversion back to the original page copy. Later, multiplexing FM carrier and data and speech compression systems were devised to make greater use of the trunk lines to help speed up the nation's communication system.

In 1960, the Telex system came into being. This is a direct dial, subscriber-to-subscriber net used by many businesses throughout the world.

Today, voice, telegraph, facsimile, and telex circuits are carried worldwide by landlines, microwave facilities, submarine cable, and orbiting communications satellites. The first telephone conversation via satellite occurred over SYNCOM on August 23, 1963. Since that time communication links to the moon and into deep space have become commonplace.

The United States today leads the world with 857 telephones per 1000 inhabitants, followed by Sweden with 594, Switzerland with 560, and Canada with 528.

Countries like Britain, Japan, and Australia are in the middle range with about 350 phones per 1000 persons, but other Western nations show much lower rates of telephone availability. For example, only 1 in 5 Greeks owns a phone, while in France there are only 217 telephones per 1000 inhabitants.

With all of these advances in electrical communication one thing stands out. For the first time, scientific theory and technological development have caught up with themselves and have become inseparable.

CONCEPT FOCUSER

- Rubbing **amber** was the **earliest** source of **frictional electricity**. This was followed by rubbing diamonds, opals, and sulfur balls.
- The natural **"leading stone"** of Asia Minor was the earliest known **device** used for **navigation** on land or sea.
- Today **ceramic magnets** outnumber **ALNICO magnets** in most applications because they are cheaper to manufacture and use less of our strategic materials.
- The "pile" was the first **reliable battery** used by the early experimentors.
- Seebeck's **thermopile** produced **electricity by heating** dissimilar metallic junctions.
- Development of **early** electrical telecommunication **devices** was mostly **accidental.**
- No matter how complicated they may be, all electrical **telecommunication devices** are made up of **resistors, condensers** (capacitors), **conductors, insulators, switches,** and **coils,** connected together in different configurations and having a power source.
- Because of **advancing technology** the United States has the **most telephones** per capita in the world today.

FOOD FOR THOUGHT

1. Explain why invisible magnetism was once believed to cause diseases.
2. If you found a lodestone, how would you use it to travel in an easterly direction?
3. For what purposes are electrostatic generators used today?
4. Explain Galvani's belief in the existence of animal electricity.

5. Which one of the following power sources would you choose to operate a simple telegraph circuit?
   a. Voltaicpile
   b. Thermopile
   c. Compositepile
   d. Nuclearpile
   e. Electronpile

6. If you wished to increase the capacity of a condensor, which factor would you change? Explain your answer.
   a. Dielectric thickness
   b. Plate thickness
   c. Plate area
   d. Applied electrical force
   e. Size of the circuit conductors

7. Explain the following concepts:
   a. Resistance
   b. Capacitance
   c. Electromagnetism
   d. Insulation
   e. Conduction

8. What does the resistivity table of copper wire (Figure 6.17) tell the circuit designer?

9. From which segment of society did most of the early inventors and discoverers of electricity come? Why?

10. What prevented early experimenters in England from exchanging technical data or information with American inventors of the same period (1600–1880 A.D.)?

EXPANDING EXPERIENCES

1. Select any of the early innovators or inventors listed in Figure 6.1 and write a paper about his life, his experiments, and the significant contributions he made toward the advancement of technology-based electrical telecommunication systems.

2. Explain to the class how the early telegraph and telephone system works. Draw a simple bubble diagram with connecting lines to represent a telegraph and telephone network for a city. Trace telegraph and telephone messages from a sender to a receiver through a central office within the network.

 LOCATOR TOOLS

Brown, Anthony. *Great Ideas in Communications.* New York: David White Company, 1968, pp. 57–74.

Brown, Ronald. *Telecommunications*. Garden City, New York: Doubleday and Company, 1970

Fabre, Maurice. *A History of Communications*. New York: Hawthorne Books, 1963

King, W. James. *The Telegraph and the Telephone*. Vol. 228, No. 29. Washington, D.C.: Smithsonian Institute, 1962, pp. 273–332.

Module
SEVEN

TECHNOLOGY-BASED ACOUSTICAL SYSTEMS

Module Seven is designed to present the various techniques used in the creation, transmission, storage, and reception of acoustical information. **Acoustical information** is any type of information in the form of sound, both audible and inaudible to humans.

Historically, the use of acoustical information was a major part of primitive communications. Grunts and groans must have accompanied gestures to relay messages. Through the development of human language and the capacity to interpret naturally occurring sounds, such as thunder, rushing water, and animal cries, humans used their natural sense of hearing.

The tradition of the human species to extend its physiological capability to communicate is apparent in the area of acoustical information. This module is concerned with further developing our understanding of technical extensions of our sense of hearing so that we might more effectively transmit, process, and receive acoustical information.

ACOUSTICAL MESSAGES

To anyone who has ever watched an old Tarzan movie, the idea of using acoustical information to transfer messages is a common one. One can note, however, that in the deep jungle, that good old Tarzan yell would soon be absorbed by the surrounding plants and trees despite what the movie makers want us to believe. Tarzan would have been better equipped if he had had a portable loudspeaker attached to his leopard skin. Or would he?

As we recall from Module Three, the human voice can project only certain frequencies of sound waves. These waves exist naturally for only a short period of time and can travel at a limited speed through certain substances like air, water, and solids. These facts reveal some of the reasons behind the development of musical instruments, which can generate various frequencies of sound, for the transmission of acoustical messages.

Throughout the world, people have used numerous types of noise-making instruments to communicate with one another. In the past, Africa has been the setting for a very sophisticated signaling network using instruments. Percussion instruments, those in which sound is created by striking, have been a part of the African culture for many centuries. Used to send messages great distances over dense terrain, drums were the source of most coded acoustical information. In fact, the drum sounds became the second language of many native tribes. Children were often given a drum name as well as a spoken name to facilitate long-distance communication via percussion instruments.

Acoustical information in the form of martial music assisted the Continental Army during the American Revolution. Daily camp life and battlefield commands were conveyed by drum and fife tunes signifying such activities as reveille, attack, retreat, or taps.

THE NATURE OF SOUND

Sound is a very interesting phenomenon whether the acoustical information is heard, like class bells, for example, or is beyond the human range of hearing, like ultrasonic sound waves. Sound, whether it is audible or inaudible, is created when there is a disturbance in any medium (solid, liquid, or gas) that possesses both elasticity and mass. There can be no sound in a vacuum.

The qualities in a medium necessary for sound—mass and elasticity—may best be explained by thinking of a row of dominos standing on end, each positioned a few centimeters from the next. If you were to push the end domino into the next, a chain reaction would occur, owing to the momentum of the **mass** of the first domino set off by your gentle push. As each domino collides with the next, it transfers its momentum over and over again, creating a wave of impacts until the last domino has fallen.

This system of dominos has mass and can transfer power, but it lacks elasticity. In order to transmit sound we must have **elasticity**. By anchoring each domino with an elastic cord that would return the domino to its original position after it was struck by the preceding one, we could expect each domino to travel back and forth about its point of anchorage. By continually striking the end domino, the row of anchored dominos would shutter back and forth transmitting momentum in a harmonic motion. As before, a wave of motion would travel down the line, followed by another and another until the source of motion (you striking the end domino) was stopped. These waves of motion represent the movement of sound through a medium.

Another example could be created by dropping a pebble into a pool of water; ripples create a disturbance across the surface of the pool until they reach the bank or until they just fade away. The body of water never really moves; the ripples merely travel across it. Sound waves, then, never really create movement of a particular medium (solids, liquids, or gases) but are carried through the medium, as long as the medium has mass and elasticity.

This brings us to another important characteristic of the transmission of sound—**velocity**. The velocity of sound waves through a medium is a function of the mass

176 TECHNOLOGY-BASED ACOUSTICAL SYSTEMS

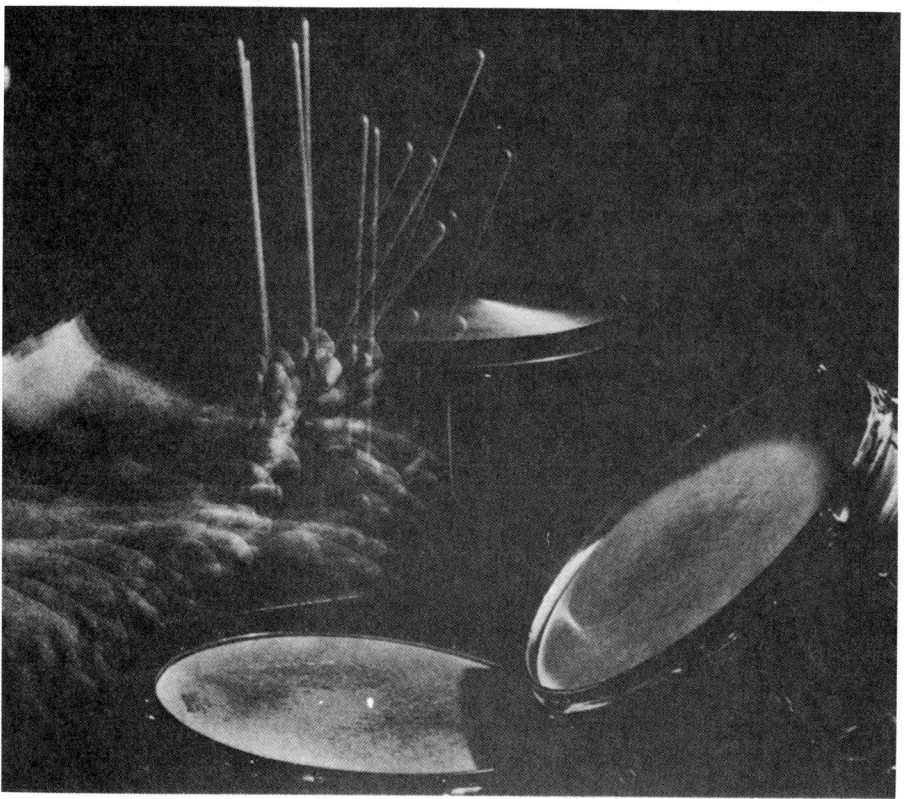

Figure 7.1

Percussion instruments have been used throughout history for ceremonial, entertainment, and communicative purposes.

and elasticity of that medium. The velocity, or speed, of sound through water would differ from the speed of the same sound through the air or through a solid. Solids and liquids are much denser than gases, which suggests that sound would travel more slowly through them. However, solids and liquids have much higher elasticity than gases do. The velocity of sound is greater as density decreases and elasticity increases, and the elasticity factor outweighs the density in most instances. This is why the wise old Indian put his ear to the ground to hear approaching horses. The Indian could hear the sound of approaching horses through wave vibrations transmitted through the ground much sooner than he could hear those same vibrations transmitted through the air.

The sound of an approaching train would be carried faster through the steel tracks than through the air. The velocity of sound in steel is about 5050 meters per second, in salt water it is around 1500 meters per second, and in air around 340 meters per second. As communication devices go, the old string-and-tin-can telephone wasn't such a bad idea after all. With a solid (string) as a transmission medium, sound would travel faster than words uttered into the air.

It was during the early 1600s that a Franciscan friar, Marin Mersenne, conducted some of the first scientific experiments concerning specific characteristics of sound. Mersenne, along with later inquirers like Jean Baptiste Biot and Daniel Calladon, did the early research necessary for the identification and utilization of various scientific concepts that led to a more complete understanding of acoustical communication. However, a classic experiment conducted in 1845 enabled us to explain certain phenomena of the nature of sound.

Christian Doppler explained the change in frequency of an approaching and receding source of sound as the relationship of velocity of observer and the sound source. In other words, if a friend were to ride his bicycle past you playing a tuba, you would hear a drop in frequency just as he passed you. The condition of this drop would depend basically on the velocity of the bicycle. But of what importance is this **Doppler effect?** It is used quite successfully in acoustical communication by the television and motion picture industries. The sounds of an approaching jet aircraft or a speeding motorcycle simulate movement and velocity; more dramatically perhaps, the Doppler effect is used to simulate the sound of something, or someone, falling from a high-rise building. The emotional effects on the viewer are achieved when the initial cry or scream drops in frequency and seemingly disappears among other buildings. According to the viewers' auditory sensory systems, they were right there when the action occurred.

INFORMATION TRANSMITTED BY ACOUSTICAL ENERGY

If we imagine someone playing a drum as a source of acoustical information, we can begin to build an interesting example. As the source of acoustical information beats out a message, the sound waves generated by the instrument radiate in all directions. The message is carried, or transmitted, via the sound waves for a certain distance (depending on the power of the sound). This acoustical information transmitted via sound waves remains basically unchanged except by slight interference from objects (trees, buildings, and the like) or by natural disturbances.

Next, let us further imagine a telephone receiver positioned 1 meter from the source of acoustical information. The mouthpiece of the receiver picks up the sound from the source just as a human ear would; however, the acoustical information is now transformed into electrical pulses in order to be transmitted over telephone lines to a second telephone some distance away. Once the electrical pulses reach their destination, they are decoded and heard in the earpiece as bits of acoustical information. The second part of our example has shown acoustical information transmitted via electrical pulses.

The drum and the telephone are both technical extensions of human beings involved in acoustical modes of communication.

The next part of this module deals with information transmitted by acoustical energy (sound). Later sections deal with acoustical information transmitted by forms of energy other than sound.

Techniques of Music

As the human capacity to communicate via acoustical systems increased with language development and enunciation details, musical instruments added to the store of communication methods and offered more possibilities of message transfer. A historical study of music and architecture reveals the early history of acoustical development. The Greek culture not only offered the word **acoustics** as a derivative from the word meaning 'hearing', but also provided many studies of and observations on music and harmonics.

Throughout history the use of music as a source of acoustical communication has been clearly defended. Various techniques in scaling and even the development of new instruments have broadened the scope of investigation. **Scaling,** or scales, is a succession of tones that increase or decrease according to a fixed interval. It is the combination of tones that creates music. Single tones mean very little musically. Music begins when a pattern of tones occurs. It is the changing relationship of tones that yields sound patterns of a pleasing or irritating nature. This relationship between any two tones is called a **musical interval.**

When one investigates musical techniques in any depth, the physics of music should be explored. From the time of the Greeks, early theory evolved into the mathematical study of musical intervals and ratios of tones. The foundations of today's modern, tempered scale were developed about the time of Johann Sebastian Bach (1685–1750). Any scale is just the pattern of musical intervals between tones. There must be a starting point from which to establish a home, or standard, note. The frequency of this note, like any sound, can be measured. The **standard frequency,** or pitch, used by musicians today is the note A = 440 Hz or cycles per second.

Instruments

The sound-producing parts of a musical instrument perform two distinct functions. Whether the instrument is a primitive wood and string lute or a modern steel and plastic clarinet, each instrument technically has a **generator,** where sound vibrations

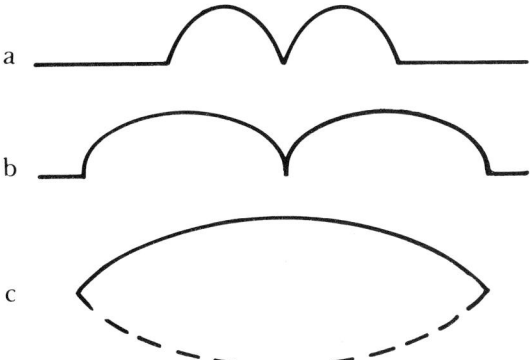

Figure 7.2

Harmonic vibrations of a string change as the strength of the force increases.

are initiated, and a **resonator,** where the sound is amplified and controlled. The following examples show familiar combinations of generators and resonators of sound: your vocal cords and mouth cavity, the strings and sound body of a guitar, the reed and body tube of a clarinet. The tonal quality of any instrument is mainly due to the relationship of the generator and resonator. Of course other elements, such as the construction methods and materials selected, require attention to maintain the quality of each instrument.

The three families of musical instruments are classified as to the types of generator and resonator used to produce sound. Although instruments in one family may sound distinctly unlike, the method of sound production is similar. The three families of instruments produce sound via strings, via air columns, or via percussion.

A string, when stretched between two points, has mass and elasticity. If displaced, the string will return to its former position; however, due to momentum of the disturbance, the string will overshoot its normal point and shutter one way and another until it comes to its point of rest. This vibration can be analyzed in three stages as shown in Figure 7.2. Instruments of the string family are played in different fashions. The displacement of strings can be achieved by striking (piano), by plucking (guitar and harp), and by bowing (violin and bass).

Just as strings offer the two characteristics of a sounding medium, so does air controlled by an instrument. Instruments that produce sound from vibrating air columns do so in an interesting manner. Although we can't see it, let's imagine a round column of air enclosed in a cylinder. If it is compressed (which has the same effect as displacing a string), the column of air will expand to achieve its normal density. As it expands, the air column (like the string) tends to overshoot its normal point and reaches a compressed stage again. As the column of air shutters back and forth to retain its normal density, it vibrates. As the air vibrations are emitted from the instrument in a controlled manner, they create audible sound waves.

Vibrating strings and air columns produce harmonic disturbances of a sounding medium. The third class of instruments, percussion, produces disturbances of an inharmonic nature. Until recently, the percussion family was not considered as im-

Strings	Air Columns	Percussion
Struck strings	Lips	Stretched membranes
Piano	Trumpet	Tympani
Plucked Strings	French horn	All drums except snare
Harp	Trombone	Rods
Guitar	Tuba	Xylophone
Banjo	Edge Tones	Chimes
Mandolin	Flute	Triangle
Bowed Strings	Organ flue pipes	Tuning fork
violin	Reeds	Plates
viola	Clarinet	Glockenspiel
cello	Saxophone	cymbals
Bass	Basset horn	Gong
	Oboe	Bells
	Harmonica	Bell chimes
	Accordian	

Figure 7.3

Instrument families

portant as orchestral instruments, just because of this difference. Sounds emitted by striking stretched membranes, rods, plates, or bells are so complex and full of inharmonic characteristics that a definite pitch is difficult to achieve.

Stretched membranes (drums), which are sometimes considered to be two-dimensional strings, vibrate in various forms necessitating very accurate placement of impact point and force to achieve the same tone. Rods (xylophone), plates (cymbals), and bells produce vibrations in a similar manner, each depending upon the elasticity of the material struck, the force of the blow, and the type of support holding the material to be struuck.

Commonly associated with the generation and transmission of musical messages is the storage and retrieval of that information. The aspect of recording acoustical information will be addressed later in this module. Before that, in order to complete our investigation into the technique of acoustical information transmission via sound waves, let's proceed to a slightly more sophisticated sound-generating device than a musical instrument.

The common problems of communicating via sound waves on the surface of the earth are difficult to identify (atmospheric disturbances, distance, time, and so forth), and once they are identified they must be overcome in order to provide efficient means of communication. However, the challenges of communication in media other than our atmosphere have baffled many scientists and technologists.

Clearly, with two-thirds of the earth's surface covered by water, the attempt to communicate in the aquatic environment is a necessary endeavor. The sense of sight is of little use under water beyond a few hundred meters. Radio waves, the wonder of modern communication, can travel but a few meters in water. So just as people who lose their sense of sight begin to substitute other senses in order to communicate, so must people who wish to communicate through water. The use of acoustic waves has provided humans with a method of "seeing" under water.

One of the oldest endeavors of past civilizations was navigation through bodies of water. Sailing by the seat of one's pants with a little bit of luck and a lot of courage as one's only equipment evolved to include the use of crude nautical charts and various sounding devices.

In the United States along the Mississippi, riverboat pilots years ago would call for depth levels of water beneath their ships. The cry of "mark 4, mark 3, mark twain" often pierced the air. A riverman in the bow of a ship threw a calibrated rope with a weight on its end into the water. When the weight struck bottom, the sailor would catch the riverboat pilot's attention by shouting "mark," then state the depth of water shown on his rope, twain (2), 3, 4, or 8 fathoms (1 fathom = approximately 1.8 meters).

Ironically, for such an old art as sailing, it wasn't until about World War I that an efficient technique was developed for communicating under water. Less than a week after the *Titanic* struck an iceberg and sank in the North Atlantic (April 1912), an underwater sound device was submitted to the British Patent Office suggesting a scheme to avoid underwater obstacles.

The development and utilization of sound transmission to navigate and to avoid obstacles under water proceeded slowly until after World War II. However, during the war, military experimentation conducted mainly by the Navy resulted in devices capable of underwater transmission and reception of acoustical information in the form of ultrasonic sound waves. The term **SO**und **NA**vigation and **R**anging (**sonar**) was adopted to describe the use of reflected sound to determine characteristics of the aquatic environment.

The basic principle of underwater acoustics is echo location. In its simplest form, **sonar** is the generation of a pulse of acoustical energy that is sent out (transmitted) into the water. When the sound wave strikes an object capable of reflecting the original sound wave, small amounts of the wave are bounced back to the original source where it is detected as an echo. Information regarding the size and distance of the reflecting object is determined by how much of the original wave is reflected and by the time lapse between the original transmission and the reception of the echo. Of course all of this is beneficial only when the exact direction of the original pulse of acoustical energy can be determined.

The generation of a directional, and therefore useful, wave of ultrasonic sound is accomplished by a device that acts as an underwater loudspeaker and microphone, called a transducer. A **transducer** is any device used to convert energy of one kind into energy of another kind. In this instance, electrical energy is converted into acoustical energy. Sonar, however, remains in the classification of acoustical modes of communication because the critical function in underwater communication is achieved by the **actual** transmission and reception of sound waves. This is opposed to the transmission and reception of electrical pulses that **represent** acoustical information, as in radio, which will be discussed later in this module.

A transducer can be one of three main types: piezoelectric, electrostrictive, or magnetostrictive.

Piezoelectric transducers involve the use of crystals. Rochelle salt and quartz are commonly used because they possess a unique quality: these crystals undergo a change in molecular structure when a vibration or an electrical field acts on the crystal. When an electrical field is applied to a piezoelectric crystal, it causes the crystal to vibrate. These vibrations are then transmitted through the water, which completes the transmission of acoustic waves, since the vibrating force causes acoustical energy to move through a medium (water) that has mass and elasticity. Likewise, when a reflected echo of the vibrations acts on the crystal transducer, the vibrations create an electrical field in the crystal that can be detected on a sonar recorder.

Electrostrictive transducers act in a similar manner. Instead of a crystal, a ceramic becomes the object of the conversion of energy types. The ceramic reacts to the magnitude of the applied electrical field (whereas the crystal reacts to the polarity of the electrical field). The ceramic generates vibrations of acoustical energy in much the same fashion as the piezoelectric transducer. The electrostrictive transducer has begun to replace all other types in most applications.

The **magnetostrictive transducer** utilizes alternating current around a coil to create magnetic fields. As the fields are reversed, the core of the coil reacts by expanding and contracting, thereby causing the vibrating motion necessary to transmit acoustical energy through water. Although the device itself is easily adapted to underwater uses, it is limited in the range of frequencies of sound. Radar works in much the same way by sending and receiving microwaves through the air.

Regardless of the type of transducer used, two main functions must be discussed before we can understand the process of underwater acoustical communication. The sonar unit would be of little value if a pulse could not be aimed in a given direction. Just as a cheerleader uses a megaphone to focus acoustical information on a specific

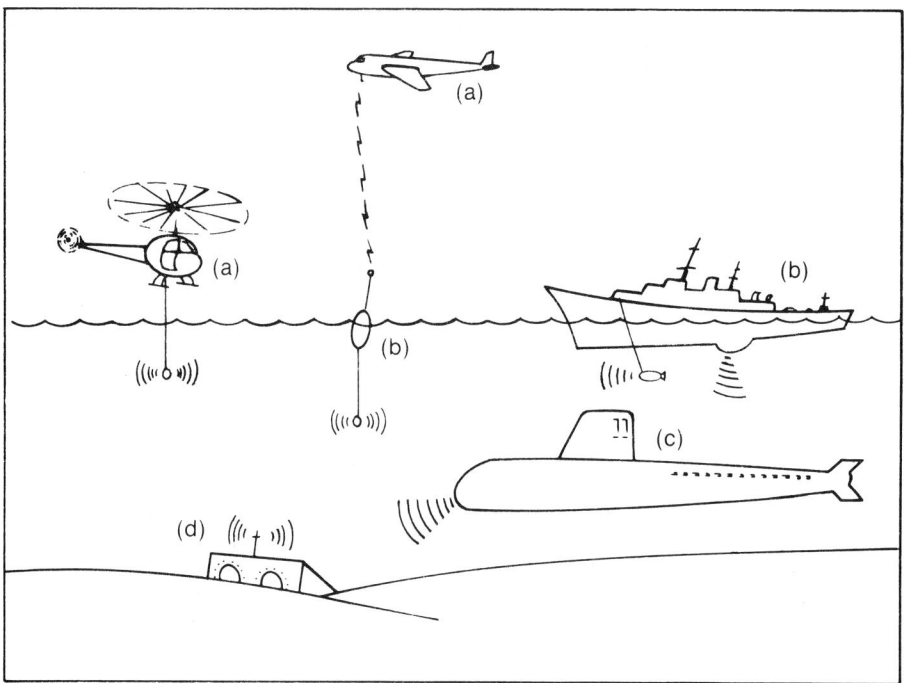

Figure 7.4

Various applications of sonar can be used to obtain accurate information about the acquatic environment: (a) aircraft, (b) surface, (c) submersible, and (d) bottom activity.

area, the acoustical energy of a sonar unit must be focused on particular areas or objects.

In order to determine the direction of underwater elements, one must be able to control the sound waves as they are transmitted or when the echo is received. The beams are controlled (or aimed) by a complex process of phase modulation called **interference.**

Once this entire signal-transmitting process has begun, it becomes necessary to see how the overall operation proceeds. As a field of electrical energy is converted to ultrasonic acoustical energy by a transducer, the pulse of acoustical energy is emitted through the water; as the sound (remember it can be inaudible to humans) strikes an obstacle, the echo bounces back to the source of the original sound, the transducer. The transducer has now been switched from a transmitting device to a receiving device by a timing switch, and it receives the echoed signal for interpretation. On board the ship a cathode-ray display screen or graphic plotter paper enables us to use the information gained.

Major applications of underwater acoustical communication are the location and identification of submerged vessels or obstacles, exploration of the ocean's bottoms, and the use by commercial fishing industries of echo sounding to locate schools of fish. Recent efforts to explore the ocean floors have brought about new developments in the use of acoustical energy in diver voice-communication under water. Miniature transducers and power packs are being used to provide individual communication capabilities via acoustic energy.

ACOUSTICAL INFORMATION TRANSMITTED BY ENERGY OTHER THAN SOUND

No communication problem attracted as much attention, or resulted in the expenditure of as much human energy and time, as the challenge of providing real-time communication over great distances. Having gone the unsuccessful route of gigantic loudspeakers and semaphore signaling towers, the trend of scientific and technological experimentation during the early and mid-1800s turned to the rage of the time, **electricity,** as a potentially useful means for communicating. The use of electricity as an energy form was the first significant technical development in long-distance communication, and it eventually led to the transmission of human speech late in the nineteenth century. However, the first steps leading to the transmission of acoustical information by energy other than sound were taken by the inventors and innovators of the electric telegraph.

Electric Telegraph

The first two decades of the nineteenth century saw electricity—which until that time had been a mere curiosity—taken out of the parlors and scientific laboratories and adopted for practical applications. The three essential elements of a telegraph system are (1) a sending device, (2) an appropriate source of power, and (3) a receiving device. Developments in power cells and batteries by 1820 solved the difficulty of consistent

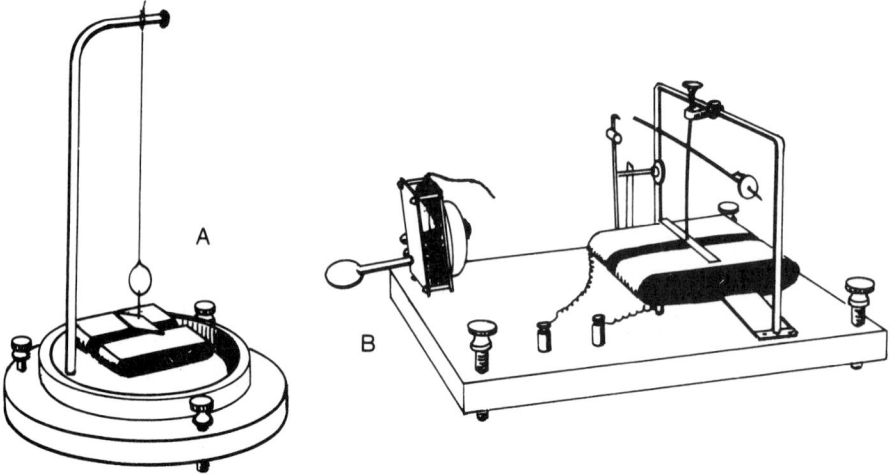

Figure 7.5

Schilling-Cannstadt's telegraph receiver: (a) indicator with fluctuating needle, (b) alarm mechanism.

energy sources for the telegraph. On the European continent two men were instrumental in advancing the understanding of electricity. Volta constructed a battery of low voltage as a continuous source of electricity; Oersted discovered the relationship between electric current and magnetism.

While development of the telegraph progressed in England and the United States, basic research continued in Europe. Paul von Schilling-Cannstadt was credited with perfecting an electronic signaling device in 1835. Schilling-Cannstadt demonstrated his device, which consisted of a telegraph that used only one pair of wires to connect a sending and receiving device, throughout Europe. The telegraph, through an electromagnetic reaction, caused a needle to fluctuate in accordance with a preselected code.

As refinement of the sending and receiving devices continued on many fronts, the incorporation of new theories of electricity brought some answers to the problem of practical application. The difficulty in sustaining the power of an electrical pulse over a long distance of wire was explained by Georg Ohm in 1827, but it was not fully understood until fifteen years later.

In England, Cooke and Wheatstone found a practical application for their five-needle telegraph in the transmission of railway and train information, first for the London and Birmingham Railroad and later for the Great Western Railway. The most striking display of the social value of the electric telegraph came in 1845. A murderer escaped via train from the English town of Slough. Armed with a description of the murderer that had been telegraphed ahead, police arrested the man as he casually departed from the train at its destination. The importance of the social acceptance of any technological innovation should not be overlooked in the overall appraisal of such an achievement.

At about the same time, new potential for electric telegraph communication was offered by the linking of bells, buzzers, and recording devices (pens and punches attached to the receiving device to create notations on a moving paper tape). This new dimension in telegraph communication coupled visual and acoustical methods of information transfer with the power of electricity. In America one of the most notable successes of telephony was the code developed by Samuel F. B. Morse. Morse's greatest contribution was a code to represent letters of the alphabet that could be simply transmitted as a dot or dash. The transmitter emitted either a short or long duration of current that could be received visually or heard acoustically as a dot or dash.

In 1843, Morse succeeded in transmitting a coded message between Baltimore and Washington over a telegraph line constructed with $30,000 appropriated by Congress. The era of electric communication had begun. Within a very short time telegraph lines extended over hundreds of miles. By the 1850s, the number of telegraph companies in America fostered extreme competition, and they often experienced more

Figure 7.6

One of the first women telegraph operators in western Pennsylvania, Molly B. Moorehead participated in establishing career opportunities for women in the communications industry.

problems of a business nature (patent holdings, rights-of-way, and so forth) than of a technical nature.

The phenomenal growth of the telegraph industry led to continual refinement of equipment and techniques. In part, as a result of the industry's consolidation under the Western Union Telegraph Company in 1856, organized technological research took new steps toward better methods of communication. Advances in electric relays, insulators, and conductor wires enabled new transmitters and receivers to send messages over greater distances. Overcrowded lines prompted the development of duplex and multiplex systems to send simultaneous messages over existing lines. Even cables under the Atlantic ocean to connect Europe with the United States were envisioned by entrepreneurs of the time.

One such enterprising American was Cyrus Field who, after many heartbreaks and serious technological setbacks, saw the successful completion of the transatlantic cable in 1866. The saga that began with the first unsuccessful attempt to link the New and Old Worlds in 1857 ended, after four attempts and millions of dollars worth of cable lost on the ocean floor, with permanent telegraph service. Interestingly, the first transatlantic telephone cable didn't provide international phone service until 1956.

The Diaphragm

The experience and devices gained through the development of long-distance communication, transmitted by electric energy, provided a foundation for the development of another means of communication by electric conduction through wires. The simple telegraph that controls the transmission of electrical pulses by a single switch is quite

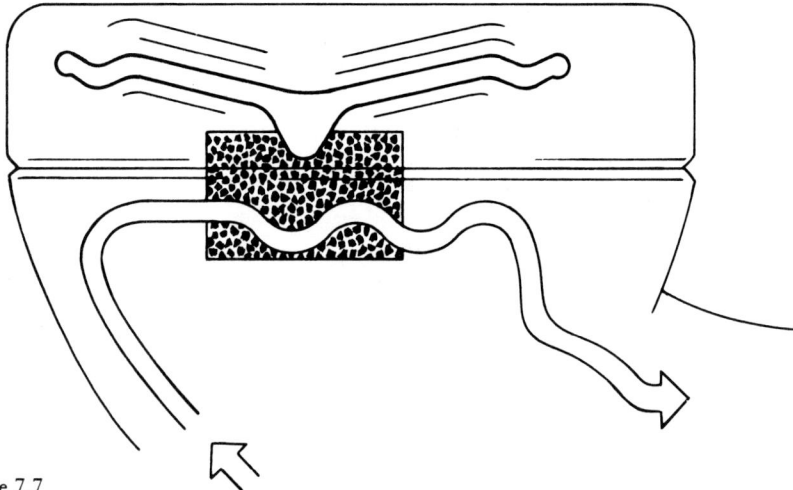

Figure 7.7

When someone speaks into a telephone mouthpiece, the sound waves strike the diaphragm, causing it to vibrate in the same manner as the sound waves. These vibrations cause the dome of the diaphragm to move in and out against carbon granules, varying the electrical current passing through the carbon. Acoustical information, which is now in the form of electrical waves, can be transmitted at the speed of light.

similar to a light switch. When the switch is open (off), the circuit is not completed; when the switch is closed, the circuit is completed and the light comes on. This type of on-off control of electric current through a conducting wire is called **pulse modulation**. However, if a continuous control of current could be achieved, an unlimited amount of information could be transmitted. This type of **continuous modulation** was achieved by John Philipp Reis when he constructed an instrument that used the vibrations of sound caused by human speech to open and close an electric circuit. Reis's use of a diaphragm as a transducer enabled sound vibrations to vary the intensity of electrical current.

A **diaphragm** is a device that consists of a flexible membrane (paper, metal, and so forth) attached to a solid frame. When acoustical energy is directed onto the flexible membrane, the membrane vibrates simultaneously with the frequencies of the original acoustical energy. If properly coupled with an electric current, the vibrations of the diaphragm modulate the current and create corresponding frequencies of electrical current, which can be carried over conducting wires. This information transfer of mechanical vibrations to electrical pulses was the process primarily responsible for the development of the telephone.

Telephone

Ironically, two patents were filed for similar telephone mechanisms on February 14, 1876. Elisha Gray of Western Electric, and Alexander Graham Bell, like his father a teacher of speech and acoustics, battled in United States courts for the initial patent grant. Many legal battles later, Bell was awarded one of the most significant patents ever issued by the United States.

The experience gained by the telegraph companies enabled the telephone to become quickly established using above-ground poles and wires to carry the electrical pulses. Each telephone had to be directly connected by iron wire to all other telephones in the system for someone to be able to make a call to any particular phone. In a community of fifteen telephones, each had to be connected to the other, since no switchboard had yet been developed to permit calls among a number of users. As commercial use of the telephone increased, the method of connecting more than two telephones evolved around the new switchboard. Each telephone was connected to a central office (still used today) in order to connect the line of one phone to the line of the intended receiver. The first switchboard was installed by E. T. Holmes in Boston in 1877.

In order to provide faster and more reliable service, an automatic telephone switching system was first used in 1892. Along with the new switching system for metropolitan areas, the telephone itself acquired a new feature, the dial. Today the touch tone and computer routing of calls provide another distinct variation in switching.

The telephone has provided a major service in long-distance acoustical modes of communication. One hundred years after the invention of the telephone more than 140 million phones exist in the United States alone, with modern switching capabilities of 550,000 long-distance calls an hour. Message transmission methods of modern telecommunications networks have changed as a result of advanced technological

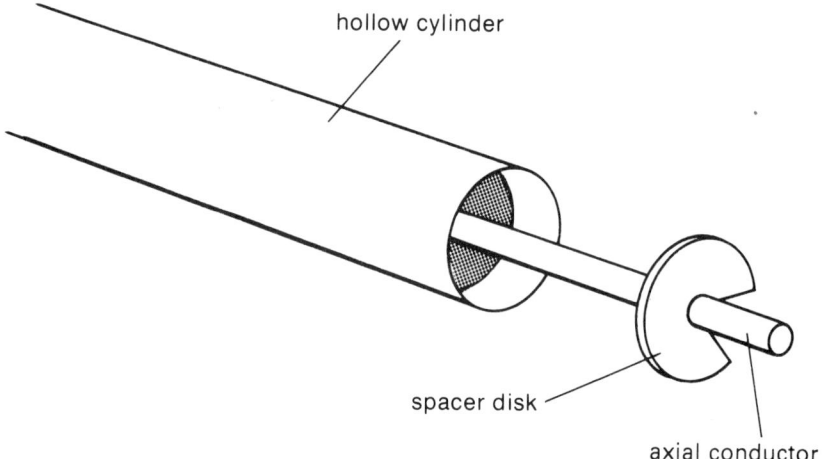

Figure 7.8

A coaxial cable is capable of carrying many speech channels or the wide frequency band required to transmit television signals. Electromagnetic energy travels in the space between the conductor and the inside walls of the cylinder.

research. Acoustical messages are currently sent via electrical pulses by many techniques besides the original iron wire.

1. **Cable.** Above-ground lines as well as underground and underwater cables provide long-distance telecommunications links. Aside from the heavily insulated single-strand copper wire, new cable techniques can provide faster and more efficient transmission of acoustical information. The coaxial cable carrier system conserves raw materials (notably copper) by using a very thin strand of metal held inside a conducting tube by plastic spacers. Long-distance transmission signals tend to weaken less when carried on coaxial cable. Bundling or multiplexing messages enable new cables of 22 coaxial tubes to carry 108,000 conversations simultaneously.
2. **Waveguide.** Hollow cylindrical tubes capable of carrying radio microwaves at ultrahigh frequencies from transmitters up to transmitting antennas, then down from receiving antennas to repeater stations are called waveguides. Necessary for directing radio waves in microwave processing stations and satellite earth stations, new waveguides are capable of transmitting acoustical information in the amount of 230,000 conversations.
3. **Microwave.** Electrical pulses carrying acoustical information that are transformed into high-frequency radio waves are called microwaves. The nature of the wave is such that it must be relayed from tower to tower or be lost in space. This is because the microwave cannot follow the curvature of the earth, nor penetrate any natural objects, such as mountains or hills. The precisely aimed microwave towers are generally in line of sight of each other spaced about 15 kilometers apart (depending on terrain) on the average.
4. **Shortwave.** Radiotelephone signals that are bounced off the earth's protective layer—the ionosphere—and then received some distance away are called shortwave signals. This technique is used to cross great expanses of water or land areas. To avoid the interference of natural phenomena and weather, stationary repeater stations are in orbit above the earth's surface.

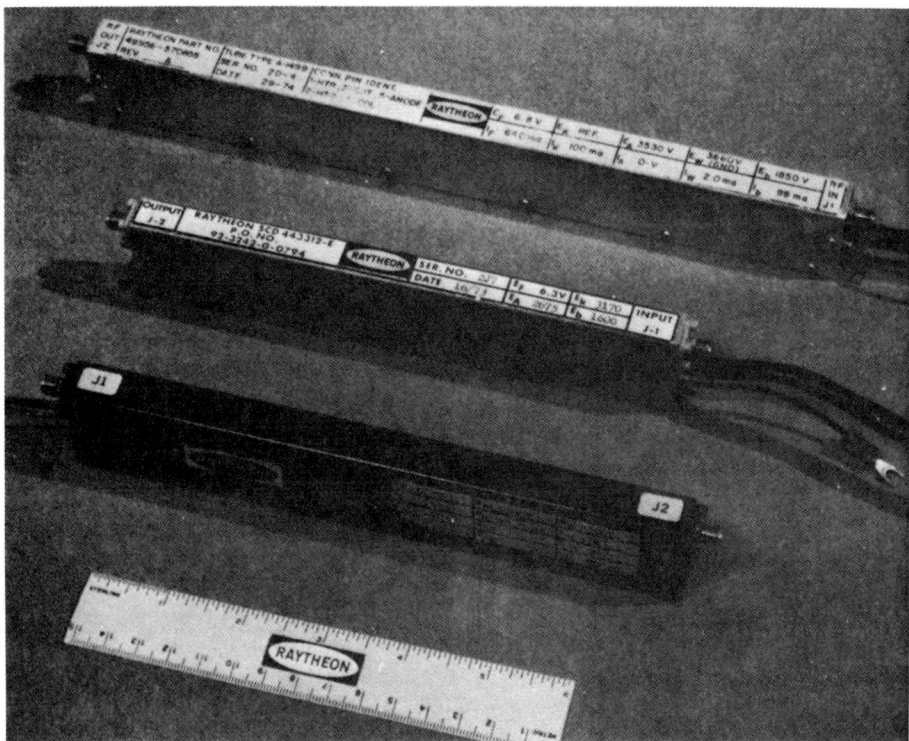

Figure 7.9

Microwave guide
Courtesy, Raytheon Company

5. **Satellite.** Communication satellites carry much of the international telephone service. As towers in the sky, satellites can either bounce microwave signals back to earth (passive) or amplify and then relay stronger signals to earth stations (active). **Early Bird**, the first commercial communications satellite, was launched on April 6, 1965. Today the global satellite system consists of more than 325 satellite pathways. NASA forecasters predict that 40 domestic satellites alone will be launched during 1980–2000 by ten major countries.

Radio

Beginning with wireless telegraphy, the radio has been popular throughout the world. The number of persons who are informed and entertained by the radio approximates the number of people who can be reached by the printed word. Reduced costs, compactness, and quality performance of modern radio receivers and transmitters have been the result of constant technological refinements.

Just as the telegraph and local telephone systems use wires to carry acoustical information in the form of electrical energy, the radio can broadcast acoustical information in the form of electrical energy without wires. For this reason it has become known as wireless communication. Tracing a unique chain of experiments and dis-

Figure 7.10a

Guglielmo Marconi is pictured above with the equipment he used to receive the first radio signal sent across the Atlantic. Note the battery, tuning coil, and coherer on the table.
Courtesy, The Marconi Company, Ltd.

Figure 7.10b

A replica of Marconi's first radio transmitter, which he used in his earliest experiments in Italy in 1895. Note the square copper sheet he used for the antenna (top center), the output wires connecting the induction coil (center) with the antenna, the wire going to an earth ground (near left table leg), and the two battery wires (near right table leg) leading down from the "key" to the battery box on the floor (bottom right).
Courtesy, The Marconi Company, Ltd.

coveries conducted by a half-dozen men, one can recognize Guglielmo Marconi as the major contributor to finding a practical application for these discoveries. Marconi, an Italian, succeeded in transmitting signals up to 3.75 kilometers on his father's estate between 1894 and 1896. This wireless telegraphic system contained elements similar to modern radio communication. Information, whether transmitted through coded signals or the human voice, must be changed, or transduced, into electrical signals. A telegraph-type key may achieve the process when sending a coded message. A transducer-type device, or microphone, similar to the diaphragm of a telephone, can be used to convert acoustical energy in the form of the human voice into electrical pulses.

Once converted, the original information, which is now in the form of electrical pulses, is carried to the transmitter. In the conversion of human speech, the electrical pulses are really an arrangement of electrons that move within a magnetic field. The movement of the electrons is representative of the frequencies of the original information carried by the human voice. When the information reaches the transmitter, it is broadcast on invisible electromagnetic waves similar to the magnetic fields created by the electrons. As the electromagnetic waves radiate through the atmosphere, they can be detected by a receiver tuned to receive the frequency of the transmission. Different transmission frequencies enable simultaneous transmission and reception of many radio signals. This is quickly illustrated by the tuning dial of your radio. You are really scanning the frequency range of a part of the electromagnetic spectrum when you try to find a particular radio station.

Once the signal is received, it is amplified to strengthen and improve its quality and is then carried to another transducer that changes the electron energy back to its original form—acoustical energy. This is heard as sound from the speaker.

Through continued improvements in the radio of Marconi's era, it became possible to transmit and receive human speech. In America, Reginald Fessenden improved his equipment with the help of the National Electric Signaling Company, and on Christmas Eve, 1906, radio operators aboard ships along the coast of Massachusetts heard voices and music over the radio for the first time. World War I stimulated advances in radio communication for point-to-point transmission. It wasn't until efficient transmitters and electronic devices could function at higher power levels that broadcast transmission became commercially feasible.

The improvements of radio technology bring out the interesting relationship between pure scientific discovery and technological innovation. Early radio (1890-1906) could attribute much of its success to the pioneers in the theory of electricity. The study of electromagnetism yielded the basic concept of radio transmission. The radio was actually developed by people like Marconi and Branly, whose main contribution was the **coherer,** a moderately sensitive device to detect radio waves and alter them into a distinguishable message. It got its name because of the way the metallic filings in a glass bulb fused together, or cohered.

At times, the practical developments in radio technology helped explain problems in electrical theory that had baffled the scientists. Significant developments in radio receiver technology could be closely associated with (or responsible for) the formulation of many scientific theories prior to about 1950. Transmitter and receiver techniques are discussed in much more detail in Modules Six and Eight.

Let's focus our attention on methods of transducing acoustical energy into elec-

192 TECHNOLOGY-BASED ACOUSTICAL SYSTEMS

trical energy. Thomas A. Edison's microphone of decades ago has found different uses throughout its history. There are three transducing techniques commonly used by recording and broadcast industries today: dynamic, condenser, and ribbon (or velocity) microphones.

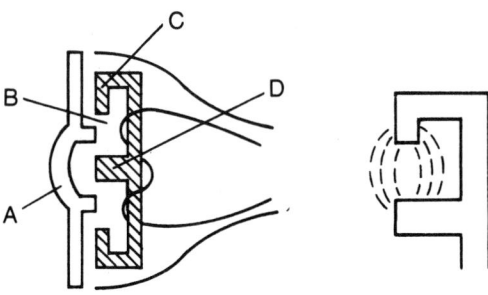

Figure 7.11

Schematic of a dynamic microphone

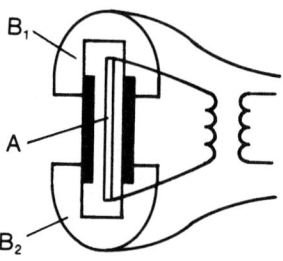

Figure 7.12

Schematic of a ribbon microphone

A **dynamic microphone** is a pressure-operated device. The change in pressure created by sound waves striking the diaphragm A (shown in Figure 7.11) cause it to vibrate in the gap B. As it vibrates, it creates a disturbance in the magnetic field (flux) between points C and D. C and D are parts of a soft iron yoke magnet. The disturbances caused in the field of flux by the vibrating diaphragm create an induced voltage corresponding to the original sound. This voltage is then amplified and fed to a speaker, transmitter, or recorder.

Another sound pressure-operated device is the **condenser microphone.** Constructed in a slightly different manner, the condenser device requires a power supply since it operates on the principles of electrostatics rather than the electromagnetic principles of the dynamic and ribbon-type devices. When sound pressure causes the diaphragm of a condenser device to vibrate, the vibrations condense and release a pressure-sensitive electrically charged plate, thereby transducing sound vibrations into electrical signals to be used by the system.

The ribbon-type device is a **velocity microphone.** A small ribbon of metal, A (shown in Figure 7.12), floats between two poles of a magnet, B_1 and B_2. The sound pressure creates a change in pressure in front of and behind the ribbon. This creates a different velocity in the air molecules that makes the ribbon vibrate, thus causing a voltage corresponding to the original sound to pass through the system.

The most obvious part of a sound system is the speaker. Unless we can receive the acoustical information from telephones, televisions, phonographs, or tape decks, we as communicators must rely on sensory receptors other than our ears. As the microphone converts acoustical energy into electrical energy, the speaker converts electrical energy into acoustical energy. This can be done by various types of loudspeakers.

The basic principle of the **dynamic loudspeaker** begins with the electric signal, which is carried to the speaker by wire (Figure 7.13a). The wire is wrapped around a permanent magnet mounted next to a diaphragm (made of metal or paper) with a cushion of air separating the two. As the electric current varies with the intensity of the encoded signal, it creates a variable magnetic field between the permanent magnet and the diaphragm. As the field varies, the diaphragm moves (vibrates), thus creating corresponding variations of acoustical energy—sound. A conical horn is generally placed around the vibrating diaphragm to improve the effect. The type of mounting that holds the diaphragm can determine the quality of sound reproduction. Dynamic loudspeakers use different types of diaphragm mountings including fixed points, resilient suspension, and floating mounts.

The two remaining types of loudspeakers, which are commonly used in combination with others for quality sound reproduction, are the crystal loudspeaker (Figure 7.13b) and the electrostatic loudspeaker (Figure 7.13c). A **crystal loudspeaker** is based on the piezoelectric effect of a crystal (quartz, Rochelle salt, or Seignette salt) that is securely mounted to a permanent housing. When the electric signal is transferred to the crystal, it causes variations in the thickness of the crystal. These variations or vibrations are transmitted to the loudspeaker diaphragm that creates the sound.

A high-frequency reproducing loudspeaker commonly used today is the **electrostatic loudspeaker** (Figure 7.13c). This speaker operates on the principle of attractive and repulsive forces of electric fields created by a voltage condenser. A series of small condenser plates arranged in front of and behind a diaphragm makes the diaphragm vibrate when voltage applied to the condensers is varied. The sound is then generated from the vibrating diaphragm, passes through holes in the condenser plates, and is emitted from the speaker body.

A speaker should reproduce a broad range of sound smoothly and uniformly. Ideally it should respond equally well to the deep bass of a tuba and the treble of a cymbal without coloring or altering the original sound. Variations in personal taste make it extremely difficult to judge how a speaker should sound. Variables such as speaker type and size, cabinet construction and materials, power output from the information source, and proper match of speaker characteristics to the power source are common areas of concern in speaker selection.

Significant advances in microphone and loudspeaker design, signal modulation techniques, automatic gain control mechanisms, and many others have been introduced by research laboratories throughout the world. One recent innovation that has offered significant advantages to established acoustical communication techniques is

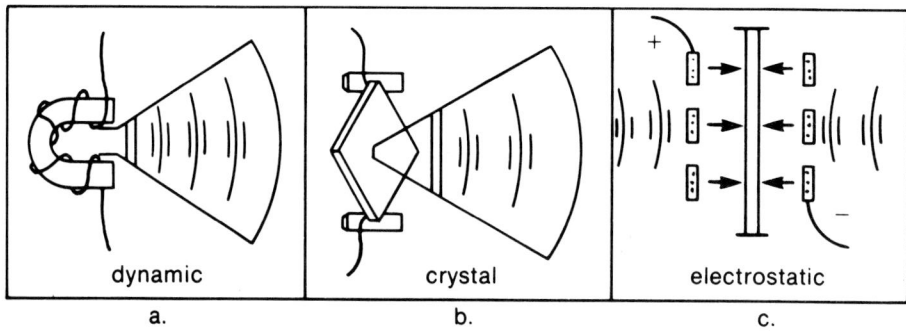

Figure 7.13

Loudspeakers and speaker dynamics

the maser. A **maser** is a device that can generate or amplify energy in manners distinctly different from a vacuum-tube amplifier. The maser operates in the microwave frequency range of the electromagnetic spectrum and offers more efficient signal-processing techniques. Due to the various applications of microwave transmission of acoustical information, and the infancy of maser devices, maser use in communications has been limited to aircraft and satellite situations.

The technical foundations of radio allowed video signals to be synchronized with radio or audio signals, making television possible. The audio portion of a television program is simply a frequency-modulated radio signal.

During the twenties, thirties, and forties, radio was a very powerful medium. With the age of public broadcasting that began in 1920 from station KDKA in Pittsburgh came a surge of stations, and also a crowding of the limited number of frequencies capable of transmitting voice communication. In America, radio stations have always been oriented toward the public, commercially sponsored, and directed toward the promotion of free speech. Broadcasting in most other countries is traditionally sponsored and controlled by the state or government. Generally, government involvement in broadcasting in America began with the Radio Act of 1927 at the request of the radio operators themselves. This act established what is now the Federal Communications Commission, which regulates and licenses stations to ensure technical quality.

LIGHT

Until this point we have discussed sound waves and electrical pulses as two distinct types of energy that are capable of transmitting and receiving acoustical information. Various techniques and devices have also been investigated that broaden the potential of acoustical communication. A third method of transmitting acoustical information by energy other than sound waves or electricity is light.

Light energy, useful for the transmission of acoustical information, is found on the electromagnetic spectrum at frequencies higher than microwaves. Originally, lasers were termed optical masers. The light energy of a laser can be used for communications because it is an orderly wave of one frequency called **coherent light.** Typical light sources produce waves of various frequencies that cancel or reinforce each other in random patterns. Typical light sources produce incoherent light.

General applications of laser beams result from various filtering methods that provide the qualities of coherency, directionality, frequency, and power. The primary advantage of laser communication is that it offers a new range of frequencies beyond the crowded low-frequency range. Also, the bandwidth of any particular message can be carried as only a small portion of the enormous area of coherent light. This opens up a totally new segment of the energy spectrum that can carry many more simultaneous messages than any others in previously exploited frequency ranges.

The reason the laser is included in this module will now become apparent. Proposed uses for laser communication center around its use as a carrier of telephone information and in space satellite systems. Both uses basically comprise the transmission of acoustical information, but lasers are also responsible for carrying other data.

Acoustical Information Storage and Retrieval

Mechanical Techniques

Long before anyone had ever heard of a radio, TV, or stereo, people enjoyed music. People loved music in the old days; pianos were as popular as the nickel beer. Even before that, it wasn't uncommon for a beau to present his true love with a curious little music box. Many of these small, wind-up devices played popular tunes and nursery rhymes to the delight of families in their parlors. The music box could be considered to be one of the first technical devices used to provide home entertainment as we know it today. (Of course things like the stereoscope and musical instruments were also present in the homes.)

A principle similar to the storage of musical acoustical information in music boxes had been used to store piano tunes on paper rolls. Instead of a raised surface on the roll representing a particular note, a square or round hole in the paper represented the information. By pumping the treadle under the keyboard, a bellows inside the piano created air pressure in lead tubes that were responsible for signaling to each hammer or note. (When a key on a piano is depressed, it causes a small wooden hammer to strike a tuned wire that vibrates to make the sound.) As the holes in the paper roll passed the ends of the lead tubes the built-up air was activated, thereby causing the appropriate hammer to strike the desired note. The faster one pumped, the faster the piano tune played—needless to say, the tempo of each piece changed with the mood of the "player."

Acoustical information is stored and retrieved differently today. **Stored** means the state of something (in this case acoustical information), which is deposited and kept for future use. **Retrieved** means to be restored to usefulness.

We can thank Emile Berliner for the shape our record collection is in today. Ten years after Thomas Edison patented the first phonograph (1877), Berliner introduced the gramophone, an invention that changed the storage surface from Edison's wax cylinder to a plastic disk.

Figure 7.14

Cut-away view of a late nineteenth century Swiss music box. A tune is played as the metal cylinder rotates against the tuned key pins. Bells and drums sometimes accompanied the metal pins.
Courtesy, Smithsonian Institution

Figure 7.15

An 1878 Edison Cylinder Recorder with the tinfoil partially recorded.
Courtesy, Smithsonian Institution

The technique of storing acoustical information on a disc in tiny wave undulations has remained a basic concept in information storage. Currently, there are three basic formats used to store information in such a mechanical or physical state. With this method one can see the waves of information in the record grooves, as opposed to magnetic-type storage, which we will discuss later.

The first, and oldest, disk format used to store information was called **monophonic**. A close look at the grooves in a monaural record shows tiny waves along the sides and a flat bottom. Each wave represents a frequency of sound. The original disk recording was made by a transducer similar to a diaphragm that changed sound vibrations into mechanical side-by-side vibrations, which were cut into the sides of a groove in a soft plastic or vinyl disk. A phonograph pick-up device can be used to retrieve the stored information from the record grooves. The pick-up device is in the tone arm of the record player; it is here that a needle or stylus is attached. The stylus tracks in the grooves of the storage disk. The mechanical vibrations of the needle caused by the grooves in the disk are changed into electrical pulses and transferred through the rest of the phonograph, eventually to be heard as sound.

Slightly more complex are the storage and retrieval techniques of **stereophonic recording**. Surprisingly—because we as humans naturally hear in stereophony—stereophonic recording didn't become practical until large-scale experiments were conducted in the early 1930s. The stereo groove is V-shaped at about 45° from the vertical on both sides (commonly referred to as the 45/45 disc recording method). When recording stereo information, the cutter head is suspended so that it can move up and down. It is controlled by two small rods attached to either side of the cutter. When information from one track (there are two tracks on stereo) is recorded, the respective rod vibrates the cutter head causing a hill-and-dale track to be cut on the inner groove wall. Information from the other track is cut into the opposite groove wall. Since information is usually cut simultaneously onto both walls of the groove, different frequency patterns are easily recognizable. Cross-talk between tracks sometimes occurs when the information of one side of the groove is picked up on the opposite track. This phenomenon is characteristic of a single-cutter head for stereophonic disk recordings.

Stereophonic retrieval of a disk recording is almost the reversal of the storage technique. In all cases a single stylus tracks the V groove. The material, shape, and operation of the stylus and stereo pick-up device that offer perfect reproduction are not universally known at this time. Hence, the many audio equipment corporations remain in constant competition for your consumer dollars.

The third, and as yet technically undetermined, format for disc recording is the reproduction of four distinct tracks of information, or **quadraphonic recording**. The product of research laboratories around the world, the development of quadraphonic sound systems has been heralded as the supreme achievement in engineering of the seventies. This is a promise that has yet to be proven, since the development is still in the primitive stages. The intent of quadraphonic sound is to simulate the sound in a concert hall or auditorium. Stereo reproduces sound from the front of a performance; quad attempts to reproduce sound from all directions. The term used to define this characteristic is **ambience**—reflected sound that reaches the listener's ears from all directions.

Nearly one half dozen companies are fighting for the, as yet, unresolved model quadraphonic system. Of these various approaches to the issue of storing and reproducing near-perfect sound, two basic methods exist.

1. **Matrix.** The matrix disk storage technique begins with four distinct channels of information from an original recording. The information is squeezed onto two channels and cut into a V groove similar to stereo. When reproduced, the information is retrieved from the two tracks and separated into the original four tracks of information. To avoid tremendous cross-talk, a logic circuit in the pick-up identifies the main channel and "favors" its signal. A problem arises when the main signal occurs at the same time but on different channels.
2. **Discrete.** The discrete disk storage technique inscribes a pair of signals on each wall of the V groove. Therefore, each of the four quadraphonic signals are discretely stored and retrieved. One pair of signals on one side of the groove is called a **base-band signal,** and it is recorded at normal audio frequencies. The other, recorded at very high frequencies, is called a **carrier-band.** The occurrence of two separate, yet simultaneous, signals is similar to the multiplexing of a telephone line carrying two conversations at the same time. By the action of a demodulator as part of the pick-up device, the signal bands are reprocessed as four separate channels of information.

Favorable and unfavorable characteristics of each method (matrix and discrete) exist. At this writing, at least one major consumer organization has identified the discrete methods of quadraphonic reproduction as being able to fulfill the promises made to audio buffs. Quadraphonic sound is a system of the future, but at present it may cost about twice as much as existing stereo systems.

The technical excellence of all three formats (mono, stereo, quad) of disk recordings and disk retrieval devices often centers on an established checklist of characteristics such as: noise, audio distortion, frequency range, balance, dynamic range, tracking, and on and on. It is difficult, at best, to compare one system against another according to any list of criteria. The international competition among manufacturers of audio disks and equipment rivals any competitive product in existence today. English, German, Spanish, and Japanese companies are on a par with, and often surpass, United States-based firms in terms of quality products.

Magnetic Techniques

One of the more versatile reproduction techniques and one which can be used by almost anyone, is magnetic recording. The idea of storage and retrieval of information using magnetic fields on physical material first was implemented with the wire recorder in 1899. A Danish experimenter named Valdemar Poulsen expanded his interest in some similar German developments of the time and succeeded in developing the first practical magnetic recorder using steel wire as the information storage element. The steel wire was capable of conducting and holding various charges, yet it was flexible enough to be wound around holding reels.

The most commonly used storage materials for magnetic recording today are ferris-oxide and chromium-dioxide plastic base tape, vinyl discs (similar to mechanical-type storage discs), and cards. By far the most popular and affordable magnetic storage material is the magnetic tape, particularly the cassette tape. Considering all audio tapes, the basic format is generally one of two major types.

1. **Full track or monaural**—on the typical 6mm tape the total magnetic surface is available to carry information. As we will see later, the recording/playback head corresponds to the appropriate tape format.
2. **Multitrack** (stereo, quad, and so forth)—the width of the track is generally smaller than full track when considering multitrack tape. Between each track is a guard band that prevents cross-talk from track to track. This also increases tape-head tracking accuracy. Some professional recording tapes can carry up to twenty-four tracks on 5cm tape but most multitrack users are limited to the 6mm tape.

One of the most fascinating processes of modern communication technology is magnetic recording. It seems that there are as many storage and retrieval devices as there are fish in the sea; however, the basic concepts of the magnetic recording process are universal. When an acoustical signal is transduced to electrical energy through a microphone, the process begins. The current is carried by conventional circuiting to a recording-head lamination, which is a minitransformer. Here the current is transformed into a magnetic force that flows through the pole pieces to the gap. The magnetic field, which has replaced the current flow, is called the magnetic **flux.** When the flow of flux reaches the pole of the head, it searches for a way to cross the gap. At this point the magnetic tape is in contact with the head and acts as a bridge across the gap. Since the flow of flux seeks the path of least resistance, it does not radiate through the air and jump the gap but follows the moving tape as a bridge. Since alternating current is used, the magnetic field is broken and reversed, causing patterns of flux corresponding to the original sound to be stored on the magnetic surface of the tape. For each track a separate lamination containing a similar head, one stacked on top of another, is used. Stereo recording is done by using separate microphone inputs to each of two recording-head laminations, simultaneously creating two distinct flows of flux onto a moving two-track tape.

To retrieve the stored information, the magnetized section of tape moves past the playback head, which produces a magnetic field in the coil. The coil then transforms the magnetic field into a current that corresponds to the original acoustical information. The current is amplified through the remaining part of the tape recorder and is eventually heard as sound.

The importance and complexity of acoustical communication have often been ignored. However, technological extensions of the human capacity to use acoustical information have played an important part in the development of modern commu-

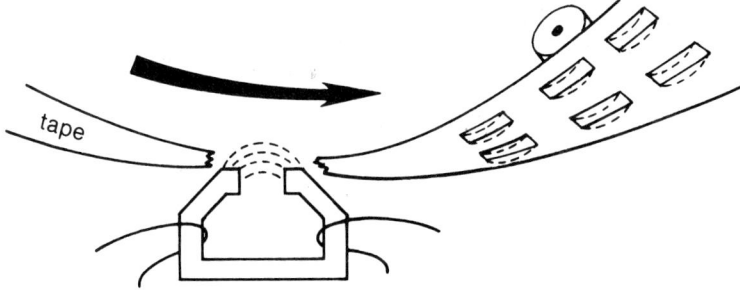

Figure 7.16

Magnetic tape record head lamination and flow of flux.

nication systems. Modern equipment and techniques of acoustical communication are the results of early experiments into the nature of sound and the development of transmission and reception techniques of acoustical information by energy sources other than sound.

Technical advances in transducers to convert energy from one form to another, in electric relays and insulators, along with conduction and radiation techniques, enabled acoustical information to travel over great distances with no (or little) time delay. The telephone and radio are common elements of communication technology found in many homes today. Acoustical storage techniques, such as disc and magnetic tape recording, have been simplified so that even a young child can use them.

All in all, the many systems used for acoustical communication have much in common. When one understands how acoustical systems work, it becomes much easier to use this technology to communicate more effectively. Each system exists for specific purposes; these can include information encoding, transmission, storage, reception, and decoding.

Concept Focuser

- **Acoustical information** is any type of information in the form of sound, both audible and inaudible to humans.
- **Sound** is created when there is a disturbance in any medium (solid, liquid, or gas) that possesses both **elasticity** and **mass.**
- Acoustical information can be **transmitted** by **acoustical energy** as well as by other **energy sources,** such as electricity and light.
- **Transducers** are devices that can convert one type of energy source into another. Microphones and loudspeakers are two basic examples of transducer action.
- Acoustical information can be **stored** (and retrieved) by **mechanical** and **magnetic** means using various **format** configurations such as monophonic, stereophonic, and quadraphonic.

Food for Thought

1. How do you account for the existence of sound beyond the range of human hearing?
2. What was the first major technological extension of the human capability to communicate with acoustical information that used electricity as an energy source? Explain your answer.
3. How does a diaphragm convert acoustical energy into electrical energy?
4. How does a loudspeaker convert electrical energy into acoustical energy?
5. What five basic technical systems are used to transmit acoustical information across long distances?
6. What are the basic differences between four-channel mechanical and four-channel magnetic information storage techniques?

EXPANDING EXPERIENCES

1. Research and report on the role of women in the telegraph and telephone industry.
2. Using an experimental approach, improve the efficiency of a string telephone.
3. Visit and observe a local telephone switching center.
4. Plot on a map nearby telephone trunk lines or microwave towers.
5. Design and construct a musical instrument.
6. Attend a concert to identify and report on the types of instruments, the location of microphones and speakers, and the general acoustics of the concert hall.
7. Obtain recordings of the same music on different disc and tape formats and test the frequency range of various reproducing systems.

 ## LOCATOR TOOLS

Chedd, Graham. *Sound, From Communication to Noise Pollution.* New York: Doubleday & Co., 1970.

Runstein, Robert E. *Modern Recording Techniques.* Indianapolis: Howard W. Sams & Co. and the Bobbs-Merrill Co., 1974.

White, Frederick A. *Our Acoustic Environment.* New York: John Wiley & Sons, 1975.

Bell Telephone Laboratories, Murray Hill, N.J. 07974.

U.S. Navy, Public Information.

Your local telephone company.

Module
EIGHT

TECHNOLOGY-BASED ELECTRONIC TELECOMMUNICATION SYSTEMS

THE BEGINNINGS OF ELECTRONIC TELECOMMUNICATIONS

Modern electronics arose from very crude beginnings to become one of humankind's major technological achievements. These technical achievements could not have happened without the hard work, inventiveness, and genius of the many pioneers of early radio. Module Eight will trace the developments of these early inventors and their inventions and culminate in the state of the art of electronic modes of telecommunication.

Early Radio Developments

The history of radio development is actually a history of the discovery and application of electronic phenomena by the early experimenters. The rate of advance of electronic technology was in direct proportion to the speed with which the new ideas were communicated to other inventors of the day (see Appendix B). Actual progress could be measured in terms of how fast an inventor could apply these new ideas to his own experiments.

As landline telegraph nets continued to spread across the world a new electronic phenomenon was discovered that was destined to accelerate even more the ability of humans to extend their telecommunication capabilities. Discovery of the phenomenon of electromagnetic waves led to the development of the wireless or radio communications.

Radio systems consist of two parts, the transmitter and the receiver. The **transmitter** sends out signals in the form of electromagnetic waves into the atmosphere.

The radio **receiver** picks up the electromagnetic waves sent out by the transmitter and converts them into the message that was originally transmitted.

It all started when Professor Fedderson discovered that electrical oscillations could be generated in a conductor and end in a spark when a charged condensor was allowed to discharge through the conductor. Nothing much happened to this new idea until H. R. Hertz was able to produce, detect, and measure the electromagnetic waves generated by the sparks from his induction coil.

It remained for Edouard Branly to invent the first radio receiver, or coherer, to detect Hertz's transmitted signals. The **coherer** detector was a small glass tube that contained metallic particles of iron. A primary battery was connected to the top and bottom of the column of particles. When a strong nearby electromagnetic wave was transmitted, it caused the metallic particles to stick together, or cohere, thereby reducing the internal resistance to the flow of current through the particles.

Through further experimentation with different materials, this crude radio detector was improved by the substitution of silver particles, which permitted more battery current to flow when the particles stuck together.

One problem remained before this could become an effective receiver. That was the question of how to unstick the particles when the transmitted electromagnetic signal stopped. The solution to this problem was a small electrically controlled hammer that struck the side of the small glass tube, thereby loosening the silver particles and decreasing the battery current flowing through them. This hammer became known as the tapper. The improved coherer detector became the world's first radio receiver and remained in use for a number of years.

With a method of generating, transmitting, and receiving electromagnetic waves, it became an easy matter for someone like Sir Oliver J. Lodge to figure how to send coded messages from one point to another by the interruption of the spark-generating process. However, it was Guglielmo Marconi who perfected this technique by adding a switch, or key, which allowed him to produce short or long bursts of electromagnetic waves in a coded form to the circuit. To improve the range of his transmitted signal, he used Stepanovitch Popoff's idea and attached one end of his induction coil to an elevated metallic object (for the antenna) and the other end to a metal plate, which he buried in the ground (for the ground). As in the coherer detector, a primary battery was used to power the transmitter. Thus was born the first practical radio transmitter, which was destined to remain in use for a long time.

As more and more technical refinements were made and the range and power of the radio transmitter was extended, it soon became the newest mode of electronic communication. The first distance record for radio transmission was 1 kilometer. With further improvements made in the height of the antenna and increases in power, the transmission path was increased from 1 to 14 kilometers. All that remained was to extend the range of the radio system from 14 kilometers to the distance across the ocean.

This was accomplished by yet another technological advance—the tuning coil.

Marconi's discovery of the tuning coil increased the range of his transmitter by increasing the resonance of the circuits.

In 1901, Marconi succeeded in sending the first radio signal across the Atlantic—linking Cornwall, England, with Signal Hill on the coast of Newfoundland. This successful transmission and reception of an electromagnetic signal proved the long-

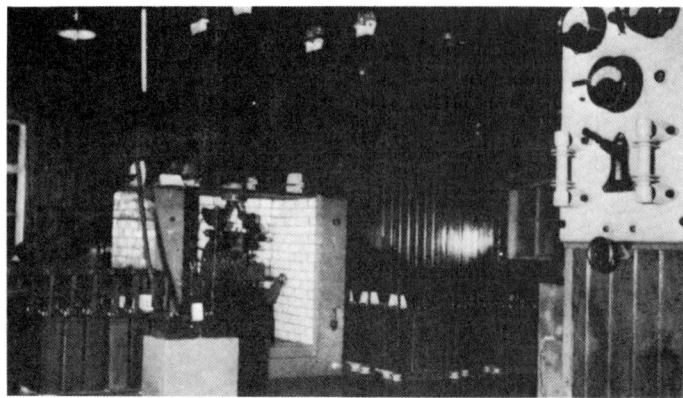

Figure 8.1a

Huge rotary spark discharge transmitter located inside Marconi's Poldhu Wireless Station in Cornwall, England. Note the large coil at top, left, center. Courtesy, The Marconi Company, Ltd.

Figure 8.1b

Fan-shaped antenna system at the Poldhu Wireless Station, which helped to send the first radio signal across the Atlantic to Newfoundland in 1901. Courtesy, The Marconi Company, Ltd.

Figure 8.1c

Sketch showing the use of a kite to achieve the greatest height possible at the Signal Hill Receiving Station, Newfoundland. The three dots of Morse code standing for the letter S were sent from England and received here. Courtesy, The Marconi Company, Ltd.

range point-to-point possibilities of this early mode of technology-based electronic communication.

Marconi was a very shrewd businessman and soon built a chain of transmitting stations to cover the well-traveled sea lanes. Because radio knew no frontiers or boundaries, it became of immediate interest to maritime companies. The first Marconi radio was installed on an American liner and had a Marconi radio operator aboard to work it. Soon, many countries installed radio sets in order to communicate with ships and with those land-based stations within range. The first airborne radio stations were installed in a Bleriot airplane and a French dirigible in 1910.

Early Regulatory Attempts

With the increased use of the wide-band spark sets, or rock-crushers as they were called, the necessity for control of this newest mode of electronic communication soon became apparent. Like some of the citizens band (CB) users of today, a few of the early radio operators monopolized the airways to the detriment of others. Often, important messages could not be received because of this human-created interference. Many people believe the 1503 people lost on the Titanic, when it struck an iceberg in 1912, could have been saved had good radio procedures been in existence then.

This disaster dramatically brought the problem to the attention of world leaders, nine of whom sent representatives to Berlin in 1913 to establish the first international rules for the regulation of radio transmissions. This was followed by other meetings in which many of the problems of this emerging technology were discussed. Such problems were the allocation of specific frequencies (or wavelengths) for certain types of radio services as well as establishment of technical standards. The representatives at these meetings agreed that future international conferences of this type were essential if all countries were to share the limited airways.

Amateur radio operations began in the United States with the organization of the Amateur Radio Relay League (ARRL) in 1914. This group of technical innovators performed many useful functions as well as experimenting and developing new technology in the higher frequencies—which later found its way into commercial and military equipment. This electronic experimentation continued in both the professional and amateur sectors and was published in the professional journals of the day.

Thermionic Emission

During his early experiments, Thomas Edison realized that he had to find many new methods for manufacturing lamps. These methods included the development of vacuum systems and glass envelopes. While experimenting with incandescent lamps, he found that the carbon filaments he was using broke rather easily. To strengthen the filament, he constructed a metal support within the evacuated lamp. For some unknown reason, he connected the metal support to the positive side of the battery and the filament to the negative side. To his surprise, he noted that a current was flowing through the evacuated lamp. As nothing much was known about the flow of electrons, this phenomenon went unnoticed for twenty-one years until J. A. Fleming learned the true significance of that accidental discovery.

Figure 8.2

Today's electric light bulb and yesterday's radio tube were both the result of Thomas Edison's early experiments with electricity. In 1879, Edison successfully produced the first usable electric bulb by passing current through a carbonized cotton thread. Except for the replacement of the thread with tungston wire, the basic principle of this early bulb is the same as used today.
Courtesy, Westinghouse Electric Corp.

While working with the Edison Electric Light Company in London, Fleming modified one of the lamps by placing a metal plate around the filament. When he applied an electromagnetic signal to the filament and connected a galvanometer to the metal plate, he noted that a strong current flowed through the lamp. Inasmuch as the current flowed only one way, from negative to positive, Fleming called his modified lamp a "valve," a term which is still used today to describe a vacuum tube in England.

Two years later, and independently of Fleming, Lee De Forest placed a wire grid between the filament and plate and noted that a weak signal, introduced at the grid, proportionately affected the current flow through the tube, and effectively amplified it. He called his tube an audion, and he is credited with inventing the triode amplifying tube.

The basic principle behind these developments is the boiling off of electrons on the cathode and their attraction to the plate. This is accomplished by coating the cathode with a rare earth material that is rich in electrons. When a heat source is applied to the cathode, electrons are released into a sort of space charge. If a positive charge is placed on the plate, then a current flows through the tube. This driving off of electrons by a heat source is called **thermionic emission**.

With the combined discoveries of Edison, Fleming, and De Forest, technology-based modes of electronic telecommunication were advanced more than in any previous period. Soon, millions of vacuum tubes were produced and used in all types of different configurations. Tube technology progressed from the diode to the triode, the tetrode, and the pentode. Eventually, certain specialized tubes had as many as twenty elements all enclosed in a single glass or metal envelope. There were more than 1500 different types of vacuum tubes developed for as many different types of applications. Today, semi-conductor technology has made most of them obsolete.

Electronic Circuits

There are three basic types of electronic circuits: rectifiers, amplifiers, and oscillators. Any combination of these circuits will produce an infinite number of different functions or system possibilities at any frequency. Each of these electronic circuits is made up of circuit elements, such as capacitors (C), resistors (R), conductors, coils (L), switches (SW), crystals (XTALS), tubes and semiconductors.

The three basic circuits may be recognized by their electrical qualities.

The **rectifier**, used in power circuits or as a detector in radio circuits, changes an incoming signal to a fluctuating signal of the opposite polarity.

The **amplifier** circuit takes a very small voltage or incoming electromagnetic signal and increases it to the point that it can be heard, seen, or otherwise used.

The **oscillator** generates a steady, predetermined frequency of electromagnetic energy to be used in a variety of applications. The output frequency of the oscillator can be changed by merely changing the values of the capacitor and coil mentioned above.

When we connect electronic equipment to a household or repair-shop electrical outlet, that outlet normally delivers an average of 120 volts of alternating current (a.c.). Unfortunately, this is not always the type of voltage needed to operate semiconductor circuits. Therefore, it must be transformed into filtered direct current (d.c.) of the proper voltage.

The graphic symbol for the diode, whether it be a vacuum tube, metallic rectifier, or a semiconductor, is:

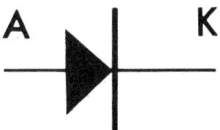

The letter A is the positive anode; the letter K is the negative cathode. Electron flow through a diode is always from K to A. The cathode is generally marked with a wide strip or dot. It may be pointed to by an arrowhead, or it may be designated by the threaded end of the diode.

Diode rectifiers as well as other types of semiconductors are identified by numbers such as 1N339. Semiconductor manuals present a complete listing of all types of solid-state devices, as well as their breakdown voltages and other relevant information.

Modern Radio Receivers

The early coherer detectors had many faults. They were too wide-banded, that is, they would receive all strong signals together but would not react to weaker ones. In the early 1900s, experiments were being conducted with many different types of crystals that seemed to have rectifying properties. Among the lead-salt type was the galena crystal, which proved to be suitable for the new crystal-set. This newest advance in radio technology soon made the early coherer detector obsolete.

Crystal Set

A crystal set consists of an antenna, a tuned circuit (L_2 & C_1) a galena crystal detector (D_1), a wire whisker, and a pair of earphones. The antenna picks up an electromagnetic (RF) signal from the air, and feeds it to the tuning circuit. The crystal, which functions as a detector, allows the antenna currents to flow on every positive half cycle of the incoming signal, but blocks the negative half cycle from going through the circuit. The positive half cycle of the incoming signal passes through the detector and the wire whisker, which makes contact with the crystal and passes the signal to the earphones where it is converted to sound energy.

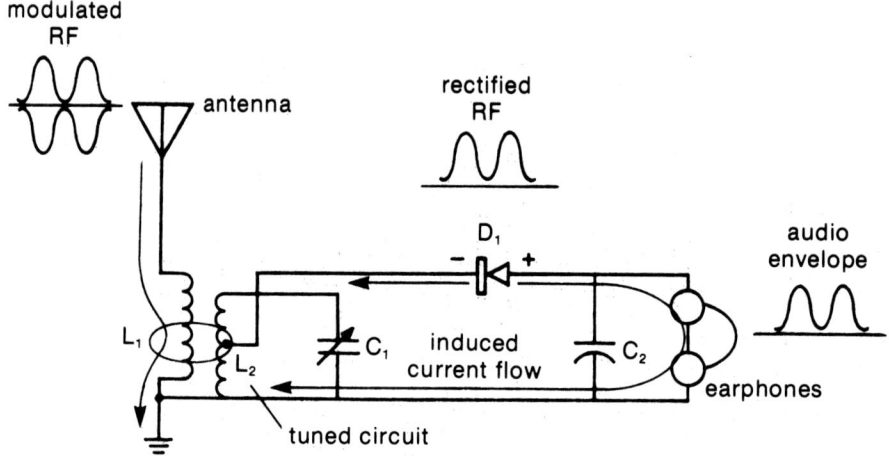

Figure 8.3

Schematic of a simple crystal set receiver showing how the crystal detector D1 rectifies the incoming radio frequency wave. The earphones can only follow the audio envelope and reproduce that sound.

Although it functioned much better than the tricky coherer detector, the sensitivity or tuning ability of the crystal set was poor and it could not be used very far from the transmitting station. Today, these sets are museum pieces and have no practical value.

Tuned Frequency Receivers

By 1920, crystal sets were being replaced by another technological advance. This was the **tuned frequency receiver** (TFR), which used the new vacuum tubes and was, therefore, more sensitive and selective to incoming signals. **Sensitivity** is the ability of a receiver to pick up weak signals, while **selectivity** is the ability to select desired signals or to reject undesired ones.

In the TFR set, the incoming electromagnetic signal was amplified and detected with only the positive half cycle amplified and passing to the earphones for conversion to sound energy. Although effective, it was destined to be replaced by an entirely new technical concept, the superheterodyne receiver.

Superheterodyne Receivers

The most common type of modern receiver used throughout the world is the superheterodyne, which was developed by Major Edwin A. Armstrong. In this receiver, the electromagnetic signal is received in the antenna circuit and amplified in the radio frequency (RF) amplifier stage. A local oscillator produces a known frequency, which is mixed with the incoming signal and produces a resultant intermediate frequency (IF) signal. The IF signal is amplified, detected and the resultant audio frequency (AF) is then amplified and fed to the earphones. If enough stages of audio amplification are added, then the earphones can be replaced with a loudspeaker. A well-designed superheterodyne receiver has better sensitivity and selectivity qualities than the TFR.

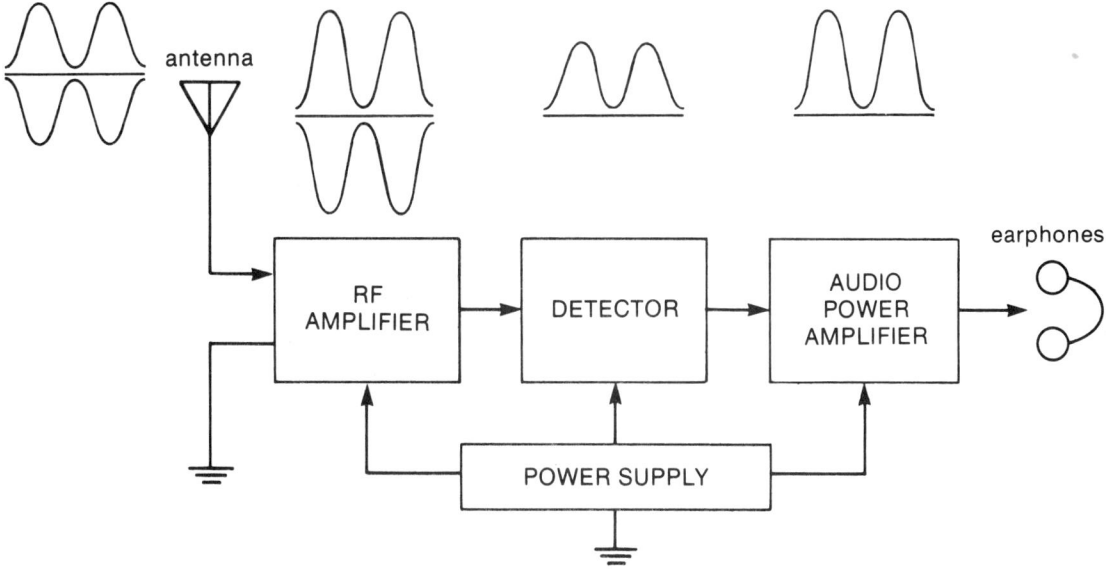

Figure 8.4

Block diagram of a tuned frequency receiver (TFR) showing the amplication of the incoming radio frequency signal, the detection function, and the audio amplification of the resultant signal.

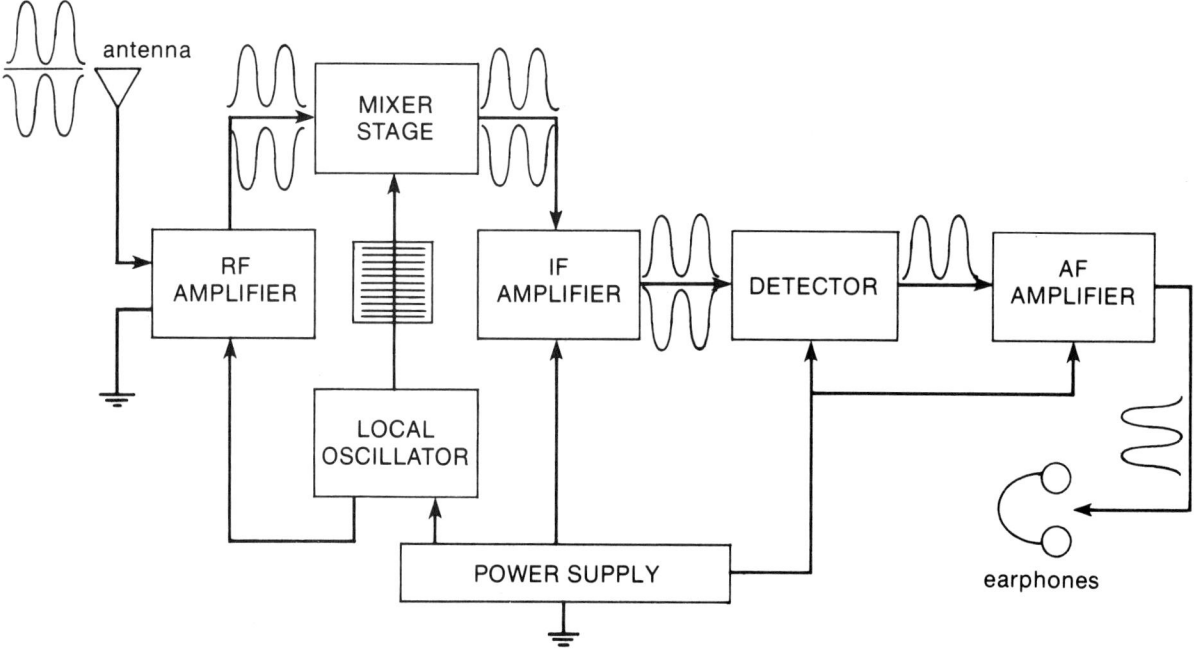

Figure 8.5

Block diagram of a superheterodyne receiver showing the effect each stage has upon the incoming radio signal.

Modern Radio Transmitters

As technology continued to advance, the early wide-band spark transmitters soon proved to be ineffective. In 1930, attempts to outlaw spark sets met with only marginal success. Therefore, the federal government permitted a few low-powered spark sets to remain on some ships; however, they succeeded in outlawing the production of any new spark sets. This ended the spark transmitter as a mode of communication and relegated it to the museum.

The simplest type of a modern radio transmitter as used in radiotelegraphy consists of an oscillator, which generates a radio frequency that is fed out to the antenna. The oscillator is controlled by a key, which produces dots and dashes. Using Morse code, a message can be transmitted to a distant receiving station. To convert this system to radiotelephony, we merely replace the key with a microphone and add a modulator stage, to produce an amplitude modulated (AM) signal. Changing the values of Figure 8.7 basic circuit elements and rearranging them in a different pattern can produce Frequency Modulation (FM), Single Side Band (SSB), or Pulse Code Modulation (PCM) transmitters.

It is difficult to tell exactly when broadcast radio branched away from point-to-point telecommunications. Both use the same type of equipment and serve the same people, but they do it in different ways. Broadcast radio became the entertainment

THE BEGINNINGS OF ELECTRONIC TELECOMMUNICATIONS 211

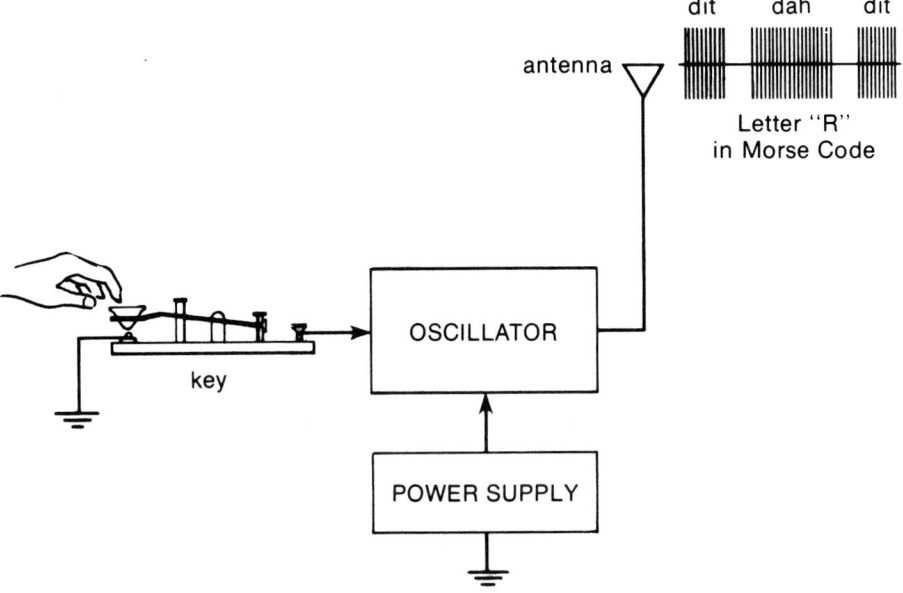

Figure 8.6

A simple block diagram of a radio-telegraph CW transmitter circuit. This circuit operates only when the key makes contact to complete the circuit.

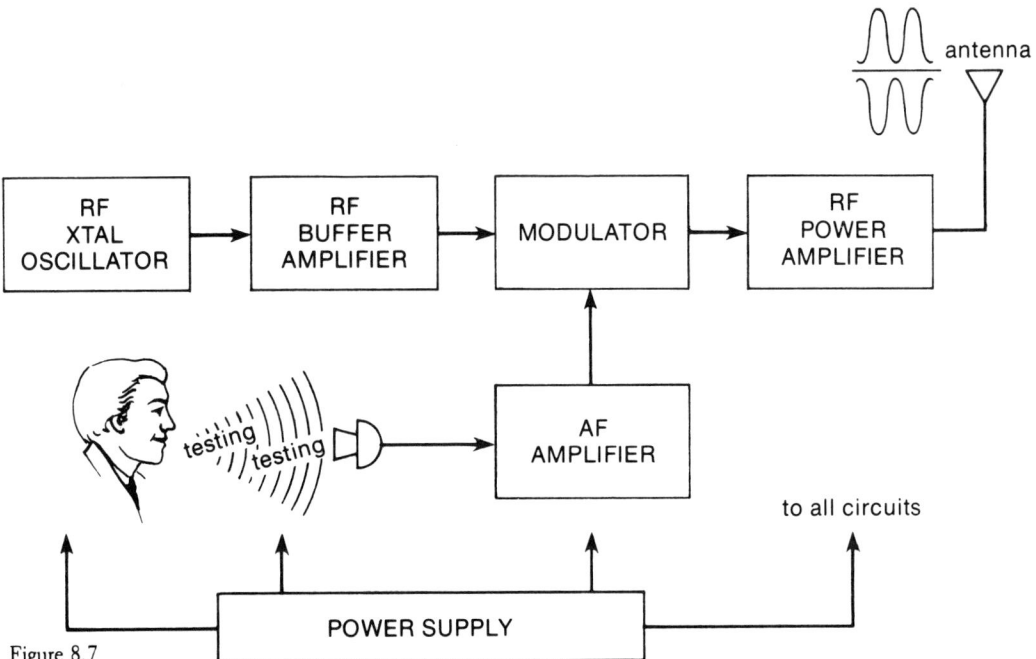

Figure 8.7

Block diagram of a radio-telephone telecommunication circuit which converts the voice frequency into electrical impulses that modulate the output of the radio frequency crystal oscillator; thereby transmitting the "intelligence" or message through the air to a receiving station.

medium, while point-to-point communications continued to expand and serve the telecommunication needs of people.

In 1920 effective broadcasting of entertainment became a reality in the United States, Germany, England, and the Soviet Union. The first radio broadcast in the United States occurred in Pittsburgh, Pennsylvania, when station KDKA came on the air for the first time. It has been on the air ever since. By 1922 there were about 400 licensed broadcast transmitters in the United States. By 1927, this figure had increased to well over 700. The National Broadcasting Company (NBC) was formed in 1926, followed by the Columbia Broadcasting Company (CBS) one year later. The old "Blue Network" of NBC became the American Broadcasting Company in 1943.

Anticipating the growth of its biggest competitor, the American Telephone and Telegraph Company extended its landline facilities in 1934 to take care of the expanding landline requirements of broadcast radio.

By 1938, radio broadcast was commonplace and occurred throughout the world. It has continued to grow at a rapid pace and will be around for a long time as one of the world's principal media for entertainment.

Television

Television may be described as the instantaneous reproduction, by electronic means, of distant scenes for visual observation. This involves subdividing a scene into a number of picture elements, transmitting them to a distant point, and reconstructing them into the original scene. This technique was first used by P. G. Nipkow and is still valid today.

Nipkow developed the first mechanical scanning system to transmit pictures. Basically, he made use of a pair of synchronized revolving discs that had a series of equal-sized holes punched in a spiral pattern. At the transmitter end, the picture was projected on the scanning disc image area, which revolved in front of a photoelectric cell. As the holes traced out a series of horizontal picture elements at sixteen times per second, the current through the photoelectric cell fluctuated accordingly. Inasmuch as the photoelectric cell at the receiving end was connected in series with the transmitting cell, it reproduced the same fluctuations and, when viewed through the receiver scanning disc, appeared as a coarse-grained reproduction of the original picture. Experimentation with size, number of holes, spiral patterns, and disc speed improved the picture quality immensely.

Human vision is slow to react to light stimuli and, therefore, sees light impulses at less than 1/10 of a second rate, as a continuous picture. This is called the **stroboscopic effect**, or retention of vision, and is used extensively in cinematography and television.

Nipkow's basic mechanical system was improved by John Logie Baird in 1923 but was later discarded in favor of the newly devised and simpler electronic scanning system. V. K. Zworykin developed the iconoscope (camera tube), which was improved many years later by Isaac Shoenberg. The early cathode-ray tube (CRT) of Carl Ferdinand Braun became the principal method of displaying the recombined picture elements. Thus, modern television became technically feasible, but it remained in the laboratory until after World War II. Following the war, television emerged from

Figure 8.8a

Early Pilot Television Set using a 6.62-cm CRT.
Courtesy, Florida State University

Figure 8.8b

Top view of the Pilot television set with the cover removed. The twin lead wire over the 6.62-cm CRT is the antenna lead-out. Note the larger tubes at the bottom of the picture and the smaller tubes at the top. This represents technology in that the smaller glass tubes soon replaced the functions of the larger ones with the exception of the power circuits. The tuning condensor located below the support bracket (top, right) is typical of the coil-condensor tuning system used in the earlier sets.
Courtesy, Florida State University

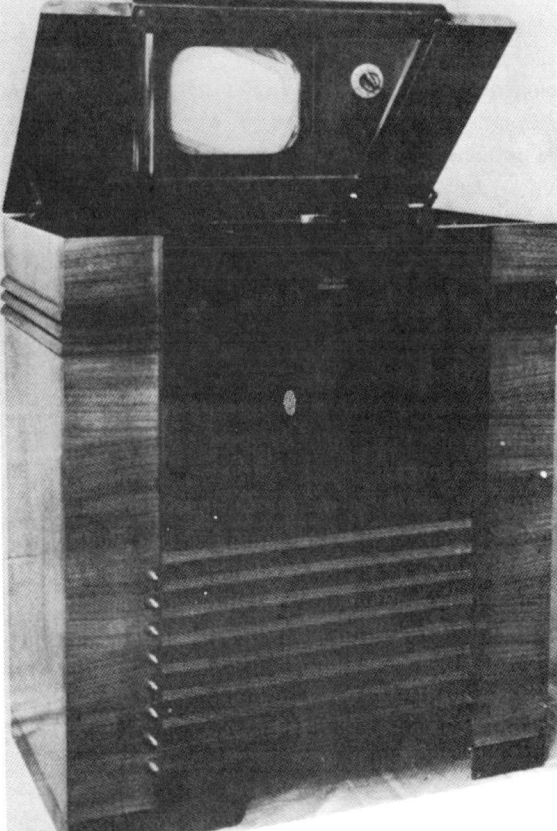

Figure 8.8c

The first "big" screen television set was manufactured by Radio Corporation of America in 1939. It used a 31-cm TV tube and had a three-band, all-wave radio built in as part of the set. It used 36 vacuum tubes and two kinescope tubes to produce an indirect image on the viewing screen. The set sold for $600.00.
Courtesy, RCA Corporation

the laboratories to become a new technology-based electronic telecommunication system.

Regular black and white telecasts in the United States began in 1950 with 105 licensed stations located in thirty-eight states. This made television available to half the population in the United States, when TV started to rival broadcast radio as the most important means of mass communication and entertainment.

The development of color television and the many new types of color video tape recording systems represented major technological breakthroughs in the period 1950–1960. Technical improvements included the zoom lens and instant video playback capability now used during major sporting and news events.

Following the earlier pattern of broadcast radio, television is financed by commercial advertisers who sponsor the many programs telecast today. In many other countries, television is government operated and controlled, as are their radio stations.

Radar

Some of the periods of rapid advancement in technology-based electronic telecommunication systems can be directly attributed to the needs of war. These advances were later modified for use during peacetime. Radar is an excellent example of this. Early radar experiments conducted by the Germans in 1934 led to the development of the first public video telephone service between Berlin and Leipzig in 1936.

The impending war in Europe rapidly changed the world's technical development priorities. In telecommunications, more powerful radio transmitters and more sensitive receivers were required. Radar research was intensified by Germany and Great Britain. When a team of British scientists successively tracked an aircraft up to 120 kilometers away using radar, it suddenly became a top secret project.

The word radar is a compounding of the first letters in the phrase Radio Detection And Ranging.

Basically radar works by the transmission of timed pulses of high-powered electromagnetic waves of short duration; time is allowed between the pulses for these electromagnetic waves to reflect back from an object, and the received echo is shown on the face of a CRT. This technique provides distance and direction information for any object detected in a circular airspace of 300 kilometers. Using radar to determine the distance of an object is something like standing in the center of a long canyon and shouting for a half second and then listening for the return echo before shouting again. If you were to calculate the amount of time it took the echo to return and divide it by two, you would know the distance to the side and end of the canyon to within a few meters.

Radar functions just as well in the dark or on rainy and foggy days as it does in daylight. However, it can play strange tricks on an operator when a temperature inversion occurs or when a strong source of radio interference is received. Today, both ground and airborne radar work around the clock tracking aircraft (air traffic control) and spacecraft in collision avoidance systems, as well as detecting severe atmospheric disturbances and storms for the National Weather Service.

Radio Astronomy

The Crab Nebula, part of the Milky Way, exploded in A.D. 1054 and is still expanding. Although over 4000 light years away from the earth, it is one of the strongest sources of electromagnetic radiation ever received from outer space. Other less active "radio stars" are the constellation Cassiopeia, Cygnus, the Great Spiral, Venus, and the sun.

Radio astronomy is a relatively new mode of passive electronic telecommunication, that is, a one-way communication system designed to receive faint signals from deep space. In 1933 Karl Guthe Jansky accidentally discovered that the huge clouds of hydrogen in our galaxy emitted radio signals on 1420.40 MHz. On the basis of this discovery the 1959 Geneva Conference of the International Telecommunications Union finally allocated the 1400–1427 megahertz radio band for exclusive use of radio astronomy.

Figure 8.9

Photograph of the radio telescope at Arecibo, Puerto Rico. The feed mechanism (top center) is shown positioned at the focal point of the giant reflective dish built into the ground. The support structure and feed mechanism weigh over 495 metric tons. The feed mechanism is 30 meters long and must be taken down during hurricane weather.
Courtesy, International Telecommunications Union

It is believed that these radio signals are caused by a reversal in the electron spin of the hydrogen atom. Although this event occurs only once in every 11,000,000 years per atom, when we consider the number of atoms in these huge hydrogen clouds, it is mathematically conceivable that the number of reversals that could occur in our galaxy is sufficient to be detected by supersensitive radio receivers on earth. Due to the Doppler effect, even small variations of the frequency can be detected, and can thus provide some indication to radio astronomers as to how far and in what direction the hydrogen clouds are moving with respect to our solar system.

Giant radio telescopes are located in Green Bank, West Virginia; Lima, Peru; Boulder, Colorado; Arecibo, Puerto Rico; New South Wales, Australia; Manchester, England; and the Crimea, Russia.

It is believed that if there are other intelligent beings in the universe, strategically located radio telescopes will let people receive the most important radio message ever sent.

Modern Advances in Telecommunication Systems

In the air, on land, on and beneath the sea, point-to-point telecommunications services have become an essential part of our environment. Telecommunication refers to the transmission, emission, or reception of information, largely by electrical, electronic, or electromagnetic modes. Thanks to the continued search for new and different types of technology-based electronic modes of communications, many new telecommunications systems have been devised.

Microwave Transmission

One such system is microwave transmission. Microwave transmission was developed in the 1940s and was first used in support of antiaircraft radar installations during World War II. It proved to be a highly reliable communication system because the microwaves could be focused into narrow beams of electromagnetic waves and used very little transmitter power.

Masers

It was not until the invention of masers that practical low-noise, solid-state microwave amplifiers could be developed for point-to-point microwave communications. Maser is an acronym for **M**icrowave **A**mplification by **S**timulated **E**mission of **R**adiation. It is excited into operation by incoming microwaves of the very highest of frequencies. The maser has the ability to amplify a very weak, short radio signal and reproduce it with a high degree of fidelity, yet not introduce any background noise in the process. As a dividend, this wide-band system permits the transmission of several thousand simultaneous voice communications. Because of these technical advantages, microwave links soon spread across the United States with line-of-sight towers located every 20 to 30 miles depending on the terrain.

Figure 8.10

Carrying the bulk of cross-country communications channels are these high performance microwave antennas (left top & bottom) installed on towers 140 meters tall and located about 30 kilometers apart, depending on the elevation of the terrain. Each "dish" is a parabolic reflector with a fiberglass protective cover. The two stick-type antennas (top of picture) are part of the Improved Mobile Telephone System (IMTS) available in many areas of the country.
Courtesy, Central Telephone Company of Florida

Forward-Scatter Systems

Another telecommunication development makes use of the ionosphere region, located between 100 and 300 kilometers above the surface of the earth. By bouncing powerful electromagnetic signals off the ionosphere, reliable long-range telecommunication services can be maintained. These large installations are called tropo-scatter or forward-scatter systems. There are essentially brute-force methods of transmitting tremendous amounts of signal power to the ionosphere and receiving the scatter from the bottom layer at a distant location.

Pulse Code Modulation

With the continuing growth of these new types of telecommunication systems, it soon became necessary to seek other methods of getting more use out of each channel. From the research laboratories came the Pulse Code Modulation (PCM) and time-division multiplex techniques, which helped expand the capability of existing systems.

PCM, an important concept in data communication and processing, is a type of time-sharing system based on the binary system. In this system, speech is changed into the binary code, transmitted over telephone networks, and decoded at the other end. This permits many more messages to flow during any given transmission time, while reducing background noises or interference.

Figure 8.11

Research scientist is shown adjusting the gas flow into a high-powered gas laser used for telecommunications research. The laser, which uses mixed helium, carbon dioxide, and nitrogen gasses, produces continuous outputs of high power over long periods of time without shutting down for repairs.
Courtesy, Bell Laboratories

The Time Assignment Speech Interpolation (TASI) technique is another method of time sharing of a telecommunication channel. Research shows that a person in a normal telephone conversation actually uses only about 40 percent of the total calling time and is silent about 60 percent of the time. The TASI system takes advantage of this very human characteristic, and with sophisticated electronic sampling and switching techniques, expands the usefulness of the channels by utilizing the 60 percent silent period for other conversations.

Lasers

Another new technique for increasing the number of communications channels led to the development of the laser. Lasers have opened up the limited electromagnetic spectrum for point-to-point communication by being able to carry a very large part of individual telecommunications channels at the same time. It has the theoretical ability to carry all of the information presently carried by telephone landlines in the world today.

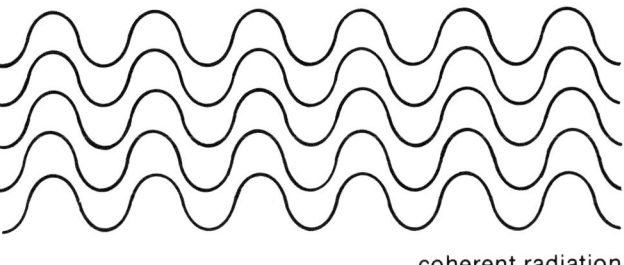
coherent radiation

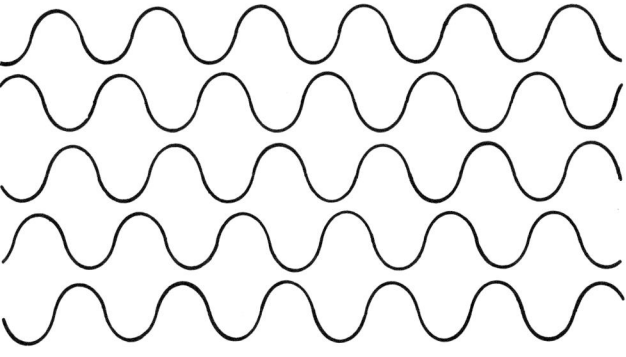
incoherent radiation

Figure 8.12

Sketch of coherent lightwave radiation versus incoherent lightwave radiation. The laser produces coherent light, whereas the ordinary electric light bulb produces incoherent light.

The word **laser** is an abbreviation for **L**ight **A**mplification by **S**timulated **E**mission of **R**adiation. It produces a narrow beam of monochromatic, coherent light —that is, all of the light waves produced are in the same order and have a single, closely defined wavelength. This differs from the common electric light bulb, which radiates in all directions on many different frequencies at the same time. Lasers differ from masers primarily in the way they are energized into operation and their outputs. Lasers amplify visible light; whereas the maser amplifies microwaves at much higher frequencies than was ever before possible.

The laser beam can be optically modulated by telephone, radio, or television signals and demodulated at the distant end. Although it can be interrupted by fog, clouds, or rain, the perfect vacuum of space would permit man to communicate for astronomical distances. For example, a laser beam projected from the earth could be detected as far as 100 light years away. Lasers are destined to become one of the most important electronic modes of telecommunication.

Space Communications

When the USSR launched Sputnik 1 on October 4, 1957, it immediately began sending out bleeps as it circled the world. On that day space communications was born.

Space communications is divided into the four separate functions of tracking, telemetry, command, and control. Each of these functions is combined into networks as shown in Figure 8.13 A, B, C, and D. The tracking function provides information on the exact location of a satellite, manned rocket, or deep space probe at any point in time.

Telemetry sends back radio signals of measurements and data to a central receiving station on earth. The information-bearing signal must be sensed, recorded, encoded, transmitted, received, decoded, and the information presented on some type of read-out device.

Control implies the ability of a ground station to direct a spacecraft to any point in space that it desires in order to successfully complete the planned mission.

Command means the transmission of a coded radio signal from a ground station to the spacecraft that instructs the spacecraft to start or stop data transmission, engines, or cameras.

Communication Satellites

Communication satellites fall into two general classes: the passive satellite which reflects signals beamed to it, and the active satellite, which receives a signal on one frequency and retransmits it on a different frequency. Echo 1, a 30-meter diameter aluminum cloth sphere launched in 1960, is a passive communications satellite. Telstar 1, launched in 1962, was the first active American communications satellite. Within hours of launch, live television, telephone conversations, and telephoto transmissions were beamed across the Atlantic and received in France. Other active synchronous satellites positioned 42,000 kilometers above the earth now extend

MODERN ADVANCES IN TELECOMMUNICATION SYSTEMS 221

NASA'S WORLDWIDE COMMUNICATIONS NETWORK FOR PROJECT APOLLO

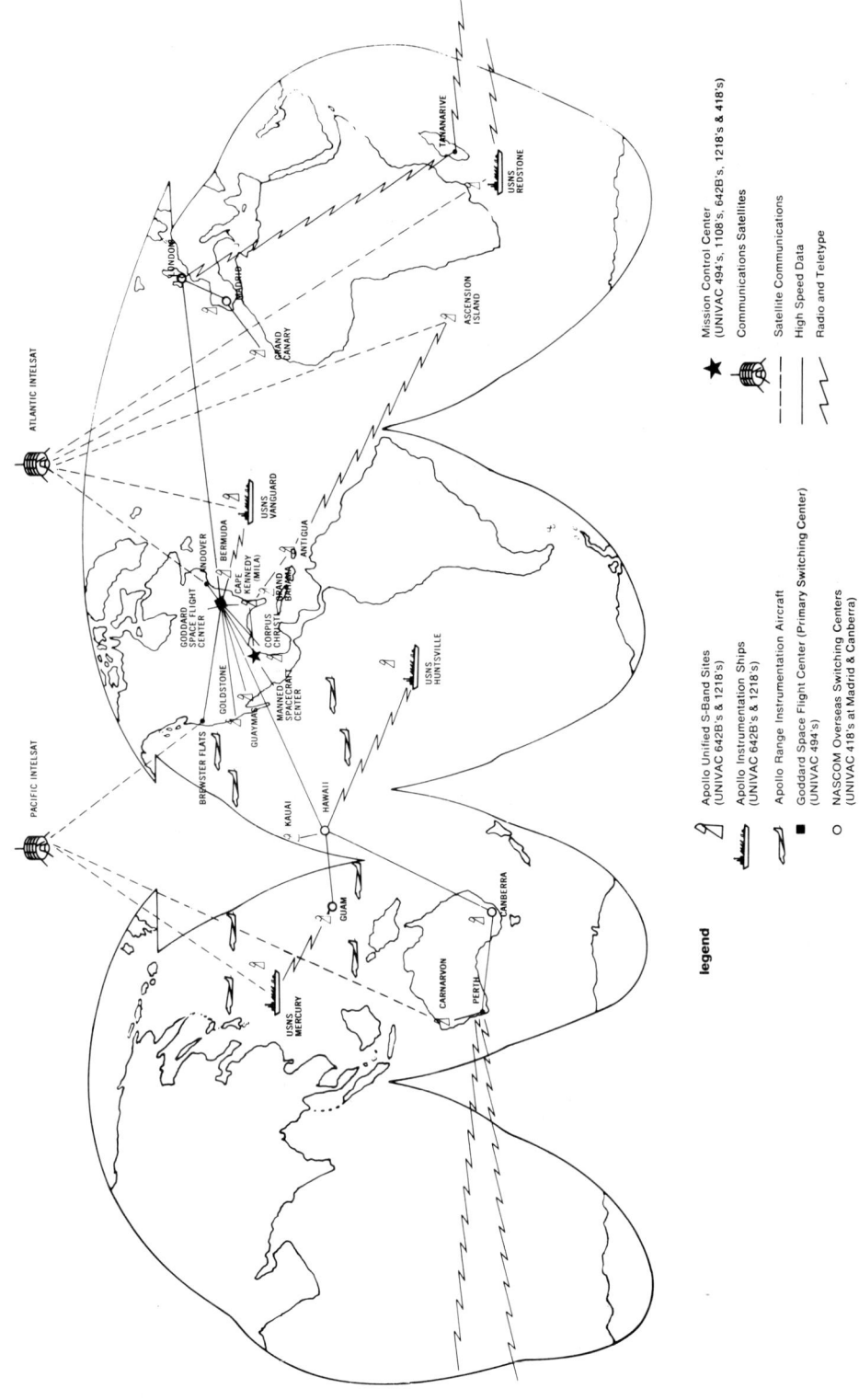

Figure 8.13a

Worldwide NASA Telecommunications Network for Project Apollo, Space Shuttle, and later deep space missions.
Courtesy, NASA

Figure 8.13b

As noted on the NASCOM chart, the USNS *Vanguard* is located in the Atlantic recovery area between Antigua and the Canary Islands in the event of a loss of communications in that area. Other instrumented ships are located in the Pacific Ocean to provide vital data on a spacecraft's location when it is out of range of the ground stations. The ship is leaving its dock at Cape Canaveral, Florida.
Courtesy, U.S. Air Force

Figure 8.13c

A close-up of the huge tracking antennas aboard the USNS *Vanguard*.
Courtesy, U.S. Air Force

Figure 8.13d

Also shown on the NASCOM chart are airborne radar and communications aircraft flying over the Atlantic and Pacific Oceans. This is one of the Range Instrumentated Aircraft that track spacecraft in Earth-parking orbits or just after a spacecraft re-enters the Earth's atmosphere. The aircraft passes its data back to the Manned Space Flight Center in Houston, Texas, for further analysis.
Courtesy, U.S. Air Force

MODERN ADVANCES IN TELECOMMUNICATION SYSTEMS 223

Figure 8.14

The TELSTAR II Communications Satellite. Built by Bell Laboratories, the satellite weighs 175 pounds and has a diameter of 34½ inches. There are 3600 solar cells on its surface. The two rows of microwave antennas around the center receive signals sent up to the satellite and relay them back to earth. On the panel at left center, just below the microwave antennas, is a radiation measuring device. An electron detector, it measures electrons in the range of 750,000 to 2 million electron volts. Telstar II was launched from Cape Canaveral by the National Aeronautics and Space Administration for the American Telephone and Telegraph Company. All tracking and launching expenses, including the cost of the DELTA launch vehicle, Courtesy, AT&T

humankind's telecommunications capability around the world. Such advanced electronic modes of space communications as developed by NASA have stimulated the development of many new technologies, such as the laboratory "growth" of semiconductor materials.

Basic Elements of Electronic Telecommunication Systems

Semiconductors

The simplest type of semiconductor is the *diode*. One of the most widely used diodes is the silicon rectifier, which has a wide range of current carrying capabilities. The tunnel diode is used for amplification, switching, and pulse generation. When a second junction is added to a semiconductor diode, then a basic transistor is formed that can provide power or voltage amplification in circuits. In addition, it can be used for a wide variety of control functions such as amplification, oscillation, and frequency conversion. MOS (metal-oxide-semiconductor) field-effect transistors have metal control electrodes to modulate the conductivity of the device. They are especially suited for voltage amplifiers in all types of electronic circuits.

Technical details on the less familiar types of semiconductors may be found in the many semiconductor manuals on the market today.

The semiconductor is a solid-state element that controls the flow of electrons in a circuit. Most semiconductors are neither good conductors nor good insulators. The ability of semiconductors to conduct electricity depends on the number of electrons and holes it contains. To understand how the electrons and holes flow in a semiconductor, it is necessary to review the theory of the atom.

Review of Semiconductor Physics

It is believed that all matter is composed of three basic building blocks: electrons, protons, and neutrons. Electrons have a negative (−) electrical charge, protons have a positive (+) electrical charge, and neutrons have no electrical charge at all. Protons and neutrons bind together in a tight compact mass called the nucleus. Electrons orbit around the nucleus, much as the earth and plants orbit about the sun. All of these combine together to form an atom of a material.

An atom is considered to be the smallest particle of an element that can exist and still retain all the properties of the element. The number of protons, neutrons, and electrons in an atom determine its physical and chemical properties. Hydrogen, for example, is the lightest element and consists of a nucleus containing one proton and one orbiting electron. Carbon has six protons, six neutrons, and six orbital electrons. The heavier the element, the more protons, neutrons, and electrons it has.

Normally, each atom has an equal number of protons and electrons. Since the electrical charges on protons and electrons are opposite, they balance each other and the atom is said to be electrically neutral. Under certain conditions, electrons of some materials can be made to leave their orbits and travel to other atoms where they in

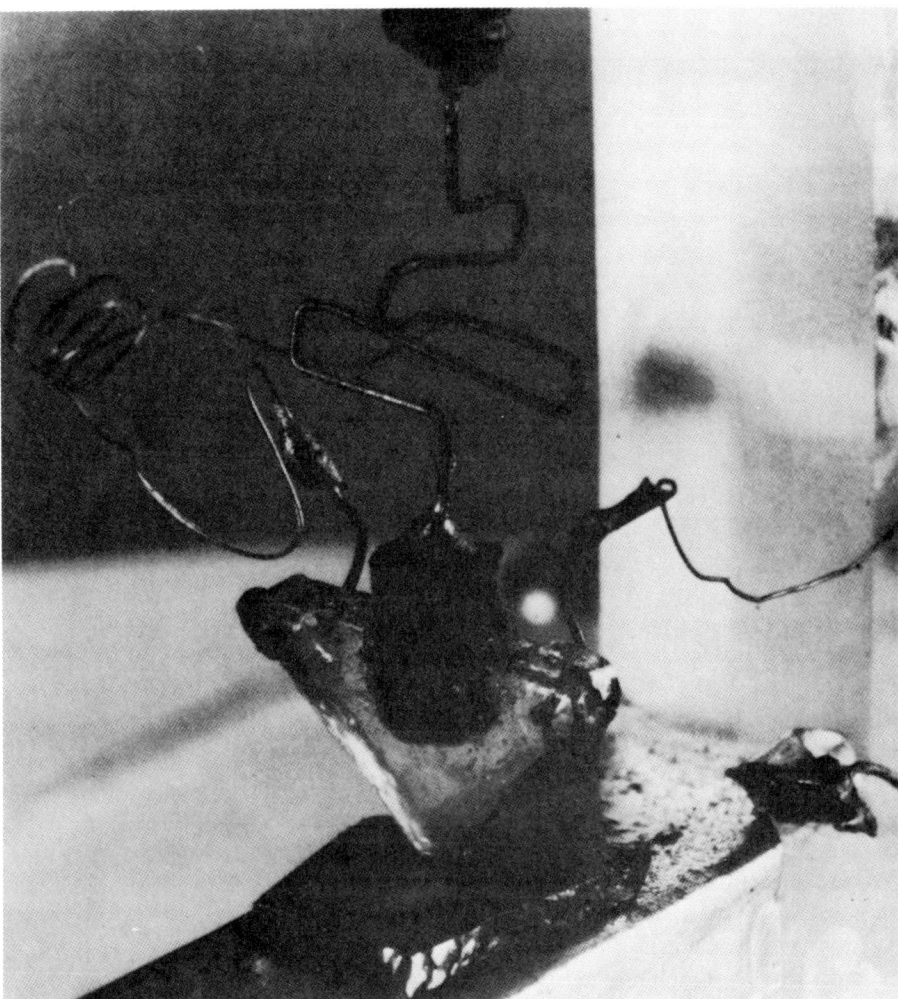

Figure 8.15

The first transistors were primitive by today's standards. Yet, they revolutionized the electronics industry and changed our way of life. For this achievement the inventors received a Nobel Prize. The above photograph shows the first transistor, a point-contact device that amplified electrical signals by passing them through a tiny piece of germanium semiconductor material. Basically, this is the same principle used today in the more sophisticated transistors.
Courtesy, Bell Laboratories

turn displace electrons. An atom having more electrons than normal exhibits a negative charge; one having fewer electrons than normal exhibits a positive charge.

In electronic modes of communication, we are concerned with the movement of electrons from atom to atom. When electrons move in an orderly fashion from one point in a circuit to another, we say that an electric current is flowing. An important point to remember is that the movement or flow of electrons is sometimes called current flow or electron flow interchangeably. This flow of current or electrons ap-

Diodes	Transistors	Others
Junction diode	Point-contact *	Hall generator (Experimental stage)
Silicon junction	Junction transistor (Bipolar)	Photoelectric cells
Photo type	N-P-N type	Photoconductive
Light Emitting Diode (L.E.D.)	P-N-P type	Photovoltaic
Solitron	(Common base)	Thermistor
Special Types	(Common emitter)	
Hot-electron diode	(Common collector)	
Laser diode	Power Transistors	
Microwave mixer diode	Special Types	
Tunnel diode	Frigistor	
Zener diode	Insulated gate FET (IGFET)	
Trysistor	MOS field-effect transistor (FET)	
Silicon rectifier	Photosensitive transistor	
Triac	Spacistor	
Varactor	Tecnetron	

*Now obsolete

Figure 8.16

Semiconductor family of devices

proximates the speed of light, which is 300,000 kilometers or 3×10^8 meters per second.

The absence of an electron is called a **hole** because it seems to act like a vacancy. Hole movement is the opposite of current flow. It moves in the opposite direction. When an electron breaks loose from its atom and wanders through a semiconductor, it leaves a hole that is soon found by another wandering electron, which has also left a hole. As electron flow moves from negative to positive, hole movement is obviously from positive to negative.

Semiconductors are crystals of pure material grown in a laboratory. In its pure, or intrinsic, state the crystal acts much like an insulator. Let's assume that we have a slice of intrinsic germanium crystal. The degree of purity is one part of foreign matter to 100 million parts of germanium. During the manufacturing process, one million atoms of an impurity such as arsenic is added. The resulting crystal is no longer pure and is referred to as having been doped. Selective doping of an intrinsic crystal permits the addition of a positive appearing P-type material or a negative appearing N-type material, as desired. The P designator comes from the word "ac*cep*tor" and the N from the word "do*nor*." P and N designators are much easier to remember than the words they came from. N-type materials are considered negative, while P-type are considered positive.

When both N-doped and P-doped semiconductor materials are grown together to form a single P-N crystal, a p-n junction semiconductor is formed. This is the basis for both diode and transistor action. If some of the relatively free N-type material moves into the positively charged holes in the adjacent P-type material, the area at the junction becomes slightly negative on the P-side and slightly positive on the N-side. This produces a barrier area. What has been formed is a germanium diode, which is now ready to be inserted in a circuit and function as a rectifier of current.

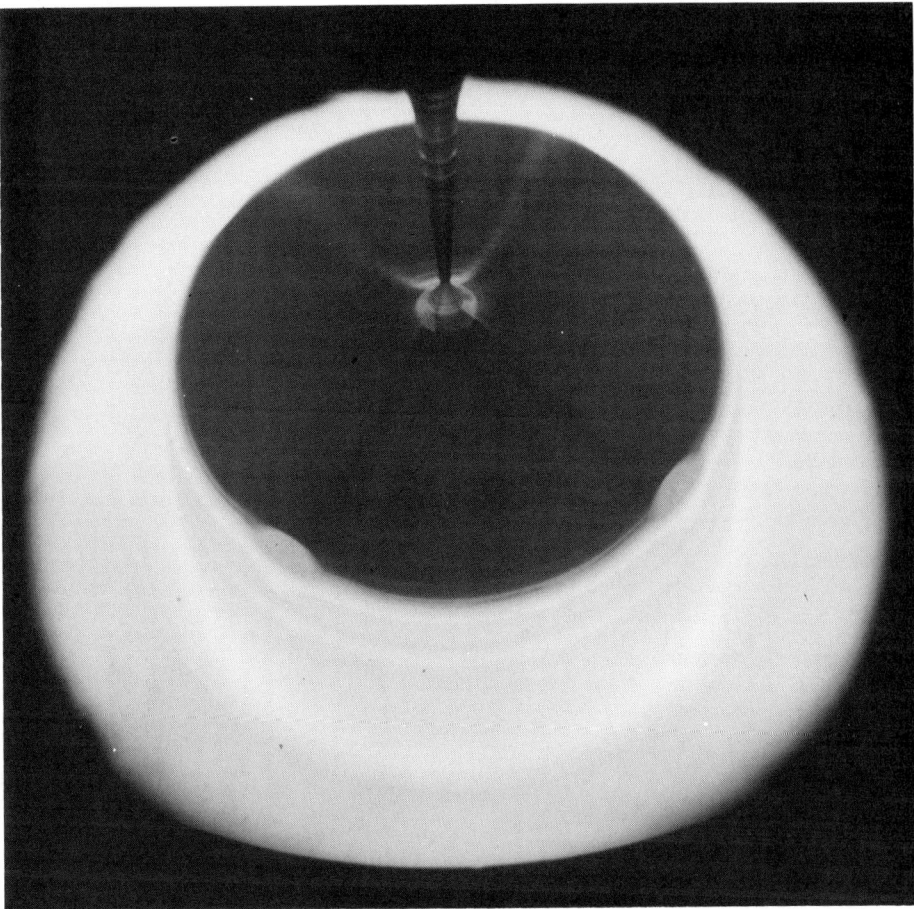

Figure 8.17

Silicon crystal being grown from a molten mass in Dow Corning's laboratories by the Czochralski method. Courtesy, Dow Corning Corporation, Midland, Michigan

Semiconductors normally have a small bias voltage in the circuit to help the electron flow. If the negative terminal of a battery is connected to the N-region, or side, of the diode and the positive terminal to the P-region, or side, of the diode, then it is said to be forward-biased because it will neutralize the barrier area and permit current to flow through the circuit. If the positive terminal of a battery is connected to the N-region and the negative terminal connected to the P-region, then it is said to be reverse biased and no current will flow in the circuit.

More simply stated, reverse bias of a diode will not permit current flow in one direction through the circuit, whereas forward bias will aid electron flow through the circuit. Although there is always a small leakage of current in both directions in any semiconductor, it is generally too small to be of much concern.

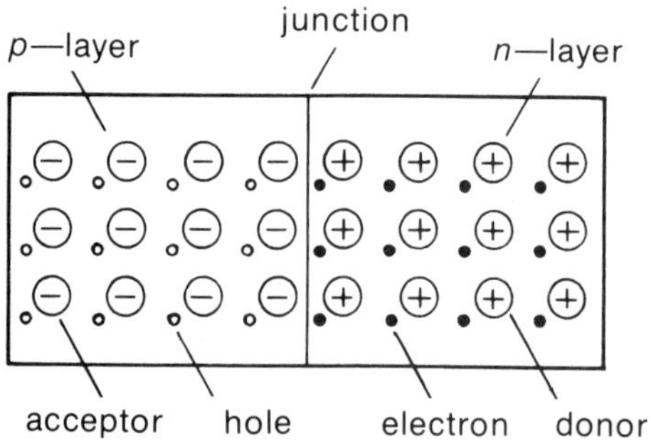

228 TECHNOLOGY-BASED ELECTRONIC TELECOMMUNICATION SYSTEMS

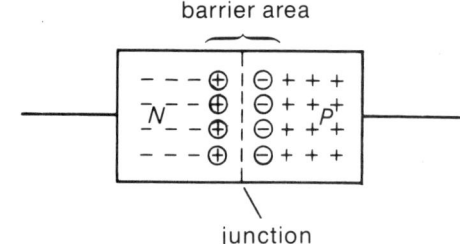

Figure 8.18

Composite sketch of a P-N-type crystal having a junction, acceptor holes, and donor electrons.

Figure 8.19

At the junction between the P-N crystals, the electron and hole carriers tend to fuse, which produces a barrier area or potential hill. A barrier/potential hill area can be formed in the manufacturing process to prevent the other electrons and holes in the crystal from combining. This is done, for example, in the rectifying diode.

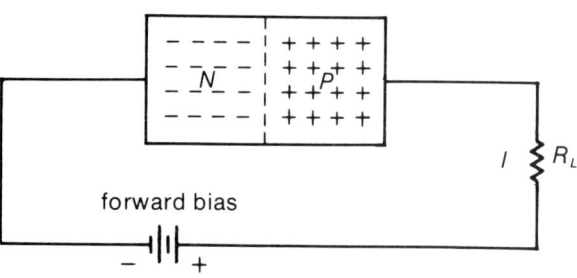

Figure 8.20

Forward-biased diode circuit

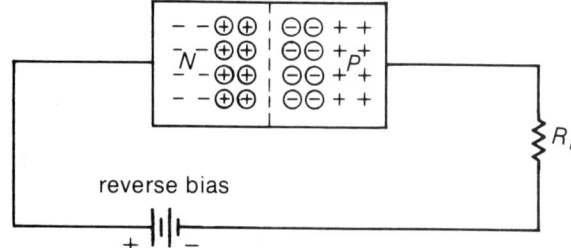

Figure 8.21

Reversed-biased diode circuit

The circuit in Figure 8.21 has the battery connected for reverse bias. It functions like this. The negative pole of the battery drives the electrons into the holes of the P-region, while the positive pole of the battery attracts electrons from the N-region. The barrier area of the junction widens and, therefore, no current can flow in the circuit. In this condition, the diode presents a very high resistance to the flow of current in the circuit.

The bias battery in Figure 8.20 is connected for forward bias and operates like this. A negative-to-positive electrostatic field is developed by the battery connected across the junction, and it overcomes the junction barrier voltage, thereby allowing current to flow in the circuit.

Semiconductors function as amplifiers, rectifiers, thermistors, modulators, memories, oscillators, switches, particle detectors, lasers, imaging devices, photodetectors, and light-emitters. The list of future possibilities for the semiconductor is almost endless.

Molecular Electronics

One of the biggest steps in technological progress since the invention of the transistor was the development of microminiaturized circuits. This technique made it possible to combine many separate electronic circuits on a small chip of material. It was called an integrated circuit.

Integrated Circuits

The **integrated circuit** (IC) is simply one in which the various circuit elements such as conductors, resistors, capacitors, transistors, diodes, and coils are all interconnected as a complete unit during the manufacturing process. There are two types of ICs: monolithic curcuits, and hybrid circuits. They are characterized by the difference in their manufacturing process.

In the **monolithic circuit**, the active and passive components are fabricated simultaneously by selective diffusion. **Diffusion** is the process of heating the semiconductor wafer in the presence of a suitable impure vapor. In this way, P- or N-type layers of controlled thickness are formed just below the semiconductor surface.

The **hybrid circuits** utilize the technique of electrical isolation of circuit elements by using low-dielectric materials and interconnecting them by internal bonding techniques, such as thermal compression or ultrasonics.

The grouping together of many thousands of ICs into a functioning system, such as an electronic calculator, is called large-scale integrated circuits (LSIC). This technique has effectively speeded up the processing of data by computers because it: (1) reduced the size of circuit elements, and (2) shortened the conductor path between them.

Today, the microminiaturization of circuits has made possible small calculators and wristwatches having the ability to give time, day, and date, as well as a wide range of computational capabilities to help you calculate the speed and acceleration of your wheels. Small wristwatch-type radios are now available in some specialty houses. The wristwatch TV set is still on the drawing board and will be available only when the market is ready for it; the technology to produce it is already known.

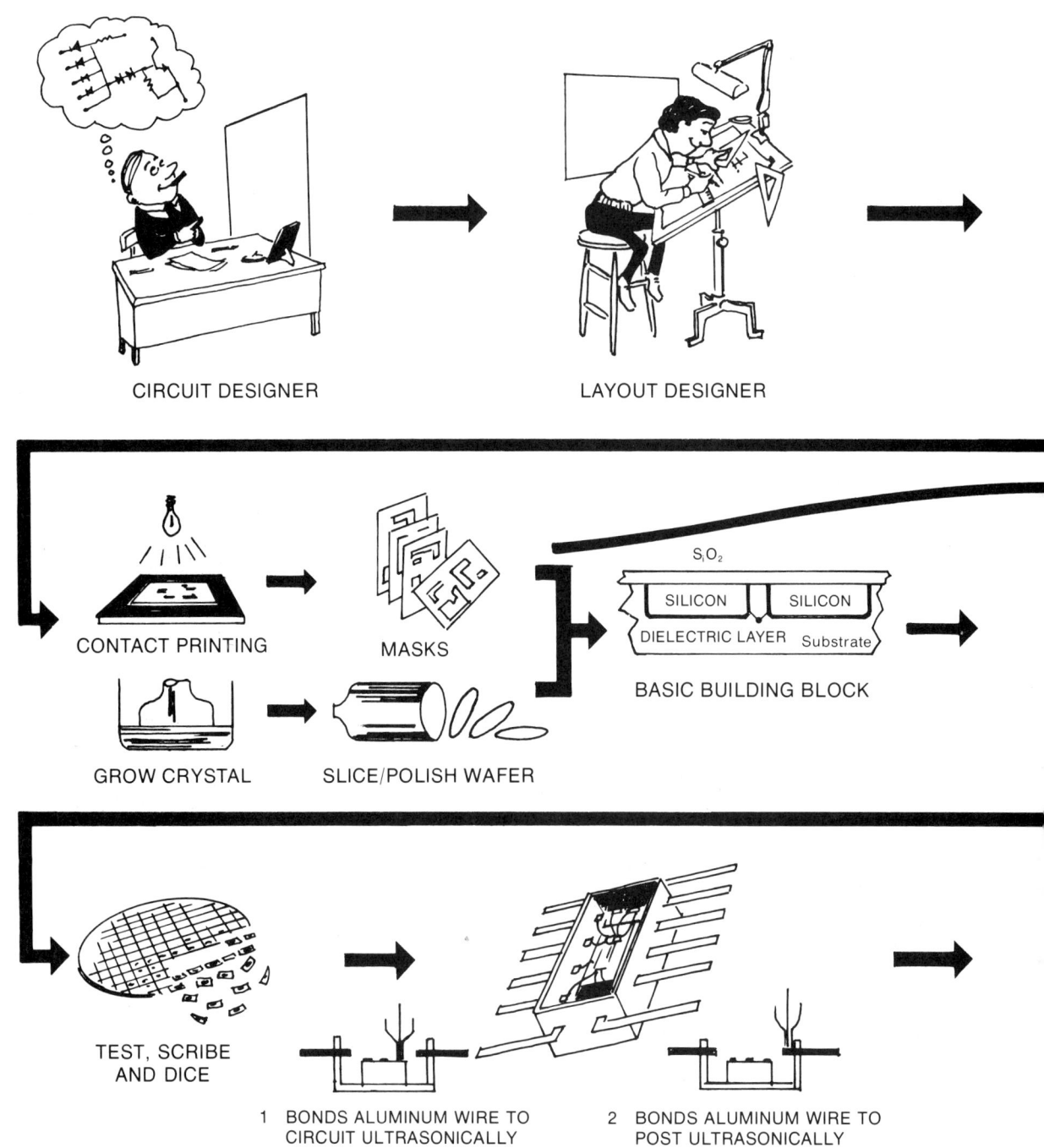

Figure 8.22

Integrated Circuit Manufacturing Process. Courtesy, Harris Semiconductor

BASIC ELEMENTS OF ELECTRONIC TELECOMMUNICATION SYSTEMS

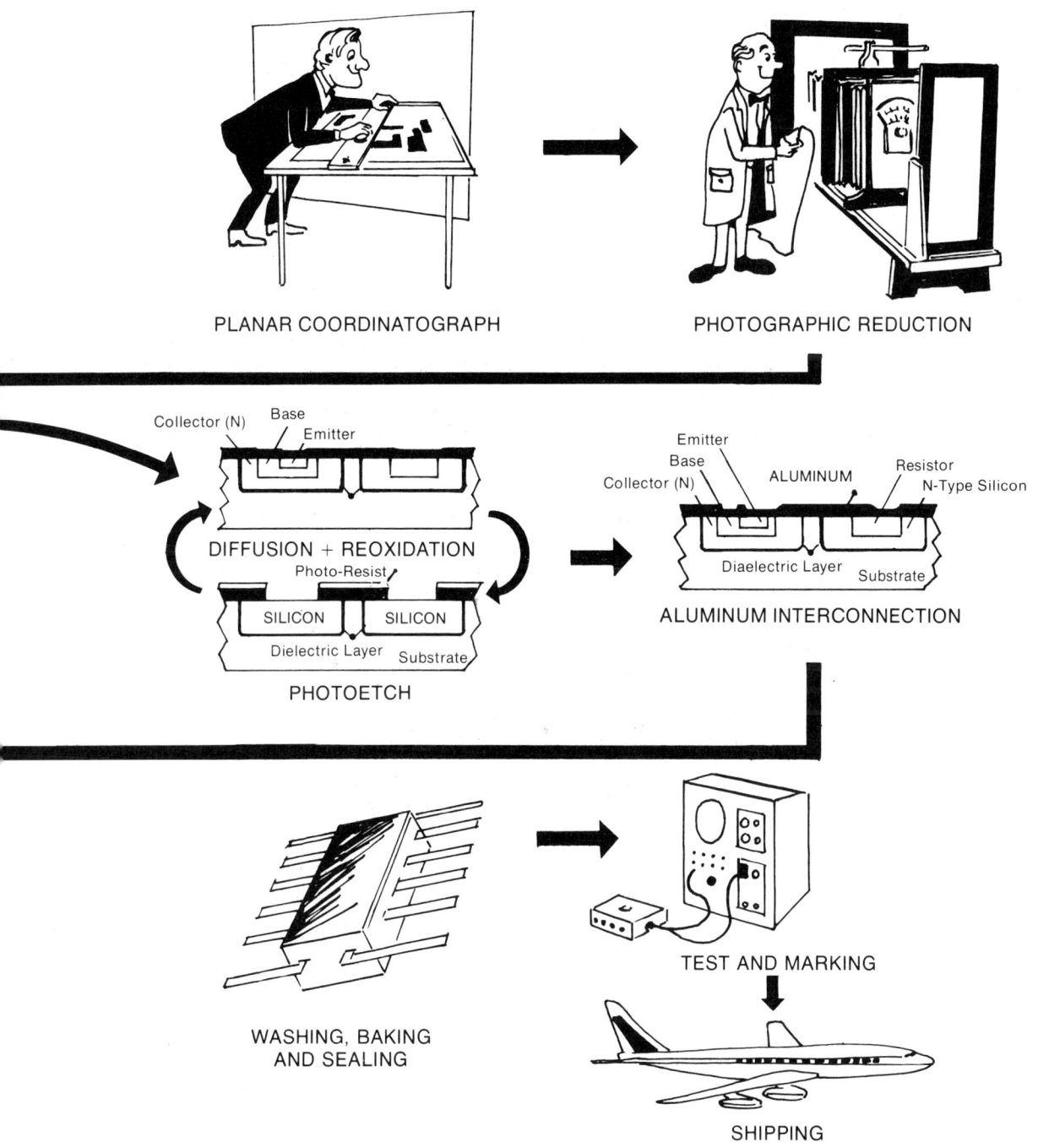

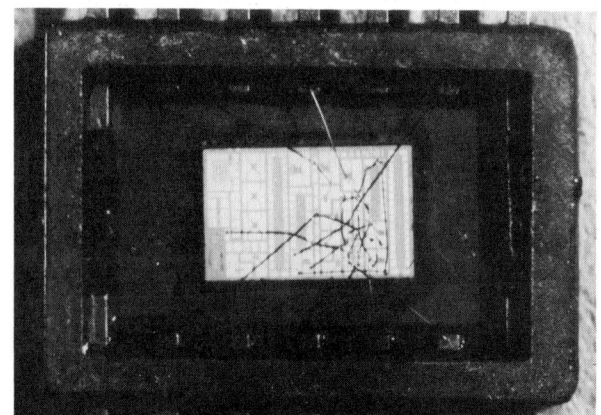

Figure 8.23a

A flat-pack integrated circuit such as this contains electrically, all of the electronic circuit elements in use today — that is, resistors, condensors, coils, transistors, leads — often in complete circuit form such as amplifiers, oscillators, detectors, multivibrators, counting circuits, and so forth.
Courtesy, Honeywell Inc.

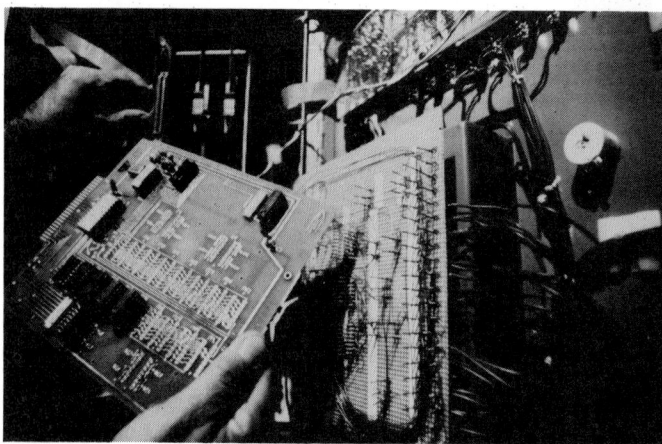

Figure 8.23b

Covers and bases are added to the flat-pack integrated circuits and are then soldered into a photo-etched circuit board as shown above. Hundreds of circuit boards like this are used in computers that control everything from your bank account to the traffic flow in the cities.
Courtesy, Honeywell Inc.

Figure 8.23c

Connecting large numbers of integrated circuits together like this is called *large scale integrated circuitry* or *micropackaging* of circuitry. One 80-mm square of micropackaging is the equivalent of all the circuits that can be crowded on a 31-cm x 31-cm circuit board. Because of the high density of circuits, a heat-exchanger (heatsink), through which liquid coolant circulates, is attached to the back of each micropackage, eliminating the need for airconditioning in larger and more advanced computer systems.
Courtesy, Honeywell, Inc.

BASIC ELEMENTS OF ELECTRONIC TELECOMMUNICATION SYSTEMS 233

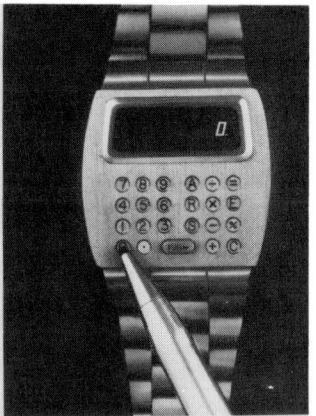
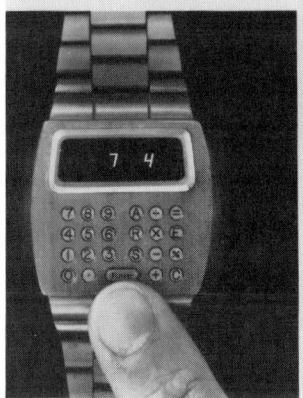

Figure 8.24a

The Pulsar wrist calculator performs as a time-keeping device accurate to within 60 seconds per year and has a month/date function as well as a six-digit display for a twelve-digit memory capability. It contains over 4500 transistors, an example of large-scale integrated circuits at work.
Courtesy, Time Computer, Inc.

Figure 8.24b

TI-30 portable calculator with forty-eight separate mathematical functions.
Courtesy, Texas Instruments, Incorporated

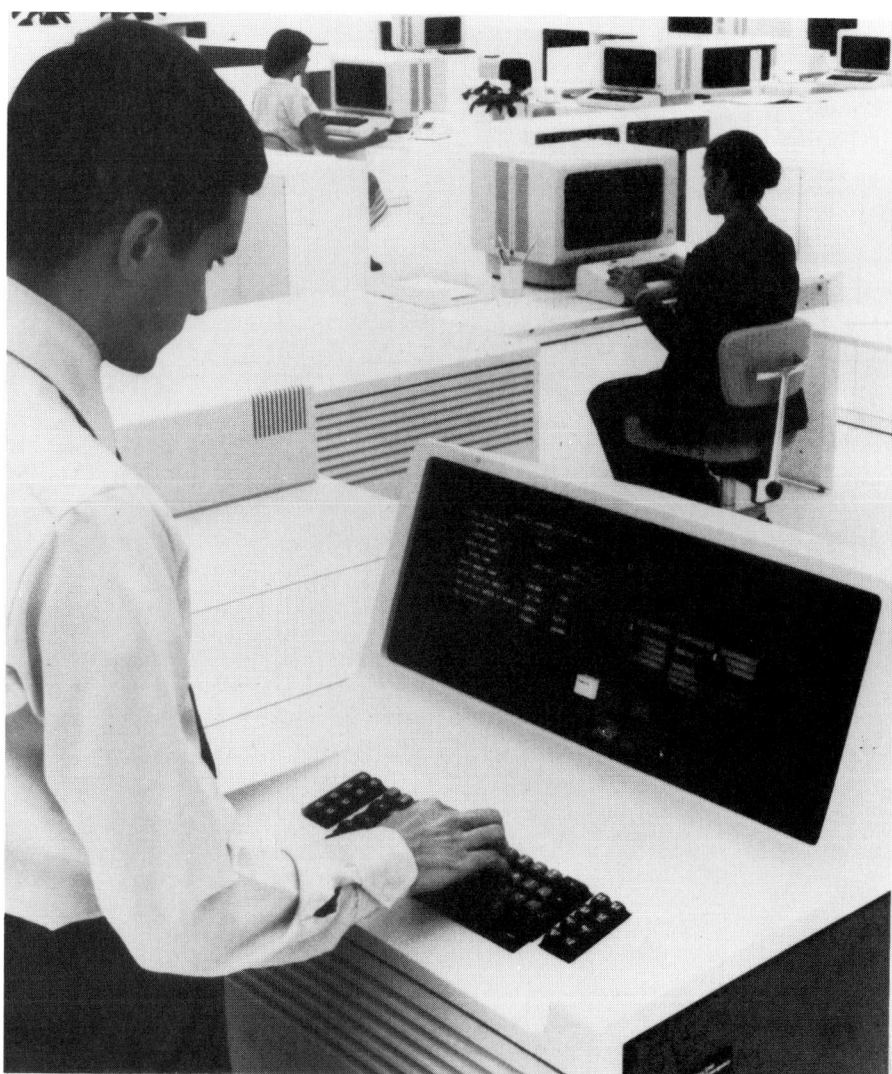

Figure 8.25

Incorporated into the small, new-technology System 138 are advanced functions — such as data base, virtual storage and computer-aided programming — that make work station applications easy to design, install and maintain.
Courtesy, IBM

Computers

Next to communication satellites, no other technical development has made such inroads into our technical society as the computer. It has changed our methods of doing business, diagnosing diseases, accomplishing government procedures, and even educating people. It affects each of us whether we are a student or the president of a large corporation; and it's only the beginning.

The principal advantages of the computer are its speed and memory capability, which are used to gather and analyze large quantities of data. These are essential to living in a highly complex technological society where data is generated at an exponential rate and digested at an arithmetical rate. Computers handle a variety of functions and perform a variety of uses for humankind.

Law enforcement agencies, through a nationwide network of computers and remote terminals, help police to check on wanted criminals or stolen vehicles. Urban planners use computers as an aid in developing solutions to the problems of pollution, transportation, and urban redevelopment. Computers free doctors and nurses from routine clerical work and allow them to give their patients more personal attention. Computer-based information retrieval systems help lawyers know about previous decisions in similar cases that could change their defense strategy. During legislative sessions computers are used to provide the up-to-date status of any bill of interest to your legislator, which helps him or her do a better job.

With computer simulation, some products can be tested before they are ever built. Mathematical models are used to check out airline operations before new routes or flights are added or old ones cancelled. Economists use models of the total economy to study interaction among the elements that effect it. A bank depositor needs accurate, current information about his checking or savings account, as does the bank teller. Inventory management in large warehouses uses computers to maintain a constant location and stock level for better customer service.

On automobile and tractor assembly lines, hundreds of parts have to be ordered, shipped, routed, and converged at the assembly point at the right time if manufacturing costs are to be kept down. Computers help meteorologists analyze huge volumes of weather data from satellites and hundreds of reporting stations around the world. Other users are realtors, credit bureaus, stockbrokers, and school systems. These are but some of the ways computers are used. Yet we are only beginning to learn how this device can better serve humankind.

The first all-electric digital computer was ENIAC. Built in 1946, it could perform 5000 additions in 1 second. It had over 18,000 vacuum tubes and 500,000 electrical connections. Although it performed its calculation function well, the large number of tubes destined the device to much downtime and it soon became a maintenance nightmare.

Since ENIAC, digital and analog computer technology has advanced at a rapid pace. Vacuum tubes gave way to semiconductors and speed was increased by using microcircuits.

The basic principle of the computer is similar to an electric light bulb. It operates in an "on" and "off" mode. Each on and off condition represents a bit of information when assigned a symbol. The symbols used in the computer are the binary code. By proper arrangement of the digital bits, any combination of numerical, alphabetical, or special symbols can be programmed rather easily.

No computer can think for itself. It is only as smart as its human programmer. Therefore, it must receive its input from cards, magnetic tapes, typewriter, voice, or by data communication links with other computers. It stores its data in card decks, on a magnetic tape, or in a memory core.

Because of the high development, production, and retirement costs of the computer, time-sharing techniques had to be introduced. Under the time-sharing plan,

Figure 8.26

World's first all-electronic digital computers, built in 1946. Named the Electronic Numerical Integrator and Computer (ENIAC), it used up at least a pail full of red-lined vacuum tubes each day due to overheating. Although it had a lot of downtime, it could perform up to 5000 additions per second, which outmoded any previous electromechanical machine.
Courtesy, Sperry-UNIVAC

the computer automatically divides its time among all of the users in a scheduled sequence. Now, many more people can make use of the most up-to-date computers for a fraction of the cost.

Electronic Measurement and Instrumentation

Of the many different types of electronics test instruments on the market, none is more useful for analyzing electronic circuits than the digital volt meter (VOM), the signal generator, or the oscilloscope (scope). The combination of VOM, signal generator, and scope can be found in nearly every electronics laboratory or service shop in the world. We will discuss each of these instruments in turn.

Digital Volt Meter

This widely known instrument is still called the VOM even though most of them are all solid-state. It is useful in measuring AC voltages as well as DC signal levels in different stages of electronic equipment. It is used in servicing transmitters, receivers, high-fidelity amplifiers, tape recorders, as well as in many industrial control applications.

Figure 8.27

This new solid-state digital, VOM provides instant measurement readout in resistance (ohms), AC volts, DC volts, DC amps, and AC amps. Courtesy, Dynascan Corporation

The Signal Generator

The signal generator is another widely used instrument to test electronic equipment. Its principal use is to align receivers for maximum gain. As its name implies, it produces an a.c. voltage that is especially useful for tracing signals through an electronic system. The generator develops sine wave or square wave at most frequencies for use in aligning receivers as well as checking their audio sections. In most generators, there are provisions to modulate the RF signal and the AF signal for checking the IF and detector stages of a receiver. Other generators have a provision for substituting the negative voltage for the automatic volume control (AVC) of a receiver. All RF signal generators have a means of controlling the amplitude of the RF signal output; however, the audio signal is of a fixed amplitude and frequency.

The Oscilloscope

In the field of electronic communications, the use of an oscilloscope, or scope as it is more commonly called, is as essential to the technician or engineer as fuel is to the automobile. This test instrument is designed to display electronic phenomena that cannot be studied by any other means. The scope consists of a cathode-ray tube (CRT) and associate circuits.

The electron gun contains a heater, cathode, control grid, focusing anode, and the accelerating anode. The electron gun shoots electrons at the screen of the CRT. The purpose of the screen is to make the electron beam visible. When the electron stream strikes the screen, it gives off light, the color of the light being determined by the composition of the phosphor coating.

The remaining part of the CRT is the deflection circuit. Two types of deflection are generally used: electromagnetic or electrostatic. TV picture tubes commonly use electromagnetic deflecting coils; whereas scopes use electrostatic means. The associated circuits amplify input signals and develop wave shapes to control the electron beam.

While there are many manufacturers of the type of equipment we have just discussed, the basic principles and operation of each of them are much the same. You will find them all to be very versatile test instruments. We will learn to use them in the ACT manual.

Let's stop for a moment now to review what we have learned.

CONCEPT FOCUSER

- The history of technology-based electronic telecommunications systems is actually a **history** of early experimenters' **discoveries** and **applications**.
- The **spark transmitter** set sent radio's **first signals across** the Atlantic. This was also the first **radio technology breakthrough**.
- **Disasters** at sea focused attention on **need** for international **radio regulation**.
- Fleming's **Valve** and De Forest's **audion** were the next technological **breakthroughs for** modern **radio**.
- **Worldwide radio broadcast** was **commonplace** by 1938.
- Black and white **television** was in **half** the **American homes** by 1950.
- Electronic **technology advanced rapidly** because of **war needs** and **produced** radar, CRT, picture-telephone, and **high-powered telecommunications** networks.
- **Radio astronomy** developments opened the way for **interstellar telecommunications**.
- **Amateur radio** experiments with the higher frequencies **opened** up **new channels** for telecommunications.
- Lasers, masers, and space communications **technology expanded** humankind's **growing telecommunication** links.
- Discovery of **semiconductor technology** was the next major technology **breakthrough**.

- Computer-technology advances were responsible for developing many new industries.

FOOD FOR THOUGHT

1. What was the first discovery of an electrical phenomenon that extended humans' telecommunication across the Atlantic?
2. Could the coherer detector receiver be used to detect today's high-powered transmitters?
3. Marconi was recognized as a very shrewd businessman. Why?
4. Rank order the following events in terms of their direct contribution to the advancement of radio technology (1 — most important; 5 — least important):
   a. Concept of thermionic emission　　　　　_____
   b. The sinking of the *Titanic*　　　　　_____
   c. Early ARRL operations　　　　　_____
   d. The rock crushers　　　　　_____
   e. Establishment of technical standards　　　　　_____

5. What is the difference between SSB and PCM transmission?
6. Which inventor is considered the father of television?
   Name the father of the digital computer.
7. If you had a choice of only one test instrument to repair all types of electronic telecommunications equipment, which *one* would you choose? Explain the reason for your selection.
   a. Oscilloscope
   b. Signal generator
   c. Digital volt meter
   d. Cyclometer

EXPANDING EXPERIENCES

The technology-based electronic achievements of the past hundred years have been a history of individual or small-team inventions. Select any one of the innovators or inventors listed in Appendix B and write a paper about his life and about how his particular technical contribution advanced the state of the art of technology-based electronic modes of communication.

LOCATOR TOOLS

Amos, S. W. *Principles of Transistor Circuits*. London: John F. Rider Publisher, 1961.

Buban, Peter and Schmitt, Marshall. *Technical Electricity and Electronics*. New York: McGraw-Hill Book Company, 1977.

Cataldo, J. T., ed. International Rectifier Corp. *Engineering Handbook*, El Segundo, Calif.: International Rectifier Corp.

Dunlap, Orrin E., Jr. *Communications in Space: From Wireless to Satellite Relay*. New York: Harper & Row, 1962.

From Semaphore to Satellite. Geneva: International Telecommunications Union, 1965, pp. 159–203, 275–335.

O'Donnel, C. F., ed. *Applied Micro-Electronics*. Washington, D.C.: American House, 1966.

RCA Transistor Manual. Somerville, New Jersey: RCA Semiconductor and Materials Division, 1979.

COMMUNICATION TECHNOLOGY AND ITS EFFECTS ON SOCIETY

Module **NINE**

This module investigates the general influence of technology on society. More specifically, it examines the effects of communication technology on the conditions of human beings having social relationships with each other. The use of technical communication devices in highly industrialized countries like the United States is increasing. Developing countries have also become involved in the use of communication technology. It is important that we become more aware of the immediate and long-term (or hidden) effects of the use of such devices on society as a whole, as well as the psychological effects on the individual.

Module Nine will deal with the topics of communication technology as a stimulus for social change, the ethical and legal aspects of common techniques used to achieve specific goals in the communication process, and the issue of control and regulation of modern communication technology.

TECHNOLOGY AND SOCIETY

As the ascent of civilization occurred, so did the growth of technology. The relationship between humans and this technology became increasingly complex. From a primitive state, the development of tools and weapons provided our early ancestors with clear-cut extensions of their bodily capabilities. For example, a flint-edged axe could benefit its user in two ways. First, the hard, sharp edge of the cutting tool could inflict a more critical blow to a target than an open-hand karate chop — whether that target was a tree or the skull of an enemy. Second, the handle of the axe acted as a lever and permitted more force to be transmitted due to shoulder and wrist action of the user. This idea of a tool as a technological extension of humans might be carried to a bow and arrow that enabled its user to overcome such obstacles as distance. Instead of sneaking up on game, one could attack from afar. Also, the combined strength of the bow with tensioned string permitted the condensed force of the arrow's impact to be more effective than slapping the dangerous beast with one's bare hands.

As tools, weapons, and techniques (technology) developed, different, sometimes improved, conditions were created for the user. Development of the bow and arrow, in combination with human language skills, enabled hunting parties to form and plan expeditions that yielded more food, at less risk, than an individual hunter could. It was, perhaps, this type of group experience that began the early sparks of civilization. Surely, it was this type of utilization of technology that created change in the way things were done. Later, wandering food-gathering and hunting societies began to settle in groups and produce their own food. It was in part the knowledge of planting and harvesting, but also their development of tools, that enabled them to work the earth.

Once settled, many of these small groups evolved customs, rules, and governing techniques in order to make easier the daily chore of group existence. But as hunting parties journeyed farther and farther and the planting areas became less fertile, the nomadic villagers moved to other sites, leaving behind alterations, however small, to the physical environment.

As different technologies are developed and used, they affect the user, the society, and the environment. Technology creates change. The invention and adoption of technological innovations appears to be a natural process of human beings. This process can be identified with various intellectual development stages that exist throughout the world in societies having varying degrees of sophistication. Current Third World, or developing, countries are involved in stages of intellectual development and technology utilization that have previously been experienced by more industrialized countries. The pattern of economic and social growth is always influenced by the technology found within a particular society.

In order to better understand the different influences of technology on society, it might be beneficial to identify historical stages of technology. It is possible for all stages to be practiced today somewhere on our spaceship Earth. Least probable is the existence of the first stage of technology.

Stage 1—Primitive Era

Primitive technology was characterized by being narrow in scope. Methods, tools, and organization were limited to hunting and weapons, providing clothing and shelter, and magic. Magic was practiced with such a high degree of sophistication that it has been considered a form of primitive technology. Magic was used to explain many of the physical/metaphysical problems of the time. Technology was used to fulfill immediate need. Work was not like it is today; all human energies were expended just to exist. Primitive technique was practiced only in a local manner, therefore providing effects or benefits for the immediate user. There was little transfer of technology; thus, technology developed very slowly. The effects of technology were directly related to specific uses. For example, if a tree was chopped down and used for construction of a shelter, the effects of using a stone axe were readily observable.

Stage 2—Craft Era

Although there was still little transfer of technology, techniques of the craft stage improved. Emphasis was placed on the application of old skills and tools along with local refinement and improvement. A worker's talents were improved to compensate for deficient tools. A broader application of existing tools is perhaps the best description of the craft stage. The effects of craft-age technology (home weaving, carpentry, farming, blacksmithing, and so forth) contributed to local economies and used local materials. People remained in control of technology, thereby retaining a choice in all of its applications. Tools and techniques were a way of life.

Stage 3—Mechanical Era

The mechanical stage of technology redefines the word progress—in this stage, bigger is better. Elements of the craft stage were incorporated into a mode of development and invention. Satisfaction was gained, not by perfection of old skills, but by development of machines to improve the process. Mass production changed the old formulas of economic growth. Consumption and production rates kept pace with the development of artificial energy sources (steam and electricity). Workers faced unfamiliar situations with dangerous machines and threatening factory environments. Work became a major portion of a person's life. The social level of human life was improved. Technology became knowledge-based, and the transfer of information from culture to culture stimulated further invention.

Effects of the mechanical stage of technology presented indirect consequences. The steam engine consumed coal. Coal production led to coal company towns and subcultures of workers and families that depended totally on the mines and company store—the chain went on and on.

Stage 4—Modern Era

Modern technology decreases physical labor and is capital intensive (it uses a great amount of capital). The most efficient method becomes the only method. Technology becomes self-motivating, being transformed and improved almost without the intervention of humans. Progress is irreversible. Techniques are linked together to form an autonomous system, somewhat independent of values and morals. People become maintainers rather than direct controllers of the process. Social effects are far-reaching and frequently unpredictable. The effects of technology are abstract and timeless; they are not tied to its original application.

Going back to an earlier point, technology creates change, it is important to point out that the rate and degree of change depend on the rate of adoption and the level of technology any society employs. Reflecting on the short descriptions of the major stages of technology, one can easily guess that social change would occur more rapidly and more frequently in stage 4 than in any other.

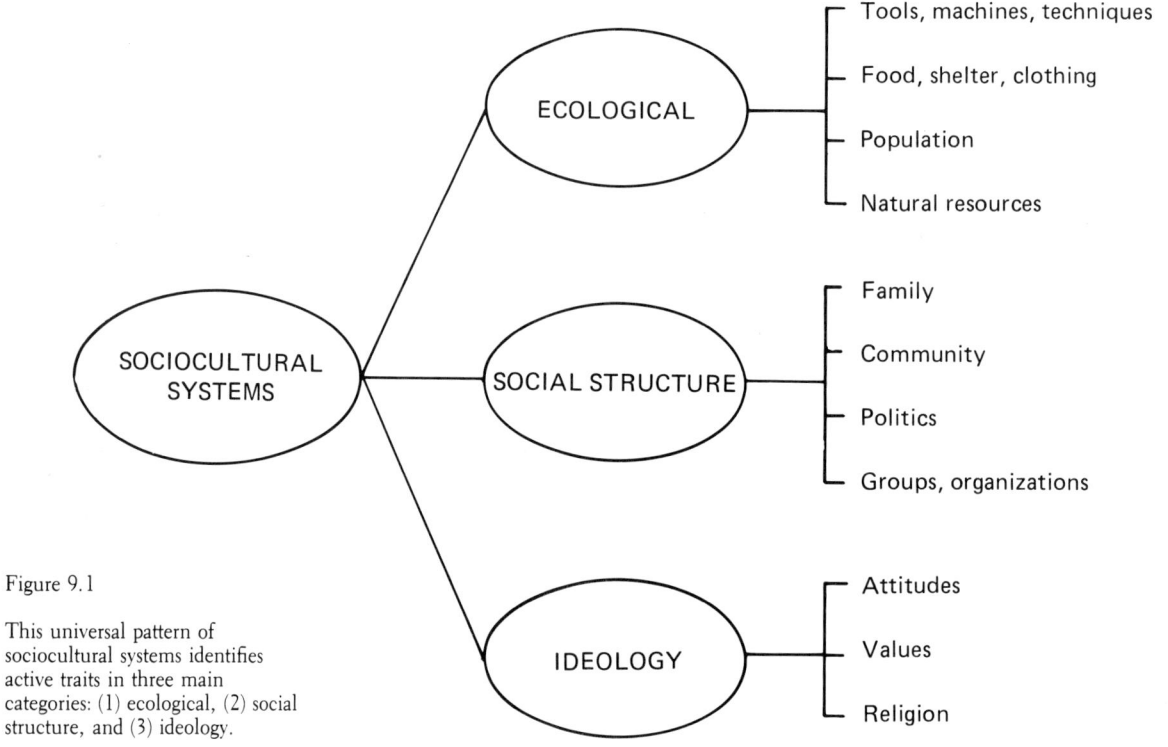

Figure 9.1

This universal pattern of sociocultural systems identifies active traits in three main categories: (1) ecological, (2) social structure, and (3) ideology.

Modern civilization is based on women, men, and children living together, working together, and otherwise depending on one another. Community, rather than isolation, is the rule—often dividing inhabitants into classes according to worldly goods, skills, or political beliefs. Modern humans live in communities or tribes, which generally have distinct cultures and which predominate within certain boundaries. Traditional Eskimo villages, for example, depend on the sea for their existence. They hunt and fish by methods unique to their heritage; their tools and weapons are designed of available material to accomplish specific tasks. The economic and political (family and chiefs) aspects of the village are firmly established in tradition.

All of the factors depicted in Figure 9.1 represent elements of society. Indeed, these factors change according to natural cycles, such as seasons and weather conditions, sickness, and death. But social change stimulated by technology creates change in two principal ways. As one example, the transistor radio has long since been introduced to the Arctic environment. Strategically located transmitter stations broadcast news and weather conditions as well as music. The broadcasts provide entertainment during the long Arctic night. Weather reports, which could save lives, warn villagers of threatening storms. Under these conditions, communication technology has created social change by offering new possibilities to the inhabitants of the region. This is the first principal kind of change. However, technology and its applications can also generate new problems and produce negative effects. Technology itself carries no value. The use of technology has both positive *and* negative effects, and they usually occur at the same time.

To continue our speculation as to the effect of radio on Eskimo culture, let's look at some negative features. First, the radio could alter family structures and a villager's appreciation of his or her place in life. Before radio, the long winter days were consumed with tales and stories about the heritage of the Eskimo. This interaction renewed and strengthened the family as a single unit, thereby providing incentive to accomplish the daily tasks of existence. With radio, a kind of superficial entertainment took place, eliminating the transfer of ancestral information or skills of daily life. In this manner, there is the possibility of a culture permanently losing some of its skills and history.

Advertising could also have a detrimental effect, particularly on the young of isolated Eskimo villages. Attitudes and values could develop that would create hostility to the ideas of older adults, who in Eskimo society form the spine of the culture. This youthful counterculture of new values and ideas (about consumer products, leisure activities, attitudes toward sex, and the like) would be, in part, developed by the accelerated rate of information accumulated by the young. Bombarded by information that they are unable to evaluate properly, the young can be beguiled by visions of a new life, free from traditional restraints. Just such an accelerated rate of information acquisition occurs in many industrialized countries of the world today (particularly the United States).

Lastly, the negative aspect of technical failure, poor reception, or failing batteries could frustrate anyone in a remote area who was unable to get the radio repaired.

Change stimulated by technological development becomes the only element of technological development that can be anticipated with certainty. The kind of change cannot be predicted, but only that some kind of change will occur. As discussed in Module Three, societies were built on efficient means of communication between individuals. Therefore, the effects of communication technology on society have greater implications than first perceived. Not only must an awareness of the techniques, devices, and processes of communication be gained, but also a thorough understanding of the effects of communication technology on humankind must be realized. How technology affects people — that's what it's all about!

Many years ago (1910) an American doctor of medicine practicing in London murdered his wife. The doctor, Hawley H. Cryppen, then buried her body in the cellar of his home and ran off with his secretary. The secretary, disguised as a boy, booked passage for herself and the doctor on a steamship to America. During the crossing, the captain of the ship became suspicious of the pair after reading an account of the crime in a London newspaper brought on board before sailing. Fortunately, or unfortunately for Dr. Cryppen, the liner *Montrose* was one of the first to be equipped with Marconi's wireless telegraph. The captain telegraphed Scotland Yard and a detective was dispatched on a faster ship to arrest the couple as they arrived in America. Eighteen months later all British passenger ships were required by law to have wireless telegraph equipment installed to provide fast communication. The moral of this little story is not "Don't run away with your secretary," but "Beware of the effects of communication technology on you."

Communication Technology Utilization

In order to gain a broad perspective on the use of communication technology in various societies other than our own, it is beneficial to examine utilization in many different areas of the world. Practically **two-thirds** of all countries on earth are considered developing countries in terms of sociopolitical activities, economic stability, technological bases, and cultural enrichment. Only **one-third** of all countries, (among them France, Canada, Japan, and the United States) are considered to be somewhat stable in these categories. In order to examine the use of communication technology on a broad spectrum, Figure 9.2 shows the latest compilation of data on the number per 1000 (or 100) inhabitants of television receivers, radio receivers, cinema seats, daily newspapers, and telephones in six areas of the world.

What this may indicate can be shown in this example. From Figure 9.2 one can easily see that in 1975 for each 1000 inhabitants of the continent of Africa there were available, on the average, 6.2 television sets. In Europe during that same year, 241 television receivers were available for use for each 1000 inhabitants. This could mean two things: (1) Europe could be considered one of the technologically advanced areas of the world, and people who live there have a better opportunity to secure television receivers; and/or (2) there is more information and entertainment to be broadcast in Europe. This assumption would mean that Africa, with only 6.2 television receivers per 1000 inhabitants, is: (1) a developing continent, not yet able to provide the technical or economic base for mass acquisition of television receivers, or (2) that there is not much information or entertainment to be broadcast.

Although the number of television receivers in a certain area of the earth can be misleading, it at least shows the actual accessibility of a certain technology. This kind of statistic, by itself, cannot show whether a country or area is not developed because it does not have adequate communication systems or whether that country cannot provide adequate communication systems because it is underdeveloped. This type of information does, however, give some indication of the relationship between the availability of communication devices and the sociopolitical and economic status of a country or area of the world.

1975 World Communication Statistics

	TV receivers per/1000	Radio receivers per/1000	Cinema seats per/1000	Daily newspapers per/1000	Telephones per/100
Africa	6.2	70	4.8	21	1.1
America	285	900	35	209	69.5
Europe	241	327	39	289	24.6
USSR	216	480	98	437	6.6
Asia *	27	80	8.6	90	2.6
Arab States	24	120	7.4	30	—

*Excluding Peoples' Republic of China
Source: 1977 UNESCO Statistical Yearbook

Figure 9.2
1975 World Communication Statistics
Courtesy, 1977 UNESCO Statistical Yearbook

What is the probability that you, as a student, have your own radio, television set, or stereo? Do you have access to a telephone to call any of your friends or relatives? If you thought for only a minute, you could probably list dozens of persons you know who have telephones. This would be true for many areas in the United States. But, according to Figure 9.3, many people throughout the world are not as lucky.

The charts shown in Figures 9.3 through 9.7 identify specific information on communication devices from sample countries around the world. Frequently shown are data identifying the changes in the number of devices (per inhabitant) between specific years. This information may be used to determine trends in sociopolitical or technological development, or just in the utilization of a particular media.

Radio Receivers per 1000 Inhabitants (Selected Countries)

	1973	1976
Kenya	41	37
Algeria	46	173
America	1,752	—
Panama	162	157
Ecuador	—	—
Guyana	198	351
Kuwait	238	487
Saudi Arabia	—	28
Bulgaria	263	314
Denmark	333	365
Italy	227	232
USSR	442	—

Source: 1977 UNESCO Statistical Yearbook

Figure 9.3

Radio Receivers per 1000 Inhabitants (selected countries) Courtesy, 1977 UNESCO Statistical Yearbook

Daily Newspapers per 1000 Inhabitants (Selected Countries)

	1973	1975
Kenya	8	10
Algeria	17	17
America	300	287
Panama	92	79
Ecuador	46	49
Guyana	88	—
Kuwait	85	—
Saudi Arabia	11	—
Bulgaria	215	232
Denmark	364	341
Italy	120	113
USSR	373	397

Source: 1977 UNESCO Statistical Yearbook

Figure 9.4

Daily Newspaper per 1000 Inhabitants (selected countries) Courtesy, 1977 UNESCO Statistical Yearbook

Cinema Seating Capacity per 1000 Inhabitants (Selected Countries)

Country	Year	Value
Kenya	1976	1.8
Algeria	1975	11.3
America	—	—
Panama	1974	86.4
Ecuador	1974	16.5
Guyana	1975	48.4
Kuwait	1975	13.0
Saudi Arabia	—	—
Bulgaria	1975	84.5
Denmark	1975	25.2
Italy	—	—
USSR	—	—

Source: 1977 UNESCO Statistical Yearbook

Figure 9.5

Cinema Seating Capacity per 1000 Inhabitants (selected countries) Courtesy, 1977 UNESCO Statistical Yearbook

Number of Telephones per 100 Inhabitants (Selected Countries)

Country	1973	1976
Kenya	0.9	1.0
Algeria	1.4	1.5
America	65.7	72.1
Panama	—	9.0
Ecuador	1.9	2.9
Guyana	2.3	2.8
Kuwait	10.7	13.6
Saudi Arabia	1.0	2.1
Bulgaria	7.4	9.7
Denmark	40.0	49.4
Italy	22.9	27.1
USSR	5.7	7.0

Source: 1977 UNESCO Statistical Yearbook

Figure 9.6

Number of Telephones per 100 Inhabitants (selected countries) Courtesy, 1977 United Nations Statistical Yearbook

Television Receivers per 1000 Inhabitants (Selected Countries)

Country	1973	1976
Kenya	3	3.6
Algeria	16	30.0
America	523	—
Panama	—	108.0
Ecuador	—	41.0
Guyana	—	81.0
Kuwait	204	—
Saudi Arabia	—	14.0
Bulgaria	160	176.0
Denmark	304	323.0
Italy	208	220.0
USSR	197	—

Source: 1977 UNESCO Statistical Yearbook

Figure 9.7a

Television Receivers Per 1000 Inhabitants (selected countries) Courtesy, 1977 UNESCO Statistical Yearbook

United States Media Financial Data ($ Millions)

		Revenues	Expenses	Income *
AM/FM Radio	1977	2,274.5	2,028.4	246.1
Television	1977	5,889.0	4,488.0	1,401.0

*Before Federal Income Taxes
Source: 1979 Broadcasting Yearbook

Figure 9.7b

United States Media Financial Data ($ Millions) Courtesy, 1979 Broadcasting Yearbook

An interesting point to examine after reviewing this data is the influence of the United States on international communications. Due to increasing world trade and the growth of multinational corporations, the information moving between nations is usually of an economic, competitive, or political nature. Logically, a pattern of heavy influence develops around the countries that have the strongest communication-technology base.

Before we leave this topic, we should look at the actions of international communication organizations like INTELSAT. As of 1974, there were seventy-four earth stations capable of receiving satellite signals of a wide assortment of telecommunication systems in countries across the globe. However, the technologically advanced countries of the world hold controlling interest in the operation of this type of organization. This kind of control may be justified when one considers the expertise necessary to build and operate such advanced communication systems. These few controlling countries (of which the United States is one) then form a hub of institutions and systems around which developing countries attach themselves, forming a worldwide communication system. International communications then progress from being a support element of international affairs to an actual instrument of foreign policy.

Clearly, then, the actual type of information (the content of the program or the nature of the message) is as important as the fact that the communication system itself has been organized, provided, and controlled by certain powerful countries. Yet the impact of the message is a difficult thing to assess because a person's access to a television receiver does not mean that that person is exposed to what is on it. The receiver must be turned on and a specific channel tuned in. The set must be in proper working condition and the viewing condition must be favorable. (Have you ever tried to watch television with six little brothers and sisters around?) Remember, too, that exposure to the message does not mean a person will accept and act on the information provided. If so, we would all drive Chevrolets and eat at McDonald's. The relationship between access, exposure, and message impact is shown in Figure 9.9.

EFFECTS ON SOCIETY AND THE INDIVIDUAL

The use of communication technology is generally assumed to be related to mass communication. This is not completely true. Communication technology in its broad interpretation can also assist in interpersonal communication with corrective devices like hearing aids, eyeglasses, or synthetic larynxes. Other communication devices, like information processing machines, do not have mass audiences, but they do affect

Figure 9.8

Communication satellite earth stations in different locations must be compatible with each other to insure accurate transfer of messages.

people. Utilization of the electronic computer affects society in general, as well as specific individuals. Many of the influences resulting from the use of this technology will be discussed later in this module.

Returning to the idea of mass communication, it is apparent that in modern society an individual (or society in general) is confronted with many channels of information. Due to the increased amount and diversity of information, it is possible

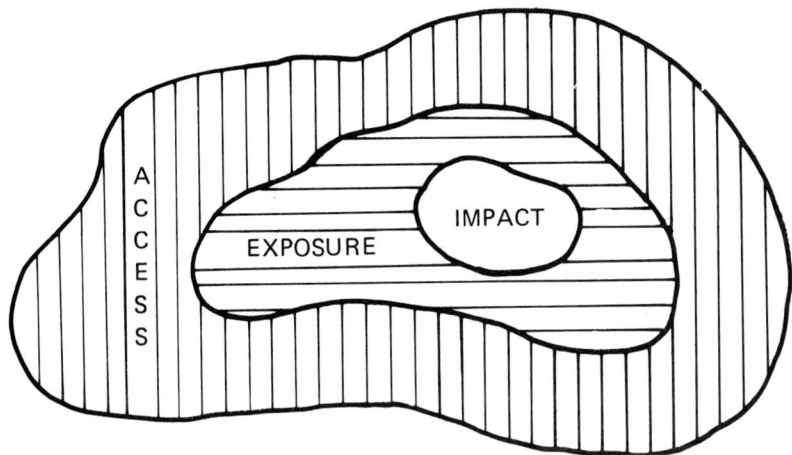

Figure 9.9

Topological model of communication showing a message's impact in relation to its accessibility to a population and the amount of exposure the message has in the population.

that the amount of information equals or surpasses the receiving capability of humans. This situation has been called **information overload.** It is very difficult to say that one channel, or source, has a particular effect over another. Therefore, carefully designed studies or controlled observations have, over the years, provided us with a knowledge base surrounding the effects of communication. Contributors to this field of study include Wilbur Schramm, Marshall McLuhan, I. de S. Pool, and David Clark.

Different opinions exist about the effects of communication. At the extremes (1) the information presented has no effect, but the medium itself creates an effect, or (2) the content, sequence, and format of information has an effect on the receiver. Regardless of what really causes what, the new communication technology has been blamed for deafening young people with rock music — if not also corrupting their morals — of contributing to delinquency by violent TV shows, and of changing mating customs with drive-in theaters. These are heavy charges.

EFFECTS ON INSTITUTIONS

To avoid generalizations, let's look at the effects of communication technology on some structural units of society. The basic units, like the state, church, and family, are recognized as areas of social activity that accept change, yet continue to exist in some form. These institutions have changed with the times. Today, modern America offers some alternatives to the traditional institutional division of society. Although alternative lifestyles and subcultures, too, have institutions (some form of government, family arrangements, and so forth), this analysis deals only with the effects of communication technology on the mainstream of American life.

Government

Prior to his inauguration, one of our recent presidents made long-distance telephone calls to leaders and heads of state in several European countries. This action could be interpreted as an attempt to keep the gears of international politics running smoothly. Seeing the need for personal contact, but dealing realistically with problems of time and money, he transcended transportation needs and, instead, used communication technology to deliver his message.

The effects of communication technology on government range from streamlining operations to microfilming documents to getting elected in the first place. The initiators of these effects fall into two main categories: (1) the communications industry, and (2) the government's use of communication networks and systems. From an industry point of view, the government has established agencies that control and regulate certain aspects of the industry. On the other hand, as a powerful commercial business, the communication industry often lobbies governmental decision-makers to enact laws and rulings favorable to their industry.

The government uses communication technology in a two-step flow of information. The government distributes information via many different media. Drivers' licenses are printed, agricultural reports use aerial photos, and TV press conferences are recorded to transmit information to the public. The second step of information flow is from the public to the government. In a representative form of government, it is important for the elected representatives to remain in tune with their constituents. It is also beneficial for the voters to know what the people in public office are really doing! In recent years, a few government officials have been driven from office by the media's embarrassing reports of their activities.

All in all, the proper use of modern technology should make the government more responsive to the American people. Data processing and computer information-storage techniques can efficiently reduce the voluminous amounts of information needed to operate a government. Domestic and international affairs can be dealt with quickly, and military operations can be controlled by high-level personnel with communication links to personnel at the operational level.

Remember, the use of technology can have both positive and negative effects at the same time, but it almost always creates change. An example of this can be found in the military. In order to respond to potential crisis, the military has developed excellent communication systems. One subtle side effect of real-time communications has had an interesting effect on the U.S. Navy. Traditionally, the commander of a ship has had total control of and responsibility for the vessel, particularly in time of crisis when training and experience offer information for split-second decisions.

Before modern communication systems, this type of responsibility offered a challenge and degree of excitement. It also stimulated junior officers to work hard to become commanders of their own vessels. However, current technical developments have enabled military and political leaders thousands of miles away to become immediately involved in crisis decisions that were once made only by the officer in charge. This action can, at times, erode the command prerogative of the on-board officer and reduce the role to one of merely carrying out someone's orders. Whether this is good or bad for the country does not concern us here, but it might explain the diminishing attractiveness of command at sea.

United States Media Financial Data ($ Millions)

		Revenues	Expenses	Income *
Am/Fm Radio	1972	1,407.0	1,272.6	134.3
Television	1973	3,464.8	2,811.7	653.1

* Before federal income taxes
Source: 1975 Broadcasting Yearbook.

Figure 9.10

1975 Broadcasting Yearbook

Economics

When investigating the effects of communication technology on economics, one's first instincts would be to list the amount of money that changed hands within the communications industry. This amount appears in Figure 9.10 and is an indicator of the industry's importance, but this topic should deal with economics in general, not just the economics of the communication industry. **Economics** means the production, distribution, and consumption of commodities. We are interested in the effects of communication technology on the production, distribution, and consumption of these commodities.

First, modern communications systems have influenced the production technologies since the 1950s in a very basic manner. From the production of wool sweat socks to gasoline, modern communication technology controls and monitors the machines and techniques necessary for production. In the automobile industry, the design and planning of new models is accomplished with electronic computers that have graphic capabilities. Engineers use electronic calculators and sophisticated testing instruments to determine materials and manufacturing techniques. Many parts are machined and shaped by numerically or computer-controlled machines. Automated assembly lines are controlled by the clock. Computer selection of parts prevents blue doors from being put on red bodies. Even the workers' paychecks are prepared by computers and other office machines. Modern communication technology provides for faster production with a higher level of standardization at a greater initial cost. There is, however, a degree of inflexibility in the performance of such production systems.

Communication systems provide a more efficient accounting and shipping network for complex distribution of commodities. This distribution depends on communication and transportation technologies. (At times these may be one and the same.) Consumer-market surveys to determine what particular type of product should be shipped where often are done by telephone. For instance, it would be foolish to ship 10,000 air conditioners to Nome, Alaska, in November. Once distribution points are established, shipping arrangements must be set up and an accurate product accounting procedure established. This accounting, if it is done on a large scale, will be handled with the help of a computer.

With accurate monitoring devices, production schedules and inventory levels can be precisely controlled. The chances of over- or underproduction are reduced with faster and more accurate assessment of demand and distribution. Equipment to computerize accounting and distribution of products is expensive, but it provides for a

Figure 9.11

Computer filing is fast becoming a necessity for efficient management of storeroom and information services.
Courtesy, AVCO Financial Services

close interface with the production phase. Also, a more specialized workforce is needed to operate and maintain communication-technology-assisted distribution systems.

Advertising plays a major role in the consumption of a commodity. Various media approaches are designed to present the product in its most attractive manner. It seems that advertisers today believe that sexy, pretty girls can sell anything. In some instances, advertising is given credit for the free commercial-broadcast industry that exists in the United States. The broadcast industry is not dependent on government underwriting. Advertising, in conjunction with printed assembly and maintenance booklets, incorporates many types of communication devices and techniques.

A modern industrialized economy is quite dependent on communication technology. The use of this technology has a wide spectrum of implications, but surely its use helps to keep the economic marketplace moving smoothly.

Family

Increased change in today's modern technological society has contributed to family instability measured by a marked difference in family structures of today, as compared to those of a generation ago. Many of your parents, and surely your grandparents, remember a time when television did not exist or when only a few neighbors had telephones. Traditionally, family members had designated roles — the man worked, the woman took care of the house and children, and the children respectfully obeyed their parents.

Many families today are different! The family as a group and the individual members who compose it have tremendous freedom. All family roles but childbearing are susceptible to change, and now the choice to have children or not is a common one. Generally better educated and more affluent than a generation ago, today's families own more equipment that enables them to participate in communicative efforts. They also engage in more technical communication activity in their work and play.

The effects of communication technology on the family unit are difficult to determine. However, the increased freedom of family members coupled with the growing number of devices and opportunities to communicate lead one to believe that it is possible for each member to receive selected information of his or her choice. The awareness gained by each individual contributes to the dynamics of the family and, perhaps, also to the dissension among its members.

For example, most households in America contain one television and one radio; many contain at least two televisions, a number of radios, and record or tape equipment. If one family member tunes in certain information on one type of media, other members are free to choose different content from other sources. If this happens often, a pattern of interests and attitudes develops that can be isolating. Pushing this example to extremes, these tactics could eventually split the family unit if other stimuli were also pushing in that direction.

As all technology has good and bad effects, so does communication. The modern family can strengthen its ties around home entertainment carried by communication systems. A family can be overjoyed by a telephone call or saddened by a telegram. The use of communication technology provides information that permits (or is responsible for) adaptive change in the family structure.

Education

With all of the progress in the field of technical communications, education has just crossed the threshold. It is only now beginning to utilize communication systems that can assist students to learn. Whether the focus is on individual instruction or on a classroom of 300 students, systems exist that can offer interesting and enjoyable learning experiences.

The proper use of communication technology within the context of specific educational goals and objectives can have very positive effects. Devices like film loop projectors, audio tape playback units, and computer-assisted instruction allow a student to learn at his or her own pace. Large-group instructional technology — viewing motion pictures or television, for example — offers the advantage of giving everyone an "up-close" look at material. Both students and teachers are affected by the use of communication technology; it can provide learning experiences that bridge time and space. Instead of just reading about the medieval barter system, it's possible to travel back in time through visual and audio forms of media and observe a reenactment of the process. Experimental studies have shown that a higher level of efficiency in learning occurs with the use of visual and audio media in teaching.

Although it can be more time-consuming for the teacher to use media, the use of technology in education also releases the teacher from certain tasks in time that can be used better planning and creative teaching. The use of communication technology in education has been accused of altering the student's relationships with others. Instead of interacting with another human being, the student interacts with a machine, and thus the educational process is dehumanized. Perhaps this does occur, but only as a side effect resulting from the improper use of technology.

Religion

Religion is one of civilization's oldest institutions. Religious activities in primitive societies quite frequently incorporated communication techniques via ritual dances and symbolistic art forms. Religion today is affected by the use of communication technology. Like government or the family, religion as an institution changes as society changes.

Just as laws and a Constitution are basic to our government, values and beliefs are basic to religion. Due to the use of mass communication techniques, religious beliefs held by individuals are confronted with unwanted and unexpected information. Flashy billboard signs, risqué magazine covers, and violent or blatantly sexual television programs occasionally offend. A pious world this is not! Because it sees its function as the transmission of information, the mass media accepts content on almost all subjects; values are often laid aside while an attempt is made to enhance the objectivity of information or news. This is exercising the American right of free expression. However, this right of free expression is also exercised to provide information with religious connotations.

Religious-oriented radio and television programs reinforce individual beliefs. Spot announcements and advertisements of activities and programs appear in newspapers. A wealth of religious tracts are published each month, possibly to counteract antireligious information, but more likely to help others "get the message."

In this world of modern media when immediacy is a cherished possession, information and news often concern the bizarre and describe the evils done by people. The possibility that persons are or could be subconsciously indoctrinated to act has long been investigated by researchers. Regardless of beliefs, the enormous amount of information made possible by modern communication technologies has at least broadened the awareness of many persons.

EFFECTS ON THE INDIVIDUAL

Many people have said that the most powerful effects of communication technology are invisible, particularly the impact on human consciousness and individual behavior. The effects on each individual are varied since individual experiences provide different information and each individual receives, processes, and stores information in a different manner. There are, however, a number of areas in which the effects on the individual can be studied.

Values and Attitudes

Each individual has some form of values and attitudes, regardless of whether these values are the same as or different from ours. Values are difficult things to explain.

They can be identified as ideals or customs that a group of people hold in regard. Topics such as freedom, cleanliness, respect, cruelty, and crime are of general interest to many people. Different groups of people generally have different regards toward the same value. For example, during the late sixties and early seventies, there grew a social movement in the United States that taxed the values and attitudes of every young person between the ages of 13 and 25. In fact, this transitional period into adulthood often becomes a time for individuals to sort things out, to develop and establish their own set of values. Anyway, these decades were also influenced greatly by the mass media of television, radio, newspapers, and magazines. A movement of the young spread across the country. They were called flower children, hippies, and yippies (among other things); these young people established their own set of values.

Kids from all walks of life ran away from home and adopted their own way of dress — army fatigues adorned with patches, beads, and bells became the uniform. Scarves and bandannas held back long hair. Personal cleanliness was not considered important, and strong feelings toward human rights and antiwar activities became the province of the young. These "new values" were proclaimed as signs of a youth culture separate from the established values of an older society. These new values were also the focus of the mass media. Reports, essays, and live coverage of the new value movement adorned every household across the country.

This use of communication technology reinforced the tendency to explore new values. Media coverage of youth groups that proclaimed new values probably did not cause anyone to adopt these values, but it certainly did present a variety of values and lifestyles. Individual tendencies to adopt the new and the radical would certainly be reinforced. Conservative youth from small towns and rural areas were exposed to new, radical ideas from which they had been sheltered. But let us remember that while the media popularized new attitudes, they also trivialized them. The opportunity for a meaningful shift in values often became merely the adoption of new trends in speech, in dress, in lifestyle.

Perceptions

An individual's perception, how that person views the world, can be affected by communication technology. Television is notorious for its suspected ability to alter one's perception. First, it has been said that many people watch television to relax, to get away from reality. Programs have been blamed for blurring the distinction between what is real and what is fantasy. The popularity of soap operas has been attributed to the need of individuals to live an exciting, dramatic life secondhand, while they remain safe in their accustomed place in life. Certainly children have difficulty distinguishing fact from fantasy while viewing cartoons and simulated programs.

Communication technology can distort the sensory reception of visual information. Any time a decision is made to show something on television, a decision is also made to not show something. For instance, when a political figure makes a speech and the television cameras show people in the audience cheering and applauding, the television viewer could easily perceive everyone to be in favor of the speech. However, while the decision to show the happy, cheering audience could have been objective, it might also have been a decision to not show the protesting signs and outraged members of the audience. This type of coverage conveys accurate information, but not *all* of the information. It is for this reason that viewers must be aware that not all perceptions and not all information provided by the mass media are a totally accurate view of reality. The people who make this type of decision are called **gate keepers**. They control what information goes in and comes out.

Emotions

Studies to determine if the emotions of an individual can be affected by communication technology, and if they could lead to undesirable actions, have been inconclusive. The effects on emotions of certain types of scenes, particularly of violence, are very easy to generalize; however, these generalizations are not always accurate.

Experiments have been conducted with a number of groups of young children. One group would watch a short film or television program that showed lots of violence; other groups viewed a nonviolent film. These groups were then observed immediately afterward for signs of aggression or violence. Some studies have shown children imitating the viewed aggression, especially if it was performed by the good guys — cowboys, police officers, or detectives — who were rewarded for being violent.

National studies of the effects of television have revealed little conclusive evidence. The relationship between media viewing and behavior seems to be only casual. In fact, the television industry claims that violence acted out on television reduces violent tendencies of viewers. They could be right. Years ago some observers indicated that heavy viewers lose their alert stages of consciousness and lapse into a trancelike posture with eyes glued to the tube.

The effects of communication technology on individual emotions range from one extreme to the other. Only a careful examination of the experimental research in specific areas can offer conclusive answers.

Learning

When Evel Knievel performed his daredevil motorcycle jumps on film and live television, he was accused of "teaching" viewers how to become rich and famous by jumping motorcycles over dangerous obstacles. The resulting announcements made by Knievel warning viewers not to attempt anything like the jumps he performed are evidence that some people believe the influence of communication technology on learning is strong indeed.

The effects of the use of communication technology on learning outside of an educational setting are incidental. Small children often pick up the lyrics to an advertisement on television or radio and sing it over and over. This is an example of incidental (indirect) learning. The mass media are oftentimes overrated as to the amount of information they supposedly help viewers learn. Surely children's programming like **Sesame Street** and **Mr. Rogers' Neighborhood** informs viewers, but perhaps the real value of these shows in respect to individual learning is that they prepare the viewer to learn. The degree of information learned from these programs depends, in large part, on reinforcement by the child's family. If parents discuss the program, encourage the child, and help the child respond, more learning will accrue.

Incidental learning can occur within any age group and in any setting. The computer programmer, for instance, can learn a new symbol or command just by seeing its use in another context often enough. However, this form of learning occurs more often with young children, particularly while they are watching television or films or reading a book. Often parents avoid upsetting situations by explaining, "It's only a story!"

THE LAW

1. Consider a book that charged that anyone who participated in dancing, hunting, or play-acting contributed to a devil's device. This might not have been so bad; but it so happened that when the above book was printed in England in 1623, that country had a queen who was fond of plays. In fact, this very same queen had recently taken part in a play at her court. The queen, being rather angry, punished the printer, William Prynn. Prynn's book was found to be seditious criticism against the queen, and he was fined. He was also branded on the forehead, had his nose slit, and both ears chopped off. But everything worked out in the end. The Long Parliament found his trial to have been illegal and released him from prison. Alas, in the meantime they had burned his book.

   A printer's life was truly interesting in those days! One not only had to select the appropriate typeface for a particular press run, but one also tried to guess who might be offended and how one could escape capture. The days of the Court of the Star Chamber are over, thanks in part to the many printers who gave their lives in seventeenth-century England in the attempt to unshackle printing from licensing and censorship. The Court of the Star Chamber controlled the process of printed communication as did the Stationers Company (a licensed printing guild for the government) established by the Tudor monarchs.

2. Recently the city of Memphis, Tennessee, filed charges against an actor in a pornographic film, not for the content of the explicit sex shown, but for being a conspirator (since he accepted money for his part) in a plot to distribute the film across state lines. The charges could lead to extreme curtailment of film distribution and production. At the time of this writing the charges have been met with countercharges and appeals. The final outcome may not be resolved for years to come.

3. In November 1974 the American Telephone and Telegraph Company was charged by the U.S. Department of Justice with "monopolizing and conspiring to monopolize" telecommunications service and equipment. The Justice Department charged AT&T with violating the Sherman Antitrust Act. AT&T responded that the purpose of the government's action was to break up the Bell System. AT&T's pledge to fight a vigorous case against the government means that the entire case will take years to come to a conclusion.

4. Imagine that some time tomorrow, state and federal Pure Food and Drug agents place you under arrest for lying about a local bubble gum scandal. Without your knowledge a new kind of lie detector is used to analyze a tape recording of your voice, which was taken during the interview. The lie detector measures certain frequency changes in the human voice that are undetectable to the human ear. If generally adopted, this remote lie detector could become an instrument for control and surveillance, a step toward a Big Brother from whom nothing could be hidden.

5. The local record and tape store always seems to have superlow-priced copies of 8-track and cassette tape recordings of the hottest sounds going. The only difference besides the cost

between that tape and the same tape at another store is the absence of the flashy printed label. So what—you buy the tape and get into it, not knowing you have contributed to one of the biggest rip-offs in the music industry. Pirated, or dubbed, copies of existing copyrighted recordings or performances are illegal. The artist or record company never receives its share of the money, and the bootlegger usually makes all the profits until he or she is caught.

These are five examples of the relationship between communication technology and the law. The first and second deal with the concept of freedom of expression and censorship, the third with monopolization of a communication industry, the fourth with the invasion of privacy, and the fifth with violation of a copyright. All are serious charges resulting from the use of some type of communication technology and its effect on society.

Amendment I: "Congress shall make no law respecting an establishment of religion, or prohibiting the free exercise thereof; or abridging the freedom of speech, or of the press; . . . "

Amendment V: "No person . . . shall be compelled in any criminal case to be a witness against himself, nor be deprived of life, liberty [to speak or write], or property, without due process of law; . . . "

Amendment XIV: ". . . nor shall any State deprive any person of life, liberty [to speak or write], or property, without due process of law; . . . "

Figure 9.12

Amendments I, V, and XIV, of the United States Constitution.

Whatever its faults might be, the democratic, capitalistic system of the United States offers more individual and societal freedom than most other countries on earth. The United States also ensures citizens' protection from some governmental processes and state laws related to communications. The first 5 months of 1979 saw 15 states introduce legislation to deal with the social/legal effects of communication technology. The three main categories of legislation dealt with were computer crime, credit reporting and criminal records.

FREEDOM OF EXPRESSION

A major test of a nation's freedom is the degree of liberty to speak, to write, and to publish that it guarantees its people. The key to self-governing societies is people's access to a maximum flow of information. The development of technology that can provide fast, accurate, and almost unlimited information to people across an entire country contributes to the literacy of all. The Bill of Rights of the United States Constitution provides three amendments that have been interpreted as granting some aspect of freedom of expression. The First Amendment grants "freedom of speech and press," the Fifth Amendment deals with personal "liberty," and the Fourteenth Amendment protects citizens so that no state shall deprive anyone of life, liberty, or property without due process of law. Liberty has been interpreted to include liberty of speech and press.

The American press broke free of serious governmental control prior to the Revolutionary period by providing a medium for Loyalists and rebels to voice their differing opinions. Freedom of speech became the backbone of internal rebellion through America's history. The antiwar movement that opposed the Vietnam war in the sixties and early seventies utilized the media and mass protests to the fullest. Investigation of a gigantic government scandal was touched off by a Washington, D.C. newspaper, and that investigation eventually forced President Richard Nixon to resign from office in 1974. Ironically, the most damaging evidence against then President Nixon was a collection of tape-recorded conversations of Nixon and others. The recordings were made by Nixon's own recorder, hidden to gain evidence on others!

Figure 9.13

Freedom of expression permitted underground antiwar newspapers and mass demonstrations in the United States during the Vietnam War. Courtesy, *Berkeley Barb*

RIGHTS OF PRIVACY

Privacy has been loosely defined as "the right to be let alone." Privacy, and the threat of losing it, has recently become an issue of great concern to Americans. Modern communication developments have produced cameras and film that can record photos at night. Long-range telephoto lenses and supersnoop directional microphones have already threatened the privacy of celebrities and politicians. Use of telephone wiretaps to obtain information has been limited to specific law enforcement agencies, which must first secure a court order from a judge. All of these are examples of obvious uses of technology to invade individual privacy; but potentially the most dangerous threat to society is wide-scale data collection and information storage practices.

Long-term effects of information dossiers containing vital statistics on individuals could be catastrophic to a free society. In the United States today, many credit bureaus and governmental agencies collect data on millions of persons. The danger comes from the potential misuse of this information—all of which could easily be cross-referenced and stored in computers for easy access. It would be possible, for example, for a governmental agent or a private individual to identify all persons who had ever owned a gun, had an automobile accident, served in the military, or possessed certain skills. The remote possibility of living in a police state capable of exploiting or repressing individuals because of something in their data file is frightening.

Laws to protect one's privacy exist. However, these are not uniform. Federal laws differ from those of the individual states, and there are many differences between states, as well. When courts deal with issues of privacy, they are attempting to balance the right to individual privacy against the public's right to know.

Freedom of Information

A self-governing society needs to know what its government is up to, and whether the government is protecting the public interest. The United States federal government is a reservoir of information. But, owing to the complexity of government agencies, these sources of information are difficult for the individual citizen to obtain. Data such as facts on the nutritional value of processed foods, product and safety tests on many goods, hints for home construction and energy conservation are available at no or little cost.

The federal Freedom of Information Act was passed in 1966 and amended in 1974. It was written to allow the public to pry hidden information from the government about a wide range of topics from big business to our national forests. Subject to nine exemptions (issues of national defense, and trade secrets are among them), the public has a right to have access to and copies of documents and files kept by any agency or department of the federal government.

To secure any records or files, an individual must send a letter of request (see Figure 9.14) and reasonably describe the information they seek. For instance, if you wanted to identify the kinds of industries in your area that contributed to pollution of the environment, you would need to state that you would like to see the surveys of industries in your area in terms of environmental impact. The government has the right to charge for copying and search time but must respond within ten working days after receiving a request.

Censorship

It's been said that one problem with freedom of expression is that it's not always healthy for a society to permit uncontrolled expression without regard to values or good taste. American courts have long been searching for that fine line of "good taste" for printed material, films, television — almost all forms of communication. What separates obscene material from constitutionally protected freedom of expression has never been, and may never be, resolved.

SAMPLE REQUEST LETTER

(Name and Address
of Government Agency)
(Washington, D.C. or your local branch office of the agency usually will do for address)

Dear Sir or Madam:

    Pursuant to the Freedom of Information Act, 5 U.S.C. 552, I hereby request access to (or a copy of) (describe the document containing the information that you want) .

    If this request is denied either in whole or in part please inform me as to your agency's appeal procedure. If any expenses in excess of $_____ are incurred in connection with this request, please inform me of all such charges prior to their being incurred for my approval. If you do not grant my request within 10 working days, I will deem my request denied.

    Thank you for your prompt attention to this matter.

Very truly yours,

Figure 9.14

Copy of the letter used to secure information from the United States Government.
Source: Freedom of Information Clearinghouse

    Newspapers, books, and magazines enjoy the most liberal privileges from licensing or censorship. There are no censorship laws except during a time of war. Newspeople and photographers sometimes are prohibited from printing information or photos about criminal cases. This recurring issue of free press affecting the right to a fair trial process generally stems from a court order violation. However, the "distribution" of printed words or pictures may be illegal if the material is found to be obscene. Film and broadcast media fall under a different category of communication and are subject to controls (lots of people in the industry and government do not like the word **censorship**). If obscene or offensive material appears in film or over the air, it is generally snipped out or bleeped. This is not done by any legal agency but by the industry itself. Self-censorship exists mainly because prior censorship by any legal agency is prohibited. This means that the Federal Communications Commission (the FCC is a government agency that controls radio and television) cannot prevent a certain program from being shown. But if that show is obscene, after it is shown the agency can revoke the station's license. Therefore, most broadcast stations impose strict censorship of their own. Some persons feel that formal censorship laws should be enacted so that the self-control of the industry doesn't overreact and present only very bland programming.

    Cable television companies do not fall into the same categories of law as do over-the-air broadcast stations. In fact, a New York City cable company regularly produced its own late night talk show, which generally exceeded the FCC limits of offensive programming.

    The film industry in America has adopted a unique form of self-censorship. All films shown in this country are rated by a letter code—G, PG, R, or X—to indicate the type of audience permitted to see the film. Of course, many forms of underground and pornographic films still exist.

Figure 9.15

Films in the United States are rated according to the amount of explicit sex, violence, and foul language they contain.

REGULATION AND CONTROL

Along with the economic, technological, and bureaucratic growth of the United States, the masses grew as consumers. There have always been laws (unwritten and written) that have attempted to ensure equal value for the exchange of goods and money. Consumption became identified with the exchange of money as people stopped producing their own goods and turned to the mills and factories of the industrial age. As our nation became more industrialized, the relationship between the individual consumer, the industrial process, and the natural environment became more impersonal.

Local, state, and federal law developed to prevent exploitation by the ferryboat owner, the water company, and the postal rider. These laws helped to protect the

"I'M WITH THE FEDERAL COMMUNICATIONS COMMISSION. DO YOU HAVE A LICENSE?"

Figure 9.16

consumer of goods and services. As the country grew, so did the governmental inadequacies. The body of the federal government closest to the people, the Congress, was delegated to enact regulations to protect consumers.

Congress created various agencies to regulate specific industries and services. Each agency began small with clarity of purpose. With the increase of technological development and its influences on social change, the original aims of the regulatory agencies changed.

The competitive free enterprise system of the United States has stimulated the development of technology that is the main pillar of the broadcasting industry. Radio and television have utilized the electromagnetic spectrum to broadcast information over the air. The phenomenal growth of radio, and later television, used many of the frequencies available to carry their broadcasts. By 1926, the limited number of frequencies that make up the electromagnetic spectrum were utilized. Overcrowding of the airwaves by too many radio transmitters created interference in message transmission and reception. The radio listener could not be sure of tuning in a particular station and having clear reception due to the overlap of frequency and power variables of many transmissions. It was at this point that the broadcasters themselves asked the government to develop fair and acceptable regulatory measures for commercial radio stations.

The Radio Act of 1927 established the Federal Radio Commission (FRC) and in 1934 Congress passed the Communications Act to broaden the regulation and control to include television. The 1934 Communications Act changed the FRC to the Federal Communications Commission (FCC), to ensure that radio, television, and telephone industries operate in the "public's interest." The FCC is an independent federal agency charged with regulating interstate and foreign communication by means of radio, television, wire, cable, and satellite. The object of FCC regulation is:

> to provide for orderly development and operation of radio services (including television and other broadcasting uses), to make available a rapid, efficient, nationwide and worldwide telegraph and telephone service at reasonable charges; to promote the safety of life and property through the use of wire and radio communication; and to employ communication facilities for strengthening the national defense.

INTERNATIONAL CONTROL

The evolution of global communications has reached new dimensions in terms of technical sophistication. World demands for communication satellites will increase dramatically by 1984. The technology of communications has made possible the utilization of the ionosphere and the moon, as well as artificial satellites, as reflecting surfaces capable of relaying message transmissions anywhere in the world within seconds. Technical devices and the accompanying social effects of advanced telecommunications between countries demand consideration of the legal aspects of international communication. The development of international radio communication systems has stimulated parallel developments in international and space law.

Legal consideration was given to domains beyond the planet earth before Sputnik was launched by the USSR in 1957. It was about that time that the slowly developing body of knowledge about law in outer space flourished. The international flavor and competition of space exploration warned that regulatory procedures must exist in order to ensure peaceful cooperation for the general welfare of humankind. Without regulation it would be something like playing a rival high school basketball game without officials.

Figure 9.17

This control panel at Intelsat Headquarters in Washington, D.C., represents the type of sophisticated equipment necessary to monitor an international communications network.
Courtesy, COMSAT

Fortunately, the United Nations was ready to accept the challenge. The United Nations established an Ad Hoc Committee on the Peaceful Uses of Outer Space on December 13, 1958. In a report a year later, the committee recommended international agreements on: (1) the use of radio frequencies, (2) the registration of orbital elements, (3) continuing radio transmissions, and (4) removal of spent satellites.

In addition, a private multinational corporation was established in 1964. The International Telecommunications Satellite Consortium (INTELSAT) was created by international interim agreements. These agreements have since been superseded by the Definitive Agreements of 1973.

As of 1974, INTELSAT had eighty-six member nations. The organization owns satellites and associated ground-control equipment and leases the use of satellite communications units to member nations. Each nation pays for the use of the system in the amount equal to its actual use on a monthly basis. The global system of communications satellites has comprised four Intelsat IV satellites operating over the Atlantic, Pacific, and Indian Oceans. Soon, a new fleet of Intelsat V satellites will be launched to handle the anticipated communications traffic growth requirements for 1980.

Copyright

Late in 1976, President Gerald Ford signed into law the first revision of the 1909 copyright law. Copyright law serves as a "guarantee of rights" that protects literary, musical, or artistic work. The new copyright law (effective January 1, 1978) protects copyrighted works for fifty years of the lifetime of an author plus fifty years, during which no one may photocopy, show, or use the material unless granted permission. Limited copying may be done by teachers, students, researchers, and libraries under certain conditions.

Until the recent revision of the copyright law, modern communications technology had made it easy to abuse copyright rights. Office and school photocopying of books, articles, and worksheets could be done instantly. Records and tapes could be pirated with sophisticated audio recording equipment, and cable television companies could monitor and then sell the programming of over-the-air broadcasts to subscribers. All of this was done without any payment of royalties to the original creators. Aside from the immediate effect of lack of recognition and economic return, intense copyright violation could discourage artists and authors from producing any original works. This would be a sore loss to any society. However, the new law should preserve and encourage creative works in the fields of music, literature, and the arts.

Advertising

Advertising is a product of industrialization. Accurate and fair advertising is healthy for the open market. Fraudulent advertising is dangerous to the producer and harmful to the consumer. In an effort to reach as many viewers as possible, advertisers are heavy users of the mass media. The competitive market of today demands the use of fast and effective communication techniques to distribute the claims of commercial products and services.

Not unlike the Old West medicine shows, when peddlers promised tonics that could cure everything from worms to stinky feet, some advertisers tend to stretch the truth or omit the facts. In order to protect consumers from untrue or incorrect advertising, the federal government established the Federal Trade Commission (FTC) in 1914 to regulate advertising. In the case of a fraudulent advertisement, the person or company who placed the ad can be held responsible. If prior knowledge of the inaccuracies can be proven, the publisher or station who ran the ad can also be held responsible.

In the past it was easier for cheats and rascals to rip-off the public through illegal advertisement than it is today. Many persons in the communications industry have realized their responsibility and obligation to ensure truth in advertising.

Antitrust

Suppose you live in a small city that has one television station, one daily newspaper, two radio stations, and three movie houses. Also, suppose the one person who owns or controls all of these concerns is chairperson of the PTA committee that selects your school district's textbooks and is a partner to the owner of the local telephone company. It doesn't take a lot of imagination to guess that it would be very easy for this person to control the flow of information for the entire city. Granted, the effects of mass communication seldom go beyond the awareness stage; but such a lopsided influence on the selection and presentation of information could be dangerous.

The federal government prevents this type of monopoly of business under the Sherman Antitrust Act. Cross-media owners, print and broadcast, face changes in the law that could prevent their ownership of more than one type of outlet in any one community. Other aspects of the law prevent common carriers, such as telephone and telegraph companies, from gaining a monopoly on services or equipment production. Usually, communications firms are ordered to divest their holdings by the Antitrust Division of the U.S. Department of Justice.

American television networks and broadcasting corporations have a unique arrangement with television and radio stations across the nation. The three major networks, NBC, ABC, and CBS, are carried by individually-owned stations — something like the local fast-food chain. But U.S. newspapers offer a more interesting example. Newspaper monopolies, or chains, are allowed to exist. In fact, it seems that big business is the way to success. In 1973, 1015 daily newspapers were members of one chain or another; 734 were independent dailies.

The linking of communications industries may be necessary to provide for the fast, smooth, and inexpensive flow of information to the people. However, we must make sure that any concentration of communications industries does not hinder the free exchange of ideas and news.

The ability of technology to influence social change is often underestimated. Irregular relationships between sociocultural elements and technical elements prevent the establishment of hard-set rules that pertain to all peoples of our globe. Trends in communication technology utilization across the world affect the amount and type of information that is exchanged. This, in turn, creates changes in our perceptions of social institutions (family, church, state) and individual values, attitudes, and emotions.

The main purpose for studying the effects of technology on society is to become more aware of this phenomenon. Only in that way can technology be controlled to provide benefits to humankind. The challenge of controlling a technology, whether it be communication, transportation, or production, must begin with a firm understanding of all the underlying concepts. Only a technologically literate society can plan for the future, a future that will be increasingly influenced by technology.

CONCEPT FOCUSER

- The use of technical **communication devices** in highly industrialized countries across the world **is increasing.**
- Along with increased use of communication technology comes a greater **influence** of this technology **to create social change.**
- Social effects of technology are **far reaching** and often **unpredictable.**
- These **changes** resulting from technology can have both **positive and negative effects** at the same time.
- The value assigned to technological change represents existing **human values** of a particular time, location, and society.
- The **effects** of communication technology are found in **structural agents of society** (government, church, family), as well as in **individual values, perceptions, and learning.**
- The key to **self-governing societies** is people's access to a maximum **flow of information.**
- This flow of information must respect the rights of individuals and governments. It is for this reason that the relationship between **communication technology and law** is important.

FOOD FOR THOUGHT

1. Why does the adoption of complex technology create different types of social change than the adoption of a more primitive technology?
2. Does the availability of communication technology and information flow affect the sociopolitical atmosphere of a given country? Why?
3. How do international communication systems create the concept of the "global society"?
4. What are the legal foundations that support free and open communications in the United States?
5. What are the four areas of individual behavior that can be affected by communication technology?

6. List five American institutions that are susceptible to heavy influence by communication technology.

Expanding Experiences

1. Interview couples married less than 5 years, married 20–25 years, and married more than 50 years. Collect a list of communication equipment each possess. Ask what are their earliest childhood recollections of communication devices. Report to the class and discuss your findings.
2. Establish a panel to discuss and answer questions on the effects of communication technology in your community. Invite a member of the clergy, editor of a newspaper, movie theater operator, manager of the telephone exchange, attorney, and others.
3. Divide the class into three groups and select an evening time period, 30 or 60 minutes, to view television. Assign one major television network to each group and ask the viewers to watch and record (write down) all examples of television's influence on values and attitudes during the program and commercials. As a class, first develop a form to be used by all observers. Compare and discuss results.
4. Compare the use of communication technology in other countries with the political atmosphere of each nation. Identify trends in democratic, socialistic, and communistic forms of government.

Locator Tools

Clark, David, and Blankenburg, William B. *You and Media — Mass Communication and Society.* New York: Canfield Press, 1973.

Mesthene, Emmanuel. *Technological Change.* New York: New American Library, 1970.

Nelson, Harold, and Teeter, Dwight. *Law of Mass Communication.* Mineola, N.Y.: The Foundation Press, 1973.

UNESCO. *World Communications.* New York: Unipub, 1975.

COMMUNICATION TECHNOLOGY AND THE FUTURE

Module
TEN

At Home, A.D. 2030

Innovations in the field of communication technology have been so numerous that we can now accomplish what was only dreamed of just a few years ago.

In Module Six we learned about developments in electrical systems and the evolution of telegraphic and telephonic communication. In Module Eight we advanced to the electronic age, which was characterized by the inventions of radio, radar, television, and satellites. In this module we will project ourselves into the future to the year 2030 and learn how solid-state communications will have extended the human senses to even greater horizons. In addition, we will make some technological forecasts based on the anticipated technical breakthroughs in this field in the years to come.

The Automated Home—A Scenario

In the year 2030 all people in technologically advanced countries will live in automated homes, where all of the chores will be prescheduled on kitchen microcomputers and accomplished electronically. The temperature, humidity, and amount of electrostatically cleansed fresh air will be monitored continuously and automatically adjusted to the desired levels. All the houseperson will have to do is to program the necessary tasks into the computer, and obedient automatons will take over from there. With the automated home, everyone in the family will have much more free time to enjoy the entertainment center as well as many more outside activities. Let's take a look at what you might encounter if you were living in 2030.

It's Monday morning and the tape-alarm system in your bedroom has just awakened you with the announcement that today you are to review for tomorrow's final examination in Communications Technology. You are reminded by the tape of some of the major concepts that you are supposed to know before you take the examination.

272 COMMUNICATION TECHNOLOGY AND THE FUTURE

Figure 10.1

Shown above is the kitchen of the future with its microcomputer system that holds thousands of receipe selections and data for balancing the diets of the entire family. In addition, it handles such other home management chores as budgeting, checkbook balancing and family games. Cost of the system is less than $800.
Courtesy, Radio Shack, a division of Tandy Corporation

Your mother, who manages a local wholesale supply store in town, was awakened by the separate tape-alarm in her bedroom and notified of the orders that came into the office during the night.

Breakfast has just been announced by the kitchen computer as the dishes slide from the programmed microwave cooker onto the table. After breakfast, the plastic tableware is swept into the washer-compactor recycling machine that makes new plastic utensils for the next meal.

After brushing your teeth, you go to the home learning center and check into school. On the desk, you have a CRT/keyboard console, a desk-top microphone, a microcomputer, and one of the new low-cost facsimile-duplicator units. It is 8:00 A.M.—time to turn on the CRT for a few announcements by your homeroom teacher. After the announcements you begin to review for the final. This is relatively easy because it has already been programmed into the computer. All you have to do is to clip on the learning electrodes, depress R on the keyboard, and sit back and listen. The learning experience will involve your ears, your eyes, and your sense of touch, smell, and taste.

AT HOME, A.D. 2030   273

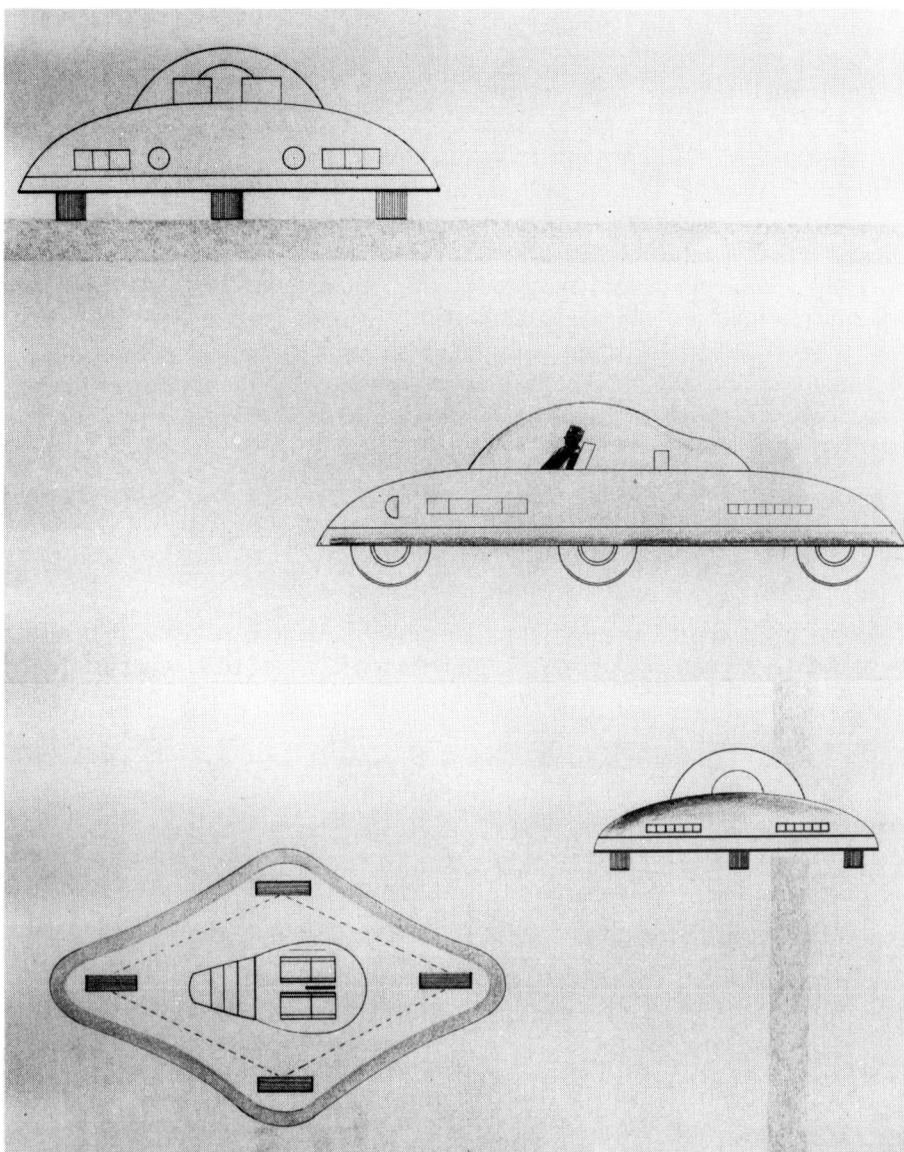

Figure 10.2

Development of the antigravity car was a major technology breakthrough. The car is functionally designed, with comfort and safety features built in as standard equipment. Wheels are used only for resting purposes, to back out of a garage, or to park in a parking space. The vehicle normally moves at different levels of elevation above the ground. Passing is accomplished by changing elevation levels, not going around other vehicles.
Courtesy, E. G. Berger

Your mother leaves the house about 8:00 A.M. and walks to the garage. As she opens the doors, she admires the shiny new fiberglass vehicle that will take her to work. Discovery of how to control gravity has made it possible for everyone to have a car while eliminating those last century cars that emit noxious fumes from ten dollar per gallon fuel. Since 2000 only antigravity cars, or those fueled with hydrogen gas, have been permitted on the streets. Engineers say that developing the antigravity car was much like designing a Ferrari to get 52 miles per gallon, hold twelve people, and still cost less than a Volkswagen to operate.

Traveling to work in her antigravity car, your mother reflects on what the family will do next weekend. She has been on a four-day workweek for the last few years, and everybody in the family seems to enjoy it. Automation has made all this possible.

She notes how the traffic moves smoothly and rapidly through town as the traffic lights work in perfect synchrony. The traffic system has street-corner radar/microcomputers, which are connected to a central traffic-optimizer system. Traffic light changes, lane adjustments, speed, and even changes in direction of traffic are computed from patterns of previous traffic flow stored in the computer's memory bank. This system maximizes the overall flow of traffic for every possible traffic situation.

Diagnostic and Prescription Computers

Unfortunately, your little brother was feeling sick when he arose this morning. Perhaps it was because his tape-alarm reminded him of a test he had to take during first-period class today.

After breakfast, your father dialed the family computer-based diagnostic and prescription system that delivered spoken information. With the critical shortage of doctors, this system has been a big help to persons with minor ills. The person/machine conversation went something like this:

> **Computer voice:** Good morning. This is your home diagnostic and prescription program for the treatment of minor ills. Do you have descriptive information about the program? Please key-in your response by using the touch-tone buttons and the appropriate code on page 4.
> Father keys in code for word **yes.**
>
> **Computer voice:** Good. To begin the program, please key in the national identification number, sex, and age of the patient.
> Father keys in national identification number, sex, and age of your little brother.
>
> **Computer voice:** Thank you. Using the code on page 5, please indicate the symptoms.
> Father keys in **headache, warm forehead, sniffles.**
>
> **Computer voice:** Any other symptoms?
> Father keys in code for "no."
>
> **Computer voice:** Thank you. Now please take patient's temperature and key in proper code.
> Father keys in code for 37.5° Celsius.

Computer voice: Based on the input symptoms, the patient is apparently suffering from a mild case of nasal pharyngitis, or the common cold. Recommend patient rest at home for one day, drink plenty of liquids, and take one aspirin every three hours. Repeating the instructions (machine repeats last sentence). Did you understand the prescription?
Father keys in code for word **yes.**

Computer voice: Good. We hope the patient feels better tomorrow. If not, be sure to contact your family physician for further instructions. It has been a pleasure to serve you.

Although this computer-based system can only be used for minor ills, plans are moving ahead to expand it to many of the more serious areas of human disease, in which constant monitoring of medication is essential. Even physicians are using this memory-jogging device in their offices to assist them in handling diagnoses faster and more accurately. In addition, the system maintains a complete medical profile on each of its patients and performs all billing.

The Automated Plant

Your mother has just arrived at her office. During transport she had a chance to be tape-briefed about the orders that came in during the night, especially the high-priority industrial orders. Instead of going directly to her office as she usually does, she goes directly to the shipping/receiving dock where the orders have already been filled, packed, billed, and stacked for shipment. An order for replacement items is now being processed by the office microcomputer.

Noting that the trucks are coming to pick up the shipment, she rides back to her office on the people-moving walkway that runs throughout the plant. Arriving at her office, she notes on the electronic appointment board that she is scheduled for a teleconference with the corporate president, who is located in a distant city. In her office, she had a CRT/keyboard console built into her desk, as well as a TV camera recessed into the opposite wall. Her secretary also has a desk-top CRT/keyboard, which she uses for filing purposes. As all supply orders are received electronically, she has no need for filing cabinets. All data is now contained in a small memory bubble unit, which is connected directly to the CRT. The only other piece of equipment is her voice-operated typewriter used for dictation or instructions. A small cable connects the plant offices with corporate headquarters on a leased-line basis. Because of the use of advanced communications technology and better business methods, only three people are needed to manage this large, but highly automated facility effectively.

It is 9:00 A.M. and your mother's secretary has signaled that the conference call is ready. Looking at her desk-top CRT, she sees the corporate headquarters staff at a similar table in what was once known as San Francisco. After the usual pleasantries and comments about the controlled weather at each location, the president reviews the profit and loss statements and outlines sales projections for the next fiscal year. At the end of the teleconference, your mother can't help but think of the advantages of communications technology as a substitute for travel and the many valuable hours that might have been wasted if people still had to travel.

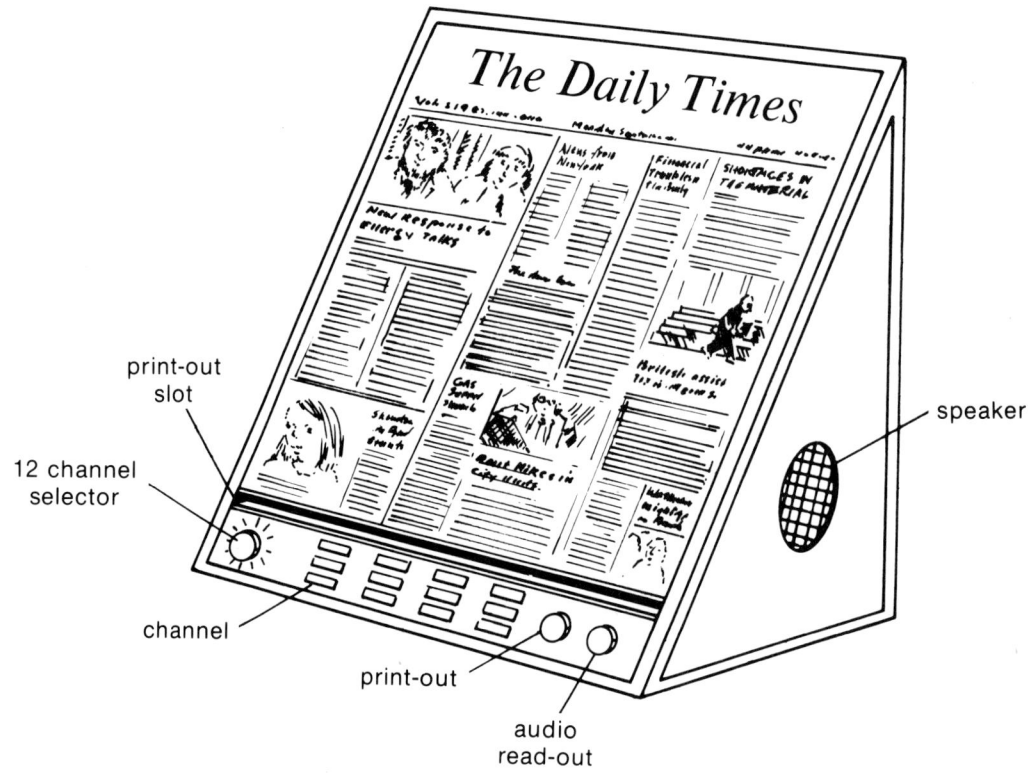

Figure 10.3

The slow scan instant newspaper is radio transmitted directly to the reader and optically displayed for easy reading. A wide selection of English and foreign language papers from around the world are available at the turn of a dial. Other features include a page print-out capability, as well as audio readout for the blind or disabled.

Shopping from Home

Meanwhile, back at home, your father has just given the prescribed medication to your little brother and is reading the morning paper over the new slow-scan system, which produces one complete frame-image for each page. Noting a special sale on food items, he immediately consults the home microcomputer for the caloric content of each item to see if it matches the balanced diet for all the family members. There are so many good items in so many stores that it would be very difficult for him to visit each store to take advantage of the specials. He punches the hard-copy button on the slow-scan newspaper system and immediately receives a hard copy of the advertisements. This is necessary because the specials are listed by code, which also contains the price of the item. Dialing supermarket A on the touch-tone handset, he orders several food items and then repeats the process for specials from the other supermarkets. His telephone orders appear on the CRT read-out of the kitchen microcomputer and he is pleased with his purchases. He has just saved several dollars by selective buying—all without having to leave the house. Punching the input button, the entire transaction is entered into the internal memory bank and the household

AT HOME, A.D. 2030

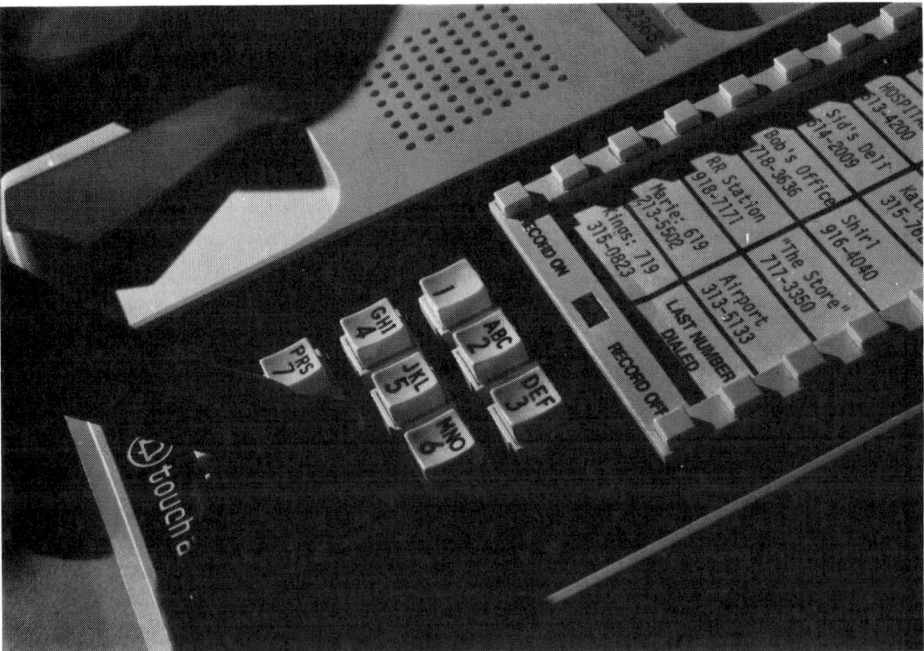

Figure 10.4

Touchamatic telephone sets like this one provide customers with instant contact with other subscribers anywhere in the world.
Courtesy, Bell Laboratories

accounts adjusted accordingly. Payment for the transaction is automatically transferred to the bank, which debits his account and credits the appropriate accounts of the supermarkets. His thoughts shift to the joys of living in a cashless society. He wonders how his neighbors are doing with the new and more economical speech-recognition microcomputer they have leased. Using it, they can tell the microcomputer what they want ordered from where and the computer does everything else. They can even vote on their home computer.

Returning to the hard copy of the morning paper, he reads about a new shopping service available to subscribers having the touch-tone system. With this device, it is possible to order all types of household items from one's own armchair. It is called the Tele-Vid system and is connected to the two-way closed-circuit television cable system that serves the home. According to the ad, the user can tone-dial up a display that appears on the television set in full color. Black-and-white television sets are no longer used except for display purposes in museums. The ad lists the operating instructions for the system. They read like this:

1. Turn your TV set to channel S.
2. Tone-dial your local Tele-Vid Service Center.
3. Place your telephone receiver in the cradle provided. The Tele-Vid trademark should appear on your TV screen along with the following recorded instructions:

Computer voice: This is your new Tele-Vid shopping service designed to make your shopping a more pleasant experience. You may request a display catalog for almost any item you wish by keying in the proper code number on your telephone handset. If you were to select carpets, you would see them displayed on your screen with a code number indicating the special price, the store handling that particular carpet, and the last date for which the sale price will be in effect. Our buying service allows you to order or reserve the items for delivery by encoding the appropriate number and your national identification number. You will be billed automatically for those items you order through the Tele-Vid system. Now you may shop with your Tele-Vid electronic shopping service.

Mobile Communications Systems

Business people, if they are to be successful, must be in instant contact with their home office at all times. In 2030, they will be served by a vast computerized network enabling them to talk to any location in the world while driving down the automated highways.

Your mother's car is connected to the new High-Capacity Mobile Telephone System (HCMTS), which has been established in most modern cities across the world. It uses frequencies in the 900 MHz region with fixed, low-power transmitters located in a grid pattern over the entire area being served. The system comprises a digital computer and a high-speed switching network that is connected to the electronic toll equipment in the central office. Both voice and digital signals are used. The mobile unit fits inside the horn button and is voice actuated.

After making a few business calls to her suppliers in Tokyo and London on her mobile set, your mother returns home to rejoin the family at 6:00 PM local time in the appropriate time zone. Now all local time and zone differences have disappeared in favor of the universal 24-hour clock system. With them went the problems of constantly changing all local time by setting the clocks ahead or behind to compensate for the changing solar paths and the eccentric rotation of the earth. These changes became necessary when space travel became commonplace and based on the need for a highly accurate universal time system.

The 24-hour universal time system is based on the sidereal second, minute, hour, day, and year as measured from fixed stars. As a traveler journeys around the world or into space, the time at any given moment, at any given location, is always the same. This means that our biological clocks are no longer affected by travel—both jet and orbital time lag have completely disappeared from our vocabulary. Maintaining such an accurate time system was made possible by the invention of the hydrogen watch which soon replaced the old atomic clock.

It was a little difficult at first getting used to regulating our activities to a new time system but after a while it became a relatively small matter when compared to the advantages of the universal time system.

Home Entertainment Center

After dinner, the family moves to the home entertainment center to enjoy an evening of worldwide television while the faithful kitchen microcomputer takes over the direction of the automatic cleaning and recycling process in the kitchen.

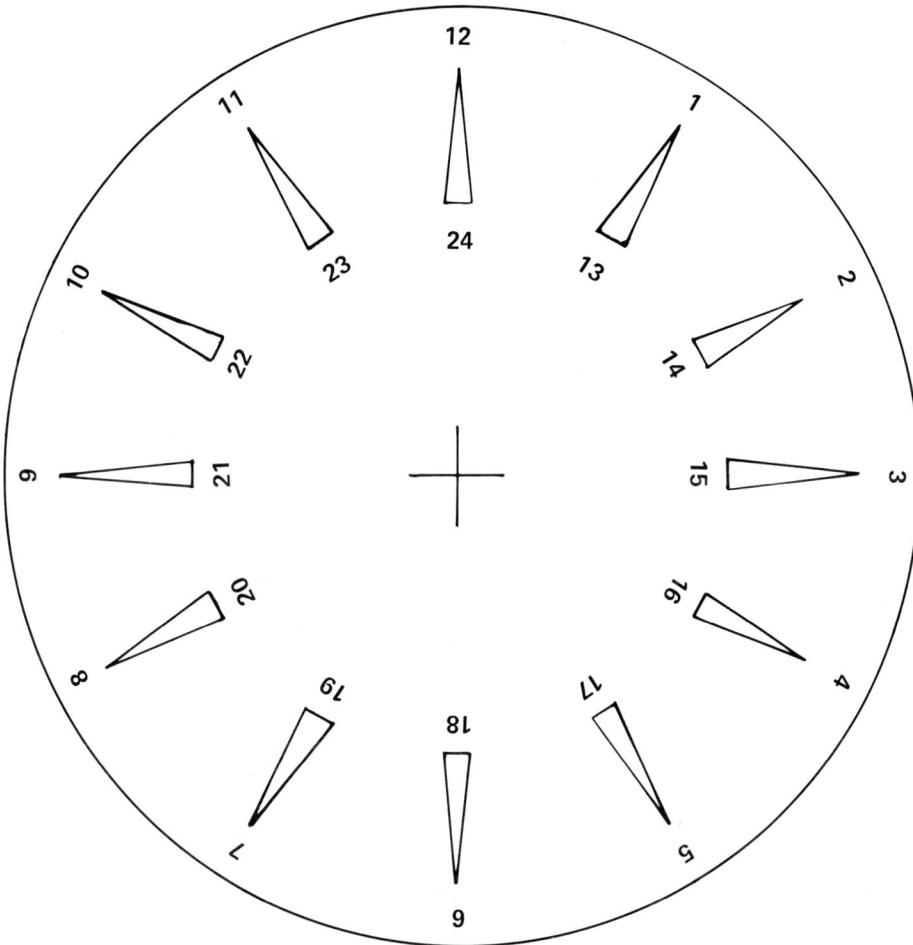

Figure 10.5

Twenty-four hour universal time system, based on the sidereal day, starts at 2400 hours each day in Greenwich, England. Solar noon is 1200 hours in the U.S. but is 2300 hours in China. Gone are the confusing time divisions of A.M., P.M., Daylight saving, and the artificial regulation of the local time zones by setting clocks ahead or behind.

Television as an entertainment medium has continued to grow at a rapid rate, with most families having a monitor in each room. The TV set of 2030 is a lot different from the set used in the 1980s. In the 1980s, the screens were flat, measuring 80-cm × 122-cm, and hanging on a wall like a picture. The receiving circuits were contained in a little box on the floor below the flat screen near a wall outlet. Because of cable TV, there was no need for unsightly TV antennas. Now, the 80-cm × 122-cm screen has given way to life-sized, electroluminescent walls which can be viewed from anywhere in the room. All video circuits are now located within the 1-cm thick screen, which for all intents and purposes looks just like the other walls of the house. The recent invention of the photoamplifier helped to make the wall-sized TV possible. Focusing and perfect color balance are achieved automatically; remote control units are located at convenient places throughout the room. Monitor screens are located in other walls of the house in case some family member would like to watch a different TV program. Most of the programs are televised in three-dimensions these days. Video recorders, which can be programmed to pick up and record a program while the family is away from home, are built into standard TV sets. The biggest problem confronting the family today is trying to decide which programs to watch from more than 100 stations available across the world.

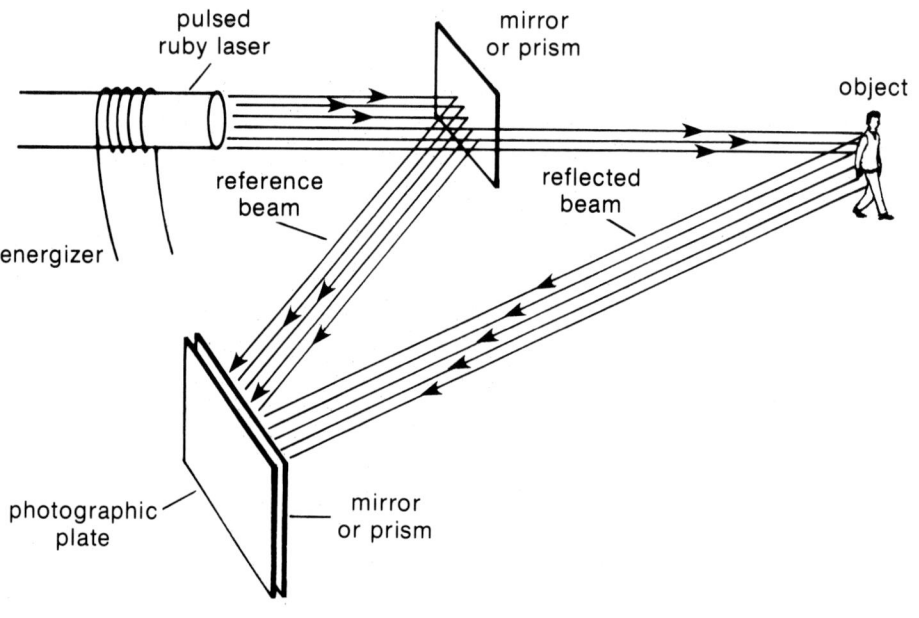

Figure 10.6

Sketch of a holographic system showing how the third dimension of any object is created.

The 3-D Television System

The technique for producing 3-D images on the TV set is relatively simple. As we learned in Module Five, 3-D images (holograms) are produced using two coherent beams of light; one that has been reflected from some object and one that has not. Illuminating the developed photographic plate in similar fashion will produce a three-dimensional image of the original object. By making a strip of holograms, and moving them at twenty frames per second, 3-D movies can be produced as shown in Figure 10.8.

Although 3-D color television does not make use of moving holographic plates, it does make use of the basic theory by producing holographic images electronically and projecting them into the room from the electroluminescent walls as shown in Figure 10.9a,b.

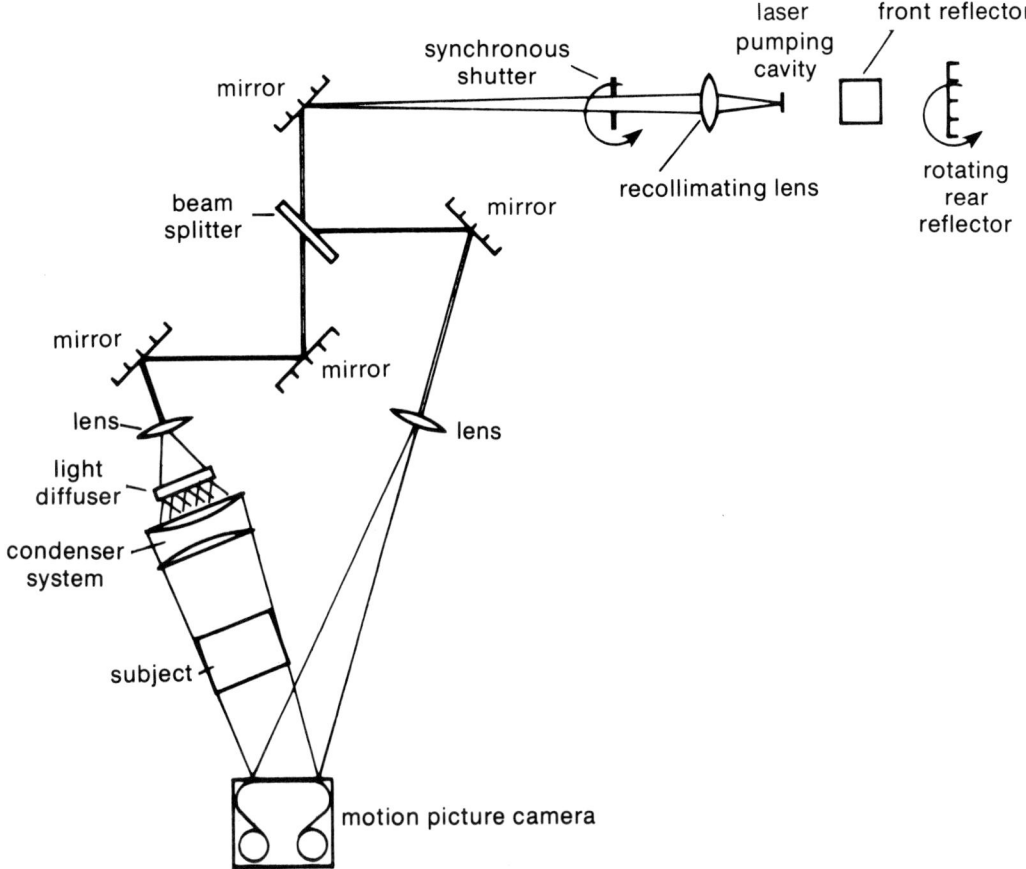

Figure 10.7

Three-dimensional movie system in which the subject and film move continuously. Through a combination of motion picture camera, mirrors, synchronous shutter, and various lenses, a true three-dimensional movie film is produced. In the sketch, the 160-pulse-per-second (pps) laser is the pumping cavity. The laser beam passes through a lens to the synchronous shutter, which reduces the pulse-per-second rate to 20 so that it can be photographed by the camera. The beam is reflected off a mirror through a beam splitter, and into another mirror and lens before it appears in the camera. The other beam is reflected into another beam splinter, through a light diffuser and condenser system, through the subject, and into the camera.

The Electronic Visitor

A telephone call has just come in for your dad on the picture telephone in the other room. Although the picture-telephone has been around for a long time, it was only recently converted for 3-D calls. As your dad switches from the 2-D mode to the 3-D mode, an image is projected into the center of the room. It is your Uncle Charlie calling from out of town, but actually, there is his complete image sitting in a chair talking to your dad. You walk around the image and notice his changing appearance. You even walk through him because the electronic visitor has no mass, just shape and image. As you walk back to watch the rest of the TV program originating in India you can't help but wonder what communication technology holds for the future.

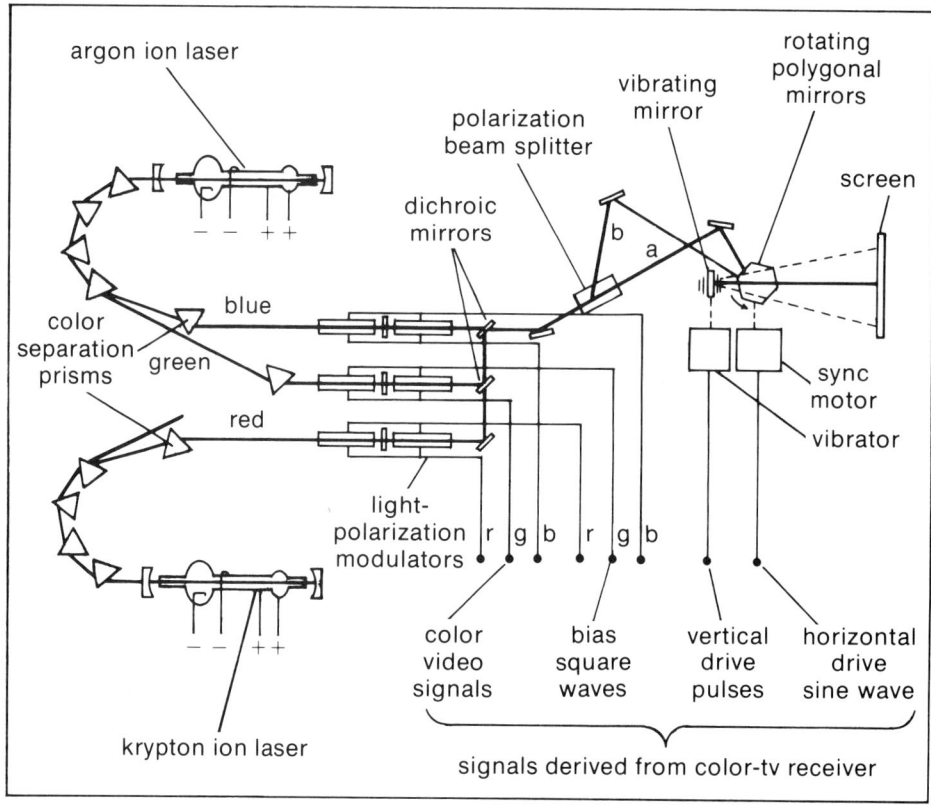

Figure 10.8

A laboratory model (sketch) of a working three-dimensional color television system showing the use of two lasers to reproduce the primary colors of red, green, and blue. The sound and pulsing signals for the system are from a standard color TV receiver. With this laser/optical display device, "off-the-air" color TV pictures can be projected on a screen.
Courtesy, GTE Laboratories, Inc.

That is a very interesting thought, and one that you will be concerned with in using a technique for investigating tomorrow—technology forecasting.

TECHNOLOGY FORECASTING

The rapid progress of scientific and technological developments described in this text can profoundly alter a person's social institutions, lifestyle, and career aspirations, for the future. What is amazing about this is not the fact that technological development has occurred or continues to occur at a rapid rate, but that it has occurred with humans having so little preparation for it.

This section focuses on the need for establishing a long-range forecasting center for the study of anticipated scientific and technological development in communi-

Figure 10.9a

This black and white photograph shows a true three-dimensional color image projected by the Unified Laser Color TV Display System from an "off-the-air" signal. An engineer at the right is adjusting the beam intensity for maximum clarity on the 91.4 cm x 1.22 m projection screen. All of the equipment contained in laboratory mock-up will be reduced and packaged in a standard-size color TV cabinet.
Courtesy, GTE Laboratories, Inc.

cations technology. Such a center would enable educational and national policymakers to stay ahead of the ever-changing course of technical events. The ability to forecast such technological breakthroughs as the car or computer would have allowed our legislators to enact laws for effective pollution control or adequate regulation of data banks so that the best interests of the individual could be preserved.

Early in 1966, the United States Air Force Office of Research embarked on such a study to determine the feasibility of using technology forecasting for the military service. The success of their venture interested other government agencies and certain industries. Since that time, many industries have used various modifications of the basic technique with varying degrees of success. At best, technology forecasting is the sum total of the best guesses by the best technical guessers. Perhaps the most beneficial thing to come out of long-range technology forecasting is a more accurate gauge of the short-term technical developments that will actually take place.

Here are some of the technological forecasts for communication technology that are to be operational in the world of 2030.

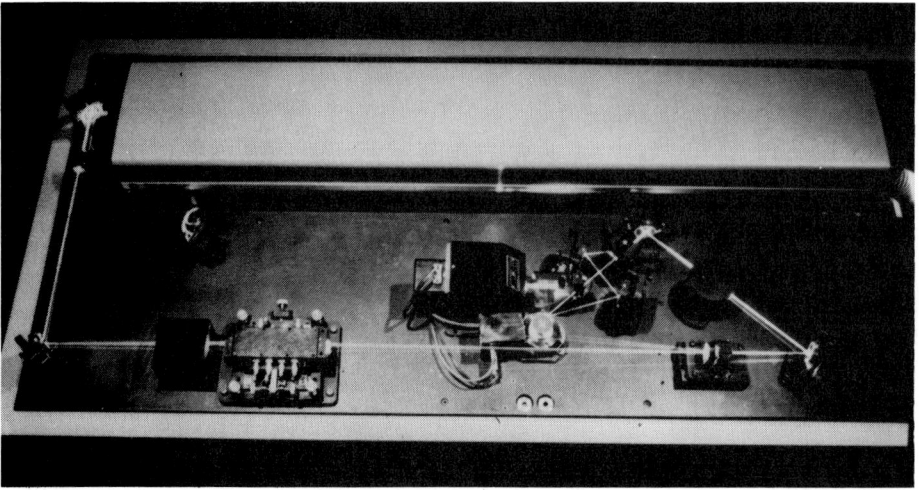

Figure 10.9b

The laser/optical subsystem of the Unified Laser Color TV display device. The large rectangular box in the background contains the multicolor laser beam source and its regulated power supply. Note the paths of the laser beam within the set. In the production model, this entire subsystem will be contained in a standard-size TV console.
Courtesy, GTE Laboratories, Inc.

Personal Communications Radio Links

Because of the major advances yet to come with large-scale integrated circuits and the relatively low cost of chips, most people will have some form of personal communication link with the world. One such link will be provided by the "wristwatch communicator." This will provide entertainment radio, color TV, and a communication link tied into the nearest grid pattern with interconnections to worldwide networks of holders of personal communications systems—very similar to the CB networks of today. For a slight additional charge, the manufacturer will add computer functions and a data storage chip. The time, day, and date function is considered standard for all wristwatch communicators.

Advances in Telecommunications

Some of the most rapid advances in technology will take place in the area of telecommunications. Many new techniques will expand the limited transmission paths already in existence, as reflected by Figure 10.11.

All local telephone equipment can be divided into two parts: the loop circuits linking subscribers to the central office, and the trunk circuits that link central offices with other central offices. In the future, most of the technical changes will take place in the loop circuits. A typical loop of the future, having up to 100 customers, will lead to a special loop unit that will digitally encode and multiplex the voice signals

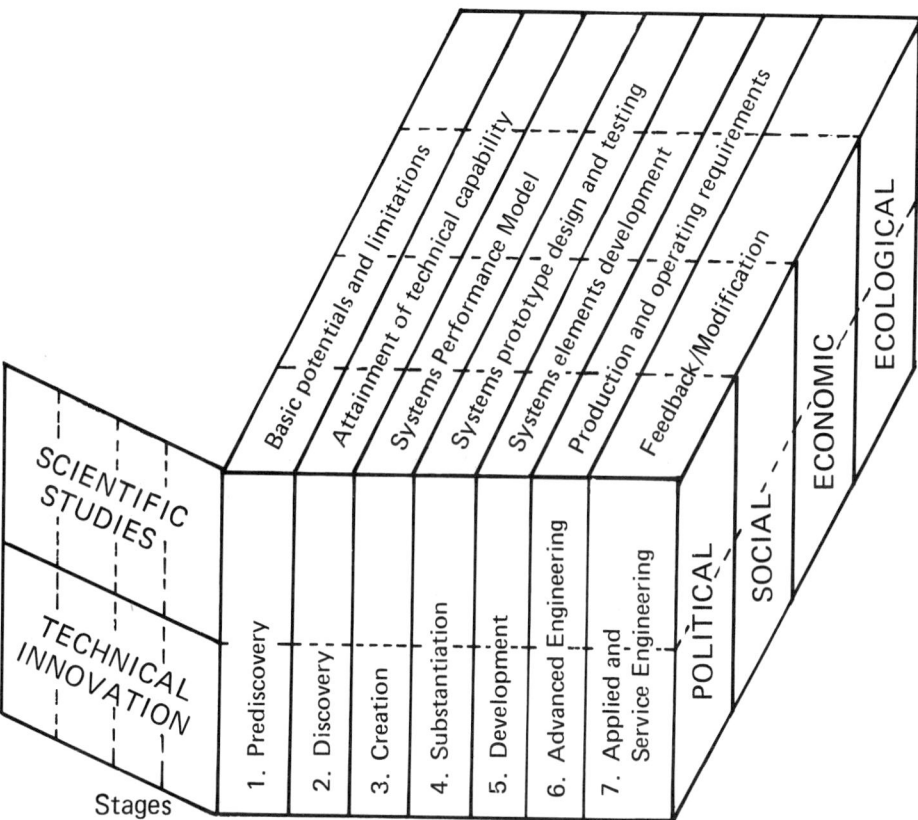

Figure 10.10

Complex matrix model for technological forecasting illustrates the variety of interrelated elements that can effect the accuracy of the forecast. In the thought process, the reader would normally progress from stage 1, Prediscovery, through stage 7, culminating in a marketable product or idea.

on a single cable leading to the central office. Here, the switching equipment would link the digitized, multiplexed signal to the trunk circuits or to another loop unit that would convert the digital signal back into voice frequencies.

World Telephone

The twelve keys of the touch-tone system on a telephone handset are presently translated at the central office and switched to the appropriate circuit. In those areas of the world where human operators are still needed to complete a telephone call, they will soon be replaced by the new, automatic exchanges so that one can direct-dial anyone in the world. The "World Telephone" will be under the direction of the United Nations and will have seventeen digits so that any phone in the world may be dialed just like a local call. It is estimated that there will be one billion phones in the world by 1990 and double that number by 2030.

Older or Current Techniques	Future Techniques
Wire pairs and repeaters	Canister microwave system
Undersea cables	Laser beam lightpipes
Landline cables	Laser beam waveguides
Coaxial Cables	Fiber lightguides
Electromagnetic waves	Muon beam
Orbiting satellites	Geostationary satellites
	High-capacity transistorized cables
	Rock strata
	Sonar nets
	Liquid electricity

Figure 10.11

Types of Telecommunications, Technology Paths

Only a few of the vacuum tubes in use today have specialized functions that may make them usable until the year 2000. They are the traveling-wave amplifier (TWA) and the impact avalanche transit time (IMPATT) type. Eventually, they too will be replaced by semiconductors that will be able to perform the same tasks more effectively and at a greatly reduced cost.

New Microwave Systems

New, inexpensive, short-range microwave systems designed to link local subscribers into long-haul communication circuits will be in operation throughout the country, possibly throughout the world. These high-capacity microwave units will transmit high-frequency digital radio signals from one canister to another. The canisters are mounted on poles spaced from 1 to 3 kilometers apart. Each canister contains complete equipment for the transmission and reception of 28,000 telephone conversations simultaneously. The rugged, self-contained units are solar powered and use the latest solid-state devices in their repeater circuitry. Unlike the huge microwave transmission systems of today, these completely trouble-free high-performance units do not require special buildings or huge tower systems. Each of the canisters holds up to seven repeaters. Costs are held down through the use of lower-sensitivity receivers operating at low power. Digital modulation with phase-shift keying solves most of the problems of this 18 GHz system that might be caused by rain, snow, or atmospheric conditions.

Yesterday's hotline between Washington and Moscow will be extended to other major countries of the world and include 2-D picture-telephones at each terminal. With these new hotlines, the diplomatic process will be speeded up, thereby lessening the chances for miscalculation by a belligerent nation.

Today, it is possible to trace the route your telephone call takes through the existing telephone transmission paths. Tomorrow, you will never know which transmission path a call is traveling because it will be routed automatically in the form of high-speed pulses through whichever high-capacity channels have the least traffic at that particular moment.

TECHNOLOGY FORECASTING 287

Figure 10.12a

The new microwave canister system
Courtesy, Bell Laboratories

Figure 10.12b

Two Bell Laboratories engineers ascend one of the masts of an experimental radio relay system near the Merrimack Valley in Massachusetts. Atop such masts are antennas and all-solid-state transmitter-receiver units. In this system, streams of digital pulses at frequencies around 18 billion cycles per second will handle more than 28,000 phone calls simultaneously. The new system may be used as a major transmission artery in metropolitan areas to meet the growing demand for voice and data communications.
Courtesy, Bell Laboratories

Advances in New Transmission Paths

Heretofore, only copper wires or coaxial cables have linked our major cities. As the use of these facilities has increased, their upper limits have been reached and people have had to look to the research laboratories for new transmission paths to help carry the nation's communications load. Once such device is the laser beam. The only difficulty with this potential medium is that it can be blocked by rain, snow, or heavy fog conditions. One solution is to encase the beam in a pipe or waveguide. In the future, laser beams encased in pipes and pressurized waveguides will carry up to 100,000 simultaneous telephone conversations or 100 television channels at the same time. Laser pipes and waveguides will supplement the existing trunk lines between cities until the older systems are phased out.

In addition to laser pipes and nitrogen-pressured waveguides, lightguides will soon enter the inventory of communications carriers. **Lightguides** are bundles of optically perfect glass fibers in which light can travel from one end to another by means of multiple reflections. In the laser beam lightguide system, tiny solid-state lasers carry information signals over individual hair-thin glass fibers. One end of the fiber is connected to a laser smaller than a grain of salt; the other end is connected to a receiver containing a tiny photoelectric detector cell that converts the light pulses into electrical signals.

The future will see these new lightguides carrying vast quantities of information—telephone calls, video programs, and computer data, for example—as a vital part of our telecommunications network. Standard typewriter-sized pages, as well as pictures, could be reduced to a tiny pinpoint of light and transmitted over the system.

Other Possible Transmission Paths

Even with the addition of laser pipes, waveguides, and lightguides to the telecommunications network, the demand for circuitry will soon outstrip technological developments unless research moves forward to explore whole new areas—areas that we have not yet considered.

One such path might be the harnessing of the seas. In the twenty-first century, we will see new undersea communications networks based on sonar principles. (Pipelines as a communication channel use fluids today.)

Another such path may be the subterranean rock strata. When communication channels become too full, alternatives such as "rock communication" will have to be utilized.

The Muon Beam

Out of the research laboratories comes a new form of a communication path—the muon beam. This beam holds a great deal of promise to supplement the overloaded communications channels forecast for the next century. The **muon** is a charged particle about 200 times as massive as the electron. It is reflected by the earth's magnetic field just enough to follow the curvature of the earth. Beams of high-energy muons are generated from the decayed products of the particle pi-meson. As soon as the problem of muon decay-strength is solved, it is forecast that the muon beam will share the communication load anticipated for 2030.

Figure 10.13a

Ultrapure glass fibers will serve as wires for a future telecommunication path. These fiber-wires carry telephone calls and other telecommunication on beams of light. The photograph above shows a reel of fiber over 1 kilometer in length carrying a laser beam attached to its other end. It takes a communication grade of 20db/km loss to be used as a telecommunication wire.
Courtesy, Bell Laboratories

Figure 10.13b

Producing laser light for the 1 kilometer long glass fiber shown in Figure 10.13a does not require a massive device. Telecommunications designers have developed a solid-state laser (center of picture) smaller than the grain of salt to its right. This "individual" laser will develop a beam of light to carry a communication channel; there will be one solid-state laser to one fiber glass channel. This is probably the most reliable, efficient, and economical source of light that can be modulated down a single fiber of a multifiber optical lightguide telecommunication system.
Courtesy, Bell Laboratories

Liquid Electricity

Research on the use of recently discovered liquid electricity as a completely new communication medium is well on its way. In the University of California at Berkeley, liquid electricity has been successfully formed by an intense laser beam, which was aimed at a crystal of ultrapure germanium held under stress and immersed in a bath of supercooled helium. A droplet of electricity was recorded by a television camera having an infrared-sensitive image camera tube. The electron-hole droplet appears to have an equal number of negative electrons and positive holes and is calculated to contain over 10,000 billion electron charges. According to the research report, the TV camera shows a collection of electrons and holes from which electrons have been dislodged. Because liquid electricity can change from a liquid to gas and maybe even to a solid, the researchers foresee a whole new world of technological development in the field of power, communications, and the transmission and storage of electricity for the twenty-first century.

After these new communications modes emerge from the research laboratory, each one must pay its own way in the form of new services or other economic benefit for the public if it is to be successful.

Computer Technology

Advances such as we have described couldn't have been created without the development of computer programming tools, such as automated equipment for the wiring, compiling, debugging, and final testing of the designs before their introduction into the telecommunications network.

Today, there are over one thousand different types of program languages, with over ten possible computer word lengths and hundreds of special character codes to unscramble before computer output can be understood. This has made it necessary to devise many complex systems for joining the wide variety of computers into intermodal systems. By the year 2030, all computer language will be converted to one compatible system so that almost anyone in the world will be able to use the computer. The owner of a small business will be able to lease a payroll/inventory machine to suit his or her special needs rather than having to share the cost and time of high-speed equipment that is overburdened with other customers' work. Huge savings will accrue to the manufacturers, as well as to the customers, as a result of bringing a high order of equipment standardization to a heretofore unstandardized field of communication technology.

In the future, the newest of these standardized machines will be fault-tolerant systems. These systems will reduce the maintenance and down-time costs. A **fault-tolerant system** is one which, more or less, carries all its own spare parts in the machine and switches to these spare circuits in the event of a self-detected breakdown. This will increase the life of the basic computer by twenty years or more. Computers will be more cost-effective.

Intermodal Systems

With the standardization problem out of the way, computer hardware will advance rapidly and will not become obsolete, as it does today, after a few years' use. Such

Figure 10.14

An enlargement of an experimental magnetic-bubble memory, which will store encoded information in the boundary between the bubbles and the surrounding material. Magnetic bubbles are like tiny islands of reversed magnetization, which can be moved around as desired. This technique permits the bubbles to be spaced closer together, thus increasing the potential density of information storage. As an example, a 2.54-cm bubble could store up to 10 million bits of information (ones and zeros), which is equivalent to a large book.
Courtesy, IBM Research Division

new techniques as self-repairing and self-generating machines will be commonplace by 2030. The self-repair function is approachable today by feeding a diagnostic routine into a computer.

The transfer of enormous banks of coded data today is a major problem for computer users. In the future, computers will be able to communicate directly with each other and trade their banks of data. Even electric typewriters will be linked together in a huge new network and will automatically write to each other. Such intermodal systems would greatly reduce the business mail that each office has to process in the course of a day. Typewriters such as these would work around the clock, speeding up business and government operations while releasing office personnel to perform those operations they do best—operations that require thought. Anyone with access to a touch-tone telephone system would be able to call up a computer in a distant location for data, provided they properly authenticated their request.

High-speed, High-capacity Computers

In most modern computer machines, the central processing unit (CPU), with its associated software, is the main information-processing tool of the system. The memory bank, however, is the heart of the computer. In the future, memory banks will be able to store up to 100 trillion bits of information and retrieve it in fractional millionths of a second. The size of the memory bank will be drastically reduced by the introduction of the **magnetic-bubble** memory cores, which will be able to store up to 1 million bits of information in a space no larger than a business card. Thousands of these memory cores would be interconnected to provide an infinite capability at the same retrieval speed mentioned above. In contrast, the human brain has 100 billion brain cells to use, compared with the infinite possibilities of the magnetic-bubble memory bank.

For manufacturers that would prefer electronic beams to the bubble technique, the future will see a new type of electron-beam memory system with infinite capabilities that may replace the bubble cores. The beam memory banks will be fed by new cryogenically cooled circuits having three to four times the speed of present-day computers.

Language Translation by Computers

As we enter the next century, we will have long since learned to program computers to put simple grammatical sentences together in meaningful responses to verbal questions and to translate them into English or other languages. This will make it possible to instantaneously translate human speech and foreign publications into an international language made up of a verbal vocabulary of 1000 basic international words. As this technique advances, students in 2030 will be using automated language translators capable of coping with idiomatic syntactical complexities of languages.

Behavioral Modification by Computer

By the next century, thanks to computer simulation, human behavioral modification will have been perfected to the point that habitual criminals will become honest citizens.

It has been known for several decades that certain areas of the cerebrum have specific functions. For example, the areas of thought, memory, and feeling are located at the front part of the brain. The area for sight is located at the back, and the area for hearing at the sides. Through early experimentation, it has been found that a weak, painless electrical charge may produce changes for as long as the current is on. In some subjects, the effects of electrical stimulation lasted for several days. Reactions such as laughter, fear, and affection can be induced even today. Tomorrow, scientists will be able to modify human behavior by selective electrical stimulation of the brain.

One of the major research thrusts in the next century will be the person/machine symbiosis, enabling humans to extend their intelligence by direct electro-mechanical interaction between their brain and the computer. The feasibility of directly recording information on the brain will also have been determined. New teaching machines using adaptive programs that respond to the student's answers as well as to certain physiological sensory responses will be in use in the public schools.

Large-Scale Computerized Data Systems

If you have flown locally or nationally, an airline computer somewhere follows your travel movements as the aircraft flies from city to city. Except for the weather or mechanical failures, there are seldom any delays. But if you fly internationally, it is a different matter entirely. For example, you must contend with entrance requirements, such as health records, citizenship, and customs, before you can enter a foreign country. Because of the growth of large-scale computerized data systems on an international scale, the future will see the international traveler debarking at a foreign port with only a small magnetic travel card. Upon your arrival at the foreign port, the inspection official would insert the international identity card into a card reader and positively identify you. The official would also be able to ascertain that you meet all of the entrance requirements. All international charges could be made against the card, eliminating the need to carry around a different currency for each country visited.

Biomedical Communications

The oldest of the technologies—communications—is now merging with the oldest of the sciences—biology. Modern medical science relies heavily on biomedical instrumentation, which it uses for recording, monitoring, and analyzing laboratory tests and for the remote presentation of the data within a few seconds to the diagnostician. In the future, computer diagnosis and prescription will become as much a part of our lifestyle as the automobile has in the past.

Today, the guide dog for the blind can be effectively replaced with an electronic "seeing" device that detects obstructions on a vertical and horizontal plane as well as any sudden changes in ground levels. In the future, new electronic eyes will scan a newspaper and change the lines into audible signals and words so that a blind person can read conventional matter as well as see the objects in the path ahead of them. The blind of the future will be able to do most of the things a sighted person can.

Today, human organs are transplanted with a fairly high degree of reception by the human body. However, there are still too many cases in which antibodies reject the transplanted human organs. By the year 2030 compact, electronically-powered, artificial organs will be available to the surgeon for replacement on a permanent basis, just as artificial teeth or hearing aids are available today. Transplants will be as common as tonsillectomies.

Global Satellite Communication Systems

Our technological prowess has now brought us to a point where we are able to communicate on a global scale, so that no person, ship, airplane, or spacecraft need ever be out of touch with the world at large. In the world of tomorrow, distance will be reduced to microseconds.

As you may recall from Modules Six and Eight, one of the limiting factors in communication technology has always been the availability of sufficient numbers of

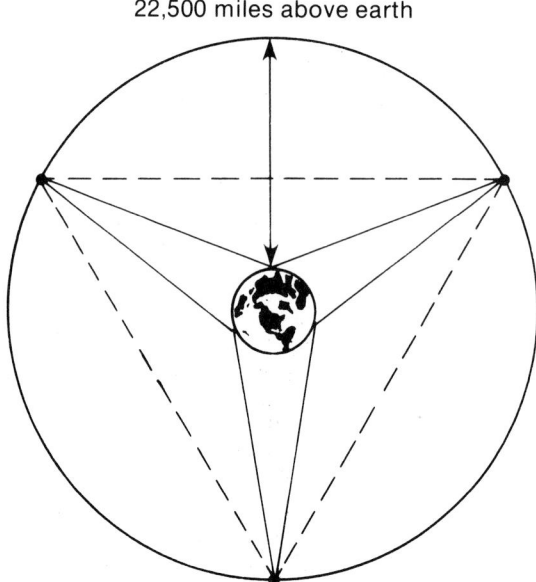

Figure 10.15

Three geostationary satellites. Telecommunication satellites in these positions would provide coverage for the entire world, with the exception of the polar caps.

channels to carry all the messages humans would like to send. The problem will be intensified in the twenty-first century with the addition of more and more people who will be using the existing communications channels. Even with the addition of new modes of communications previously mentioned, as well as compression-of-data techniques, it is forecast that the channels will still be overcrowded.

A good example of the overcrowding is the communications satellite. At an altitude of 36,000 kilometers, the communications satellite can be placed in orbit over the equator and it will appear to be stationary from any point on earth. A satellite positioned in such a manner is said to be **geostationary.** Three such geostationary communications satellites placed equidistant around the equatorial belt will provide full communication coverage of the earth. They would function as radio repeaters.

A signal from one earth station is transmitted up to the satellite (the uplink), and the signal is received and retransmitted down (the downlink) from the satellite to another earth station. So as not to interfere with other transmitting stations or satellites, the uplink and downlink channels use different frequency bands and employ channel-sharing techniques. Even with the use of digital links with single-carrier-per-channel equipment for time-division multiple access as the standard, the worldwide use of the radio spectrum depletes the frequencies available for other uses.

The problem has been further complicated by the battle for access to the available communications satellites, as well as by the host of nations orbiting their own satellites over the same equatorial region. Because of the possibility of crosstalk between satellites, there is no practical room for more than 100 satellites in geostationary orbit around the earth's equator.

By the year 2030, all 100 of the places will be filled, thereby eliminating any further possibility for expansion of space-borne communication for business, entertainment, data transmission, or international contacts on our personnel communi-

TECHNOLOGY FORECASTING 295

Figure 10.16a

With 100 satellites in space, a need exists to replace, repair, or return some of them to earth for extensive overhaul. The Space Shuttle vehicle was designed to accomplish this feat among others. With its main engines and solid rocket motors roaring, the vehicle lifts off from its launch pad carrying a telecommunication satellite in its cargo compartment.
Courtesy, Rockwell International, Space Division

Figure 10.16b

The shuttle orbiter changes its orbital path by firing its maneuvering engines as it heads for a disabled telecommunications satellite.

Figure 10.16c

With its manipular arm extended, the Space Shuttle vehicle prepares to recover a damaged telecommunications satellite and replace it with a new one. This vehicle was designed to retrieve or place payloads such as satellites in space and to perform other repair or maintenance functions.
Courtesy, Rockwell International, Space Division

cators. Space maintenance of the numerous communications satellites will be handled on a regular basis by the Space Shuttle vehicle. However, with the new circuit technology of the twenty-first century, the reliability of the satellites would become infinite.

As more and more of the communications satellites are orbited skyward for special applications, inexpensive mobile and fixed earth terminals will be developed so that the large-scale data users and businesses will have simultaneous, multiple access to them. This will be made possible by new roof-top satellite antennas connected to transmitters and receivers linked to computers in the rooms below. This technical evolution of the next century will be accomplished through the development of lower-cost receivers, transmitters in preassembled racks, and prefabricated structures. Global satellite communications will exceed all other types of technological innovations in the century ahead.

The Global Patent Office

As the global communications capability is expanded, many new applications will be included on the networks. One such possibility is that a global patent system would allow member nations to share, with the other member nations, the many inventions developed throughout the world. This, in itself, would speed up technical development as many new ideas are disseminated and new communications devices are developed. The system envisioned would receive, process, and disseminate, on a worldwide basis, applications from inventors everywhere.

The system would function like this: Each of the member nation's patent offices would be automatically linked, through the global satellite system, to a giant on-line computer in Geneva, Switzerland. Incoming data on inventions approved by the member nations would be compared with data retrieved from the on-line computer in Geneva. This computer also would search its memory for any prior patents in the same field and provide the interested inventor with a hard copy of related inventions.

Whenever an inventor filed a patent application in his or her home country, it would be flashed to the Geneva Patent Office for international recording. Holographic negatives would replace drawings because they can now be transmitted much more easily than drawings reduced to digital bits.

Today, records of the U.S. Patent Office reflect a two-year wait before inventors' patents are approved. With the future global patent system, approval time would be reduced to about five hours. As an additional benefit, the Geneva Center would become the international clearinghouse for technology, a vital service to authors of texts like this one.

Interstellar Communications

Theoretically, there is no reason to believe that when an electromagnetic signal is radiated into outer space, it doesn't continue to travel for an infinite distance throughout the entire universe. Conversely, there is no evidence to say that an advanced civilization that has been sending out signals for centuries does not exist beyond our solar system. Actually, more and more scientists are coming to believe that humankind is not alone in this galaxy. Therefore, it is forecast that the discovery of signals, other than those produced by the radio stars, will prove the existence of intelligent beings beyond the earth.

It is likely that by A.D. 2030 interstellar communications will be devised and our civilization will establish contact with beings from outer space. This will probably be accomplished by using a 1-kilometer laser beam operating at 100-nanometer wavelength in the microwave region and feeding a 10-meter transmission dish that produces 25 photons per second in some 10-meter receiving dish located 1000 light years away. A bank of 26 high-speed, high-capacity data processors are on-line and ready to record and analyze new signals received from outer space.

Other Technology Forecasts

In the future, and perhaps beyond A.D. 2030, it is within the realm of possibility that many people will be trained to use ESP for reliable short-range communications. With the addition of a hatlike device, people will be able to extend their telepathy paths to greater distances through electronically augmented communication between brains.

The use of radio teledynamics or the remote control of mechanisms will play an increasing role in the lifestyles of people living in the next century. For example, the availability of complex robots that are programmable, self-adaptive, and capable of performing household and office chores will become a fact of life and release many humans from such activities.

Before this century is ended, we will probably see the establishment of a central data storage facility on a regional basis, with wide public access for general and specialized information retrieval, primarily in the area of medical, legal, and library data. Access to the regional computer will be by touch-tone handset and available to students and professionals alike.

The Decline of Print as a Communication Mode

In the years ahead, every form of human activity will continue to produce tons of material that will find its way into publication and eventually into the libraries of the world. The computer alone generates such a quantity of paper printouts in every conceivable field that it threatens to inundate us all before too long. Unfortunately, we have generated too much data and information to assimilate, digest, and even act upon in the foreseeable future. Obviously, new ways are needed to cope effectively with this continuing paper problem.

Future Information and Data Systems

The future solution to the dual problems of paper generation and shrinking library space is the immediate conversion of hard copy into retrievable digital data. For example, old how-to books will soon be converted and placed in the information storage and retrieval facilities where they will be available at the flip of a CRT readout device or through the touch-tone system linked directly to the home-learning-center CRT console. New books and computer-generated data will go directly into the storage system without going through an intermediate printing stage.

With books, magazines, documents, and papers reduced to digital data, we will all have to modify our old ways of organizing our thoughts so as to take full advantage of the storage, processing, and retrieval capabilities of our information systems.

How Forecasting Can Help

As you have read the technical forecasting section of this module, you have probably concluded that communication technology was a vital key to human progress and technical development down through the ages and will continue to be the key for the future. We can now forecast many technical events intelligently and judge them carefully in terms of human progress or regression as the consequence of their use. For example, it can be particularly harmful to our free society when technology joins bureaucracy to control, manipulate, or modify human behavior without the full consent of the individuals concerned. Therefore, careful judgment in terms of the consequence of use of a particular technology is the best way for technology forecasting to serve humankind.

There does not appear to be anything that cannot be accomplished by technology. It's only a matter of time, talent, and materials.

⫸ CONCEPT FOCUSER

- **Kitchen** and **traffic flow regulator computers** are **available today** and will be in widespread **use by** circa **2030.**
- The **technology** needed to produce **home learning centers, hydrogen-fueled cars, diagnostic and prescription computers,** and **automated factories** is available **today.**
- **Antigravity cars** must await **new technology breakthroughs.**
- **Almost everyone** will have a **wristwatch communication link** with the **world** by A.D. 2000
- **Development of the technology** for producing 3-D home movies, 3-D **telephones,** and **3-D TVs in full color** is **underway** today.
- Technology **forecasting** and technology **assessment** will emerge as completely **new studies** in the **future.**
- New **transmission paths** such as the **muon beam** and **liquid electricity** will be developed as soon as the appropriate **technology breakthrough occurs.**
- Newer **computers** will **interface** with each other **without** the need for a special **black box.**
- **Computer technology** is **advancing rapidly** with the introduction of many new techniques such as **self-repairing capabilities.**

- The **technology** leading to a future **self-generating computer** is under **study today**.
- **Computers** can **store** and **transfer enormous** banks of **data today**.
- **Memory banks** will physically **decrease** while **bit storage** capacity will **increase** tremendously **tomorrow**.
- Design of automated computer **language translators** is **underway today**.
- **Behavior modification** by computer will become a **more common** type of medical treatment by A.D. 2000.
- **The world** will be **linked** together by **global satellite telecommunication systems**.
- **Print** as a telecommunication **medium** will **decline sharply** as data **retrieval** systems **increase** drastically.
- **Technology** forecasting is **educated guessing** by technical **experts** in the field.
- **There is almost nothing that can't be accomplished by technology given proper time, talent, materials, and funds.**
- **Technology** can become a **monster or remain the servant** of humankind. The direction it takes **depends on** intelligent **forecasting, assessment,** and appropriate **action.**

FOOD FOR THOUGHT

1. How would you feel about having a distant computer prescribe medicine for you over the telephone? Explain your reaction.
2. Because the computer never forgets, do you think your homework and school assignments would be easier to keep up with in the home learning center concept?
3. How do you think your mother or father would like shopping with the Tele-Vid system? Do you think your parent would get the best buys?
4. Do you foresee a lot more leisure time as a result of some of the technology forecasted?
5. Explain the concept of technology forecasting and how it might affect your life in the future.
6. Define the technology assessment concept and explain how it can be used to benefit humankind.

EXPANDING EXPERIENCES

Case Study. Technology assessment is a systematic study of the effects on society that may occur when a technology is introduced. Select and study any one of the preceding technology forecasts and:
1. Make a list of the anticipated first, second, third, fourth, fifth, and so on order of consequences that might occur. Be sure to consider each consequence in terms of its social, cultural, and economic impact on our free society.

2. On the basis of your selection, write a scenario in terms of how your own lifestyle might be affected if the forecast were to come true within the next twenty years.

LOCATOR TOOLS

Barnes, Norman F. *Holography: The Image Maker.* Elnora, N.Y.: Laser Technology, Inc., 1972.

Bright, James R., and Schoeman, Milton E. F., eds. *A Guide to Practical Technological Forecasting.* Englewood Cliffs, N.J.: Prentice-Hall, 1973.

Hellman, Hal. *Communications in the World of the Future.* Philadelphia, Pa.: M. Evans & Co., 1969.

CONTRIBUTIONS OR INVENTIONS LEADING UP TO TECHNOLOGY-BASED ELECTRICAL TELECOMMUNICATION SYSTEMS

Appendix A

Contributor and Nativity	Contribution or Invention	Approximate Time Frame
The Ancient Era:		
Magnes (Asia Minor)	Discovered magnetic attraction of magnetite.	Before 400 B.C.
Plato (Greek)	Wrote of the existence of natural magnets (magnetite).	400 B.C.
Thales (Greek)	Discovered attractive properties of amber.	600 B.C.
Pliny (Roman)	Second discovery of attractive properties of amber.	A.D 62
The Modern Era:		
Perregriunus (unknown)	Discovered the law of magnetic poles, which is still valid today.	1269
Christopher Columbus (Italian)	Discovered the existence of magnetic declination.	1492
William Gilbert (English)	Developed erroneous theory of electric and nonelectric material. Developed the theory that world was a giant magnet. Summarized all that was then known about electricity.	1600
Dr. J. Wall (English)	First to produce an electric spark from an electrified rod.	1650

APPENDIX A

Contributor and Nativity	Contribution or Invention	Approximate Time Frame
Otto Von Guericke (German)	Built and tested the first electrostatic (frictional) generator.	1672
Stephen Gray (English)	First to correctly classify materials as conductors or non-conductors. Developed the degree of electrification of wire and named it **potential**.	1729
Charles Francis Du Fay (French)	Announced belief in the existence of two kinds of electrical "fluids," which could repel or attract each other. Transmitted a current through a wet hempen string a distance of 420 meters.	1733
Pieter Van Musschenbroek (Dutch)	Built the first Leyden jar.	1746
Sir Walter Watson (English)	Discovered that an electrical impulse can travel over a kilometer on a wire. Ascertained velocity of electricity in a wire.	1749
Benjamin Franklin (American)	Demonstrated that frictional electricity and lightning were pretty much the same thing. Advanced present theory of positive and negative electrical charges.	1752
Swedenborg (Swedish)	First verified clairvoyant vision—of a fire 200 kilometers away.	1759
John Canton (English)	First to produce the "electrometer," or the "pith ball" electrostatic indicator.	1762
George Louis Lesagne (Swiss)	Built the first electrical telegraph instrument using a single wire to represent each letter of the alphabet.	1774
Luigi Alvisio Galvani (Italian)	Accidentally discovered bioconductivity.	1774
Charles Augustin Coulomb (French)	Proved that an electrical charge remained on the outer surface of a conductor. Formulated the first valid laws of force. The unit of quality of electricity was named after him.	1777
Henry Cavendish (English)	Experimented with iron wire as electrical conductors and developed the concept of "degree of electrofication" or potential energy as it is known today.	1785
Betancourt (Spanish)	Experimented with Leyden jars and static electricity to send signals between cities.	1787
Don Francisco Salva (Spanish)	Sent electrostatic signals 42 kilometers using Leyden jars.	1798

APPENDIX A

Contributor and Nativity	Contribution or Invention	Approximate Time Frame
Alessandro Volta (Italian)	Produced a new kind of electricity from his chemical battery. The unit of voltage was named after him.	1799
John Dalton (English)	Developed the theory of atomic structure, which is in use today.	1802
S. T. Von Soemmerring (German)	Described and demonstrated an electrochemical telegraph, which used gases from the decomposition of water in a tank to indicate letters of the alphabet. Used a voltaic pile as current source.	1809
Zamboni (unknown)	Produced a dry pile, a prototype of the common dry cell battery.	1812
J. B. Ritter (German)	Invented the electric storage battery.	1812
Sir Francis Ronald (English)	Demonstrated the speed of electricity by sending frictional electricity over 13 kilometers of wire to activate pith balls at receiving station. System used synchronized clockwork and a dial that contained the alphabet.	1816
Hans Christian Oersted (Danish)	Discovered electromagnetism. The unit of magnetic intensity was named after him.	1819
André-Marie Ampère (French)	Built the first electromagnet using a coil of wire and having an iron core inserted in the coil to intensify it. The unit of current was named after him.	1820
Dominique François Jean Arago (French)	Produced first commercial electromagnet.	1820
Bohenberg (Germany)	Developed the electroscope.	1820
Michael Faraday (English)	Formulated laws of electromagnetic induction. Discovered and produced alternating current through electromagnet induction by rotating a 35-centimeter copper disk between the poles of an electromagnet.	1820
Johann Salomo Christoph Schweigger (German)	Invented the first galvanometer.	1820
Thomas J. Seebeck (German)	Discovered thermoelectricity and produced the thermopile using two dissimilar metals. Produced a small amount of direct current from his thermopile.	1821

Contributor and Nativity	Contribution or Invention	Approximate Time Frame
William Sturgeon (English)	Built first electromagnetic horseshoe and straight bar magnets to help pick up nails around his shoe shop.	1825
Dr. Georg Simon Ohm (German)	Discovered the fundamental law of galvanic relationship that exists between voltage, current, and resistance. All circuit values today are now calculated by Ohm's law.	1827
A. C. Becquerel (French)	Discovered the double fluid galvanic battery.	1829
Michael Faraday (English)	Built the first transformer and wrote about the close relationship that exists between magnetism and electricity.	1829
Baron Pavel-Lvovitch deSchilling (Russian)	Deflected compass needle at receiving station to indicate letters of alphabet. Built the first two-station electromagnetic telegraph system.	1832
Jean C. A. Peltier (French)	Produced direct current by heating two dissimilar metals. This phenomenon is termed the Peltier effect.	1834
Heinrich Lenz (Germany) M. H. Jacobi (Russian)	Independently discovered that current in a coil is proportional to the number of turns of the coil.	1834
Karl A. Steinheil (German)	Improved on the two-station electromagnetic telegraph device of Schilling by building a two-station electromagnetic telegraph system that used a compass to indicate alphabet.	1836
J. P. Daniell (English)	Developed a constant performing electric battery.	1836
Charles Wheatstone, William Fothergill Cooke (English)	Improved earlier electromagnetic-actuated compass needle indicating system by adding five additional compasses. The device called Wheatstone Bridge was named after Wheatstone who developed it.	1837
Karl Frederic Gauss, Wilhelm Eduard Weber (German)	Constructed and used first electromagnetic-actuated compass needle to indicate alphabet for communication between their laboratories. Unit area of magnetic flux is named after Gauss.	1837
Alexander Bain (English)	Conceived an electronic device using the electrolyte principle of facsimile to transmit pictures by wires between any two points.	1842
Joseph Henry (American)	Discovered the force of induced current and the self-induced properties of coils. The unit of measurement for the electrical size of coils was named after him.	1845

APPENDIX A 305

Contributor and Nativity	Contribution or Invention	Approximate Time Frame
Samuel Finley Breese Morse (American)	Developed first practical telegraph set and transmission code. The Morse code was named after him.	1844
Gaston Plante (French)	Designed the first lead-acid battery that effectively converted chemical energy to electrical energy.	1860
James Clerk Maxwell (Scottish)	Developed theory that light is an electrical phenomenon and that Faraday's theory of electromagnetic waves existed. The unit of magnetic flux is called maxwell in his honor.	1864
Alexander Graham Bell (American)	Successfully changed mechanical energy into electrical energy and back again, as in the telephone transmitter and receiver circuits. Invented the phonograph.	1875
Thomas Alva Edison (American)	Developed the "quadrupling" method of transmitting more than one message over a circuit at the same time. Invented the nickel storage battery.	1877
Emil Berliner (American)	Developed the variable resistance telephone transmitter.	1877
Camille A. Faure (French)	Developed a storage battery, called an accumulator.	1880
Gilbert Murray (English)	Experimented with mental telepathy with one out of three verified successes.	1910–1929

Appendix B

CONTRIBUTIONS TO TECHNOLOGY-BASED ELECTRONIC TELECOMMUNICATION SYSTEMS

Contributor and Nativity	Contribution or Invention	Approximate Time Frame
Augusto Righi (Italian)	Conducted extensive experiments with early wireless devices.	1850–1920
Reginald Aubrey Fedderson (Canadian-American)	Discovered that when a condenser is discharged into a conductor, oscillations that cause intermittent sparks are developed.	1897
George R. Carey (American)	Used properties of selenium to try to transmit pictures on a wire.	1875
Thomas Alva Edison (American)	While experimenting with his early electric lamps, he accidentally discovered a flow of electrons from the hot filaments. This was called the Edison effect and was the forerunner of the electron tube.	1883
Paul Gottlieb Nipkow (German)	Developed a mechanical TV scanner, a revolving disc with a series of holes punched in it in the form of a spiral.	1884
Heinrich Rudolph Hertz (German)	Developed electrical wave radiation theory and built an exciter and a resonator. Hertzian waves were named after him.	1888
Emile Berliner (American)	Developed the microphone.	1891
Edouard Branly (French)	Invented the coherer detector, a glass tube containing iron filings. When acted upon by an electrical discharge, the filings stick together and thereby are able to detect electric waves.	1893

APPENDIX B

Contributor and Nativity	Contribution or Invention	Approximate Time Frame
Sir Oliver Joseph Lodge (English)	Conducted wireless telegraphy experiments using coherers. Patented an adjustable inductance coil in the antenna circuit to turn resonance circuits.	1894
Alexander Stepanovitch Popoff (Russian)	Independently developed the idea of an aerial ground and sent a signal over a distance of forty meters. Developed the first radio receiver.	1895
Guglielmo Marconi (Italian)	Developed an improved coherer system of wireless telegraph. Independently discovered the aerial and ground as circuits. Sent the first transatlantic wireless message between England and Newfoundland.	1895
Capt. H. Jackson (Unknown)	Developed wireless transmitter.	1896
Carl Ferdinand Braun (Unknown)	Developed the first cathode ray tubes and contributed to wireless telegraphy knowledge.	1897
K. F. Brown (German)	Reshaped the cathode ray tube by placing the cathode and anode at opposite ends so that an electron beam from the cathode could be attracted to the phosphorous-coated anode.	1897
Sir Joseph John Thompson (English)	Discovered the stream of electrons flowing between cathode and anode when the tube was energized. Formulated a theory that all matter is composed of three types of particles: the electron, the proton, and the neutron. This electron theory is still in use today.	1897
Oliver Heaviside (English) A. E. Kennelly (American)	They independently suggested that radio waves did not follow the curvature of the earth, but rather hit a layer of air (the ionosphere) above it.	1902
Valdemar Poulsen (Danish)	The first inventor to generate a continuous electromagnetic radio wave by means of an arc lamp. His device was called a radio generator. Later invented the first magnetic wire recorder.	1902
John Ambrose Fleming (English)	Invented the first vacuum diode rectifier tube, which was called the Fleming Value after him.	1904
Lee De Forest (American)	Independently improved the early Fleming Value by placing a grid between the filament (cathode) and the plate (anode) and noted greatly amplified signals. It was called the audion amplifier.	1904
Robert Von Lieben (Austrian)	Discovered and patented the first electronic amplifier tubes in Germany.	1906
Alexander Meissner (Unknown)	Connected oscillator to audion tube to produce a strong source of electromagnetic waves.	1913

Contributor and Nativity	Contribution or Invention	Approximate Time Frame
Ernst F. W. Alexanderson (American)	Developed the powerful alternator radio transmitter in New Brunswick. Demonstrated large-screen TV.	1917
Major Edwin H. Armstrong (American)	Invented the superheterodyne receiver.	1918
Vladimir Kosma Zworykin (Russian)	Invented the Iconoscope (image-observer) camera tube and electronic scanning system.	1923
John Logie Baird (Scottish)	Developed the concept of modern television and transmitted a recogni able picture with a whirling mechanical scanner. System developed 240-line picture at 25 frames per second.	1923
Commander Ferrie (French)	Invented a tube that could amplify an electric impulse a hundred million times.	1923
Dr. Shintaro Uda Dr. Hidetsugu Yagi (Japanese)	Developers of the very high frequency Yagi antenna, which is used throughout the world.	1925
Philo T. Farnsworth (American)	Developed an ingenious nonstorage electronic pickup tube called the image dissector. Although less sensitive than the iconoscope, it transmits excellent pictures.	1928
Karl Guthe Jansky (American)	Discoverer of radio waves coming from outer space. His discovery paved the way for today's radio astronomy.	1933
Isaac Shoenberg (Russian)	Improved the Iconoscope and developed an electronic picture of 405 lines at 50 frames per second.	1936
Albert Rose Harley Iams (American)	Developed the RCA image orthicon, which equals the picture quality of 35mm film.	1939
Sir Robert Watson-Watt (English)	Developed radar to detect aircraft at a height of 3000 meters and distances of 160 kilometers.	1939
J. T. Randall A. H. Boot (English)	Invented the magnetron tube, which permitted higher power at higher frequencies for radar sets.	1940
R. Varian (American)	Invented the klystron, an ultrahigh frequency microwave tube essential for increasing radar frequencies.	1943
Russell S. Ohl (American)	Developed a treated crystal that converts light into electrical energy. It is called the photoelectric cell.	1945
J. Presper Edkert, Jr. John W. Mauchly (American)	Designed and hand-built the world's first all electric digital computer (UNIVAC).	1946
John Bardeen Walter H. Brattain William Shockley (American)	Won Nobel Prize in Physics for their invention of the transistor. This invention revolutionized the electronics industry.	1948

Contributor and Nativity	Contribution or Invention	Approximate Time Frame
Paul Weimer Stanley Forgue Robert Goodrich (American)	Developed the compact vidicon picture tube, which is generally used for industrial television purposes.	1949
N. G. Bassov A. M. Prokhorou (Russian)	Described Maser (Microwave Amplification by Stimulated Emission of Radiation).	1954
J. P. Gordon H. J. Ziegler C. H. Townes (American)	Gave the name of Maser to the new device.	1955
Dr. T. H. Maiman (American)	Built the world's first operating laser.	1960
Hugh Gernsback (American)	Developer of the concept of the "instant newspaper," which is continuously transmitted to the reader by radio.	1963
P. K. Tien D. McNair H. L. Hodges (American)	Developed the triode laser, which provides a hundredfold increase in electron efficiency over standard lasers.	1965

Glossary of Terms

Acceptor–an atom of matter that tends to accept free electrons into its valence electrons

Acoustic–relating to the sense of hearing or to sound waves

Acoustic nerve–auditory nerve, serves to conduct sensory stimuli from the ear to the brain

Alnico–an alloy of iron, nickel, aluminum, and cobalt used for permanent magnets

Ameslan–the American sign language used by the deaf

Ampere–electron or current flow

Anaglyph–a picture involving two images of the same object from different points of view, usually in different colors, that when viewed through an anaglyphoscope produces a stereoscopic effect

Analog–an analog computer directly measures and transforms continuous physical quantities such as electrical voltages

Analog signal–a continuous signal, like an electrical signal

Anode–the positive pole or electrode of an electrolytic cell or vacuum tube

Anomalies–occurrences for which data are not adequate to determine exactly what is going on or what is causing it to occur. Telepathic communication is an anomalous area in communications. How it takes place is not totally certain

Anvil–a small bone in the middle ear that transfers wave vibration from the stirrup to the hammer

Aperture cards–a microform which is usually 82.5 mm × 187.25 mm (3¼ × 7⅜") in size. The card combines keypunched data and microfilm. Cards may contain a single image or up to eight images on one 35-mm frame

Arithmetic unit–the part of the computer that performs the logic and arithmetic operations

Articulation–the process of making adjustments and movements of the speech organs necessary to utter distinct syllables or words

Atom–smallest particle that makes up a material, an atom is composed of nucleus, protons, neutrons, and electrons

Audile communication–the reception of information through the sense of hearing

Aura–ionized air caused by electrostatic potential which can be viewed using Kirlian photography. The pattern, or aura, produced is found around every object, living or dead

Biofeedback–using technological devices to assist in regulating human bodily conditions

Biogravitation–a communication anomaly; also called telekinesis; moving objects with the power of the mind

Capacitor–an electrical device that controls the direction of current flow in a circuit and that can also store electricity

Cathode–the negative pole or electrode of an electrolytic cell or vacuum tube

Cathode-ray display–a large sealed tube similar to a television screen used to display both photographic and alpha/numerical data

Central processing unit (CPU)–the unit of a computer system that calculates and performs logic functions based on a series of programming instructions

Channel–in communications, the medium through which information is transmitted

Chromium oxide–material on a plastic base used for magnetic tape recording

Cochlea–a spiral passage in the ear that directs the flow of acoustical information to the brain via the auditory nerve

Coding–the process of changing information from one form to another: for example, voice signals to electrical pulses

Coherent light–light energy that is controllable and consistent in purity, color, and intensity; a laser beam is coherent light

Coherer–a device usually used to detect radio waves; early devices were tubes filled with a conducting substance in granular form that increased resistance when struck by radio waves

Communication–the expression of meaning

Communication technology–relates to our sensory extensions; the way we use tools and techniques to create, transmit, receive, process, preserve, and retrieve information

Concept formation–the second phase in the development of the visual image. The first concept is often the media that does the communicating. The final concept can take on many forms, such as photographs, paintings, or a graphic designer's comprehensive layout. Often the act of visual communication stops with this phase

Conductor–material that permits motion of a large number of electrons; the fewer the number of valence electrons, the better the conductor

Cone–sensory receptor in the retinal layer of the eye that helps transmit visual information to the brain

Context–all of the environmental factors that affect the meaning of a message

Control–the process of machines regulating or affecting the behavior of other machines

Control unit–the part that determines the sequence of operations of the computer

Cornea–the outer transparent covering of the eyeball, which covers the iris and pupil and admits light to the interior

Cryogenics–the study or use of superlow temperatures to stimulate the speed of electron flow

Cutaneous receptors–nerve endings in the skin capable of detecting sensations of warmth, cold, contact, or pain

Cybernetic–the term was coined to stand for "steersman" and refers to the science of control processes in electronic, mechanical, and biological systems

Cyclometer–an instrument that measures revolutions of an axle, wheel, or circular arc

Daguerreotype–first photographic process capable of permanently preserving a photographic image; invented by the Frenchman, L. J. M. Daguerre; image placed on copper coated with silver with an iodide emulsion

Debug–to locate and correct errors in a computer system or program

Decibel–a unit of measurement for expressing the relative loudness of sounds

Decode–the process of changing the form of information from a coded form to the original form: for example, electrical pulses to voice signals

Decoding–changing the form of a message prior to reception so that it approximates the form it had prior to encoding

Dermis–an inner layer of skin made up of elastic tissue and numerous nerves and sensory receptors

Dermo-optic–a relatively unknown sensory dimension possessed by some individuals in which ultrasensitive tactile stimulation results in visual images being recorded in the brain

Diaphragm–a device consisting of a flexible membrane attached to a solid frame; generally used to provide continuous modulation of electric current

Diazo–a reproduction process involving exposure to ultraviolet light; the emulsion surface consisting of diazo salts is then made visible after it is exposed to ammonia fumes or dry toner

Dielectric–an insulating material that separates the contact plates of a condensor

Digital–relating to numerical calculation; a digital computer represents numbers by discrete electrical states

Diode–a vacuum tube with a cold anode and a hot cathode that functions as a rectifier

Disc–a thin, flat, circular plate or object

Discrete–a system detached from others, capable of operating separately using individual parts or elements

Donor–an atom of matter that tends to give up or lose its valence electrons

Doppler effect–the change in frequency of an approaching and receding source of sound

Downtime–time lost when a communication system malfunctions (particularly in computer systems)

Duplexing–the process of sending two or more signals simultaneously over the same channel, usually done by varying the frequencies of the signals

Echo location–the process of comparing sound echos with the original sound and interpreting the differences for location, size, and shape of objects, usually underwater

Electrode–element in a cell or battery, point of contact of electric circuit

Electrostatic field–the space around a charged body that is influenced by the charge

Electrostatics–a reprographic process using a dry toner, which becomes charged with an electric current and is attracted to a printing surface having an unlike charge

Electrostrictive–electricity produced by pressure; property of certain substances, such as ceramic, to produce electricity due to magnitude of a force or electrical field

Encoding–changing the form of a message to ease the transmission, reception, or interpretation of that message

Entrepreneur–one who undertakes to carry out an enterprise or business of an innovative nature, generally taking great economic risks

Epidermis–the outer layer of skin

Facsimile–method of transmitting exact copies of visual material by radio, telephone, or telegraph

FCC–Federal Communications Commission, a U.S. government regulatory body for radio, television, telephone, and other broadcast communications; formed in 1934 to replace the FRC

Feedback–the process of transmitting information from a receiver to a sender as a result of the act of communication

Ferris oxide–material on a plastic base used for magnetic tape recording

Forward-scatter–also tropo-scatter; systems used to bounce powerful electromagnetic signals off the ionosphere

FRC–Federal Radio Commission; existed as a U.S. government regulatory body for radio and its use until 1934, when it was replaced by the FCC

Frequency–the number of cycles per second of a vibrating body or wave

Fuse–a safety device in an electric circuit that breaks the circuit flow if the circuit is overloaded

Galvanometer–a meter that measures very small amounts of voltage and current

Gilbert–unit of measure of magnetomotive force

Graphic plotter–a device capable of reproducing information into line copy or drawings on paper, often used for some kinds of computer output

Gustatory communication–the reception of information in the form of impressions through the sense of taste

Gustatory receptors–cells or taste buds capable of detecting flavors; associated with the sense of taste

Gutenberg–Johann Gutenberg of Manitz, Germany, invented the total printing system consisting of movable metal type, a wine press, paper, and ink; made books accessible to the common man

Halftone–a reproduction of continuous-tone artwork like a photograph; made by changing copy into a series of dots of various sizes through the use of a halftone screen

Hammer–a small bone in the middle ear that transfers wave vibrations from the anvil to the cochlea

Hieroglyphics–character writing; the picture writing of the ancient Egyptians

Hole–in electronics, the absence of an electron

Holography–a technique used to project a three-dimensional image in space using a laser beam projected off a series of mirrors on to a hologram

Homeostat–an automatic control device capable of regulating the speed of another mechanism

Hybrid circuits–an electronic circuit incorporating two or more types of components, such as transistors and vacuum tubes

Hydrophone–an electroacoustic transducer for listening to sounds transmitted through water

Ideation–the process of thinking creatively to solve a problem and arrive at a number of possible solutions to the problem

Image preservation–methods used to store information; primarily microform techniques

Image reproduction–the third phase in the act of visual communication; occurs when the image is reproduced, or multiple copies of the image are created for use by many viewers

Infrasonic–a fluttering sensation of wave vibrations with no sense of pitch having a frequency lower than about 16 cps and therefore below the audible range of the human ear

Instrumentation–the process of obtaining information through devices that receive data

Insulator–a material that does not conduct electricity well because stable valence electrons do not easily break free

Integrated circuit–a circuit where various circuit elements such as conductors, resistors, capacitors, transistors, diodes, and coils are all interconnected as a complete unit during the manufacturing process

Intelsat–International Telecommunications Satellite Organization; a collective group of nations that participate in a global satellite communication system with ground control capabilities for sending and receiving information

Interference–the disturbance of signals due to a variety of factors that prevent the reception of clear, coherent information

Intermodal–computer and information processing devices that can operate interchangeably with other devices and systems

Intonation–the melody or pattern of pitch changes revealed in sound or speech

Intrinsic semiconductor–a semiconductor whose operating characteristics are dependent upon the qualities of a pure crystal

Ionosphere–a region located between 100 and 300 kilometers above the earth

Iris–the colored part of the eye that is perforated by the pupil and excludes the entrance of light except through the pupil

Kinetograph–an early camera used to photograph moving images; developed by Thomas Edison

Kinetoscope–the first moving picture viewing device; invented by Thomas Edison

Laser–**L**ight **A**mplification by **S**imulated **E**mission of **R**adiation; production of coherent light capable of carrying a great amount of information

Leyden jar–a primitive capacitor with two metal plates separated by an insulator

Lithography–a printing process based on the theory that grease and water won't mix; flat or plane-surface printing; also kown as offset or planography

LSIC–Large Scale Integrated Circuits, monolithic integrated circuits of very high density, usually on a single chip

Magnetic field–imaginary lines that constitute magnetic action; these lines radiate from the North Pole to the South Pole creating a closed loop

Magnetic flux–the quantity of magnetic lines surrounding a magnetic field

Magnetostrictive–electricity produced by magnetic fields, motion (vibrations) is also accomplished by expanding and contracting a core coil as magnetic fields are reversed

Maser–**M**icrowave **A**mplification by **S**timulated **E**mission of **R**adiation; a system that amplifies very weak radio signals and reproduces them with high fidelity and no background noise, used with microwave systems

Matrix–a structure or shape that gives form to a thing or idea

Microforms–a general descriptor used to stand for any type of microfilm; most common forms are roll film (16mm and 35mm), microfiche, aperture cards, and ultrafiche

Microwave–electromagnetic wave of extremely high frequency with a wavelength from approximately 50 cm to 1 mm

Microwave transmission–developed in the 1940s; involves the transmission of a very short wave—now between 100 centimeters and 1 centimeter in wavelength; requires very little transmitter power

Mimeograph–a printing process involving the use of a prepared master; based on the silk screen process, or through-the-surface printing; generally used for up to 5000 copies

Molecular electronics–the practice of using independent elements and devices that form a total system

Monalith–a semiconductor chip containing a variety of devices that is part of an integrated circuit

Monophonic–a single track or channel of sound often used to describe sound storage and retrieval techniques

Multimeter–combination ampere, volt, and ohm meter

Network–combination of two or more components that contribute to the operation of a system

Noise–any distractions that interfere with the accurate and efficient transmission of information: for example, visual—out of focus, acoustical—static

Oersted–unit of measure of magnetic intensity

Off-line–input/output devices used to perform operations independent of the computer

Offset–lithography; plane-surface printing; the most common printing process today

Ohm–unit of measurement of resistance (working element)

Ohm's Law–the mathematical relationship between current, resistance, and voltage in an electric circuit

$$I = \frac{E}{R}$$

Olfactory communication–the reception of information in the form of sensory impressions through the sense of smell

On-line–input/output devices linked directly to a computer

Orthochromatic–refers to black and white film types sensitive to all colors of light except red. This film is "blind" to blue. This means that blue copy photographed with ortho film will not be recognized

Oscillator–generates a steady, predetermined frequency of electromagnetic energy; output frequency can be changed by changing the values in the amplifier circuit

Oscilloscope–an electronic test instrument with a display screen, or scope, capable of showing wave configurations

Panchromatic–continuous-tone film sensitive to all colors of light; must be processed in complete darkness

Papillae–small projections on the sensory receptors of humans that contributes to the sense of touch, taste, and smell

Papyrus–an early form of paper made from reeds

Parallel circuit–a circuit that provides two or more paths for electron flow

Perception–the action or faculty of recognizing or being aware of

Phonoreceptor–a device or organ that can receive or detect sound waves

Phosphor–a material that radiates light upon impact of light of varying wavelengths, glowing substances

Pictography–picture writing; the process of developing pictograms, simple drawings that transmit information to the viewer; first became popular around 20,000 B.C. and are still used today to transmit information from one person to another

Piezoelectricity–electricity produced by pressure, particularly when a crystal is subjected to compression along a certain axis or polarity

Pile–a collection of material that when activated produces an electrical charge, a battery

Polygraph–a lie detector machine used by the medical profession and police; based on the concept of fluctuating moisture readings

Psychokinesis–a communication anomaly; when objects such as laboratory balances are caused to move without being touched

Pulse code modulation–modulation of signals in which information is conveyed by a code of pulses

Quadrophonic–four tracks or channels of sound; often used to describe sound storage and retrieval techniques

Quadruplexing–the process of sending four or more signals simultaneously over the same channel

Radar–**R**adio **D**etection **A**nd **R**anging; involves the transmission of timed pulses of high-power electromagnetic waves of short duration allowing time between the pulses for them to be reflected back from an object; the received echo is shown on the face of a cathode-ray tube

Radio astronomy–the study of the galaxy in terms of radio signals (1400–1427 MH) using large radio telescopes (receiving antennas)

Radiography–the X-ray process using film sensitive to X-rays or gamma rays; used to view the internal composition of many solid surfaces

Real time–any system that operates at a speed fast enough to receive information, perform the calculations, and output the results in time to affect the process while it is still going on

Rectifier–the rectifier is used in power circuits or as a detector in radio circuits and changes an incoming signal to a fluctuating one of the opposite polarity

REL–reluctance, resistance to flow of magnetic lines of force

Relief–raised-surface printing

Reprography–a word used to describe the communication processes used by the office, business, and quick copy printing sectors to reproduce copies of visual information usually in quantities less than 5,000 copies

Resistor–an electrical device that offers resistance to the flow of electrons, used to control the amount of current in a circuit

Retina–the back surface of the eye that receives the image formed by the lens and passes the information through the optic nerve to the brain

Rockcrushers–the first wide-band spark sets (radios)

Rod–rod-shaped cells in the retina of the eye that are sensitive to very weak light and help transmit visual information to the brain

Rough sketch–a complete design sketch showing placement of design elements, type style, and size; as complete a layout as possible without progressing on to camera-ready copy

GLOSSARY OF TERMS

Scope–a visual display screen often used in metering instruments or to display computer data

Semaphore–to signal by some system of flags or other movable object

Semiconductor–a solid-state element of pure material, grown in a laboratory, that controls the flow of electrons in a circuit; semiconductors are neither good conductors nor good insulators

Sensory–relating to impulses on, or relating to, the sense organs

Series circuit–a circuit that provides only one possible path for electron flow

Series parallel circuit–individual series circuits connected in parallel

Servo systems–control systems consisting of a sensing device, a system ensuring accuracy, and a system enabling rapid response

Shortwave–electromagnetic wave of high frequency with a wavelength of 60 meters or less

Solid state–transistor electronics, electronic systems that do not contain vacuum tubes

Somatic area–sensory projection area of the brain that receives all information from the sense of touch

SONAR–**SO**und **NA**vigation and **R**anging; the process of using reflected sound waves to determine characteristics and shapes of objects in water

Sonic–wave vibrations having a frequency within the auditory range of the human ear, from about 16 cps to 20,000 cps

Spirit duplication–aniline-dye printing, or a ditto or spirit process; the process uses a prepared master and a carbon-based image that breaks down after being subjected to alcohol

Stereophonic–having two tracks or channels of sound; often used to describe sound storage and retrieval techniques

Stereoscopic–multidimensional vision

Stippling–the illustration technique involving the use of many small dots placed close together to give the appearance of shading or visual texture

Stirrup–a small bone in the middle ear that transfers wave motion vibration from the tympanic membrane (eardrum) to the anvil

Stridulatory–a shrill or often vibrating noise

Superheterodyne–a type of radio receiver where the electromagnetic signal is received in the antenna circuit and amplified in the radio frequency (RF) stage

Synapse–the point at which nerve impulses pass from one neuron to another

Synesthesia–also known as color hearing; a sensory dimension where certain sounds provoke certain colors; an anomaly in human sensory communication

Tactile communication–the reception of information through the sense of touch

Tactile stimulation–the act or process of stimulating the sense of touch

TASI–Time Assignment Speech Interpolation; a time-sharing telecommunication system used by the telephone companies to use the silent periods in phone conversations for other conversations

Taste buds—a number of small teardrop-shaped bodies located on the surface of the tongue that assist in discriminating flavors; organs of taste

Telecommunication–the use of instrumentation and/or control devices to facilitate the transmission, emission, or reception of information, largely by electrical, electronic, or electromagnetic modes

Telekinesis–an anomaly; also called biogravitation; the process of moving objects through the power of the mind

Telemetry–the process of sending radio signals using instrumentation from a space craft to a central receiving station on earth

Telepathy–an anomaly; the process of transmitting and receiving information through thought processes; sometimes referred to as ESP or extrasensory perception

Telex System–a teleprinter system that uses an audiofrequency for transmitting teletypewriter information over telephone lines

TFR–Tuned Frequency Receiver; replaced the crystal set radio around 1918

Thermionic emission–the driving off of electrons by a heat source, one of the basic principles behind the vacuum tube

Thermistors–a transistor whose action depends on the change of temperature

Thermography–Thermofax; a reprographic process normally used for less than five copies; a heat sensitive emulsion is exposed to light causing a localized build up of heat, which creates a black image

Thermopile–a collection of materials that when activated by heat produces an electrical charge

Thumbnail sketch–a number of small designs for the same job on one sheet of paper, each representing one possibility for line placement

Transducer–any device used to convert energy of one kind into energy of another kind

Transformer–a device that transfers energy from one circuit to another; can increase or decrease amounts

Transistor–a device used to amplify an electromagnetic signal; called a transistor because it transfers a voltage across a resistor

Tropo-scatter–also forward-scatter; systems used to bounce powerful electromagnetic signals off the ionosphere

Tympanic membrane–eardrum; a thin membrane closing the cavity of the middle ear like the head of a drum; a diaphragm

Typeface–type style; the surface of the type that contacts paper

Ultrafiche–a microform that contains images greater than 90 × (90 times smaller than the original), thus permitting thousands of images per fiche; each fiche looks much like a standard microfiche, except for the smaller images

Ultrasonic–wave vibrations having a frequency above the range of human hearing, generally beyond 20,000 cps

UPC–Universal Product Code; code printed on consumer products to enable optical scan computer checkout

User–the person using the information processing or computer system

Valence electrons–the electrons in the outermost orbit of an atom; the actual "free" electrons that are responsible for electrical conduction in metals and for forming chemical bonds

Visual communication–the reception of information through the sense of vision

Visual literacy–the refinement of capabilities for creating and understanding visual messages; the essential elements of visual literacy: dot, line, texture, color, and shape

Volt–unit of measurement of electromotive force (pressure)

Voltaic pile–an early chemical battery consisting of copper and zinc discs in a solution of diluted sulfuric acid

VTR–Video tape recorder

VTVM–Vacuum Tube Volt Meter

Wattmeter–a meter that measures electrical power in terms of watts

Waveguide–a device that controls and guides waves as they are transmitted from one point to another, generally referring to microwave guides or lightwave guides

Wide banded–the capacity of early radio receivers to receive all strong signals but no weaker ones

Xerography–an electrostatic process used to reproduce copies of the original document; the Xerox process is an example

Xography–a 3-D or stereoscopic technique involving the use of a stereoscopic photograph viewed through a lenticular screen; often a popular technique to produce 3-D greeting cards

Xylography–a form of raised-surface or relief printing using wood blocks for the printing carrier

Symbols and Abbreviations

Abbreviation or Symbol	Full Representation	Most Common Use Area
AC	Alternating current	Electricity
AF	Audio frequency	Radio
AM	Amplitude modulation	Radio
⚡ (antenna symbol)	Antenna	Radio
ASA	American Standard Association Film Speed Rating	Photography
⊣⊢ (battery symbol)	Battery cell	Electricity
⊣⊢ (capacitor symbol)	Capacitor	Electricity
CB	Citizen's band radio	Radio
CPU	Central processing unit	Computing
CPS	Cycles per second	Electricity
CRT	Cathode-ray tube	Electronics
dB	Decibel	Acoustics
DC	Direct current	Electricity
FCC	Federal Communications Commission	Government, Communications
FM	Frequency modulation	Radio

SYMBOLS AND ABBREVIATIONS

Abbreviation or Symbol	Full Representation	Most Common Use Area
FRC	Federal Radio Commission	Government, Communications
f-stop	Fixed sizes of camera aperture opening	Photography
(fuse symbol)	Fuse	Electricity
(ground symbol)	Ground	Electricity
(headphone symbol)	Headphone	Acoustics
IC	Integrated circuit	Electronics
IF	Intermediate frequency	Radio
∞	Infinity	Photography
I/O	Input/Output	Computing
LED	Light emitting diode	Electronics
(magnetic flux symbol)	Magnetic flux	Magnetism
Ω	Ohm	Electricity
PCM	Pulse code modulation	Radio
REL	Reluctance	Magnetism
(resistor symbol)	Resistor	Electricity
RF	Radio frequency	Radio
rpm	Revolution per minute	Electricity, power
(single pole switch symbol)	Single pole switch	Electricity
(speaker symbol)	Speaker	Acoustics
SSB	Single side band	Radio
(transistor symbol)	Transistor	Electronics
UHF	Ultra high frequencies	Radio
VHF	Very high frequencies	Radio

INDEX

acoustics, 178
ambiance, 197
amplifier, 207
antitrust act, 268
aperture cards, 132

Bell, Alexander G., 166, 169
bees, waggle dance, 19
bifocular vision, 18
black box concept, 8

calotype photography, 119
camera obscura, 117
capacitor, 146
cave painting, 89
censorship, 262
channel, 8
chemical batteries, 145
cinema, 126
coaxial cable, 188
coherer, 191; coherer detector, 203
color, 96–97
color photography, 123
communication, process of, 5–10; definition of, 7; in bees, 19; ants, 20; birds, 21; apes, 22; whales, 21; machines, 13, 28–41; in plants, 44; deep space tracking systems, 30; law, 259
communication and law, 259
communication technology, definition for, 11
compass, 164
computer, 81–83, 234, 290–93
computer shopping, 274
computer technology, 290–93
condenser, 146
condenser microphone, 193
conductors, 153–55
copyright, 267
crystal loudspeaker, 193
crystal radio, 208
cuneiform writing, 101
current, 150
cybernetics, 80–81

daguerreotype photography, 118
Dancer, John B., 131
design, 91–98
diazo process, 110
Doppler effect, 177
dot, in design, 91–92
dry silver technology, 123
dynamic microphone, 192

Edison, Thomas, 125
effects of communication on society, 249–54
elasticity, 175
electricity, meaning of, 144
electromagnetism, theory of, 158
electron theory, 149
electrostrictive transducers, 182
encoding and decoding, 179

facsimile transmission, 168
feedback, 8
film, orthochromatic, 119; panchromatic, 119
Fleming valve, 205–6
flux pattern, 141
forward scatter systems, 217
freedom of information, 262
freedom of expression, 260
Furness, William, 22
fuses, 157

Gabor, Dennis, 133
global satellite systems, 293–96
graphic design, 91–95
gravure printing, 108
Gray, Stephen, 153
Gutenberg's printing system, 103–5

holography, 132–33
holographic television, 280
hieroglyphics, 101

ideography, 102
illusionary depth, 128
image preservation, 91, 130–32

information processing, 73–83; theory of, 77–78; cybernetics, 81–82
insulators, 153–55
interference, 183
integrated circuits, 229–32
interpersonal communication, 61–62
inventions, in communications, *see appendixes A & B*

kinesics, 67

lasers, 219–20
laserphoto, 135
law of forces between charged bodies, 149
left hand rule for coils, 160
left hand rule for conductors, 160
letterpress printing, 105–6
lightwave communication, 136
line, in design, 91–94, emotion, 95
lodestone, 140

machine to machine communication, 13, 28–41
magnetic declination, 140
magnetic field, 159–60
magnetic recording, 199
magnetism, 139
magnetostrictive transducers, 182
Marconi, Guglielmo, 190
masers, 194–216
mass communication, 100
measuring information, 79
message analysis and design, 89
microfiche, 132
microfilm, 131
microforms, 131–33; microfilm, 131; aperture cards, 132, ultrafiche, 132
microwave communication, 133, 286
mimeograph process, 114
mobile communication systems, 278
Morse code, 185
Morse, Samuel, 165
motion pictures, 124–25
moveable type, 103
muon beam research, 288

Niepce, Joseph, 118
noise, 8
nonverbal communication, 62

oersted, 158
offset lithography, 106-7
Ohm, Georg S., 149
Ohm's law, 156
oscillator, 207

panchromatic photography, 119
paper making, 102
papyrus, 102
parabolic dish, 169
parallel circuit, 151-52
personal space, ackistics, 65
person to machine communication, 12
photography, 117-21
pictography, 101
piezoelectric transducers, 181
power of resistors, 156
processing film, 120-21
pulse code modulation, 218

quadraphonic recording, 197

radar, 214
radio, 189
radio astronomy, 215
radiography, 121
raised surface printing, 105-6
receiver, 8
rectifier, 207
regulation of communication, 205, 264-66
remote transmission techniques, 114-15
reprography, 110-17; diazo, 110; thermal, 112; electrostatic, 112; spirit, 114; mimeograph, 114
resistors, 155
resonator, 179
rights of privacy, 261-62
rough sketch, in design, 98
Rowland's law, 162

satellites, 189, 220-23, 293-96
scaling, 178
screen printing, 109
semiconductors, 224-29
series circuit, 151-52
series-parallel circuit, 151-52
sender, 8
shape, in design, 91, 97
shortwave, 188
social development, 241-45; primitive, 242; craft, 243; mechanical, 243; modern, 243
Soemmerring chemical telegraph, 164
sonar, 181
speech, 67-70

spirit duplication, 114
static electricity, 142
stereophonic recording, 197
stippling, 93
superheterodyne receiver, 209
switches, 156
synesthesia, 61

Talbot, William Fox, 119
technical developments, 3-4; *see inventions*
technology forecasting, 282
telephone, 186-87
television, 127-28, 212-13
thermal process, 112
thermionic emission, 205-6
thermocouple, 146
thumbnail sketch, in design, 98
transducer, 181
transformer action, 163
tuner frequency receiver, 209

ultrafiche, 132
utilization of communication technology, 246-49

values and attitudes, effect on communication, 256
Van de Graaff accelerator, 143
velocity, 175
velocity microphone, 193
verbal communication, 67-70
visual literacy, 87; symbols, 87
visual message, 88
visual seals, 100
visual texture, 96
voltage, 150
voltaic batteries, 145

waveguide, 188

xerography, 112
xography, 129
xylography, 103

Yerkes, Robert, 22